D

CERTIFICATE OF
AUTHENTICATION

This is to certify that this casebound edition of
'Brands to Bexhill' is limited to just 984 copies
numbered 051 to 1,034, of which this copy is

No. **447**

Signed in authentication

For and on behalf of BOOKMARQUE PUBLISHING

BRANDS to BEXHILL

BRANDS to BEXHILL

Cock the shutter, engage the gear. . .
British motor racing really started here!

Max Le Grand

bmp

BOOKMARQUE
PUBLISHING

First published 1995

© Max Le Grand

ISBN 1–870519–30–2
(Limited casebound edition)
ISBN 1–870519–33–7
(Collector's edition)

....

British Library Cataloguing in Publication Data

A catalogue record for this book is available from the British Library.

Set in 10 on 12 point Times
Typesetting and origination by Bookmarque
Published by Bookmarque Publishing · Minster Lovell & New Yatt · Oxon
Printed and bound by Butler & Tanner Ltd · Frome · Somerset

Contents

FRONTISPIECE:
Max Le Grand being interviewed by Raymond Baxter and Lord Montagu of Beaulieu during the unveiling of the obelisks at Bexhill-on-Sea in September 1994, commemorating the Bexhill races which were held at the turn of the century.

To Pam and our entire family
for their love, devotion and support,
and to Stuart who gave meaning to those values.

Foreword

I DOUBT that many people associate Bexhill-on-Sea with motor racing, but Whit Monday 1902 saw the first 'Motor Derby' and first automobile speed tests staged in England take place at this Sussex town with which my family has a long association.

Other venues were considered, namely Lord Suffield's estate at Cromer and the Duke of Portland's at Welbeck Park, but the Automobile Club considered that the course should have better access to the public as well as foreign competition. With this in view the agents of my Great Grandfather, the 8th Earl De La Warr, entered into negotiations. Being a keen motor enthusiast he gladly consented and no doubt being of Norman descent welcomed the prescence of the French racers, including the illustrious M. Leon Serpollet who put up the fastest speed of the day at 54 mph.

It is fitting that the celebrated motor racing photographer and correspondent Max Le Grand, author of this fascinating book, whose own origins started at Brands Hatch, has placed Bexhill-on-Sea into the context of his own observations upon modern motor sport history.

Earl De La Warr

Acknowledgements

A FASCINATING cross-section of people over the years have unwittingly or by request searched their memories, rummaged through archives or perused scrapbooks to help muster the essential details that bind the fabric of this tome together. The outcome is by no means a historical statement, but a very personal appraisal of motor racing as I discovered it in Bexhill and found it at first-hand as a photographer and writer. Treat my ramblings as an enlightenment rather than an examination, and you will share the joy I had in the penning.

Unfortunately, I cannot acknowledge every soul, whether they are mortal or celestial. To my devilish friends I shall at the appropriate time be able to show thankfulness personally. But I fondly appreciate the acquaintance of everybody no matter how fleeting. If you recognise your contribution, then our encounter was worthwhile.

The more immediate points of reference made by people, known to me or not, have made my task thankfully easier. Anne Hinds of the Press Office at Brands Hatch Circuit who provided material which jogged my boyhood memories of the circuit, while Martin Hadwen searched the archives of the British Racing & Sports Car Club.

Concerning Bexhill and the famous 'races'. At my first stage of searching in the Town Hall there was the kind lady who sat and shivered in the bowels of the Council while allowing me to discover records of those early days. Next, my gratitude goes to John Dowling, the current editor of the *Bexhill-on-Sea Observer* for unlocking the 'great cupboard' and allowing me to dust down its photographic secrets. Other helpful sources of information were found at the Bexhill Museum, the Bexhill Library, the Sackville Hotel and at 10 Jameson Road.

On matters concerning the Bexhill 100, a huge vote of thanks to Brian Hazell, Kenneth Pope, Brian Storkey and Paul Foulkes-Halbard for making available so much original paraphernalia concerning the past and present. Major Vyvyan Harmsworth LVO, Director of Corporate Affairs at Associated Newspapers, managed to uncover photographic evidence of his forefather, Mr Alfred Harmsworth, as a pioneer at the Bexhill Races. What pleasure I had turning over old stones with Frank Nichols, Bob Curl and Lawrie Webber.

The reporters who worked on the *Bexhill Chronicle* and the *Bexhill-on-Sea Observer* in 1902, and penned such vivid first hand impressions of sporting automobilism that they did much to create the atmosphere of the original Bexhill Races.

My career as a photographer and writer on matters of concern to motor racing was entirely due to the generosity of the Press Officers at circuits the world over. To enable me to seek official accreditation at all of those international races, I am indebted to past editors namely: Gregor Grant *Autosport*, Tony Gilfrin *Motor Clubman,* George Bishop and Doug Blain *Small Car*, (which grew into *Car*), Gabby Crombac *Sport Auto*, Rico Steinamann *Powerslide*; Claes Uddgren and Hasse Adsjo *Bilsport,* Peter Garnier *Autocar*, Michael Bowler *Thoroughbred and Classic Cars*, Eric Fordham *Motor Rally and Racing Review*, Tony Rudlin *Auto,* Reuben Archer *Fast Car*, Dr Franco Gozzi *Ferrari*, Anthony Peagam *Ford Times,* Al Coppel *Motorsport International*, Alan Brinton *Motor Racing*, Karl Ludvigsen *Ludvigsen Library* and Henry Manney who was a guardian angel.

Other individuals who rummaged through picture libraries were Tony Muggridge of Ninfield for the upturned 1907 picture of a rare Bexhill accident, also Helen Wallace for her transparencies of the Bexhill 100 and Don Bostel, who admits to being a better scaffolder than photographer, for his pictures of the Obelisk unveiling at Bexhill. David Hoppit and Jonathan Buckley of *Vintage Times* magazine for promoting a good cause and giving encouragement when the writing got hard,

Along the road to over 200 international races, my humble gratitude is owed to Dick Jefferies and Vic Barlow of Dunlop; Ray Simpson the Castrol Competition Manager; Harold Theyer of Ferodo; Laurie Hands, the jovial representative of Champion Spark Plugs; Geoff Murdoch, Esso's racing manager and others in the trade who kept my wheels rolling when all else was falling apart. I am truly thankful for all spare parts supplied.

To Mike Goodhall, the photo-archive manager at Brooklands. And last, but not least, John and Denise Rose at Bookmarque, Tom Colverson and Kim Giles for the long haul in bringing this tome to fruition.

Considerable time and research was spent trying to discover the photographers of certain historic pictures in this book, however, there are some instances where I have been unable to provide a suitable acknowledgement. Also if I have inadvertently omitted to mention persons or publications please do accept my sincere apologies.

Max Le Grand, May 1995

Prelude

MEMORY, BEING that fickle archive of our individual past, may explain why I was subconsciously aware of Bexhill's motor racing heritage during my mid-twenties. This remote tinkle of an alpine bell came after a meeting with a gentleman in Austria during 1964. He was almost a centenarian while I was 24 years, an age when historical considerations have no priority over travel, girls, racing and booze. The Grand Prix caravan was then trespassing upon a new pasture at Zeltweg where a temporary venue had been set in the shadow of the Niedere hills of the Stiermark region. Jochen Rindt's star was ascending at around this time. He was ambitious to display his skill to the home crowd, so Rob Walker provided his privately owned Brabham-BRM for the young tyro. Prior to this first Austrian Grand Prix, Jochen had warned that we should not judge the airfield venue on face value because a proper 'super circuit' was being planned.

Since breaking new ground is always a refreshing experience, my flight from London to Munich was filled with great anticipation. I was met at Munich by a German colleague. We drove through captivating, mountainous scenery of lush grass and nodding crops of flowers. Eventually, the narrow mountain passes lowered us into Judenburg where we were to stay. The Osterreichring as it was presumptuously christened, was in fact a circuit laid over a defunct air-force base between Knittelfeld and Zeltweg. So primitive was the facility outlined by thousands of straw bales that I wondered how on earth the national automobile club had been granted a permit by the FIA to organise such an event.

Any shortcomings were overwhelmed by the joyous hospitality offered with open arms by our Austrian hosts. More-or-less everybody, regardless of who they were, had to 'put-up' in private houses, summer chalets, farm houses and simply camp. Lorenzo Bandini enjoyed a rare victory for Ferrari after his team leader John Surtees was forced to retire. Jochen did not figure, but the thousands of spectators drowned what sorrow there might have been, when they started the serious business of downing those intimidating steins of beer in large marquees while the thigh-slapping and bum-banging got into top traditional dance gear to the accompaniment of the local 'oompah' band.

Heaven knows how we got there, or who drove, come to that but we ended up in the Bambi Express Bar in Judenburg at 2 am Monday morning. The girls were cleaning and washing up after the last race fans had dispersed for home. I conclude that these girls must be well practised in dealing with gentlemen who have had a skinful. Without so much as a prompt, we diluted the alcohol with all the black coffee on tap before daring to crash into our private digs.

Amid this unearthly hour of restitution, a loud, rotund figure burst into the coffee bar. This huge cuddly man was grandfather to one of the waitresses. He joined us and speaking in better than adequate English, we talked about the day at the race. He himself had not joined the throngs at Zeltweg, confessing to old age and a verandah where he had slept while the Grand Prix was underway. As a young man he had worked in England, and recalled that during his posting he had attended his first race meeting somewhere along the South coast. Senility prevented him from pin-pointing the location of this past motor racing event but he was keen to have us pay him a visit to his farm lodge for further discussion on the subject later in the day.

His granddaughter roused us from our dwelling. After fond farewells to the family who had suffered our stay, we motored towards Salzburg where we turned off the main road onto dusty track to find an imposing, wooden-walled farmhouse. After a good-natured welcome from grandfather, he guided us into his study where he produced what appeared to be a leather-bound, padlocked five-year diary. The folio was in fact a well-preserved album of period photographs and memorabilia such as train passes, theatre tickets, menus and letters from many moons ago. A thumping head did not detract from my appreciation of this wondrous insight into one man's perfectly preserved past. Carefully turning the pages I stumbled upon a spread of photographs taken of friends 'hamming-it-up' while sat in a Wolseley Racer which apparently made its debut at this sporting fair.

There was no reference about the scene and much as the grandfather racked his brains in frustration, the only item of a clue that bubbled to the surface was that he attended a ball at the Kursaal after the meeting (naturally, at that time, the Kursaal meant nothing to me). He was, however, mystified as to why such a quintessential English seaside emporium, similar to a pier, should have adopted the German name of Kursaal, which by definition is a public room found at German health resorts.

Thirty years since that conversation, I have calculated that my elderly Austrian acquaintance was in his mid-twenties during 1902. So my friend, who has long since passed, must have been at the first Bexhill Races where the Wolseley Racer appeared from under wraps. If this is correct, then he undoubtedly enjoyed the splendid good fortune to have attended the sumptuous 'Automobile Ball' which was held at the Kursaal on that same occasion. Unwittingly, it seems, I had had the seed for discovering the Bexhill Races planted firmly in my mind by a jovial Austrian hunting gentleman, which I found to be really quite astonishing.

It was to be some fifteen years later when I actually moved to Bexhill-on-Sea, in East Sussex, and only after settling into a new home did I come to realise the true significance of Bexhill, a secluded backwater, and its largely

unrecognised place in the history of British motor racing. I embarked upon a
voyage of discovery that was full of surprises, none more so than the following cameo, on a brilliant summer morning in Bexhill during July 1986, will
illustrate.

A dazzling sun rose over the English Channel to render the Edwardian
buildings along the De La Warr Parade a radiant magenta. Parked along the
grass verge was a French-registered camper-wagon. A couple sat at a trestle
table on the parade lawn where they had just finished breakfast. I sauntered
by having visited the newsagent for my daily newspaper. We smiled, as strangers do, exchanged pleasantries, then monsieur beckoned me to join them.

They were both puzzled by my name and why I did not speak the President's tongue. My explanation was that I am English with a French ancestry
on my father's side of the family. As madame broke bread, offered a slice of
aromatic fromage, then poured me a drink, I further explained that really I am
as English as roast beef and Yorkshire pudding — a goblet of fine Bordeaux
rouge possibly coursed through my veins but that is all.

Within that coquettish period of familiarisation between persons unknown,
common ground emerged when madame informed me they lived in Épernay,
set amid the Champagne-Ardennes region, a town I immediately related to
from assignations to the French Grand Prix at Reims. Alas! a bus stop — no
more — along the World Championship route, the last 'numéro onze' went
through in 1966, with Jack Brabham victorious at the wheel. Their faces lit
up, not just because I had frequented the 'Musée du Champagne' in Épernay,
but we shared the acquaintance of Philippe Etancelin, the ancien pilote of the
gritted teeth, reversed cap and pugnacious driving style, known simply as
'Phi-Phi' to all his admirers and friends. The realisation dawned with the clarity of the day — we all shared more than a passing interest in motor racing.

Throughout my term of observing the sport, I found that the kindred spirit
bridged the cultural and language gaps and even closed the generation gap.
The automobile provided the catalyst between those who share the camaraderie of the sport. Put man's ingenuity to manipulate the infinite variables of
the mechanical device against his opponents, and the dash for supremacy is
exhilarating. Historically, the champions of the sport have celebrated their
victories with champagne. This effervescent marriage started from the day
when the horseless carriage was emancipated in 1896 — when 'bubbly and
brrummm' each represented the symbols of success.

My friends from Épernay were of a vintage mature enough to remember
'Phi-Phi' claim a famous win with his Bugatti at the premier Grand Prix de la
Marne over the Reims road circuit in 1927. Madame's father then worked at
Hautvillers. There, at the Abbey during the 17th century, a cellarer answering
to Dom Perignon fermented the juice of grapes to create a sparkling wine.
Madame reiterated her father's story of how monsieur Etancelin arrived at
Hautvillers to collect several crates of victory champagne before driving back
to Ille-et-Villaine. Somewhere between Soissons and Beauvais the cherubic
Rouennais racer had dispensed with 24 hours of bonhomie. Myth suggests
that 'Phi-Phi' returned to Normandy at the wheel of his Bugatti with an

14

inebriated expression, the car still laden with crates — the bottles of which were empty!

I learned that the French couple had, since the first European and British Grand Prix at Brands Hatch in 1964, made the biennial pilgrimage to the Kent circuit. In 1986 Nigel Mansell took the honours for Williams-Honda. 'A good moment for Britain' ventured my friend wryly, 'but a sad moment for us'. They judged Mansell's win as good sport. What concerned them was the manner in which Nigel, Nelson Piquet and Alain Prost wantonly sprayed champagne (what for them was their bread and water), soaking the huge crowd below the presentation dias in Möet et Chandon. It was not so much Mansell's enthusiasm in creating his own cloud burst, but that they felt Alain Prost might have shown some respect for a classic French product. Monsieur's eyes at this point turned wistfully to the old Sackville Hotel along the Bexhill promenade. 'Let me tell you', he said, 'Leon Serpollet at his victory banquet here in 1902, would lift a flute of Dom Perignon, sniff the bouquet, address the toast to his distinguished hosts, sip the champagne, savour the 'brut', bow to the vanquished, then retire with respect.'

Curious to know where he had made such a study, I was then enlightened upon the reason for their pilgrimage to Bexhill. Right along from where we sat, the Parade was the 'Course' where, in 1902, the Automobile Club organised the very first 'motor races' in Britain. At the Whitsuntide weekend, the celebrated French racing motorist Leon Serpollet recorded the fastest time of the day over the flying kilometre in his own steam-driven car.

'We come to Bexhill', smiled my friend, 'to pay our respects to the premier victory by a French driver on British soil'. The eyes of Frenchmen still go moist at that indelible moment written into early French motoring history.

Whereas Bexhill for me remains an enigmatic, rather anonymous, monument to the evolution of motor sport in Britain, there are still pilgrims for whom the promenade course is a shrine. Since I am a generation or so beyond those pioneering days, I more readily identify with Brands Hatch, a venue I watched develop throughout my boyhood from being a grass track stadium just after the Second World War, to a full-blown Grand Prix circuit.

The couple were curious about those early days of the Kent circuit and how it came to flourish within a barren valley of chalk and clay. By now, the cameo along the De La Warr Parade was becoming laughable with people who were up and about and beginning their daily work. Some glanced at the three of us hob-nobbing away while quaffing Cognac, as we kept a wary eye on the mature lady dippers as they swam in the sea. Since part of the French tradition is based upon the bicycle and most of the nation has been weaned upon the Tour de France, I noted their reaction when I told of Brands Hatch, and how it started as à cycle track for racing and pace-making. They were aghast and intrigued when I described how Ron Argent, an engineering apprentice from Sidcup, out with a bunch of cyclists on a Sunday club circuit, stopped for a breather at a junction in the Fawkham valley. It was there that Ron spotted the potential of the natural amphitheatre in 1926.

He had been constantly searching for a possible site for off-the-road races to escape the growing recklessness of motorists who brushed past them along narrow country lanes. The hollow below Brands Hatch Farm was a dream come true. Encouraged by his mates, Ron approached the landowner and enquired about the possible use of the chalk-based, thistle-infested field. To their collective amazement, the gentleman was only to pleased to set aside the rabbit warren.

By 1928, Brands Hatch had established a growing reputation in London and the South-East of England among cyclists, as 'the venue'. Monsieur observed a parallel between Bexhill and Brands Hatch in that both venues were originally cycle tracks. Aside from the swarms of cyclists who regularly patronised 'The Hatch' there were other rumblings emanating from the woods beyond Kingsdown Park House. Motorcycle scramblers had plotted a tough course through the undulating, flint-strewn terrain where the Sidcup and District MC Club organised regular meeting with a growing number of supporters who were fast out-numbering the cycling fraternity. Ever ambitious, the motor cyclists interspersed straight line drag strip meets with the cycle races. Brands soon became a mecca for the double knockers. Before the Second World War, the glorious 'nursery' had bred some great names like Eric Oliver, who eventually became the World Sidecar Champion. He and Jack Surtees waged some titanic battles. The grimy winner always celebrated, supping bottles of ginger beer before setting off together, crammed onto one or the others bike for a lap of honour. Later on, over the same dusty bowl, Jack's son, John, cut his teeth and grew to become the only man in history to claim the world crown on both two wheels and on four.

Since I was a 'war baby' born during August 1940, I was not around to see Bert Cornwall's wasteland transform into a proper grass track. My mother and father, among other staunch fans, vowed when war broke out in 1939 to carry on the Brands tradition when the 'little skirmish' was over. That small indifference between nations erupted into the Second World War and Brands Hatch was converted into a fully-manned army base. Peace was declared over Britain in May 1945 when Prime Minister Winston Churchill declared those immortal words: 'War will end at midnight — advance Britannia. Long live the cause of Freedom. God Save the King'.

As soldiers, survivors and the walking wounded returned home for demob during 1945-46, motorcycle fanatics descended upon Brands Hatch to stockpile fuel left by the army. With petrol rationing on the horizon, they cleaned up Brands and hatched plans for the future. The driving force behind the resurrection was Joe Francis, a gruff, go-getting motorcycle dealer with a heart of gold. Among other dedicated 'Brands Hatchers' he enlisted my parents to set up a proper catering unit in the Pavilion and get some order into the open grandstand along the top straight.

Childhood memories of that long, hot summer of 1947 came flooding back as unrelated stories swapped between us and coincidentally fell into place. A fascinating Monday morning was partly clouded when monsieur politely asked if he could study the progress of the Tour de France in my *Daily Mail*. A Frenchman's most sacred cow, next to his deux chevaux or out-of-town mistress, was in prospect of being won by an AMERICAN cyclist! Having bid fond 'Adieu' to the couple, I watched the camper wagon disappear in the direction of Dover. I had a feeling that Greg Lemond was not going to be the most popular winner to reap the blue riband of French sport when he crossed the finishing line on the Champs Elysées. I was happy as I strolled home (not at the discomfiture of the French) but it's not every day when, like 'Phi-Phi', one can sit down to breakfast breathing alcohol over the family.

That was motor racing . . .

1

Scholastic Oddities

'ARE YOU hard of hearing?' asked the ear specialist as he put my audio senses to stringent test. 'What!' I blurted in reply. 'Yes, quite,' he mused, 'My prognosis is that your tympanums have been exposed to prolonged periods of highly tuned combustive power. People in motor racing suffer the impediment a lot.' I was quite indignant. How could a medical practitioner have rumbled a life-long love affair with such accuracy?

Between the years 1946 and 1977 I had rejoiced to the rorty sound of tearing calico trumpeted from engines that ranged from double-knocker Norton's to the tingling scream of a Cosworth-Ford at full pelt. Frankly, whatever the doctor's diagnosis, I couldn't have cared tuppence. Aside from my enduring fondness for Dixieland Jazz, the various orchestras of sound conducted from Grand Prix cars, sports cars, Indycars, Jaguars, Yamahas or Hondas were my kind of music. So I informed the medic that I was weaned as a 'war baby' on the post-war glory days at Brands Hatch Stadium.

The Kent grass track was then a bean-shaped circumference pegged by members of the Sidcup Motorcycle Club. Mum and family were driven by Dad in the family Morris Cowley from our home in Chapel Road, Bexleyheath to Brands Hatch practically every weekend come hail or shine. It was a pilgrimage they had pursued before the Second World War. Consequently, they had gone from being devoted enthusiasts to actually helping to make the stadium function at a profit. Naturally, I had gone in tow as the petulant junior spectator. By the time I reached the age of ten I was aware that life among my playmates was strange. Dad was a Local Government Officer who seemed desperately unhappy with his lot at Bexleyheath Borough Council. Mum became known as the neighbour who kept lodgers. I never remember wanting for anything as a lad. We had a motor car, maintained a telephone which friends often toddled in to use and also harboured a television which saw a growing number of kids congregate in the front room to watch. Bearing in mind this was the late 1940s, for the average family we didn't appear to be doing so bad.

In spite of this comfortable life, Mum and Dad — especially Mum — spent all their spare time getting more involved with Brands Hatch to bolster their income. I soon learned to swell my own pocket money after each meeting. As the riders packed up to go home, I would scour the paddock for ginger beer bottles and get the tuppences back. On a good day I could return 100 bottles on average — not bad for a young lad!

While I was intoxicated by the blood, dust and thunder of motorcycle racing, most of my chums at home were content to go with their fathers to support Bexleyheath & Welling at the local football ground. A privileged few caught the trollybus from the Clock Tower at Bexleyheath to cheer on Charlton Athletic when they had home matches. I must have been in my 'thirties before I attended a league soccer match when Brian Clough and Peter Taylor took over the management of Brighton & Hove Albion. So it was without wonder that I never rose to the rumbustious enthusiasm of my mates over the progress of the 'reds' at The Valley ground. My mind was preoccupied with the 'Blue Boys'. They were my heroes who raced 'chairs' in the sidecar races at Brands Hatch and they derived their name from the blue polo-neck sweaters they wore over their thick black leather trousers and heavy-duty riding boots. In my mind Eric Oliver was the loathsome 'Dracula' who was then World Champion of the chairs. I was staunchly loyal to the Blue Boys. The fact that nobody knew what I was blathering on about at school never occurred to me. But Mum noticed my predicament because one weekend she suggested that I should invite the Jones's son Alan, from across the road, to join us on a day out at Brands Hatch. I was thrilled to bits. At last I had an ally. Many years later I encountered Alan again, a married man and still thankful for that first insight into my world. Just when I thought I had a kindred spirit with whom to share my enthusiasm at home — blow me down, we moved house.

Since Dad was tied to his job at the Borough Council, the move wasn't exactly a plunge into the unknown. With more room for Mum's lodgers and a bigger garden for me to play in, the newly acquired home in tree-lined Stephen Road at Barnehurst was just just two miles from my birthplace. Not far up the road was the Red Barn pub where George Webb, a well-known local pianist, and a bunch of his cronies formed a group that introduced this country to Dixieland jazz.

Around the time that Mum and Dad moved home, Brands Hatch underwent a metamorphosis. The chalk-based grass track during the winter of 1949-50 shed its dust-laden, divot-piled coat and acquired a tarmac road surface that measured exactly one mile. The new road circuit lay less than one hour's drive from Brooklands and The Lilliputian circuit at Crystal Palace was an ambitious project mainly inspired by John Hall the appointed Managing Director of Brands Hatch Circuit at the time. In retrospect, it was John's ambitious plunge into a dream future that would eventually see Brands Hatch become a full-blown Grand Prix circuit. For the time being, the new road surface opened new sporting horizons. Apart from offering a new challenge to the regular motorcycle fraternity, the Kent circuit became the residence of the Half Litre Club.

Single-seater motor racing with all its attendant glamour had found a new home right on London's doorstep. The open wheel racing cars were in fact purpose-built space frames powered at the front or the rear of the driver by finely tuned motorcycle engines. Apart from introducing a new generation of tigerish drivers like Stirling Moss, Stuart Lewis-Evans and his equally swift 'Pop', there were local club stars like George Wicken, the Maidstone dairy man who gave a new meaning to C'est ce bon'. There was the diminutive Don Parker, bald-headed 'Curly' Dryden, bolt-on goodies Les Leston and the quart-in-a-pint-pot Big Bill Whithouse. Even men who had built their reputations on two wheels looked over the fence and smacked their lips at the prize money. Those terrible twins from Chatham, Don and Norman Gray, purchased the ubiquitous Cooper-Nortons and Don supplemented the contents of his coffers while putting prior knowledge of racing on two wheels to good effect. Another convert was Bexleyheath motorcycle dealer and racer Bernard Ecclestone, who became the king of all he surveys in modern Grand Prix motor racing.

Race commentary was spicily embroidered by John (lick your pencils girls) Bolster, the popular *Autosport* magazine correspondent. John's eulogies often became more colourful than the racing as the pink champagne went down. Instantly identified by his deer-stalker, horn-rimmed spectacles and generous moustache, it was Bolster who encouraged the many spectators who watched racing from their cars parked on the South Bank to sound their horns when race winners performed their lap of honour.

Motor racing and Bolster's happy banter witnessed an upward change in the social status among spectators. Mum, who was by now in charge of catering at the Pavilion, noticed this change against the more 'earthy' types who loved motorcycle racing. Mind you, both branches of the sport had more than their fair share of cheeky monkeys. Mum was not beyond giving Stirling Moss a clip round the ear when she caught him pinching coconut-shredded buns off the counter show case.

At the advent of my early 'teens, I was beginning to rationalise about motorcycle and motor racing. My avid interest in the former had waned as I readily identified with the motor racing fraternity. It wasn't a whim of snobbishness, — I think that a young fertile mind was responding to a change of scene. After a few meetings thrilling to my newly appointed sport, I started to look objectively at the drivers and wondered if the time would ever come when Brands Hatch sired a potential world champion driver.

When Stirling Moss arrived on the scene his name was already established. His latent talent was there for all to see. Stirling was clearly a man to watch, which explained why he was such a crowd-puller when he appeared at Brands Hatch to drive Ray Martin's rear-engined Kieft.

Never for one moment did I dream that one fellow, who suddenly turned up at the racing drivers' school towards the end of the 1953 school summer holidays, would be a future champion.

The bloke signed on as Graham Hill. He was a stocky chap, the epitome of a cheerful, cheeky Flying Officer Kite character. Ironically, Graham reminded me sometimes of being like Dad, who had served in the Royal Air Force during the Second World War. Both men sported generous moustaches, had a rolling gait and a big sparkle in their eyes when they spotted a shapely pair of legs. At that time, Dad and Graham were akin to a couple of peas from the same pod. Mum possibly recognised this similarity. She reckoned that Graham was a raffish, but likable rogue who had a line of chat with the tea girls. She caught him on more than one occasion ordering cups of tea at the Pavilion counter, then with a wry smile and a wink, he would walk off, apparently not intending to pay for them.

In spite of Mum's opinion, I warmed to the jocular man who never walked past me without scuffling my hair. Graham then owned a Morris and appeared the least sporting type compared with the other racing-school pupils, most of whom preened like a bunch of posers who were spending Daddies' money on 'a bit of a jolly' to impress their girl friends.

The posers' eyes stood out like organ stops as Graham strove to get full value for his five bob a lap in a single-seater racing car. He described a lurid, but original, racing line around the kidney-shaped circuit which in those days was driven anti-clockwise. Clearways and Paddock Bends were joined by what were laughingly called the top and bottom straights. Graham mastered those and the vertical bends on the undulating surface with great brio. After a quid's worth of laps, he returned to the paddock slip road, the 500 cc Cooper JAP oozing oil and smoke while Graham was positively steaming with enthusiasm. When Graham Hill first became World Champion driver in the BRM back in 1962, I couldn't help but smile at the thought of the very first day I had witnessed him in a racing car.

* * *

The years 1954-55 were pretty momentous. Brands Hatch grew an extension up to Druids Hill Bend making the circuit 1.24 miles and this in turn became clockwise, a customary feature of other British circuits like Silverstone and Goodwood.

By adding those precious yards, John Hall could now expand upon the Half Litre Club's busy little bees, with classes for sports cars, saloons, and other formula including the introduction of Grand Prix cars.

Private testing shortly after the tarmacadam had dried around Druids, proved to the Royal Automobile Club that Brands Hatch was adequate to host such marques as Maserati, HWM and Connaught. John Hall had not only achieved phase two of his development of the circuit, but my cup was full as well.

Aside from all the excitement at Brands Hatch, the truth was dawning in the twilight months of my education at the Bexleyheath Secondary School for Boys.

The master at Form 4C was Mr Martin, a long-suffering teacher who had man-handled us through the most important year of our scholastic career so that we could enter the world, citizens of pride and respectability. The middle-of-the-road boys didn't have the naff of those lads in 4A, but we weren't wanting like those boys in 4D. My shining characteristics were: Conduct – excellent. Punctuality – Very Good. Attendance – Full. So when Mum and I went along to be interviewed by the Headmaster, Mr Lester, and the Local Employment Officer, I wondered what they were going to make of a goodie-two-shoes who was an inveterate clock-watcher with a 100% record for non-absenteeism? When I was asked if I wanted to be a tinker or a tailor, a soldier or a sailor, there was a vacuum of silence. Mum was beside herself with embarrassment. It wasn't as if I was lazy. How could I be with my flair for making money from empty ginger beer bottles. I had since performed numerous paper rounds, worked as a baker's boy at the Tip Top, re-wound feature films for the projectionist at the Palace Cinema and been call-boy when great stars like Anne Shelton, Billy Cotton and his Band, Derek Roy, Tommy Cooper and Wilson, Keppel and Betty featured in shows at the Regal Theatre along the Broadway at Bexleyheath. I was probably making more money before I left school than I made when my education came to an end. In fact I nursed a thespian-Mitty ambition but had the idea knocked out of me by Dad who suggested that I should work in Local Government.

In desperation Mr Lester decided that I should attend a College of Further Education to concentrate upon my natural aptitudes. My final school report variously described me as 'Too Erratic' at Woodwork, 'Bone Idle' at Preliminary Craft Work, and 'Disappointing' on Scripture. But hope sprang eternal when my strengths in English and Art were revealed.

That was it — Mr Lester surmised that I possesed a vivid imagination tethered to an all-seeing eye.

The Headmaster arranged an entry interview for me with the Principal of the Medway College of Art in Rochester. Mr Stanley Hayes discovered I was the proud owner of a Kodak Box Brownie camera and I informed him that I also processed my own films and printed the photographs at home. I was immediately wheeled into the Photography Department where I was introduced to Norman Tudgay, a bewhiskered, gnome-like Welshman, who was to become my mentor.

Before the summer holidays came to an end and I embarked upon my life as a new student in Rochester, Mum and Dad sprang a surprise on me. In 1947 we had taken the annual holiday at a self-catering flat along Wearbay Crescent, that overlooked the Leas Cliff and the English Channel at Folkestone.

I clearly recall a sunny, crystal clear morning when I stood on the balcony peering out to sea.

'What's that place over there Dad?' I pointed to a dark silhouette rising over the sea on the horizon. Dad scrambled his geographical wits about him. 'That's France over there, son'.

'Is that another world Dad?'

Learned one was temporarily lost for words, then he told me: 'Not exactly: it's another country. We live in England and we speak English. That is France, they speak French and drive on the wrong side of the road to us.' On that instant, my infantile mind was fired. The seeds of wanderlust had been sown.

I pestered Mum and Dad endlessly about going to France. For a good few years I had to content myself with breaks at 'Waterfall Cottage' in the tranquil village of Shoreham in Kent; long stays with Uncle Maurice and Auntie Margaret (my Mum's sister) at Lancing in Sussex; more holidays at Wearbay Crescent and the occasional foray into the Gloucestershire Cotswolds to stay with Aunt Flo at Ozleworth.

Then just before my fifteenth birthday, Dad asked if I would like a touring holiday in France... The family jalopy was then a beautifully-maintained Jaguar, a smashing ivory-coloured beast which Dad had acquired at a bargain price. It was the envy of our sole remaining lodger, Ronnie Carr. Since the double garage at Stephen Road had a pit, they seemed to spend hours down it working on the car. Now I knew why, so after hours of tinkering away in the midnight oil, the day came to load up the khaki marquee, z-beds, sleeping bags, primus stove, extra clothes and food supplies. Calais here we come.

Harking back to that first big step abroad, it probably sounds a totally uninspiring trip. The ferry crossing from Dover to Calais unhappily saw Mum suffer her first-ever bout of sea sickness. While Dad comforted her, I was rushing from one end of the boat to the other watching the white cliffs of Dover disappear and the promised land loom ahead. The excitement was unbelievable, you would have thought I was going to the other end of the world.

Full of imagination, Dad chose some unlikely places to 'pitch-up' for the night. Today I cannot imagine getting stirred by the thought of living under canvas outside towns like St Omer, Amiens and Beauvais, but for me it was Venice, Rome and Barcelona.

After making-do and mending along the roadside, much to Mum's relief we drove the pegs in for a week at the relatively civilised environs of a proper campsite at the Bois de Boulogne in Paris. Our immediate neighbours were the Mension family from Pontivy in Brittany. Madame and Monsieur Mension were accompanied by their gorgeous daughter Claudia. Girls at home were mostly passing ships in the early evening. At 14 years I was well aware of the other specie, but at the onset of pubescence, my feelings toward them became confused as they changed shape before my eyes. Claudia — I suppose being French, was all there, and for the first time in my life I was struck by this bewildering force which I have since learnt was sexuality.

Boys' school playground whispers about fancying some bint, being in love with a bird or having a crush on that plain Jane across the road did not adequately prepare me for the mesmerising love which I managed to summon over Claudia in the middle of Paris during those few precious days of a lad's awakening.

Dad recognised the signs and encouraged the friendship which was contrary to Mum's more cautious instinct at her son's distraction.

Love's sweet course was diverted as we upped sticks to head back home via Abbeville. The straight tree-lined routes nationales, heavenly little villages, crunchy baguettes dripping with butter and salade-de-tomate meant nothing for the time being. Back at home, within a week or so I recovered my sensibilities. There was a lot more 'over there' which I wanted to see.

My two-year course of photography at Rochester turned out to be just over three years of enlightenment upon life and provided an unexpected direction to my ultimate career. Apart from my introduction to mixed company at Pelham Road Infants School in Bexleyheath, my passage through the junior and senior schools was spent very much with 'the boys'. These days I cannot envisage a hard core of lads being lumped together in the same classes for seven years. That was precisely what happened to boys like Blonde 'Deadie', Big Al, Shy Carter, 'Stinker' Richards, 'Cocky' Webster and several more. We literally grew up from boys to become young men, right through our grades. Imagine the culture shock of Medway Art College when I walked in on my first day to find that most students were in their late 'teens or early 'twenties, and there were girls, fully blossomed girls, made up and fetching.

Norman Tudgay's sum total of full-time students was three. Pam Richards and Jan Richard were two second-year students and I was the freshman. While they worked outside on location, I slaved under hot studio lights photographing 'still life' — anything from a splinter of wood to an onion, a posie of flowers or a cheese grater. Tudgay insisted I had to learn about light on textures and general composition with a big old Soho-Reflex half-plate camera. Groping about in the darkroom with the two girls seeing how things develop was a revelation by comparison!

While Norman Tudgay was the creative photographer, Tom Buckeridge, his part-time colleague, was a brilliant technical tutor. After my first year of intensive learning, the two mentors reviewed my probationary period and recommended to Mr Hayes that I should stay on in order to realise a potential talent.

Pam and Jan left college, so I became the senior student to a handful of freshmen in 1956. One of the newcomers became a friend for life. Unbeknown to Peter Anderson, a young man of Scottish blood who lived in Gravesend, he was to have a terrific influence upon where I was to target my career.

Peter arrived at Rochester with a good track record in amateur photography. I was amazed when I found that he shared my enthusiasm for motor racing. I discovered his expertise when he showed me a folio of his motor racing photographs taken at Brands Hatch. Peter's work was brilliant considering that he had none of the advantages of the accredited photographer working on the inside track.

Suddenly a purpose dawned upon my life, I had not seen the wood for the trees. It had never occurred to me that by combining photography with motor racing, I could placate a yearning to travel and perhaps make a living. Peter had given me ample food for thought.

I overstayed my two-year welcome to Medway by just over a year. Tudgay nursed an ambition to start a course of colour photography and reckoned that this would enhance my chances in life if I could show a combined ability to handle both monochrome and colour work. The course never materialised in my time.

A year or so after we had moved to Barnehurst, Mum's weekend job at Brands Hatch began to impinge upon the weekdays as well. Since she never learned to drive a car and Dad was still occupied at the Borough Council, Mum decided to cycle from Stephen Road to the racing circuit for work on general practice and private test days.

The combined return distance of some 26 miles over a very hilly route through Crayford and Horton Kirby before reaching Brands along a steep back lane was quite a trial of strength, even for a lady of Mum's stamina. While she insisted that the cycling and walking up the hills was good for her constitution, what she omitted to mention was the long hours she spent on her feet all day dealing with the likes of Stirling Moss and Graham Hill.

At this time, John Hall had employed the services of George Pennington as the on site track manager. He was responsible for the condition of the circuit road surface, curbing, keeping the infield grass low, replenishing protective earth banks, supervising marshals' points and overseeing all the spectator amenities. And that was only half the job.

George, his wife and two strapping sons, Keith and Colin, lived in the cramped accommodation attached to the rear of the Pavilion. Their rooms mostly overlooked the Paddock which had been relocated from the infield at Paddock Bend. So the dawn chorus on practice and race days can be ima-gined!

The Penningtons were at everybody's beck and call. Often they had late nights with riotous tramps' suppers, board meetings, film shows and other social events. John Hall was well aware of this toll on the Penningtons' private life. It was one heck of a job with nobody close by to provide relief.

Sometime during 1957 Mr and Mrs Hall vacated their converted apartment at Kingsdown Park House which stood proud in woodland half way up Druids, One weekend at Brands Hatch, Dad and I wandered over to the big house. 'How do you fancy living here, son?' he asked, barely able to conceal a Cheshire-cat grin.

I stared open-mouthed, aghast at what appeared to be baronial mansion, Park House was situated in a beautiful spot, several miles from towns like Rochester, Gravesend, Dartford, Sevenoaks and Maidstone. My initial feeling was of isolation, I didn't fancy being cut of from all my chums and places that were familiar to me.

On the other side of the coin was the thought of actually living at Brands Hatch. Since I was a teenager, a bit of pride came into play. Golly — wouldn't Peter be impressed! I warmed to the idea and then Dad returned me to practicalities. No — we would not have the run of all sixteen rooms. The first-floor apartment was the section on offer and that included the three maids' rooms on the second floor — minus the service! That still left ten rooms for us, overlooking a splendid view of Fawkham Valley. Druids and Paddock could just be detected through the trees of what I had chosen to be my bedroom. I was there already.

The move to Brands Hatch saved a great deal of wear and tear on Mum, and for the first time in years the Penningtons could take days off together while we held the fort. Dad had to drive to work while I cycled to Longfield railway station to catch trains to Rochester for College.

2

Occupational Hazards

GEORGE PHILLIPS was the staff photographer for the British weekly racing magazine *Autosport*. Since I had been inspired by Peter Anderson's work, I made a point of talking with established motor racing photographers about work. Some of the freelance chaps were unforthcoming, no doubt anticipating a threat to their own livelihoods. George was a gruff fatherly figure, prepared to pass the time of day with me. I told him of my aspiration to join the ranks of motor racing photographers in the future.

Straight away George placed a friendly hand on my shoulder, then he looked me straight in the eye and said: 'Listen my lad, don't just stick around here, people who matter will think of you as a Brands specialist. Go to other circuits. Put yourself about with the editors. Let 'em know what you want to do. See you at Silverstone next week — eh?'

I was well aware the 1958 British Grand Prix was taking place on the Northamptonshire circuit the following Saturday. I didn't have a car. Cycling there would take an age. Instead I opted for the thumb.

Lady Luck must have smiled favourably as I stood on the A20 road outside the main entrance to Brands Hatch on a brilliant Saturday morning. A chappie from the Maidstone area pulled up in his Jowett Javelin. It was five o'clock and his cheery welcome answered my request.

'Silverstone, you're in luck, Jump in'.

This was just before motorways were opened, so our motoring enthusiast with great dexterity picked a route through London to join the A5 arterial road to the north-west. Even at this unearthly hour, race fans were out in their numbers as traffic bottled up, filing through towns like St Albans and Dunstable. By the time we reached Stony Stratford, traffic was coming to a crawl which signalled to my acquaintance to pull off and wend his way through a hotch-potch of country lanes in the Whittlewood Forest to temporarily join the jam getting into the circuit. Matey informed me that he had been attending the Grand Prix at Silverstone since 1951, which explained his knowledge of the back routes, Nevertheless, I was astonished that we were parked and ready to face the big day as the cock crowed at 8 am.

I had been spoilt by the excellent viewing facilities at Brands Hatch; but the layout of Silverstone over airfield perimeter roads with its limited horizons still came as a surprise to me.

I homed in upon the paddock inside the circuit and caught the officials at the 'Motor' bridge napping as I waltzed past them into the pits area. What a pleasant surprise to find a few familiar faces among the marshals, the mechanics and the racing drivers. It dawned upon me that this was what was euphemistically called the 'circus'. These were the tight nucleus of folk who travelled to all the races throughout Britain and Europe.

I caught sight of the big transporters that disgorged flaming Ferraris, verdant Vanwalls and the privately entered Maseratis. I had taken my ancient Rolleicord and invested in a single roll of film. Instead of being the eager photographer, I spent so much time staring in vacant admiration at this kaleidoscope of automotive wizardry that, when the film was processed, I had taken only eight exposures from a reel of twelve all day!

Amid the general melée I singled out George Phillips, who welcomed me like a son. He was delighted that I had shown the initiative to break away from the apron strings of Brands Hatch. By way of a reward, he wangled me a press pass. Before bustling off to work, he strongly advised: 'This circuit is bloody fast. If you get on the infield, keep your eyes open. Cars spin off at a rate of knots. I'll be at Copse early on. If you see me, stand behind, I don't want your backside in my pictures. Remember, just keep walking until you're stopped. You'll be alright'.

That last piece of advice remained deeply ingrained. It was the most effective way of dealing with officialdom at circuits.

The British Grand Prix wasn't so much a race, more an opportunity to soak up all the images, to study photogenic angles, to see the opportunity to practise Tudgay's light, texture and composition. I was aware of colour, of the drivers' expressive faces showing piercing concentration. Above all, I looked for the maximum effort when racing cars are being driven to the brink of disaster. It was soul-stirring and I became more than aware of the human aspect of motor racing rather than the mechanical side of the sport. The internal combustion engine and all its ramifications held no spell over this mind which had never understood the nuts-'n'-bolts of how it worked. I could appreciate a piece of machinery put together with tender loving care by a mechanical genius. For me to grapple with spanners was beyond my ken. My ignorance of what happened 'under the bonnet' had a bearing upon my future life as an observer of motor racing when I came to write about the sport.

Days after the race I collected the mounted slides and in a quiet corner of Park House meticulously viewed them. I was enveloped in disappointment. Oh, the photographs had come out perfectly: so they damned well should, after all my training. I could not comprehend how I had exposed such mundane pictures in my effort to capture some of the Silverstone colour.

My pride and joy was a shot of the Swedish driver, Joakim Bonnier, in his red Maserati, standing on the brakes before entering Copse Corner. It was the only action photograph on the reel, but it was perfectly aligned, in focus and — although I said it myself — a positive little Rembrandt. Don't forget, this was before zoom lenses, telephotos and suchlike. No wonder I was chuffed. My best independent witness was to be George Phillips. Weeks later I caught up with him at a Brands Hatch club meeting. When I showed him the sum total of my day's outing at Silverstone, George grimaced. As he peered at each picture in detail, the dour expression lightened.

'Don't let my editor Gregor Grant see these. I might be out of a ruddy job!'

* * *

Most of us experience a red-letter day, but in February 1959 I had a distinctly black-letter day. I arrived at Art College to be asked by Mr Tudgay to help tidy the studio. Then he set me the task of forming a set for a portraiture session. Word was about that the Chairman of the College Governors was making a random visit. I recognised the towering figure of authority enter the studio. Before Mr Tudgay had the opportunity to greet him, the Governor strode over to my set and in a loud voice said:

'Are you still here, Le Grand?'

'Yes sir', I replied.

'Then we'll have to remedy that', scowled the authority. Deep in my heart I knew what he was talking about, and before I broke into a cold sweat I continued to set the lights.

Later that day I was summoned to the Principal's office. Mr Hayes half looked at me; 'I don't know how to put this, Max', he paused. 'I have to expel you, and you must leave the college by the end of this week'.

The end of my course was overdue by fifteen months. During that time the college grant had been paid each term without question. I had firmly established myself within the social fabric of the College, helping to arrange dances, rag weeks, outings and even a rock boat cruise to France... not forgetting my photographic studies as well.

Mr Hayes and Mr Tudgay offered every assistance in attempting to find me a job somewhere in the Medway Towns. Meanwhile, I requested time to visit London in search of work. Nobody seemed to hold out much hope. I had amassed a good folio of work, but my tutors' report was non-committal: 'Max is at times astonishing, at other times just astonishing'. Mr Tudgay reckoned that I had made the best of myself with inferior equipment, which I took as a compliment. In spite of my brave face, I was quaking in my boots and felt nauseous with worry. How on earth was I going to tell Mum and Dad that I had been expelled from Rochester?

Full of apprehension, on the following day I stepped from a train at Victoria Station and viewed London's teeming mass with gloom. If all those people had jobs, then why shouldn't I get one, was the question I kept posing to myself as I wandered aimlessly toward the W H Smith book stall in the station concourse. I idly flicked through some magazines. One was a copy of *Good Housekeeping*, and I quickly noted that their offices were just across the road from the Victoria Railway terminal in Grosvenor Gardens. My mood hardened as I mounted the steps of the grey, Victorian edifice, studiously ignored the commissionaire (recalling George's advice — 'Keep walking') and almost succeeded in making an entrance before the gentleman of the guard halted me. I informed him of an urgent need to visit the photographic studio. He telephoned a Mr Kenneth Swain, who was the Chief Photographer. His assistant welcomed me at the reception and I casually mentioned that I was a student looking for employment. By some amazing quirk of good fortune, the fellow confided his intention to leave the studio soon to sign on for his national service.

I was taken to the basement where Kenneth Swain was finishing a 'Quickie Cook' session for *She* magazine. He then took me into his office and after about an hour of general conversation and a perusal of my folio, this wonderful Pickwickian character, with a ready laugh that was often punctuated by the snort of a pig, pondered awhile, explained the circumstances (which I already knew), then in a off-hand manner told me that the job was mine at the going rate of £8 2s 6d a week.

That was a couple of quid less than I had been earning after I had collectively completed my morning paper round, deposited ginger-beer bottles, rewound film and done the baker's round on Saturdays. What the hell, to walk into a job at The National Magazine Company and have the prospect of performing work for *Good Housekeeping*, *She* magazine, *Vanity Fair* and *House Beautiful* far outweighed financial considerations. I grabbed the opportunity with both arms. That night Mum and Dad were overwhelming in their pride at my luck. The following day Mr Hayes, my mentors and everybody at the College were delighted. Rarely had a student toasted his own future in the Principal's study, but I did. The black-letter day had turned out to be a red-letter one after all. My apprenticeship under Kenneth Swain lasted about a year and a half. I had worked with one of the best food photographers in the business. The numerous colour supplements in *Good Housekeeping* which he had illustrated over the years bore witness to this. I had joined Ken on outdoor assignments as well, and since most of the work was in colour, this made up for the knowledge which I had narrowly missed at College. I had also learned about 'back lighting' subjects, especially food, to enhance the mouthwatering flavour of the dishes. A growing number of my lunch hours were spent at The Steering Wheel Club, a Mayfair watering hole for the racing fraternity situated along the narrow Brick Street. On one occasion there I met with Gregor Grant, the cheery editor of *Autosport*. Gregor had obviously been informed by George Phillips in conversation of my ambitions. He was a man with very wide contacts in motor racing circles across Europe and in North America, where he observed most of the international events and Grands Prix.

When Gregor was given food for thought, he would often grind his jaw while his eyes rolled skywards. Over a gin-and-tonic he made a considered suggestion.

'Max, I suggest you might learn something about motor racing photography that you aspire to, if you visit Louis Klemantaski'. At that time, Klemantaski was my role master. I had spent hours studying his work in various publications. I telephoned the great man, and he agreed to see me.

While chatting outside The Steering Wheel Club before we parted to go our different ways, I noticed, over Gregor's shoulder a Royal Coat of Arms over the next door. I commented upon this and Gregor in a hushed Scots tone informed me that above the Club were the studios of Baron, the famous court photographer.

Eventually my term of service at The National Magazine Company ran down, so during a short hiatus I found myself fulfilling assignments for *Autosport* at various club meetings at Brands, working with Martyn Watkins and Chris Nixon who reported on the race meetings.

My initial black-and-white pictures were not much good. I worked then with a German Leica camera with a 55 mm lens. I ended up either centring cars in the enlarger, cars falling out of the frame, or magnifying tiny dots in the centre of the negative. I wrote long captions to explain the subject matter, which prompted Chris Nixon to suggest that I would be a better reporter than a photographer! I hated monochrome work, but I had to learn.

Wall's Ice Cream enlisted my services in 1959 to attend the British Grand Prix at Aintree just outside Liverpool. The assignation did not cover the race. Instead, I had a brief to photograph in colour a model girl mingling with the race fans in the paddock as they purchased ice cream from the newly designed kiosks which the company had made that year!

It was strange to be at such a big meeting and barely having time to focus my attention upon all the excitement around me. The World Championship race was won by Jack Brabham, a race which the model Judy and I witnessed after spending best part of the day immersed in people licking ice cream. In retrospect, it was a bonus, because I might not have gone to Aintree, a venue that was more familiar to followers of the Grand National horse race.

Aintree's emergence as Britain's second Grand Prix circuit to Silverstone was a mixed blessing. In fairness to race enthusiasts north of Pudsey, it meant that the premier event was more accessible: it was also a bonus to fans from across the Irish Sea. Those looking for a different kind of horse power seemed a trifle nonplused.

The Liverpool circuit could have been a serious rival to John Hall's third phase of development which would turn Brands Hatch into a pukka Grand Prix circuit. Instead, Mirabelle Topham's road circuit with a steeplechase course probably stung John Hall into action.

Throughout 1959-60 feverish work progressed in the woodland where the original scramble course ran through Dingle Dell, through the (real) bomb holes and through the infamous Chalkpit. Most of these features were bull-dozed, levelled and given a smooth road surface. In my spare time I earned some ready cash humping hard core, wheeling barrows of cement and bunging up rabbit holes. It was tremendously exciting contributing in a small way to the circuit's growing development.

The finished product was a 2.65-mile road circuit that encompassed Hawthorn Bend (a fast climbing right-hander), the Portobello Straight (named after a local pub), Westfield Corner and the notorious Dingle Dell which every self-respecting scrambler in the world had known as 'Flint Hill'. Tony Brooks, driving a Yeoman Credit Intercontinental Cooper Coventry-Climax, had the honour of making the first exploratory laps of the new Grand Prix circuit. He found an exciting challenge in its complex undulating layout, which was certainly different from the 'flat' circuits of Silverstone and Aintree.

* * *

At the age of twenty I had still not learned to drive and therefore I had not experienced that thrill of owning a motor car. But I religiously-maintained George Phillips's advice and somehow travelled to other British circuits. Apart from Silverstone and Aintree, I caught a train to Chichester then I made for Goodwood in Sussex to see the historic Tourist Trophy race.

My old chums Chris Casey and Peter Festorazzi of the Rochester Chatham & District Motor Club took me to the Gold Cup Meeting at Oulton Park, the picturesque Cheshire venue. I developed a huge affection for Snetterton, the airfield circuit in Norfolk, and later in my career I won awards with photographs taken at Snetterton during a miserable, rain-soaked, meeting.

People on the inside of the sport were already aware of John Webb, an amazing man who suffered from a crippling disease but it never seemed to prevent him from actually racing and eventually becoming the 'King-Pin' when Grovewood Securities became the owners of Brands Hatch and a power in British motor sport.

Before he flourished, John, among other entrepreneurial exploits, had formed the flight charter company Webbair. This service existed to fly racing personnel to various international meetings across Europe.

Shortly after I left The National Magazine Company, I decided to make my first foray to international events. I chose to attend the ADAC Nürburgring 1,000-kilometre race, followed a week later by the 1960 Monaco Grand Prix. I had booked a single flight to Germany on Webbair, so when the day in May came to assemble at London Gatwick Airport, I was shivering with nervous excitement. Not until I reached the airport did I know whether there was going to be anybody familiar in the party... apart from John Webb, of course.

Peter Garnier was the motor racing editor on *Autocar*. He took me under his paternal wing on the flight, and in a rented Volkswagen at Köln-Bonn Airport in Germany, we drove to the Nürburgring where the last deed he performed was to wangle a photographer's pass for me from the dubious press officer concerned. From then on I was on my own.

Professional writers like Peter were on expenses, whereas I counted every penny of my own money. The only publication to show a peep of interest in my adventure was *Motor Clubman*, a small magazine edited by Tony Gilfrin at his Orpington-based office.

My mood at Nürburgring fluctuated between enthusiasm and complete despair. The 14-mile circuit that cut a swathe through the conifer forests of the Eifel Mountains was forbidding and mist-laden when rain was pouring upon the scene. Like many naive travellers then I believed that everywhere south of Calais was a sun-kissed paradise. I was inadequately prepared for the soaking as I stood and contemplated the spaghetti of steel tubes that made up the space frame of the Camoradi-Maserati which was driven by Stirling Moss

31

and Dan Gurney in the pit lane.

Suddenly my wet little world went dry. I looked around to be greeted by a bespectacled gentleman with a walrus moustache holding an umbrella who muttered: 'No car is worth getting that wet for'. Henry Manny II, the esteemed Franco-American writer of *Road & Track*, the top American car magazine, had made a welcome intrusion upon my life. Meeting with Henry lifted all my apprehensions as well, because, after a long chat in the Sport Hotel, he offered to share his room with me. The sinister hills of the Nürburgring suddenly lost their satanic atmosphere.

Over the years of observing motor sport, I have noticed how Henry's enthusiasm has waxed and waned at each venue. I awoke the next day and happily informed Henry that I intended to walk the entire 14 miles of the Nürburgring. He blanched and peered at me with incredulity. 'Don't let this old critter dampen your enthusiasm', Henry mused, 'but it's trees, hills, wild swine and fuzz in jack boots out there. Allow me to drop you at Adenau Bridge, then you can walk half the circuit back against the racers. I'll see you at the hotel for tea'.

Henry left me outside Adenau to learn the facts of life. He was right, but what he omitted to mention was the dripping trees, a quagmire under foot and the dedicated enthusiasm of the Germans who stoked up camp fires and offered frankfurters and black coffee to the bedraggled English passerby. Nothing dampened their love for real motor racing amid the Eifel forests.

They adopted Moss and Gurney who handed the bacon to the Camoradi Team after an heroic drive. I was quite pleased with my colour work around the pit area, but the 'moody' monochromes that attempted to capture the vile conditions of that weekend with cars slithering through trees were just too damned arty for good photo-reportage.

So it was back to the drawing-board as I journeyed alone by train from Köln to Milano, then direct to Nice via Ventimilia. Before facing the claustrophobic environs of a Grand Prix through the streets of Monte Carlo. I had already learned that there was more to international motor racing than mere pictures.

Depending upon your social station, Monte Carlo boasts a wide variety of watering holes to suit virtually any pocket. I found a place half way up Saint Devote. This was the 'Chatham Bar' run by the adorable Rosie Balbou which was adequate to my bottom line budget. Sitting alone, squinting at the many signed photographs of ancien pilotes hanging on the bar walls was a slim man who offered an open-handed greeting.

'Aren't you the fellow who travelled with Peter Garnier last week?' chortled my new-found friend with the impish love for his sport.

Phillip Turner was another extremely short-sighted British reporter who viewed motor racing through lenses of such magnification that a Ferrari must have appeared like a London double decker bus. Nevertheless, his clear, concise race reports graced the pages of *Motor* magazine.

Phillip wore a necklace of binoculars and cameras, while on even this most balmy of Mediterranean days, he carried a plastic mackintosh 'just in case'.

Over a beer Phillip told me how he had flown back to London with his photographer Maurice Rowe to post his race report from the Nürburgring and edit his sports gossip page. He then flew to Nice on the Wednesday, and here he was, bright as a button in the strong Côte d'Azur sunshine and raring to go on this most glamourous of Grand Prix.

Open-minded to a fault, Phillip told me how he collected his notes in the pit lane, rummaged for the practice times and race results in the press office, then at the finish of the meeting how he drafted his report on the race while flying home. I commented that it must be a hard life at the height of the season. Phillip disagreed. He chortled some more, his apparently large brown eyes sparkling with glee as he related how smashing it was, and what tremendous fun he had seeing all these races in such delightful places. Phillip Turner may not have carried Bunter's rotundity, but 'I say you chaps' his enthusiasm for racing easily matched Billy's boyish gluttony for food.

According to Henry Manny, when the Grand Prix came to Monte Carlo, the rich old biddies either closed the shutters and pulled the curtains, or moved in with their bridge-playing partners somewhere below the Grand Corniche overlooking the principality. Who can blame them, the 6.30 am practice period is not exactly music even to the most dedicated. Apart from the lively social aspect of the Monaco Grand Prix, which I gather was formal in the staid portals of the Hotel de Paris and thoroughly informal, which suited me, at the Tip Top Bar half way down Mirabeau, I learned some sobering facts on motor racing photography.

Monaco on first sight is a photographic delight: lots of expensive motor cars and scantily dressed girls; and until I visited the Casino, I hadn't realised how productive the Royal Mint had been! Wonderful fun — but a potential motor racing photographer has to earn a living. Since nobody was going to enlist my services on the spot, I watched the professionals at work. A racing photographer has to plan his movements about the circuit ahead before covering an event such as the Monaco Grand Prix. Otherwise he could finish up positioned in a restricted area with no access to his next vantage point. Bearing in mind the lively social aspect of Monaco, I segregated the wide selection of photographers into four different categories. Firstly, there were the great camera artists like Julius Weitmann, Yves Debraine and Louis Klemantaski. Secondly came the accomplished specialist magazine photographers. Next the newspaper representatives I christened the 'gore mongers' whose editorial brief was simply to capture in minute detail the horrendous accidents. Last, but not least, the all intrusive 'paparazzi' whose assignation was to 'sneak' pictures of high societies 'beautiful people' as they mingled with the racing set at parties where people in uncompromising situations could often be found.

The specialist magazine photographers had to grab shots that summed up the Grand Prix and highlighted the leading contenders. They were not able to unleash their creative powers in the name of photo-reportage.

Accomplished photographers like Debraine went to endless lengths in securing high viewpoints like the apartment block that overlooked the old

Station Hairpin at Monte Carlo to obtain a wide angle picture that illustrated the unique environment through which racing took place.

Even he would have to plan ahead in order to move from that location to another on the ground. For some at Monaco, actually getting back on the inside track was often prevented by over-zealous officials who manned the road blocks that closed the street circuit. Some frustrated photographers crashed the barriers while the thoughtful ones established good public relations with the officials before proceedings burst into action... a procedure that stands the passage of time.

If the Monaco Grand Prix had been a field education, then my visit to Louis Klemantaski at his town house in London served to qualify the curriculum I had set myself in Europe.

This aspirant found intriguing parallels with the early part of Louis' career. He started out with a Box Brownie, then after a couple of seasons actually racing, he turned his hand to a trusty Leica.

I envied Louis his 'inside knowledge' gained not just from competing, but later from co-driving the likes of Reg Parnell and Peter Collins in the Mille Miglia, the 1,000-mile race over the highways of Italy. His shots from the driver's viewpoint had me drooling. I also woke up to the fact I couldn't even drive a car at this stage!

What captivated me were the pre-war days when Louis literally worked on the roadside with drivers like Dick Seaman hurling a Mercedes, full throttle at 170 mph, towards his naked lens: foolhardy days, but what exhilaration.

I was constantly amazed to find that Klemantaski's post-war colour photography was exposed with a 2.25-inch square twin-lens reflex camera: no telephoto lenses. Louis opened a folio of his work taken at the Le Mans 24-hour race. There was one file of brilliant shots taken of sports cars powering through the Esses after the swoop downhill from under the Dunlop Bridge.

Every photograph was perfect in exposure, and in its balance of light and shade, and each car filled the centre of the frame. Not one picture had been composed in the enlarger which is a luxury for many monochrome photographers'. What I saw in each picture was exactly what he spotted in reality. He was right there, the sports cars whistling beneath his nose at 130 mph. To freeze that action, immobilise the driver's face and capture the attitude of the car, was the work of a great camera artist with a rare power of anticipation. I wondered how I had the gall to be in the same room as Louis Klemantaski. What standards to reach!

On the way home from London I had purchased a *British Journal of Photography*. There, in the 'Situations Vacant' column, I saw advertised the job of Studio Assistant at Baron Studios.

While the Managing Director of Baron Studios interviewed me he had come out with all kinds of facts concerning the illustrious studio. Back in 1955 Princess Margaret, under enormous pressure, decided against marrying Group Captain Peter Townsend, a commoner who was equerry to her late father, King George VI; not that this landmark in the nation's modern history had anything to do with me. But the consequences lightly brushed my life when a predecessor in my new job, Antony Armstrong-Jones, had served his apprenticeship under the great court photographer. My new boss, Mr Gwyer Gibson, went on to explain that Antony Armstrong-Jones had taken his departure in order to embark upon a freelance career at a small studio he established in Pimlico.

Rex Coleman, with whom I would attend sittings, jokingly informed me that everything I would touch had a brass plaque inscribed AAJ and it was up to me if I wished to replace them.

So I moved into a job that not only enhanced my prospects, but would also bring me into contact with royal personages, figures of state, the titled, and stars of show business. Given a platform I might appear to be a gregarious being, but in truth this essentially shrinking violet in front of the great and noble was too shy for words. So the job would do my confidence a power of good, and the privilege of lunches in The Steering Wheel Club should improve my own career no end.

Life was always interesting at Baron's where (unlike other studios,) we had to work with suits, clean shirts and ties.When state leaders were attended, I often had a quick lesson in etiquette, because one of the many reasons why leading personalities sought special sittings at the studio was that members of its staff knew how to address them politely: not just the fact we had the best photo-finishers and retouchers in the business who possessed the skill to lighten the furrows of power and obliterate the warts of age.

I often wondered what kind of man or woman relished the reigns of leadership over a nation. My first opportunity to encounter such a person came when President Nkrumah of Ghana invited us to his suite at the Savoy Hotel. He later faced two potential assassinations and a coup, and yet to me he was quiet, dignified and fastidious about his dress for the state pictures to be used for the Royal visit by The Queen and the Duke of Edinburgh in 1961.

Almost a year after Prime Minister Solomon Bandaranaika of Ceylon died from a murder attempt in 1959, the slight, almost diffident figure of his widow, Mrs Sirimavo Bandaranaike, arrived in London as the first woman Prime Minister in the world. The state required official pictures of the new Prime Minister, so we had to be extra careful with the lighting while a lady escort primped at her dress for what that seemed an eternity.

One of the most memorable sittings Rex and I attended was at the Carlton Tower Hotel in Knightsbridge. We were welcomed by armed guards at the appointed suite of rooms. They searched our equipment before allowing us inside to prime the set. While I searched out power points for our lights and extended the tripod, mounted the camera and placed the half-plate slides, Rex searched the rooms for an appropriate seat.

Before the leader arrived, the two guards again glanced around our set before standing aside to salute the entrance of His Beatitude, The Archbishop Makarios, Leader of the Greek Cypriots.

The sitting went without a hitch, apart from one amusing moment of paranoia when Rex went to press the shutter release for the first exposure. One of the guards spotted that a cable from a spotlight trailed beneath His Beatitudes habit. I honestly believe that the poor man thought we had a detonator. I hastily removed the cable to give the chair a wide berth. To make things worse, in making my profuse apology to Archbishop Makarios I blurted out: 'Sorry to inconvenience you Mr Battitude'. The leader laughed out aloud at my gaffe. I found out that heads of state do have a wry sense of humour. My stay at Baron's was worthwhile, if only from that point of view.

Lunchtimes often witnessed an exodus of racing folk to The Steering Wheel Club, many of whom represented the trade in motor sport. Over a good many 'jars of halves' I fell into conversation with gentlemen like the convivial Dick Jefferies (competition manager for Dunlop) and Laurie Hands (the benevolent chief at Champion Spark Plugs), who were always full of likely suggestions for work. I struck a very productive relationship with Harold Theyer from Ferodo Brake Linings whose works were at Chapel-en-le-Frith, and Ray Cunningham entrusted me with a big Shell promotion at the London Racing Car Show. I could envisage platforms upon which to use my talents other than photography and later writing about the sport. There was a crust to be earned ultimately, so I worked upon the assumption that from crumbs grow the real bread. I could get a slice of the action as a freelance.

While I was talking with these influential representatives within the sport, one problem became more apparent. Here I was, up to my neck, becoming more and more involved with motor racing with each passing day, and yet I could not drive a motor car! Where had I gone wrong?

The situation had to be remedied forthwith, otherwise I might have to build my reputation on 'the thumb' — not the best way to win friends and influence people in this game!

From the initial driving lesson at Gravesend in August 1961 I took part in an onward-going saga that became almost Whitehall farcical: it lasted for a laughable two and half years until I passed my Ministry of Transport Driving Test in Sevenoaks during March 1964.

My college of learning was spread between Dartford, Bexleyheath and a wide variety of hybrid, rally-tune cars and Motor Racing Stables whose staff-members kindly allowed me to practise driving over the service roads at Brands Hatch. What complicated the issue was that I had school instructors like Tony Lanfranchi and Syd Fox teaching me how to double declutch, how to heel and tow on braking and gear changes. I was more proficient at hand-brake turns and taking a smooth racing line around Brands Hatch with my arms straight, and my hands at ten-to-two on the steering wheel than I was at driving on the open road.

In fact, I was driving safely and efficiently but not sufficiently well to impress the test examiners: I failed the MoT driving test five times! The Examiners were not enamoured by smoking wheels as I drove away from traffic lights and the hand-brake being tugged and the wheel being yanked over when I should be performing a text-book three-point turn in some quiet cul-de-sac. Mind you, I had the Highway Code off pat — all I had to do was to drive properly.

Totally exasperated, I was assigned to the Phoenix Park races outside

Dublin in 1963. Peter Proctor, that virtuoso of racing and rallying and I stayed as house guests with Ireland's best rally-driver, Rosemary Smith. She suggested that I overcame my problem by calling in at City Hall, where I could purchase an Irish Driving Licence over the counter for £1, which would validate my driving in the United Kingdom for one year until I qualified for my full licence. Until I actually drew a curtain over my shame by passing the test in a dual-controlled Morris 1000 in Sevenoaks, the Irish licence sufficed. What I thought was a perfect Irish accent was sometimes suspected by the strong arm of the law, especially when I borrowed a Fiat 600 to cover the 1963 RAC Rally of Great Britain and the police stopped me for loitering on steep hills!

Mum and Dad were so relieved that I was at last legal that they treated me to a second-hand Hillman Minx. At last, I was independent.

* * *

What is this romance that pounds away in the hearts of so many motor racing enthusiasts? Talk to a mechanic with his oily rag and a brace of spanners — he will shrug his shoulders. Study the brow-beaten features of any team manager and he will question your sanity. Watch the marshals at their posts on the most rain-soaked of days and they appear to have been jilted. But scrutinise the wide-eyed features of drivers like Peter Collins, Mike Hawthorn or Innes Ireland — then you will catch the romance of motor racing.

If the 'fifties were an era of flamboyance, ne'er-do-care, live today and the pox on tomorrow, then I missed the bus during the so-called 'permissive sixties'. Strange how the rest of the world was always ten years behind the break-neck speed lived by the racing fraternity. Juan Manuel Fangio must have felt the veritable senior citizen when he passed judgment upon those virile young lions, Collins and Hawthorn, as they habitually deflowered damsels around the circuits of the world. The verdict on the five-times World Champion was 'Probably guilty... of envy'. But then he was twenty years ahead of his time.

Although I just caught the dying embers of that romantic era at the 1958 British Grand Prix, on reflection, the swinging sixties still maintained a rumbustuous air for a callow youth. Every dog has his day. What I missed out upon in the 'fifties, I certainly made up for during my era — a time I reflect upon with rose-coloured affection. So I shrugged off the nostalgia of respected scribes such as Denis Jenkinson, Bernard Cahier and even Henry Manny II who thought that the days of hairy-chested drivers went with Fangio's pension and kindled my romantic era firstly with admiration for Stirling Moss.

The Tring lad was the sole survivor of the 'fifties, while the likes of Mike Hawthorn, Peter Collins and Stuart Lewis-Evans had already ascended to the great circuit in heaven. Moss was very much the 'big star' of the early 'sixties. 'Coming Men' like Graham Hill and Scotland's Jim Clark were still snapping at his heels. I was already cutting my photographic teeth at Easter Goodwood in 1962 when I attended a non-championship Formula One race witnessing a horrifying accident in which Stirling Moss very nearly lost his life. Moss was driving a Yeoman-Credit Lotus Climax which had been suffering some kind of mechanical trouble, causing him to make two pit stops. Graham Hill was the race leader while Stirling was two laps down, but going like a shot-from-a-gun. I was at Fordwater watching the hair-raising pursuit. With no hope of winning the race, Moss — as ever — was giving the spectators full value. The lime-green Lotus bore down upon the BRM of Hill with incredible speed as Moss darted out to overtake Hill and unlap himself. I saw nothing of the impending accident and continued wandering back to the pits.

It was not until the next lap that I realised Moss was missing. As I passed a marshal's post, there was a great deal of agitation and concern. Only then did I know that something dreadful had happened.

Back in the paddock I encountered Michael Cooper, a freelance London photographer. He was totally distraught. Not only did he see the accident, but he captured the horrific crash on film. Mike was no 'gore-monger', he loved the sport and like me found the idea of capitalising upon a driver's misfortune totally abhorrent.

He last saw Stirling being extricated from the mangled wreckage of the Lotus by marshals and St John's ambulance staff. Mike reckoned that the impact was so hard that Stirling was a 'goner'.

This was to be the first time I experienced the 'down-side' of motor racing. Although I had witnessed accidents at other circuits, Stirling's terrifying shunt threw the sport into a completely different perspective for me. Remember, that afternoon, nobody knew whether he was dead or alive. Hardened men in the paddock choked back tears. Women stared, eyes red with crying, into a world of their own. Stirling had escaped before, We all recalled another awful accident at Spa during the Belgian Grand Prix the previous year. Moss hung on so tight that he bent in half the steering wheel of Rob Walker's Lotus 18. In that limbo of not knowing Stirling's fate, funny things trickled through my mind, like the memory of Mum chastising him over the shredded coconut buns at Brands Hatch. Since those early days, Stirling's life had become full of races, faces and so many different places. Everybody told me that in spite of his mercurial life-style, he always had time for people. I felt on the periphery of his life, although later on we always got on well together. He never let me down, and beneath that dashing persona was an extraordinarily humble man. Stirling Moss did survive and after a return to Goodwood to find that the old magic had gone, he retired. A picture I took of him on the grid at Goodwood that Easter Monday has now become very special. It was my last picture of Stirling the racing driver.

Not having a mechanical aptitude for motor cars, meant that my affair with the sport was stimulated more by the individual skill of the drivers.

How the man controlled the obstinate beast intrigued me more than the practicalities of high-performance machinery.

I tried to fathom what kind of mentality could sanely lower itself into the confine of a racing car cockpit, and then try to wring the beast's neck. Were these fellows off their rockers knowing, in those days, that the next race could be their last? Or did they emerge from the same mould that cast test pilots, mountaineers and the SAS? I guessed that racing drivers fell between the lot. Observers always trotted out the excuse that by living right on the brink of oblivion, racing drivers were entitled to their 'life of Riley'.

This attitude to life influenced some of the camp followers who adopted the drivers cosmopolitan existence. Just being a mere witness to their skill and bathing in reflected glory was a balm to their ego.

This was not to say that we did not suffer at the death. So I assume this inveterate romantic joined the roller coaster because everybody relished the excitement.

I was often financially embarrassed at the embryonic stage of my career. So not unnaturally I was indebted to Christopher Nixon who continued to enlist my photographic services for *Autosport* while the amiable Tony Gilfrin ran a series in *Motor Clubman* titled 'Wheel to Wheel' whereby I had the job of interviewing established club drivers like John Whitmore, Jack Sears and Chris Craft. My minuscule power base also encompassed a new magazine originated by Maurice Newbound called *Motor Rally* for which he retained me as the racing correspondent. Because the well-established publications like *Autocar*, *Motor Sport* and *Motor* magazine had their own staff providing full coverage of races, I leapt upon any new band-wagon going at the time. Some titles sank while others plodded on against all economic reason, providing a meal-ticket and a byline to races, to rallies and even to veteran car runs. At this early stage, the writing subsidised my photography. Heaven knows why, because the scripts I delivered were so abysmal, that publications needed a full-time sub-editor to unravel my copy into a readable story. It was dreadful, so I worked harder at the photography.

At the risk of being accused of being the craftsman who blamed his tools, I had to dump the antiquated Rollei and Leica cameras. Both instruments were doing my reputation a great deal of harm. I replaced them with a batch of Japanese equipment allegedly cloned from the real European McCoy's. I swapped the Rollei for a 2.25-inch Yashica-Mat, then supplemented its large format with a 35 mm Contax and was careful to make an astute choice of lenses. I wanted a simple life. Since zoom lenses had not been invented, I opted for a 200 mm Long Tom for the action, a 55 mm lens for general work about the pits and for drivers' portraits, and lastly a 21 mm lens for working in confined spaces to create wide-angled shots.

I employed the Yashica for photographs that would grace the front covers of magazines or — better still — double-page spreads in the centre. At that time, magazine printers were wary of accepting 35 mm colour slides on the assumption that they were too grainy to provide a sharp definition and that they lacked proper colour saturation. I fought tooth'n'nail against some art directors to convince them how wrong they were to allow themselves to be dictated to by the printers. We won in the end. I found two staunch allies in Charles Pocklington, the art editor of a brazen new magazine called *Small Car*, and — across the Channel — Gerard Crombac, the editor of the French magazine *Sport Auto*. Both magazines were bold enough to use my colour work, and they opened the flood gates. By nature I was never a person to follow trends. If I had been, maybe life would have been a lot easier. Instead I tried to plough my own furrow in motor racing photography.

As I travelled further afield to assorted events that included the Grands Prix, Indianapolis 500, Le Mans 24-hours, various rallies and twenty two London to Brighton Veteran Car Runs, my insatiable desire to explore and to meet people was gradually being placated.

The people in motor racing were perhaps far more important to me than the sport itself. I formed long-standing friendships with race marshals, with the mechanics, with gentlemen in the trade and with the many race fans. Racing drivers and team managers were important factors, but I always felt like a 'spare part' trying to nuzzle into a world that was beyond my ken. Certainly when it came to happy 'working relationships' with the hierarchy of the sport, I had to steel myself at the initial stages of my career. Working with Baron Studios should have knocked that last ounce of shyness out of me. So I was content with palling up to the supporting cast, and to be honest I found them a lot more informative when it came to my writing.

Photographers like Michael Tee, Lynton Money, Michael Cooper, Maxwell Boyd and David Phipps were basically motor racing enthusiasts lured to the sport by the creative stimulus of action, colour and the variety of backgrounds with the cast of great characters. Technical boffins revelled in the chromium-plated sculpture of the machinery. They were fulfilling a role of their own choice, where I was never 100% dedicated because I did not have that open choice.

As a child I was carried along with the parental flow. It was not my choice to visit Brands Hatch every weekend of my boyhood, but the alternative was to be left at home, which was impossible. As it happened, I enjoyed growing up in the competitive atmosphere. When it came to leaving school, and all else failed, my hobby of photography bubbled to the surface — again, not from choice. It was deemed by the powers that be that I should develop a latent creativity through the seeing eye. Further education was the easy option for the educational authorities in dealing with an apparently unambitious pupil. Since destiny, fate — call it what you like — had pre-ordained my respective paths of photography and motor racing, you may appreciate why I felt like the proverbial square peg in a round hole.

The reality of my situation was based upon travel right from infancy. From an early age I was fascinated by television as a medium. I nursed a desire to make programmes about people existing within their own native environment — seeing how they coped, learning ethnic work skills, studying parochial pastimes and finding out how their nationality shaped their character. When Alan Whicker embarked upon his circumnavigations of the world, I got extremely frustrated with people who told me to forget ideas that were above my station. Any ambition I harboured at 'trying my luck' was surreptitiously chiselled away. Anyway, I was carving a niche for myself by adopting the happy compromise, and I had set myself targets to which I could aspire. It was great fun to learn, but it was not all plain sailing.

3

Colour, Clarity & Competence

'THERE I was all crossed up with 9,000 on the clock and this bloody photographer pokes a camera in my face': words uttered tongue-in-cheek by Graham Hill to a rapt audience at a guest night organised by Nick Syrett for the British Racing and Sports Car Club above the *Paviours Arms* at Westminster. Such occasions were often a font of highly exaggerated stories related by well-oiled raconteurs like Graham — who was one of the best. At the time, he was referring to the 1960 British Grand Prix at Silverstone when, after a bad start, he shot through the entire field in pursuit of race leader Jack Brabham. Graham actually edged his BRM, ahead of the swarthy Australian's Cooper-Climax and then followed a ding-dong battle into the braking area of Copse Corner which ended when the BRM spun off into the banking. Graham Hill finished up right beneath my feet, and I have never heard such a string of blasphemy uttered. No wonder: that was to be his best chance to win the home race.

Right from the first time I set eyes upon Graham Hill at Brands Hatch, he seemed to impose his will upon a car by literally man-handling it around the circuit. The sheer effort and determination he poured into becoming a racing driver was legendary.

Some drivers like Stirling Moss and Jim Clark often 'performed' for the camera. If they spotted you all teed up for a shot, they gave a wave, set headlights blazing or tossed the car into a lurid oversteer which was the last thing I wanted. Graham swore blind that he never 'clowned' about for the photographers, since he was not blessed with the natural ability to control a racing car, every spare ounce of his effort and concentration went into winning. Hill's eyes were dark and piercing, his mouth a mean thin line, every racing mile was born of blood, sweat, toil and tears.

Graham was an extremely photogenic man, both in and out of the car, which explains why I came to rue the introduction of the all-enveloping Bell helmet introduced by Jackie Stewart at Watkins Glen during the 1968 United States Grand Prix. Suddenly, a lot of the character went out of motor racing photography as each driver adopted the 'egg-head' look.

Before that time Graham had attended the opening of an exhibition of my racing photography at Kodak's Regent Street showroom in London during 1966. While perusing the pictures, he observed one of himself and commen-

41

ted: 'What a miserable git I look when I am driving!' As soon as the Bells were donned we missed those dramatic expressions of wide-eyed, open-mouthed concentration when the clowning had to stop and they drove at ten-tenths for a victory.

One of the most marketable events for almost any publication in the world is the Royal Automobile Club's London-to-Brighton Veteran Car Run. Every November this unique annual cavalcade of emancipated carriages, all constructed before 1904, chug, hiss, pop and bang their journeys from the shores of the Serpentine to the popular resort in Sussex-by-the-Sea.

In 1959 Doug Eatwell was a staff photographer on the *News Chronicle*. When the world was at peace with itself, and Doug had a free Sunday, he would toddle from his home at Hartley to Brands Hatch to sniff out a potential picture story.

One day in November 1959 he called and invited me to join him to cover the 'Old Crocks Run' — as it became known. I was dubious, because antique motor cars had never caught my attention. Anyway, I went along with Doug in his black Austin A35 for the day out.

To say that I was completely overwhelmed would be a gross understatement. I had not realised how picturesque veteran cars were and what characters drove them. I became utterly smitten by the event and attended the run on twenty-two different occasions thereafter.

The RAC reckoned that whatever the weather, over one million spectators cheered the participants along the 56-mile route down the A23 arterial road. The spirit of the Veteran Car Run was typically evoked in 1971 when Graham Hill was accompanied by actress Dora Bryan on a charity-collecting mission for Oxfam. He was driving a 1903 7.5 hp Wolseley. Like most competitors un-accustomed to the idiosyncrasies of the horseless carriage, Graham was having a rare experience juggling with the clutch on the right foot and the brake to the left while attempting to control the velocity with the advance-and-retard ignition device.

He spotted me just outside Redhill, shot a broad grin my way (which belied the steely racing-driver image) and waved a two-fingered sign before having to jump on the brakes to stop the Wolseley from crashing into a stationary modern car. From the mayhem emerged Dora, shuddering but not shaken, while the Wolseley suffered what Graham described as 'a bang up the chuff' in the melée.

The hard-luck stories on the run amount to a legion each year, only to be equalled by the towering resolve to actually cross the finish line along Brighton's Madeira Drive in some semblance of order. Overseas readers lap up this typical cameo of pure British eccentricity.

Enthusiasts often assumed that Monaco was the most attractive venue at which racing photographs could be taken. I go along with that opinion. A person would need to be a hard case not to feel the claustrophobic excitement generated by racing cars zapping through the narrow streets. There were stretches of road where you could see driving skills being exercised — like the harbour chicane, Tabac, the 'S' bend through Casino Square, and the hump going down to Mirabeau. The trouble is that some of these places might have been inaccessible. Monaco for me was a place for 'pretty pictures' and it was always fun wondering whether one year someone on the front row of the grid would 'collect' Louis Chiron (who started the race) as he performed frenzied antics on the line with seconds to go before the 'off'.

Different venues inspired varying degrees of creative stimulus. I found that airfield circuits like Sebring, Florida, Snetterton, Silverstone and Goodwood came alive in certain incongruous conditions.

It was Snetterton on a dreadful, grey stormy day when I had the inspiration to take the photograph that won the Ford 'Colour Photograph of the Year' in 1966. I remember standing for some time in pouring rain, camera akimbo, watching the impassive face of Chris Amon as he sat in his mighty AC Cobra being sheltered by his New Zealand chum, Bruce Abernathy, who held an umbrella over the driver. The scene summed up just how everybody felt that day and obviously my photograph of it won the approval of the judges.

While travelling to the circuits, I amassed a certain knowledge of each venue where I knew the drivers were being put to the ultimate test of having to drive to the limit — on the brink of disaster on testing terrain.

My heart's desire was the French Grand Prix at Rouen-les-Essarts, a spectacular road circuit set in the region of Haute, Normandy. The incredible downhill series of curves with an embankment to the left and a precipitous drop to the right reached from the start line to the cobbled hairpin, contained all the ferocious whiplashes that sorted the champions out from the chaff. Louis Klemantaski caught a fantastic shot of Fangio in his Maserati in a high-speed over-steer drift — one of the greatest photographs taken of the maestro at his miraculous best in 1957.

The 1.5-litre cars were too underpowered to be as dramatic as Fangio's. So I settled for the infield at the hairpin which was a cobbled, adverse-camber surface. Drivers would arrive here from a fast left-hand sweep and in a matter of yards had to brake, rush through the gearbox to first or second, then haul the car back to the left-hand side of the road to make a correct approach to the hairpin. Not even Jim Clark had time to wave at this point. When he was under extreme pressure, the Lotus 25 would loom into view with wheels locked up, tyres smoking as he scrabbled about in the cockpit attempting several things at once. It was the one place where his immaculate driving skills were pushed to the limit.

Zandvoort, where the Dutch Grand Prix found a home, was planned in an imaginative series of high-speed curves, a straight and two hairpin bends. The circuit was planned over the sand dunes that are so much a feature of the Dutch North Sea coastline. There was a swift section of undulating curves which the 1.5-litre Grand Prix cars were driven virtually flat out. Standing high on a dune, I focussed on the cars as they screamed past below my feet. Using the 200 mm lens I panned into the action. Blue Dunlop racing overalls shimmered in the wind. I could see the drivers fighting to control power slides by their deft handling of the steering wheel. A Ferrari hove into sight. John Surtees was on full song and his cockpit filled the view-finder. Every detail was crystal clear as he darted beneath me at 165 mph. This was before the days of motor-driven cameras, so this was a once-in-a-lifetime shot. I released the shutter of the Pentax and felt sure that I had captured a tremendous picture. I followed through by focusing upon other cars, but like a skeet-shooter aiming upon a clay, with the same inkling of time to react. I missed other shots by a yard or so in the frame. Upon returning to London I was dead keen to see those photographs. The picture of John Surtees stood out like a Rembrandt. Such crucial moments have to be savoured — they are few and far between.

Over the years of working in the Ardennes forests where Spa-Francorchamps posed the greatest examination at the Belgian Grand Prix, Henry Manny and I habitually spent at least one practice session cooped up in the doorway of a house between Malmedy and Les Coombes. Cows grazed in fields of buttercups and it was through this rustic scene that the racing cars swept along the fastest curves of the quickest road circuit in the world. Henry described it as real 'tippy-toey' stuff where only drivers of great virility nerved their way through with hobnailed boots on! Henry tuned me in to his private audio show. We listened for the slightest sign of a driver feathering his accelerator. If it was a pole position lap then we would delight in the pure sound of eeeeeee EEEEEE OOOOOOOOOOOOO WWWWWW wwwwww. On the other hand any driver suffering the hee-bee-jee-bees would betray a sound like eeeee EEEEOOOOO (gasp) OOOOO wwwwww. We sometimes got rural pictures of cows chewing the cud, barely distracted the racing cars, or just kept on listening, then wagging our fingers at drivers back at the pits.

Early September in motor racing parlance translated to Monza and the Italian Grand Prix. The prospect always triggered a quasi-religious melancholia. To enter the autodromo early in the week of the race, could be likened to a pilgrimage to the Lombardy shrine. By Friday, enthusiastic Italians arrived by the thousands to pay homage to the Great God — Ferrari.

Back in the 'sixties Dr Franco Gozzi, a bear of a man, attended the public affairs of Scruderia Ferrari. In 1966 John Frankenheimer, the Hollywood film director, had managed to extract a budget of millions of dollars out of Metro Goldwyn Mayer to make the film 'Grand Prix'. The entire production had provided a colourful distraction to the real thing throughout that season. Frankenheimer had achieved the near impossible by securing location shots right within the Ferrari racing headquarters. The film director took me along for the ride — an opportunity I was not going to miss.

Under the guise of seeking potential sets, Frankenheimer asked Gozzi to show him around the entire factory, a facility rarely granted to even the most respected customer, let alone a Hollywood mogul. As I ogled the production line of Formula One Ferraris being prepared for the Grand Prix, Gozzi took me by the arm and informed me what a lucky man I was to be hanging on to Frankenheimer's long coat tail. When the time came for the director to discuss the terms for the facility, Gozzi led me to a quiet corner and eulogised poetically about the magic of Ferrari at this time of the season.

'Do you know what Ferrari means to the Italian?' murmured Franco: 'I tell you. Take a beautiful red rose, plucked in the morning dew. Watch the sunlight glint on each individual petal. Count the colours of the spectrum in the droplets of moisture. Then take the rose to your nose and savour the fragrance. That, for the Italian, is 'bello figuro'. I was enchanted but at the same time taking forbidden photographs of the race mechanics preparing the cars. Franco turned a blind eye. I felt that this was the Vatican of privilege to car buffs the world over, and the Doctor was a brilliant public relations director.

Several years later, in 1974, *Fast Car* magazine assigned me to a weekend with Scruderia Ferrari at the Italian Grand Prix. I was welcomed by the team manager Luca Montezemolo at the Hotel Sant Eustorgia which is situated next door to a Roman Catholic church in Arcore, just up the road from Monza.

I sat down on this balmy evening with Luca and his chief engineer Mauro Forghieri and talked over the race to come. Niki Lauda sat at an adjacent table with his wife Mariella. Luca was continually being called to the telephone, since mobiles were not in service then. It meant that he was always having to go into the hotel. During one of these intervals, Mauro pursued the theme which Dr Gozzi had started in 1966, concerning the Italian psyche and the motor car. Mauro was a demonstrative man, full of passion — this came across in his statement: 'Italian man will go without pasta for a whole year in order to purchase a motor car which will be beyond his means of extended credit. You can see this, just look at the new cars parked outside dreary tenements. You will judge his home is not his castle like it is in England. Niki Lauda overheard these comments, and leant over to me with a cynical grin and said: 'What a load of rubbish. Half the cars are stolen'.

Suddenly the convivial atmosphere was shattered by the venomous sound of a multi-cylinder motorcycle engine changing down through the gears as it approached the hotel. I had been aware of the youths who craned their necks over the hotel boundary wall keeping a vigil on the comings-and-goings at the hostelry. A figure astride an MV Augusta motorcycle thundered through the gateway to the hotel which signalled the cry 'Scarrozzo Clay Reg-azzon-iii'. The instant excitement generated around the grounds was quite deafening as the motorcycle blatted to halt and the hunched figure of Reg-azzon-iii switched off the MV, propped it up and — like a great orchestral conductor — moved into the lighted part of the gardens.

Before the hotel was overwhelmed, security guards had hastily closed the gates to the sacred land of Lambrusco and Ferrari. By now the choir of chanting voices over the wall was being augmented by the church bells sounding for twenty minutes.

That weekend of Italian madness was, to the humiliation of Commandetore Enzo Ferrari, an utter fiasco. Neither Niki Lauda nor Clay Regazzoni could vanquish the Imperial weed. The John Player Special driven by Sweden's blond national hero delivered the suckling pig amid cries of NO-NO-NO bellowed by the fervent partisan throats in the main grandstand. The mood was 'brutto' — ugly — and since the Latin by nature either rises in ecstasy or falls suicidally, there is no mezzanine floor for respect and humility in defeat.

Monza has always been something of an enigma among photographers. Motor racing history lingers at every corner. The trees stand sentinel witnesses to great battles that stretch back to the 'twenties when the autodromo opened. Ghosts may haunt the Lombardi circuit, but unfortunately they cannot be recorded alongside the modern charioteers. A photographer has to work hard for a masterpiece, but without a telephoto lens you are professionally dead. Before the chicanes and the armco barriers, Monza was a slip-streamer's race, where a shake of the dice at the 180° Parabolica bend leading to the home straight decided which drivers would be victoriously acclaimed. When Monza lethargically moved with the times of safety, a more sinister monolith loomed. The armco barrier that was designed to deflect errant racing cars, made a posthumous World Champion of Austria's Jochen Rindt when he flew off the road in the Gold Leaf Lotus 72 Ford. Ronnie Peterson, driving a similar car, lost his life at the chicane after the pits. At Monza, if the favoured team could not win, the safety appliances betrayed the circuit as well.

Just across the A20 main road from Brands Hatch, 'Red', as she was then known, ran a boarding house for racing drivers like the *enfants terribles* Tom Pryce and Tony Trimmer. One night in 1969 I dropped by for a night cap when I was introduced to Claes Uddgren, a short-stay guest. He was a Swedish journalist who had just started to publish *Bilsport*, a motoring bible for racers and rallyists. Before the night was over, I shook hands with Claes to seal a long and lucrative relationship as the magazine's international correspondent.

For those of us beyond Scandinavia, Sweden represented one of several things: a fir-tree-clad land of granite populated by blond, blue-eyed men and women who lived on a diet of free love. In reality, the Swedes in their own bland open-minded attitude, take sex with the cornflakes and discuss the subject much as we relish tomorrow's pork chops. Sex was open for all to see in newspaper features, Swedish drama on television and radio, sex shops and porno-shows. The only man I encountered who had a red-blooded, wide-eyed attitude was in Malmo, and he, during the time of the local racing car show, delighted in taking me to every 'live sex show' in town.

As for the blond, blue-eyed stereotype, I suppose that Ronnie Peterson and Reine Wisell lived up to the misconception spread about the world.

Motor racing in Sweden has a fairly long tradition, so you would think that hosting a Swedish Grand Prix would be no trouble. A group of enthusiasts in the Jonkoping region of Sweden came together under the charismatic leadership of the un-Swedish cigar-touting figure of 'Smokey' Asberg. He helped form the Scandinavian Raceway at Anderstorp. Here a rather featureless circuit was laid within an area of deforestation where legend had it that an old wire maker called Anders had built his wooden 'torp' cabin around which a small community had grown.

Sven (to address 'Smokey' correctly) got his mates, Sven-Ake Klint, Rune Anderson and Birgitta Bernving, around a table to form the Scandinavian Raceway committee. Their dream was to host a Grand Prix. Against all the odds, a cynical Government confronted the monarchy of King Carl Gustaf and Prince Bertil who between them gave the royal nod of approval. Thereafter, this tiny community reverberated to the sound of Grand Prix cars.

Sponsors like Gislaved Tyres, Texaco Oils and Polar Caravans each year gave the committee grey hairs, before ultimately giving much-needed finance at the Cinderella hour in case they fell foul of the Government.

Another member of the committee was a dark-haired, bearded Viking. Bertil Sanell was a driving force behind the Swedish Grand Prix. He telephoned me in England one day in 1974 when winter chilled the air to inform me that Polar Caravans had agreed to sponsor the 1975 race and to ask if I could be enlisted to help co-ordinate a promotion. I soon found out that the Grand Prix itself was an anticlimax compared with the fun we had at the prelude.

Polar Caravans was a small manufacturer established by Bertil Holmquist. The factory was buried in the wastes of Vastabotten, just below the Arctic Circle at Dorotea. A press conference to launch the association was arranged for November when Lord Alexander Hesketh, a private Formula One entrant, had been invited along with his driver James Hunt and a Hesketh-Ford racing car to add noblesse at a time when Ingmar Johannson, the heavyweight Swedish boxing champion, was declared a non-person by Olaf Palme's Socialist Government because he partook of a 'dangerous' sport. Lord Hesketh was the English aristocrat invited to lend respectability to motor racing, and to quell rumours that motor racing was also to become a 'non-sport' in Sweden.

Contrary to popular assumption that the press conference would be held at a five-star hotel in Stockholm, the bewildered party of Scandinavian motoring writers was bustled onto an overnight train to Ostersund. Sweden in midwinter can seem a very inhospitable place, and we were still heading in a northerly direction towards Lapland! The coach ferried us to a remote ski-hotel at Borgafjall where sundry guests were welcomed by Lord Hesketh and Smokey Asberg. James Hunt had beaten a hasty retreat to perform some testing in a sunnier clime. I had a feeling that his Lordship felt he was neglecting his duty to the team as well because night temperatures dropped to 48°F below freezing.

Nevertheless our hosts, Polar Caravans and Scandinavian Raceway, provided a tremendous weekend. We were lavishly furnished with venison, vodka and virgins and treated to snowmobile safaris, outdoor barbecues, skiing, deer driving and a night out in a Polar caravan with Bertil Holmquist.

The Polar Grand Prix of Sweden was duly launched from this most unlikely setting where for the first time Swedes cast aside their bottles of Class One Beer for the Russian fire-water, and we saw the blue eyes of the blond men turn wild and red.

Monday dawned with customary darkness as I wandered down to the reception hall to find an anguished Lordship who tugged me aside and uttered 'Max, for heaven's sake, fresh snow has blocked the roads — get me out of here!' Until the snow-plough rescued us, it was back to the venison, vodka and virgins. The Swedish Grand Prix by comparison was never so much fun.

Ever since the Vingt-Quatre-Heures Grand Prix d'Endurance was originated in May 1923 along a road circuit outside Le Mans in the Sarthe region of
France, legends and myths have evolved — not the least concerning the
supreme athleticism of the drivers, a fact that bypassed me until I made my
debutant visit to Le Mans in 1963. Then I witnessed drivers with varying
degrees of fitness scamper across the road when the tricolour was dropped to
start the race. Their cars were parked in echelon in front of the pits. Approximately sixty drivers had to try to identify their own cars, then leap into the
driver's seat, fire up the engine, and — like sixty bank robbers making a fast
get-away — they screamed off as if the Keystone Cops were about to give hot
pursuit from around Maison Blanc.

Stirling Moss made the Le Mans start his speciality. The only times I saw
him were at Nürburgring 1000K's and Goodwood to start the Tourist Trophy.
He would leg it across the road, step aboard his steed and screech away
before the door was closed. I believe that safety belts killed one of the great
spectacles of motor sport in 1970, and Le Mans was reduced to a rolling start.

Jacky Ickx, the Belgian driver who won Le Mans a record six times, sat
down with me prior to the 1969 race and asked me why Moss made such a
show of the start when he had 24 hours in which to settle into the race. I suggested that some team managers used him as a 'hare' to draw the opposition
into blowing up early in the race. Ickx thought that this strategy was a total
waste of a motor car.

As if to prove the point in 1969, Jacky and his co-driver Jack Oliver won
the race. What made Ickx's point clear was that at the drop of the flag, while
fifty-nine drivers rushed like beach donkeys to avoid a rip tide, Ickx strolled
across the road to his Ford: a sight I shall never forget, especially since he
could have been killed in the melée.

I observed seven Le Mans Grand Prix races and savour many happy memories — like the year when Mark Konig privately entered the Bob Curl-
inspired Nomad-BRM with Tony Lanfranchi. To be competing in the Le
Mans 24-hours was a dream come true for Mark, who for months had
laboured painstakingly over every detail in order to ensure that the team
would finish. Then as he ambled up to his spot for the start, he went to pull on
his goggles to his chagrin discovered that he had forgotten them!

One year I positioned myself at the Esses at that magical time when dusk
turns to darkness. Officious gendarmes often instructed me to move along the
safety bank. When I stood my ground, I avoided confrontational situations by
asking them to feature in the compositions which made them a silhouette
against the oncoming headlights.

There were no Rembrandts this time but on one roll of 35 mm film I shot
30 Le Trec's which gave me a lot of pleasure back home.

Since flashlight was not permitted at the roadside or in the pit area at night,
I learned to handle available light when some high-speed pit stops took place.
What helped to dramatise proceedings was when over-zealous mechanics
whose job was to refuel a car, sometimes spilt petrol onto hot exhaust pipes.

At the end of the Mulsanne Straight, the cars went into the 50 mph Mulsanne Corner where pit signals were established because it became increasingly hazardous for drivers to read pit signals amid the confusion of the illuminated pit area.

Watching some of the faster cars brake from 200 mph down to cruising pace within 400 yards or so was extremely dramatic. Brake discs glowed in the dark and hot rubber was left on the track, especially when a hapless driver had to make for the escape road.

There was always a good story to come out of Le Mans, often totally irrelevant to the proceedings. As a typical example, imagine this scene at the notorious gentlemen's toilet behind the pits, where the cocktail of a million piddles created a stench not to be savoured.

On a fog-laden morning, A J Foyt was awakened to complete his darkness-to-dawn stint in the Ford he was sharing with Dan Gurney. With a head full of candy floss from sleep, Foyt sidled over to the toilet and was confronted in the entrance by an Englishman, much the worse for a skilful, fumbling with his fly buttons.

The indignant Indianapolis champion told the fellow he couldn't just stand there and pee, to which the wavering Englishman replied 'I'm nosh goin' to pish 'ere, I'm goin' to pish rightoooovvv-eeerrr tthh-eeerrreeeee' and duly pointed Percy at the porcelain.

Sunday at dawn bore witness to all of life's basic manifestations around the tented village down by the Esses. While some spectators religiously attended mass, drunks puked at your feet, couples made love in the dewy grass, bleary-eyed fellows emerged from tents and peed against trees, haggard females bent over primus stoves cooking baked beans, canvas latrines reverberated to a symphony of open bowels. Squeals of laughter issued from bivvies alive with 'mumps', deflowered maidens cried rape — all this against the background of racing cars droning ever onwards so that a car manufacturer could reassure customers that victory at Le Mans indicated that the same reliability, space, grace and pace could be found in your showroom model.

* * *

Residing at Park House within the sound of multi-cylinders circulating around Brands Hatch became something of a mixed blessing. There was the occasion when the sound of a Grand Prix car clearing its throat would percolate through my bedroom window. When the car started to lap at what I thought was a respectable pace, I used a stop-watch while reclining in bed and got approximate lap times by the sound of distant thunder reverberating off a certain tree before the driver turned into Druids Hill Bend.

As the schedule of events at home and abroad got heavier with each passing season, being met with the sound of hybrid machinery at home — music though it was to the ears — I found the need for interludes away from the sport. I would sneak off to watch the Wimbledon Lawn Tennis Championships, and relished the atmosphere of the Golf Open. The razzamatazz of Derby Day at Epsom, so refreshing, where talk was of different horse power.

Away from any big events, nothing satisfied me more than to be with personal friends who had little to do with motor sport. We often went for days along the south coast or picnics overlooking a panoramic view of our green and pleasant land.

The tranquillity of Beckley in East Sussex where Bob Curl, a fibre glass fabricator and designer, lived, was very soporific. I met Bob when I joined Mark Konig's little team that went to Le Mans with the Nomad BRM. We found a kindredness not only reflected through motor racing, but we shared a simple appreciation of the countryside. Bob was always rock solid, dependable and never changed — which was a complete contrast to my own scattered life. I remember arriving at Beckley to find him working on a plasticine model. I was the very first writer to see the model of the new Hesketh-Ford, and watched it being secretly made in virgin white fibreglass at the coachwork shop of Marchant and Cox in Hastings. Gosh, it was fun, going to races with that knowledge and that I was months ahead with an exclusive story.

Shortly after the Grand Prix circuit was completed, Brands Hatch was taken over by Grovewood Securities. John Hall relinquished his managing directorship to John Webb. The Grovewood stronghold on Brands Hatch provided an entrée to Oulton Park, Snetterton and Mallory Park. This 'empire building' by Grovewood was cynically viewed by many outsiders as a wedge for the finance house to invest in prime land for future property development — a scare that proved to be contradictory. The company really did have the interest of motor racing at heart and gave John Webb virtual *carte blanche* to run the Grovewood circuits on a thoroughly business-like footing. Brands Hatch was obviously the star in the galaxy and was slowly groomed to provide a second home to Silverstone for the British Grand Prix.

John Webb was a tough businessman and a true motor racing enthusiast who, in spite of his disabilities, actually raced a Jensen. He made as many enemies as he cultivated friends. He nursed innovative ideas as to how he could control motor racing profitably. He inspired formula that were an alternative to Formula One and Two and Three — the international FIA formula which was regulated by the body in Paris and provided a logical ascent to Grand Prix racing for drivers who were ambitious enough to mount that ladder. Webb thrust Formula 5000 upon the unsuspecting world. Nobody knew whether these ostensibly formula one monocoque cars with big yankee power were meant to be a stepping stone into Formula One, or to provide an alternative. Whatever the intention, John Webb had total control over his series of championship races which were run on Grovewood circuits and other venues who took a race on board.

These races featured a motley collection of Formula One might-of-beens or has-beens. Perfectly able drivers like Peter Gethin, who became King of the Bastard formula, Mike Hailwood, the impish motorcycle champion, David Hobbs, Tony Lanfranchi (who would drive anything for a crust) and wild foreign characters like Sweden's Ulf Norinder made up the cast. Occasional walk-on parts were made by Brian Redman, David Prophet, and Ray Allen who was a prodigy of motor racing stables.

Gethin was perhaps the one driver who benefited from his race craft in Formula 5000 in that he got occasional Grand Prix drives for McLaren and a guest appearance in a Yardley-BRM in the 1971 Italian Grand Prix at Monza where he won a thrilling slip-streamer against Ronnie Peterson, Françoise Cevert, Mike Hailwood and Howden Ganley. To give John Webb his full credit, he became the John Blashford-Snell of motor racing in that he explored parts that no other race promoter would dare to venture. He organised a Formula Ford series of races in Brazil which turned out to be a massive fiasco. Everybody enjoyed the adventure in the rain forests — it was a pity about the racing! Having established my own minuscule kingdom in motor racing from an eyrie in one of the maid's rooms at Park House, it became obvious that I was a thorn in John Webb's hide. Not only did I have direct access to the circuit, but I sometimes scooped his own publication *Motor Racing*, which was the official organ of the British Racing & Sports Car Club. The monthly publication was edited by Alan Brinton and John Blunsden. I suppose that having a member of the opposition 'within' supplying stories and pictures and using complete editorial freedom to say what he liked about the Grovewood circuits in *Autosport*, *Small Car*, *Motor Rally*, *Auto News*, *Sport Auto*, *Bilsport*, and *Powerslide*, was too much. So I approached John Webb to remedy the situation.

Life became less 'prickly' when it was suggested that I should contribute likely stories and cover photographs to *Motor Racing*. Another olive branch came from Rothmans of Pall Mall who mounted an array of my colour photographs over the bar in the Brands Hatch pavilion. The status was now ante bellum because I also had a big photograph dominating the club bar at Silverstone, by courtesy of the British Racing Drivers Club

After I had carved a niche at the international level of motor racing, there were Sunday afternoons when I strolled through the woods from Park House to enjoy a sociable afternoon at a good old 'clubbie'. The crowd-puller then was saloon car racing when the 1.24-mile club circuit proved ideal to see combat waged between the Jaguars driven by Sir Gawainne Baille, Michael Parkes and Jack Sears. These desperados of Tommy Sopwith's equipe tried to stem a marauding swarm of works Mini-Coopers which were thrown about in their wake by the likes of Sir John Whitmore, John Rhodes and John Love. There was a Queen Bee among them to add spice to the rampant competition. Christabel Carlisle was a cut-glass Kensington girl who drove Don Moore's red Mini-Cooper which he tuned at Cambridge. Christabel wreaked mobile havoc on three wheels and often two at Paddock Bend when the works boys gave her a wide berth — not wishing to be parties to inverted snobbery. In time, the likes of Whitmore came to realise the girl had genuine driving skill.

Where the Jaguars rocked and rolled around Brands like screaming banshees in a cloud of tyre smoke, the minis defied all front-engined logic by scrabbling around the bends in oversteer. It was 'posh' stock car racing which I enjoyed with rollicking good company when we invariably ended up in the bar after the meeting.

I spent many happy hours supping pints with the BRSCC course marshals.

Whether they ended the day returning to the Pavilion looking like drowned rats or as red as lobsters, they unleashed their responsibilities in the bar. David Venables was a lawyer who played the straight man to Graham Wrangles, a cigarette representative. Aided and abetted by chaps like Andrew Longden, Peter Anderson and John Woodington, they concocted outlandish stories of fighting off photographers, or restraining crumpet from climbing the spectator barrier to get their hands on the lads, pulling out drivers from upturned cars and telling a newcomer that the red and yellow striped flag for oil on the course was the flag used to warn a driver that he was about to be overtaken. These sessions lasted into the night, long before the breathalyser put paid to this harmless aspect of our social intercourse.

Now and then fellows like Andrew and John would cadge a lift and share the petrol costs with me to attend a Grand Prix in Europe. I never refused their company, and often got into considerable trouble for my hospitality. There was the instance when the coloured signs pointing to the car parks for the French Grand Prix at Clermont-Ferrand, somehow got switched around in the night — and who got caught up the telegraph pole while these bods scarpered to the nearest bar!

Monty Terrell was the Chief Fire marshal who suggested that I should attend a full-blown course on fighting petrol fires. He thought that a regular photographer like me could be more than useful at race meetings in the event of an emergency to supplement local marshals. It was a brilliant idea: there were times when I had witnessed awful fatalities amid fire where on such occasions the local marshals were not up to scratch.

Unfortunately, the one time when I was in a position to assist marshals in aid of a stricken driver, the fire extinguishers did not work. The driver perished as we all looked on, totally helpless.

Race marshals work on a voluntary basis. As total amateurs in those days, they willingly placed themselves at risk to save others: they were the unsung heroes of motor racing.

Norman Wisdom, the comedian who achieved worldwide fame as the helpless little 'gump', was a racing enthusiast. I became a fan of his when I rewound films at the Palace Cinema in Bexleyheath. I saw *Trouble in Store* fifteen times, and knew the story almost chapter and verse. I spotted Norman and his straight man Jerry Desmonde at a sodden Brands Hatch club meeting. They were sitting on the roof of a Riley. The time came for them to make a hasty departure to London for a performance at the Palladium Theatre. Such was the quagmire along the top straight, no matter how Jerry tried to reverse out of the glutinous mud, the Riley dug itself in still deeper. I summoned help, and with Norman jumping up and down on the rear bumper and other bodies manually lifting the car, amid great guffaws of mirth and merriment, we extricated them from the morass. The scene would have done justice to an Ealing comedy. I told Dad about Norman's keenness on racing, and he allocated him a seat in the VIP box of the main grandstand from there on. I often wondered if the cheeky chappie enjoyed himself as much among the 'nobs'.

By the time that I met Norman again, I was turned 30 years and was courting with Pamela Easterbrook, the love of my life who eventually became my wife. Shortly after our initial romantic attachment, I took Pam to the Wood-ville Halls at Gravesend to see a Norman Wisdom show. After the perfor-mance we ventured back stage to Norman's dressing room. In no time the conversation turned to the subject of cars and straight away he informed us with enormous pride that he had just purchased a brand new BMW.

Life was volcanic with excitement in July 1964, not just because Brands Hatch was honoured with the mantle of hosting the European Grand Prix, but Beatlemania was reaching proportions that had the entire world agog. HRH Princess Margaret lent royal approval to the mop-haired four by attending the premier of their film *A Hard Day's Night* in London. Four days later Liver-pool was deluged in 150,000 screaming fans of The Beatles — John Lennon, Paul McCartney, George Harrison and Ringo Starr — who made a home return after taking the world by storm. This potent distraction prompted Basil Cardew, the doyen motoring correspondent of the *Daily Express*, to quixotic-ally observe that maybe the race should have been at Aintree where the action was for the 'Beatlemania Grand Prix'. As it was, George Harrison, a Beatle car-fiend, watched the Grand Prix disguised as Gandhi.

To have the Grand Prix circus descend upon the doorstep filled me with enormous pride. I had watched since a boy this acorn grow into the oak tree. Since the days when I painted white the pegs that marked out the grass track, I witnessed each development of the circuit and experienced the heartache when local protesters fought hard against the noise, the inconvenience caused by traffic. Even hooliganism was reported in local pubs — which was ridicu-lous. Local traders at Kingsdown, Farningham and Wrotham rubbed their hands with joy at weekends when bars were crammed, hotels bulged, shops turned over a trade from campers and petrol stations were run dry.

Standing at the infield entrance to the paddock tunnel, I recalled the hun-dreds of rabbits which were stricken with myxomatosis and clubbed to death at the warren just inside Paddock Bend. Where the circuit was dressed in it's Grand Prix regalia, I looked at the most notorious bend in British motor racing, where the likes of Jim Clark and Graham Hill were about to wage battle, I could see the 'Blue Boys' powering up the chalk-dusted hill with Eric Oliver spitting grit.

That weekend the family worked side-by-side. Mum was rushed off her feet in the Pavilion, Dad was allocating people to their rightful seats in the main grandstand and their off-shoot was earning his crust among the fratern-ity I had come to identify with from all over the world.

I felt strangely ill at ease with my situation when Henry Manny turned the tables by enquiring about the best audio stand point.

So we wandered out into the country where I showed him the fast climbing right-hander at Hawthorn Bend, Standing there, I wondered how little old Brands Hatch measured up against circuits like the Nürburgring, Rouen-les-Essarts, Spa-Francorchamps and Monza. I sought his independent assessment. Henry knew that I was involved, so when he sniffed the air, then mused that it was like standing on the downhill rush to Aremberg at Nürburgring, I was happy. From that day on I thought of Brands Hatch as the little Nürburgring.

During the week of the Grand Prix, I seemed to accumulate friends galore. The call for 'freebies' was unending. I could have slept half the crowd at Park House. Since I had been allocated four 'house guest' tickets by the Royal Automobile Club, a lot of people were disappointed. Even I had a terrible time reaching Park House when I popped into Fawkham Green for groceries. The drive of Park House had been taken over as an entrance to the South Bank. Before I had fumbled about for my pass, I was being charged an entrance fee to my own home!

The race will be remembered as one of 'stalemate' when Jim Clark in his Lotus-Climax headed Graham Hill's BRM who had John Surtees's Ferrari in tow.

For 212 miles it was a high-speed roller-coaster which had the crowd on its toes wondering which of the great British champions to cheer on. As it happened at the end of the 1964 season, John Surtees won the World Championship — the first man to do so on two wheels and on four. When Big Jack boxed his son's ears, I felt sure that it was because the father wanted only the best for John on motorcycles. Little did the old man dream that the same grit and determination to succeed would achieve the double crown.

The talking point of the weekend occurred after a qualifying season. The teams were packing their chattels in the pits in order to return to the paddock. From out of the blue, Jim Clark's Lotus-Climax burst the silence and was driven onto the circuit. All eyes in the pit-lane focussed upon the Team Lotus Chief, Colin Chapman.

Had 'Chunky' wangled an illicit test period for his star driver?

Graham Hill watched the Lotus from the rear of the pits as it cruised around the South Bank Bend on to the Grand Prix circuit. To his bewilderment the number one driver realised, that it was not Clark at the wheel, but Ken Tyrrell's star Formula 3 driver Jackie Stewart.

I watched Hill stride over to BRM team manager Tony Rudd and demand to know 'what the bloody hell is going on?'. Rudd shrugged and with a wry smile implied that Lotus had 'done the dirty'. Other teams had solicited Jackie's skilled services and assumed that the door was still open. Chapman had already been forced to place Mike Spence as the Lotus number two driver after Peter Arndel had suffered a dreadful accident in a Formula 2 race at Reims. So what was the Lotus Chief up to?

Motoring writers were absolutely agog. Speculation was rife. Telephone wires were almost aglow in the sunset. What happened was perfectly simple. Jim Clark had asked Chapman if Jackie could sample a ride. Chapman didn't know that Jackie was already signed with BRM for a two-year contract. So what on earth were the Scots playing at? No one was willing to say.

Unbeknown to everybody, those few enthralling laps by Jackie were performed with the blessing of BRM. So you can imagine the Bourne team's satisfaction as rumour countered rumour that Lotus were going to serve up a 'double Scotch' for 1965. Such blatant mischief right under Fleet Street's nose almost created the sensation of the weekend. Such a shindy could never happen in these days, not with the hessian bags full of cash which drivers now require for services rendered.

Wielding a camera at the home race was for me akin to having taken holiday shots along the Algarve, Côte d'Azur and the Red Sea Resorts, then returning to familiar old Wearbay Crescent at Folkestone. I knew practically every angle, bump and camber at Brands Hatch. Yet to my surprise my inspiration was not dulled by familiarity. Having the 'circus' on terrain which I knew seemed to 'raise the game'.

Brands Hatch is a busy circuit where drivers get very little respite. To cut down the angles along the club circuit, I spent more time exploring the country aspect. On the inside of Hawthorn bend I could see cars dash down the slope from beneath the Shell bridge, hit the bump stops in the dip when drivers jabbed the brakes, to squirrel across the road with power just about full on. Another fruitful spot was on the outside of Dingle Dell as the cars rose from the valley, and went very light on the crest just when they wanted maximum braking to make the right turn into the 'S' bends. Watching Clark and Hill on the ragged edge during the pursuit made for exciting pictures. I had forgotten that we would be moving onto the Nürburgring for the German Grand Prix in two weeks. When the dust settled after the European Grand Prix, I felt a great sense of anti-climax — like being at a party you want never to end.

* * *

Race team mechanics became more than passing acquaintances. I spent many a night with them in dark lock-up garages beneath lean-too awnings watching them after qualification, strip down the cars and race-prepare them. Although I had no real understanding of the mechanical details, I could appreciate the loving care which they applied to their work. Unlike *Motor Sport* magazine's Denis Jenkinson, who unknowingly became a sort of mobile point of reference through his detailed race reports, I had to learn the technicalities parrot fashion. Chaps like Dick Scammell of Team Lotus, Willy Southgate at BRM, Tony Cleverley on Rob Walker's team and Eramanno Cuoghi of Ferrari spent time explaining finer details to me as they worked on the race cars.

Gradually I got the picture and felt confident enough sometimes to quote them — especially after a race. If a driver retired because of a mechanical fault and I got the standard 'rod stepped out of bed' information, I did have some idea of the catastrophe. Later on, if my story cross-checked with Denis Jenkinson's, I was happy. Mind you, he often wagged a finger at me if I got it wrong.

Many of the drivers were just as mechanically eloquent, so I was reassured when someone like Jim Clark tried to analyse his thoughts with me — talk about the blind leading the blind!

There was an occasion at Zandvoort when Clark first drove the revolutionary Lotus 49 Ford at the 1967 Dutch Grand Prix. He sat down in a hire car with me in a mood of total exasperation. There had been a fault with his car during practice. Chapman had got the mechanics to run a tooth comb right through the Lotus. Jimmy didn't know whether he was being a bit of an old woman, but after a lot of bitching about, he had got his way. He told me:

'I felt sure a wheel was going to fall off yesterday, and could have gone on driving today until the bloody wheel did fall off. I told them there was something wrong with the car, but over night they didn't find it. So I went out today, and still I was sure there was a fault. So I brought the car into the pits and wouldn't drive it until they found the fault. In the end you could hardly see it. A ball race had broken'.

Jim Clark had such a supreme talent at the wheel, I wondered if he was ever pushed to drive on the limit. His reply was a surprise:

'I find it very difficult to drive on the limit all the time unless I have to. I must have an incentive, otherwise I won't bother. I'm just lazy about that sort of thing. Actually it's not so much laziness — I spend time nursing the car along in a race. I'm worried something is going to break. That really worries me, especially at a place like the Nürburgring. Around there you feel you could drive the car that much harder at times. But you're graunching it so much you don't feel like doing it. Almost every lap of the 'Ring you feel there is something falling off. You hit a bump differently. Something happens. Your shock absorbers get clapped out, you start pattering across the road, and you immediately think something is coming away from the car. Around some of these rough, bumpy circuits, you're completely on edge wondering what it could be. I spend time peering about to see if everything is hanging on, and that costs me seconds per lap'.

If Clark suffered these dreadful fears and still managed to win races, it made me wonder what the other drivers had to overcome to finish at all?

The Austrian driver Jochen Rindt who became the World Champion posthumously in 1970, was made the scapegoat to an enormous controversy when instead of driving the Gold Leaf Lotus 72 Ford in the German Grand Prix at Nürburgring that year, he represented the Grand Prix Drivers Association with an 18 point programme to make the circuit safe to race upon. Because of shortage of time, the authorities emphatically told Rindt that the safety appliances requested could not be in place.

So the race was shifted at huge inconvenience to Hockenheim — where, ironically, Jim Clark had died competing in a Formula 2 race in April 1968.

I remember a very heated conversation with Jochen Rindt on this issue just before the Italian Grand Prix. I told him how Jimmy felt about driving at the 'Ring, but he accepted the examination and passed with winning colours by driving according to the conditions. If Jacky Ickx, Jo Siffert and a batch of other drivers were willing to drive at the Eifel circuit, then he must accept the same examination as well. But the GPDA were going through what in their eyes was a responsible, safety-conscious period at this time. Rindt could have been right, but after 1970 the German Grand Prix returned to a much modified Nürburgring on six occasions. To cap it all, Jackie Stewart — who initially started the massive crusade for circuit safety after his accident at Spa-Francorchamps in 1966 — drove on the 'Ring, a circuit he came to mistrust, and won the German race in 1971 and 1973 driving his Tyrrell-Ford! I thought those efforts were medal-worthy. Jackie Stewart was a driver I came to know early on in his career. When he was confounding everybody as the new 'coming man' during 1963-4, I was assigned by *Small Car* magazine to compose a colour feature on him.

Right from the word go I found Jackie an extremely commercial animal who was well aware of his own public relations. I imagine that in reality he realised his ability to drive a racing car better than most aspiring young drivers around Formula 3 at the time. He was always prodding and probing his accomplished fellow-drivers like Jim Clark and John Surtees. He made no bones of the fact that he intended to carve a better life for Helen, his family and dependents.

When I first met with Clark at this incubative period of his career, he was driving a Lotus Elite in the 3-hour, mini Le Mans race at Snetterton in 1959. Ian Scott-Watson was a racing enthusiast with whom he shared cars with his pal Jimmy. Ian soon realised his friend's superior skill. As the race went from a Norfolk sunset into darkness, Ian spoke of Jimmy over a cup of tea in the canteen and made the prophetic statement that we were looking upon a World Champion in the making. Jim won the 3-hour event and at a small celebration afterwards a look of resignation crossed Jim's face when I mentioned Ian's prophecy 'For Chrissake, you don't believe him do you?'.

There were occasions when I joined Jimmy and Jackie on the way to tests or when they were reconnoitring a new circuit. It was along public highways that their styles differed. Jimmy drove with great verve all the time, whereas Jackie played very much to the Highway Code — at least in the United Kingdom, much to the comfort of his passengers.

While recceing circuits, Jimmy had a tendency to give you an insight to his mystic, observing the racing line almost regardless of whether a 'road circuit' was open or closed. Jackie was a lot more controlled, pointing out apexes, braking points and places where a racing car might go light over humps and bumps. It was almost a guided tour: it may not have been fast, but those of us in the back got some insight into what he might be doing in a Grand Prix car.

Jimmy could arrive at a section of the Nürburgring, for example, with anchors away and a casual remark: 'Oops, I forgot that corner tightened up'. He would say this looking you in the face with a thumb crooked over the steering wheel. Jimmy drove for the sport and liked to win, but Jackie also drove for the sport and liked to win because... .

Much later on in Jimmy's career I spoke to him about being a public figure having to suffer cameras always being thrust in his face. Being a keen amateur photographer himself, the Scot didn't mind the adulation at the track — in fact he often tried to figure out who was using what kind of camera, and would always notice a chap who had replaced an old faithful with a new camera, and would want to know why.

Jackie was far more conscious of his public image and how he handled himself corporately and in front of the media. Image projection was something he came to terms with during a promotional trip to Japan in 1966. Jim

Clark, Graham Hill and Jackie arrived in Tokyo with massive publicity: the eager Nippons photographed the three heroes at every opportunity.

When people approached them for interviews or autographs, the Japanese went straight to Graham Hill and asked for Mr Clark's autograph. This juxtaposition was caused by the fact that Jim Clark was the best-known name in motor racing while Graham's face was the most distinguished. Jackie found that crisis of identity in the Japanese mind disturbing. He was determined not to have that mistake made when he had made his name.

After becoming World Champion driver in 1969 Jackie Stewart made a very big effort to project the sport beyond the avid race fan. One big coup he almost pulled off was to be the co-driver with Steve McQueen in John Sturgess's Warner Brothers film *Le Mans* !

Jackie was berated by the motoring press for even considering such a film contract. They were mindful of the Scotsman's fanatical crusade on the subject of circuit and driver safety. To be racing with a relatively inexperienced driver like McQueen, in a race that Stewart reckoned to be very dangerous because of the wide variance of skill among the drivers at high speed, especially at night, was cause for concern. The deal with John Sturgess did not materialise. Instead, Jackie was content to raise his commercial profile in the United States of America by driving the Carl Haas Can-Am Lola in the Can-Am series during 1971.

Always astute in business matters, Jackie together with McCormack's organisation, negotiated agreements with multi-national companies like the Ford Motor Company and Goodyear Tyres.

I enjoyed the 'sixties because the drivers were accessible, not just for comment, but also for fun and we all pulled together to further the sport. However, when blatant commercialism from outside the sport was allowed to encroach in 1968, things started to change, and new obligations had to be realised. As more money became available, the commercial aspect of motor racing mushroomed. During this period, writers who had enjoyed a close proximity with the top drivers had to re-adjust their approach.

At the German Grand Prix, I blithely asked Jackie if I could have a lap with him around the Nürburgring for a feature in *Small Car*. He shuffled around, looked uncomfortable, and pointed me in the direction of Jay Michaels, his American agent for IMG. 'Sure you can Max', beamed Jay, 'get your publication to front up £4,000, that's the going rate for our new World Champion driver.' I was aghast. There *was* going to be a period of readjustment then. I didn't get my ride. Motor racing was very different now. The driver who had proudly welcomed me to his family home at Helensburgh and let me leaf through his scrapbook and observe our 'Coming Man' feature in *Small Car*, was clearly in the big time.

From then onwards, the future of motor racing gradually changed from being highly diversified and drivers became more specialist in their chosen rank. Apart from the odd exception, when a driver graduated to Formula One, that was it, full stop. Men like Emerson Fittipaldi, Niki Lauda, James Hunt, Ayrton Senna, Alain Prost and Nigel Mansell no longer felt obliged to participate in other formula to supplement their incomes. Mansell moved from Grand Prix racing to Indycars in 1993, and would under different circumstances, I am sure, like to have dove-tailed the races, but it was not possible.

Skies were more open during the 'sixties. Bruce McLaren, Denis Hulme, and later Peter Revson and Jackie Stewart, thought nothing of alternating World Championship races in Europe with the North American Can-Am series every weekend.

Long after Denis Hulme retired, I stayed with his family at the home overlooking Lake Rotoiti on New Zealand's North Island. We mulled over his incredible schedules when he seemed to spend more time in jets crossing the North Atlantic Ocean than with two feet planted on terra firma. Denis was incredibly laid back and relaxed about those periods when it was a Grand Prix, a Can-Am, an Indianapolis, a bit of Formula 2 and maybe a sports car race for Sid Taylor thrown in. He admitted that the world slipped by very quickly, especially on those weekends when qualification at Monaco and Indianapolis 500 coincided. He chortled at the thought of giving a car the big rev, around the Hoosier Bowl, then having mentally to gear himself down to the streets of Monte Carlo — where, by comparison, driving was like a doddle along a country lane — all within 24 hours.

Slightly less hectic were the timetables of Jacky Ickx, Chris Amon, Derek Bell and Jean Pierre-Beltoise, when they mixed the Grand Prix with World Sports Car Championship races. At least they were mostly in Europe.

If it were possible, the mid-'sixties were even busier. Then Grand Prix drivers often featured in Formula 2, national sports car races and saloon car events. If they felt so inclined they could winter at the Tasman Series which took place in January and February, with at least eight events wending around Australia and New Zealand. The annual schedule of people like Clark, McLaren, Hill and Stewart was like a worldwide bus-stop tour and just as breathtaking.

In 1965 Jim Clark faced the starting flag over 40 times. Not only did the Scot become the World Champion that year, but he won the Indianapolis 500 as well. In these days Grand Prix drivers have 16 World Championship races per annum, a lot of testing and very little else. I wonder who would be judged to give the best value for money?

4

Rapide Femmes

IT WAS about a twenty-minute walk across the grazing fields from Park House to our nearest neighbours. They were a welsh family who had been living in Fawkham long before we moved there. Taffy Jones, his wife and two daughters, Bronwyn and Diane, lived upon a limited income in a terrace of cottages. Their neighbours couldn't stand Brands Hatch. Taffy's family were very pro-Brands and did part-time work at the circuit. He swore that he and his wife never spoke to the anti-brigade next door, which I thought was sad. After all, they resided in an idyllic part of Fawkham. When the circuit was dormant, it was tranquil, with just the sound of sheep bleating in the background.

Taffy was on welfare, but he earned his few bob extra working with my Dad in the main grandstand. Mrs Jones helped out with Mum at the Pavilion tea counter. On Monday evenings when the 'invaders' had departed the circuit, the locals at Fawkham had a brief respite from either the black leather motorcyclists or the cloth-cap MG Magnate owners. As the sun began to set, Taff and I would meet at the bottom of the drive and slowly wander down to the *Rising Sun* pub at Fawkham Green. The *Portobello Inn* at West Kingsdown on the A20 was too far to walk. Besides, there was a different kind of clientele, Kingsdown was known to harbour a few undesirables who often went away on business at Her Majesty's Pleasure.

At the *Rising Sun* we would join the local farm hands in the public bar for darts over a few jars of Black'n'Tan. Motor racing very rarely entered the conversation among these earthy types. They had no curiosity about whether I had just returned from overseas, and that was the way I liked it.

At one session word had got round about this girl up at Brands who was giving the lads a hard time. They were referring to Christabel Carlisle. That started Taffy off. This was sometimes a mistake because cherries grew into apples, which turned into melons and in the end we almost had World War Three. Taff reckoned that I should 'chat up that fast girl'. His apparently rash remark struck a chord.

When *Motor Clubman* suffered its demise, Tony Gilfrin moved on to join the sales team at *Small Car* (now *Car* magazine). He introduced me to the reactionary editor, George Bishop, and his side-kick Doug Blain, a garrulous, short-sighted Australian. Together they developed an editorial policy of hunting down prototypes of future mass-production cars, then photographing them years before they hit the market. Test drivers were turned into gibbering wrecks, because they could hardly stop along a country lane to hose down the bark for fear of a *Small Car* photographer leaping out of the hedgerows — not to make an indecent exposure, but to snap a model still under wraps.

As if that was not enough to send a creeping paranoia throughout the motor industry, George took some maniacal delight in breaking press embargoes that announced new models. It was the publication's only way of keeping up with the daily newspapers and weekly magazines — and often getting ahead of them — in the dire race for improved circulation figures. The 'respectable' journals could do nothing but religiously observe the protocols for fear of losing valuable advertising revenue.

So when I met George Bishop to discuss the idea of 'Fast Girls' I surmised a captive authority as the handle-bar moustache bristled in rampant anticipation. He requested a list of gorgeous female racing drivers, then I was to stuff them into Innes Ireland's Lotus, undo a few top buttons and photograph them. Not that George was a chauvinistic pig, but he knew that his readership responded to unannounced models, but amply pronounced models as well... all good for the bottom line figures, he reckoned. Art editor Charles Pocklington, a man of vision whose work was described in the tome *Magazine Design* as 'brilliantly lively and strongly visual', rubbed his hands at the pleasure of spreading such pictures in full colour across the pages. Thesewere my kind of people.

I deleted Pat Moss from my list, firstly because she was already recognised as a champion rally driver: her accomplishments were certainly equal to her brother Stirling's in motor racing. And secondly, I felt sure that her giant husband, Swedish rally driver Erik Carlsson, would prefer Pat to be remembered for her numerous victories, which included a fantastic win with Anne Wisdom on the 1960 Liège-Rome-Liège in the Austin Healey 3000.

Since my weekends were taken up with race meetings, 'Fast Girls' conveniently slotted into being the day job during the week. At the height of the season I ended up with no spare time at all, but with an assignation such as this, I was not in a position to complain. More often than not I would diplomatically secure dates to visit my subjects at home. This method of procuring information and getting nice photographs was preferable to seeking the girls' co-operation at a meeting — when they would be bundles of nerves, which is not conducive to nice portraits.

Apart from that I met their parents, since most of them lived at home, and I could see the rung they occupied on the social ladder. I had to admit that ladies who race were not all doing it at Daddy's behest and aided by his open cheque book. I tracked them down to terraced, back-to-back houses in Newcastle-upon-Tyne; to a remote pile that overlooked Ilkley Moor. One father worked for the *News of the World* from his detached house in its one-acre garden at Sawbridgeworth. A Castle Coombe regular lived with Mum, Dad and sister in a semi-detached house just outside Swindon.

Almost without exception mother and father gave their daughter full blessing to participate in motor sport. Fathers positively glowed with pride at their daughters' achievements, while mothers showed a lot more concern. This concern had no reflection upon the danger of motor sport, but arose from anxiety about the moral attitude of the gentlemen drivers.

None of the girls I encountered were 'butch' by any stretch of the imagination. They were feminine, cool as lemon sorbets, always immaculate in appearance before getting behind the wheel. As one innocent at large told me: 'If you look good, you go like a ton of bricks.' She never understood why the fellows stifled laughter at that remark — but I knew what she meant.

Being a girl in motor sport made you fodder for the media. The tabloids lapped up a girl who could hoodwink the lads. Until they did win their flying colours, the angle of the story was usually loaded with *double-entendre*. A girl soon caught Fleet Street's respect when she won outright *à la* Pat Moss. None of the girls could reach terms with the avid media interest, and this sometimes caused resentment among the fellows who raced year-in-year-out for barely a mention in *Autosport*, and here was I giving them a colour feature in *Car* magazine when they had hardly any track record. I explained the position by pointing out to the girls that they were participating in a male-orientated sport. In this domain there was no 'after you ma'am' in the braking area, and the chaps would slam the door firmly in their faces at the apex of a corner, then spatter their screens with dust and stones just to let them who was in charge. It was nothing personal, but a simple fact of motor sporting life is that 'when the flag drops, the bull-shit stops'. Most of the girls either relished that challenge, or went rallying. Gabrielle Konig never took any flak from a man. If Gabrielle was knocked aside by an opponent, she would sniff hard, blink, square her shoulders as if to say 'up your pipe mate', then continue to race hard at the next man in her sights. If a fellow backed off in the wake of this indignity, then Gabrielle's eyes would flicker even more and a broad grin would cross her face.

Aside from having to deal with men, the girls had their own unique problems. Daphne Freeman was a Brighton girl who took part in anything on four wheels: races, rallies, she even pig sticked in car trials. 'Daffers' — as everybody knew her — was a jolly-hockey-sticks kind of person, always bursting with enthusiasm, thrusting herself into a muddy terrain with enormous zest and glee. At car trials she yelled blue murder at the 'bouncer' in the passenger seat, to 'get the bum working' to secure the last ounce of adhesion as the car struggled to traverse a steep, slippery section.

Daffers often lost valuable points gathering herself together when flaying at the wheel and working the hand brake simultaneously, her bra-strap 'pinged' a fall-out as the car wallowed axle deep in the mire. This essentially fast girl malfunction manifested itself in other ways. So while the lads worked upon mods for their cars, the girls concentrated upon bolstering their bras. Jennifer Tudor-Owen confessed that she tried one race without a bra. Every time she got 'crossed-up' at the steering wheel, she suffered a fleshy implosion, almost squeezing her feminine assets to oblivion.

If Christabel Carlisle became a role model for other girls, then Michaelle

Burns-Greig from Duns in the Borders region (a close neighbour to Jim Clark's family), began her career in racing at a disadvantage. Racing a Mini-Cooper, Michaelle was determined to make her mark in saloon car racing but was not taken seriously, which irked her no end. Living in the shadow of a legend must have placed appalling pressures of expectancy, and being compared with Christabel could not have made life easy. Unlike the London racer, Michaelle was not protected by Don Moore who race-prepared CMC 77 for Christabel and tuned the Mini-Cooper to seriously worry the works team. To Michaelle's credit she persevered in swimming against the tide. She might have achieved greater things had she entered another class of racing, or had followed Anita Taylor's example and gone to someone like Ralph Broad, who might have considered a Ford Anglia for her. The last time I met with the Scots lass she had become Chairman of the Planning and Development Committee for the Border Regional Council at Melrose, Roxburghshire. Clearly Michaelle had the instinct to lead, but lacked the proper equipment to gain any advantage in the racing world.

Anita Taylor, sister of Trevor the Team Lotus Grand Prix driver, might have chosen another sport. The Rotherham girl was born into a race-mad family and, regardless of Trevor's prowess, she wanted to blaze her own trail — with a bit of brotherly assistance.

Between them, the lads modified a Ford Anglia in black and yellow regalia for Anita to race. This intensely blue-eyed brunette was probably one of the coolest maidens of them all. At Brands Hatch, she was racing into Paddock Bend, hell-bent upon beating off opponents in the braking area. Unfortunately she paid for her pluck. The Anglia careered off the road and landed heavily in the bank amid a cloud of dust and flint stones. Course marshals rushed to Anita's assistance and carefully helped her from the bent motor car. With mascara un-smudged, lipstick immaculate and her skin flushed but peachy, she remained absolutely unflustered and she turned to one of the lads and purred in that rich Yorkshire accent:

'You wouldn't mind getting my handbag out of the car please.' She almost got flattened in the stampede!

Rosemary Smith had known that I wanted to make her a subject of 'Fast Girls' and said that she would let me know next time she was in London. Good as her word the blonde Irish colleen arrived at Park House in a brand-new Sunbeam Rapier. She looked immaculate in a green suit, with her hair pinned back and wearing bright red nail lacquer and her face radiant. She opted to get the photographs done first, and suggested that she should toss the Rapier around some of the mud roads on the inside of the Grand Prix circuit at Brands Hatch. I thought that it would be a shame to get the car all muddied up, but Rosemary's attitude was: 'Aach to hell, you're giving us free publicity'. That was typical Rosemary. She confessed that racing around in circles never gave her the 'buzz' which rallying did when she was charging along forest tracks, through driving snow at night and conquering the twisting Cols of Europe. Ireland's best female rally driver preferred to walk on the wild side.

Rosemary drove mainly for the Rootes Group in Sunbeam Rapiers and Hillman Imps. One of her most notable results featured in the 1965 Tulip Rally. There were rumblings of discontent after her outright victory in the Hillman Imp.

Most post-war rallies observed the class improvement rule. A class win was trumpeted in the prestige advertisements with equal volume as outright victory. The Tulip organisers changed that, because some rule bending had crept into the system which surfaced when Geoff Mabbs won the Tulip Rally in 1961 at the wheel of a Triumph Herald Coupé! The modified regulations meant that a competitor had to beat those in classes above and below his or her car to win outright.

Rosemary was able to capitalise upon the revision when her Imp steamed into a time control in the high altitudes of Champagnole. Apparently a lot of entries in the classes above the Imp had incurred time delays at a road block, and were thus penalised. Rosemary simply whistled through to win. She couldn't comprehend the unsporting attitude of some drivers to her achievement. Generally speaking, Rosemary was well liked and accepted on merit.

Another long-distance driver was Denise McLuggage of America. I met Denise through Phil Hill, the 1961 Ferrari driver who became the first American World Champion. We met at the Sebring 12-hours sports car race in Florida: they were both driving Ferraris. Phil drove the works car while Denise had the privately entered model of the North American Racing Team.

The flat air-base circuit featured a variety of fast curves and slow bends. Denise would maintain parity with Phil most of the time, but she lost ground through the fast left-hander. Phil was scuttling through at 170 mph in spite of the bumpy surface. Denise clung almost to his exhaust pipes, but then suddenly the works Ferrari would pull away. She could turn into the sweeping bend comfortably, however, as she approached the elusive apex she had to back off. The sheer physical effort of holding such a tigerish beast on line virtually pulled her arms from their sockets. The will was there, but even this tough lady had to admit that the body was weak. Mildly disconcerted, she asked Phil if he had a problem holding his Ferrari on line through that bend. He stepped back in feigned wide-eyed astonishment and indicated that his right foot was buried on the accelerator with a headstone on it. Denise concluded that a shot of testosterone might help her case, but was too much of a lady to tell Phil that. After all, he had the factory car and she was privately entered. Phil let the debate settle at that point.

It was Kineton's well-known afficionado, Rivers Fletcher, who introduced me to Isobel Robinson of Guildford. She had spent eight years working with him at Rubery Owen, the parent company of the BRM racing team, and she attended a good many races making films for the company archives.

Isobel was best known when she raced a blue 500 cc Cooper-Norton which matched her crash helmet and overalls. There was a time when she held the record at the Firle Hill Climb in Sussex. Attempting to beat the clock on hill climbs bore no comparison for Isobel to the cut-'n'-thrust of racing. Her philosophy was simple: to race without glory is better than to not to race at

Most of this class at Bexleyheath Secondary School in 1952, under Mr Hicks, remained together for for four years. The author is in the middle row, second from the right.

Holiday in Folkestone 1952 with Mum, Dad and Sylvia Ticehurst, a good friend and neighbour at Barnehurst.

Paddock Bend at Brands Hatch in 1947 had two routes up the hill – the outer was faster to avoid the dust from leading riders. Note the Pavilion in the background – this is where Mum worked.

Getting Jim Clark into focus at Snetterton.

Ready for the
annual Press Trial
at Swanley in 1964.

all. She could not have cared a bent five pound note about winning. The battle was her métier whether it was for last place or somewhere in the field. It was a matter of pride that Isobel never came last, because she reckoned that a bad woman racer gets a raw deal whereas a fellow gets his brownie points for at least trying.

There were many wonderful lady drivers like Patsy Burt, Claudine Trautmann, Jennifer Nadin and the amazing Madame Laumaille. She was reputed to be the first lady racing driver in history to compete against the gentlemen in a specially prepared motor car. Madame Laumaille handled the tiller of a De Dion tricycle in the 1898 Marseilles-Nice two-day race. Monsieur Laumaille also competed and to his chagrin finished sixth in his class, two places behind his 'Rapide Dame' after she had also recorded the fastest run in her class along one section. Madame Laumaille was somewhat before Innes Ireland's time, and too much of a pioneer for candidature in the Bishop gallery.

5

Remedy for Shattered Images

WITHIN MY tenure of motor sport, three distinct facets emerged. The first concerned my creative approach, while secondly and thirdly, and of more general concern, were safety and the commercialism of the sport. These issues were influenced by midnight 1967 as the New Year approached. I celebrated the arrival of 1968 after a stock car meeting at Brands Hatch. At the Cinderella hour nobody was concerned of the bountiful future.

I had already seen blatant commercialism of the sport in North America. Mamby-Pamby images were conjured when British Racing Green would disappear under the livery of multi-national companies. BRM had already courted the favours of Yardley perfumes. We wondered if the spirit of camaraderie would disappear with the encroachment of executive public relations men. For motor racing to progress in the 'sixties, we felt duty bound to welcome the interlopers.

To understand my attitude, the classic film *Genevieve* based upon the veteran car run reflected a time in my young life which had become nostalgically entrenched in my memory as a 'good time to be around'. There were no motorways, no 70 mph limits to frustrate the sporting motorist. Traffic indicators saluted spasmodically from car door pillars. The A23 was merely an arterial road. I dreamt of Kay Kendall and Kenneth More as my favourite Aunty and Uncle. I realised that it was unhealthy for a lad to be imbued by the glow of recent history, but that was the Britain I hankered for, and still do.

To illustrate the point, one Wednesday morning in June 1965, the Tim Parnell Racing Team driver, Richard Attwood, a son of the Wolverhampton Vauxhall dealer and a free spirit to boot, arrived at Park House and parked his Velox at the front door. We had planned to travel together on a three-week working tour taking in the Belgian Grand Prix, Le Mans and the French Grand Prix.

'Tatty', as we all knew him, didn't bother to ring the front door bell. He sat on the car horn, then moved over to the passenger seat and waited for me to chauffeur him to Dover Docks. Along the A20 we passed above Folkestone, a cue for me to bore Richard with bygone memories of summer holidays at Wearbay Crescent. As we descended into Dover, it was clear that Richard was more interested in the space race. Colonel Alexei Leonev had already made history in March by becoming the first man to 'walk in space' for the

Soviet Union. NASA and the United States of America were at this stage still in the wake of the pioneering Russians. But news in June was full of Major Edward White who became the first American to make a space walk outside of the Gemini 4 spacecraft.

We arrived in the assembly area at Dover Docks. Dotted among the holiday makers and commercial adventurers were team transporters like Team Lotus's old Bedford, Cooper's big pantechnicon and Parnell's mobile workshop with Stan Collier at the wheel. So this was the Grand Prix life in the fast lane 'sixties style. A four-hour channel crossing to Ostend spent in the ferry bar. Things speeded up when we hit Belgium and headed towards Brussels along the E40 autoroute with a steady 'ton' on the clock.

We were bypassing Ghent when Richard asked for the pace to be quickened because he remembered that we had to pick up Jochen Rindt at Brussels Airport. The new Austrian hero was driving for Cooper-Climax alongside Bruce McLaren. He was flying in from Vienna and Richard had arranged for Jochen to join us for the ride to Spa.

The notorious three-lane highway between Brussels and Liège was at its most treacherous when the weather broke. Squalls intermingled with sunshine served up dazzling road conditions. What with rain, spray from the huge camions and a new highly-strung passenger shouting instructions for overtaking in the glory lane, I began to feel that my efforts at being a chauffeur were not appreciated.

Jochen offered to drive. So as I went to pull off the road for him to take over, he took the wheel and moved onto my lap while I wriggled out from under him. The Austrian desperado found the controls and bam — we were travelling. Oncoming drivers must have thought that I was being high-jacked: it provided quite a spectacle at 70 mph!

As we careered along from Liège along the N62 to Spa, the road became more twisty and interesting the closer we got to the Ardennes region. I knew both Richard and Jochen quite well as drivers, but what intrigued me was their different attitude even to driving on the road. Richard placed his faith in me and was content with my pace. Jochen was a 'goer' right from the start. Impatient to get places, out-manoeuvring other road users by a coat of paint. His limits were a hair's-breadth finer than Richard's. One became a dead World Champion, the other lived to tell the tale. We did reach Spa-Francorchamps in one piece!

Jochen was staying with John Cooper and the team in Spa. So I drove Richard around one half of the road circuit, through Eau Rouge, past Malmedy to Stavelot and eventually we arrived at our hotel just down the road from the cascade at Trois-Ponts. The team had arrived before us because of our diversion to Brussels airport. Tim and Virginia Parnell were also ensconced along with Innes Ireland, the other half of the Lotus BRM Parnell team. Judging from the number of beer bottles strewn across the tables, the spirit of the weekend had already been set by chief mechanic Stan Collier.

The Grand Prix will best be remembered as a demonstration of superiority by the two Scotsmen. Jim Clark openly loathed Spa, but he had already scored a hat-trick of victories for Team Lotus and this was his fourth consecutive win. Jackie Stewart on his debut at the circuit for BRM acquitted himself well by finishing in second place, after his team leader Graham Hill had started from pole position only to finish in fifth place.

We had witnessed uninhibited driving of the highest order — especially from Stewart, who positively revelled in the challenge of the Ardennes circuit. His performance indicated the more ambitious and adventurous approach of a 'rookie' driver willing to earn his spurs on a 'real driver's circuit'. Most members of the Grand Prix Drivers' Association at Spa accepted the unguarded monster and paid the satanical venue the same respect that a yachtsman has for Cape Horn.

In spite of the terrifying accident that befell Stewart at Spa the following year in driving rain when his 3-litre BRM careered off the road and trapped him, soaked in petrol, in his cockpit, his competitive spirit survived while his mental attitude was changed which led to his crusade for greater circuit safety and improved medical facilities.

Jochen finished a lowly eleventh, with the rev-counter of his Cooper-Climax rolling around in his lap, having become dislodged from its location on the dashboard.

Tatty was not so charmed. Virginia Parnell who was keeping the team lap chart, noted to Big Tim that he was missing. Word filtered through the forests that he had suffered a 'nasty' and there was a fire.

'Bloody hell', murmured Tim, his bottom lip pouting. 'Sounds like Richard's been and gorn and dunnit'. Innes pulled up at the pits straight after the chequered flag. 'Richard's had a hell of a shunt,' he bellowed, 'They've got the fire out. He's alive!'

I walked with Tim and Stan to the car which we drove around the sopping circuit to the scene. Richard had already been extricated and was on the road to Verviers hospital by ambulance. The Lotus BRM was almost 'T' boned against a telegraph pole. Tim reckoned that his chap might be lucky to have escaped with a few broken bones. What he had suffered in the fire nobody knew.

Tim instructed me to attend Richard in Verviers, while — phlegmatic as ever — he reckoned that he and Stan would get the wreckage back to the pits. Being the son of racing driver, Reg Parnell, Tim had learnt to ride his luck. The assumption after talking to marshals was that Richard might be okay. I told Tim that I would telephone the hotel when I had information on Richard's condition.

It took me a torrential eternity to reach Verviers. Apart from being becalmed in the jam of traffic departing from the circuit, I then had to find my way to the hospital when I reached the town.

Once there and I had identified the patient, a charmingly efficient nurse who spoke reasonable English explained that Richard was in shock: he had superficial burns to his face and back, bad bruising and abrasions. He was going to be detained at Verviers for at least a week for proper treatment, a medical examination and x-rays before he could return to England. I was then allowed to visit the poor lad and my first stupid reaction was to burst out laughing. Tatty had been exposed to sufficient heat to scorch the stubble around his mouth which had been treated with bright red mercurochrome and this made him appear like a clown. His natural one-sided grin turned to a grimace as pain contorted his features. I was able to report back to Tim that the lad was on the mend.

On Monday morning brilliant sunshine poured through the window of Richard's private room. Apart from Tim and Ginnie, there were Innes, Jochen and other friends who crowded in to wish him well. I had already volunteered to Tim that I would stay with Richard, then drive him to Brussels airport so that he could fly back to London before I continued on to Le Mans. This was generally agreed to be a good idea, so Tim gave me a huge wodge of Belgian Francs and told me to keep in touch and pay all the bills.

When everybody had departed their various ways, I returned to Trois Ponts to write my columns. The Verviers local paper *Le Jour* had kindly offered to develop my films and print what I required while Mike Spence elected to take my work back to London to be collected at Heathrow.

Richard was not wanting any family fuss. I had spoken to his mother by telephone and she was all for wishing to fly out and tend her son's needs. 'What bloody needs?' he bellowed at me one morning, 'I intend to race at Le Mans'. According to the medics that was clearly unrealistic. So Tat's recovery expectation was put back one week to the French Grand Prix at Clermont-Ferrand. I was prepared to leave that target open. Racing drivers like some thing to aim at, so I encouraged that thinking. By Wednesday, he was getting really fed-up with himself. What with me hanging about like a spare part, we had a crisis meeting with the medics in his room and the decision was made that he should fly back to England on the morrow. They didn't like it, but Tat was adamant, and I booked the flight from Brussels to London for a special medical case. Then the crunch came when the hospital refused to let Richard be driven in an ambulance to the airport.

I resolved to drive him there myself. It was a hell of a decision, but we had had enough. It was not that the hospital staff at Verviers had not been attentive. Everybody had been marvellous, but with great respect to them, I felt that their treatment was not the very best for a quick recovery. So we bade our farewells on the Thursday and I embarked upon a drive to Brussels that felt as if I had a car full of eggs, and every street was cobbled.

The attention accorded to Richard at Brussels airport was faultless. Maybe having a security chief as a racing enthusiast helped us. Soon after completing his check-in, Richard and I were provided with an escort in the Vauxhall right to the steps of the flight to London. Once the lad was safely aboard, I then telephoned Tim in order to unload my responsibilities onto England. From then onwards I was at liberty to motor across Northern France to the small village of Cleres just outside Rouen.

Veteran and vintage enthusiasts will recognise this rustic corner of the Seine Maritime where Jackie Pichon is not only the ebullient host of the Hotel du Cheval Noir, but he also owns the infamous Auto Musée across the village high street. Just to the rear of the hotel is a big old tithe barn where he restored his collection of antiquated vehicles.

Had events gone according to plan, Tatty and I were going to spend a day at Cleres driving some of Pichon's veteran cars along the surrounding rural lanes for a *Car* magazine feature. In the event I arrived in solitary splendour to be greeted by Jackie, who was clearly upset about Richard's accident.

Jackie had been my host previously when Rouen was the venue of the French Grand Prix in 1962 and '64, Rivers Fletcher of BRM nearly always made the Hotel du Cheval Noir the base for the team at these events.

I frequented Jackie's hostelry when I missed channel ferries out of Dieppe to Newhaven. One memorable occasion cropped up after an April Le Mans test weekend. Along with David Piper and Liz Michel we arrived at 3 am on the Monday morning amid a massive storm. Light sprang eternal from the hotel bar, Jackie welcomed us and without a turn of his black wavy hair he hustled us into a party where plenty of soup, wine and broken bread was available. We dug in, joined in and departed at daybreak somewhat the worse for wear.

Jackie was quite adjusted to the ways of his mad motoring friends. I compiled a lovely feature on the museum and drove an attractive local school teacher around the area of the zoological gardens in something decrepit, to complete a frivolous story.

The drive from Rouen to Le Mans was always fun as the weekend of the 24-hour race approached, when the N138 was enriched by a steady procession of 'sporting types' converging upon the Sarthe circuit. The Dutch whined along in their orange-painted variomatic Dafs. They gave adequate berth for the Mercedes 300SL gull wing job which had the headlights blazing, thereby turning the variomatic bands of the Daf transmission to molten rubber. Proud owners of what was then the new 1.6-litre Lancia Fulvia skimmed past me, but they were getting in the way of the Alfa Romeo Giulias. Then came a regiment of three British-registered motorcars that appeared to be tied to each other and were performing manoeuvres similar to synchronised swimming as they dipped in perfect unison in and out of the slow lane. Their leader was a beautifully maintained Jaguar XK-SS, the road-going version of the 'D' type, followed by angry-sounding florid Ford Mustang whose occupants were being blown to smithereens by the draught. The rearguard of this train was a Porsche 911 Targa that whined in contrast to the other two baritones. As against the aristocratic Le Mans enthusiasts, the fun-loving British race fans in their Ford Anglias and Austin Mini-Coopers were lucky to get a look in on this mobile classic car show. All were festooned with Les Leston's bolt-on goodies, plastered with chequered tape and black insulation cross patches covered their headlights, They might, have looked speedy, but the fans were, having fun getting nowhere slowly.

Knowing that this colourful cavalcade would come to a grinding halt long before making Le Mans, I diverted from the N138 at Alençon and careered along the 300 through Courgains and Ballon to reach the Automobile Club de l'Ouest so that I might claim my credentials before closing time.

Paul Frère, the respected Belgian motoring writer and one-time winner of the 1960 Le Mans (with his compatriot Olivier Gendebien) in a Ferrari, passed me the comment: 'The essence of Le Mans does not change with each year — only the winning car and its driver'.

I go along with Paul in that the drama unfurls against the same distracting background, but for me the mood of each '24-hours' is set by the weather, the casualty rate and whether the winning manufacturers are French, Italian, German or British. In 1965 there was a landslide victory for Ferrari. The Scruderia had been unstoppable since Aston Martin won in 1959. This time the Ferrari was driven by Masten Gregory, (the bespectacled American driver with a voice from Etna) and Jochen Rindt. Unbiased though written observers were supposed to be, I was honestly pleased for Jochen because his short entrée into Grand Prix racing with Cooper had been fraught with mechanical maladies. He was unable to display his latent potential which we had witnessed in Formula Two racing.

Considering his 'win-at-all-costs' mentality, I thought that Jochen's attitude was not conducive to 'the patience game' which long-distance drivers have to play at Le Mans, where to perform at 6-7-tenths is sufficient to pay dividends. So his partnership with Masten Gregory on this occasion was inspired, and indicated that the Austrian did have control over his impetuosity.

During that weekend I encountered Jochen after Masten had taken over early on Saturday evening. He took me to his 'bunk wagon' where — instead of grabbing some sleep — he was more concerned about Richard Attwood's welfare. After I had related the full story, Jochen was furious and vowed that he would tell his team-mate Bruce McLaren before the next meeting of the Grand Prix Drivers' Association. Jochen reckoned that an injured driver deserved prompt aid and the fastest method of transportation to reach specialist treatment,

Events accelerated after Jackie Stewart's accident at Spa in 1966. Key people were gradually galvanised into creating the mobile Grand Prix Medical Service, which was unkindly described as Louis Stanley's big 'white elephant' which trundled around the international circuits.

After Le Mans had been won, Denis Druit, the Racing Manager of BP, unloaded a surplus of petrol into Tatty's Vauxhall and I proceeded to follow my nose to Royan on the French west coast at the estuary of the mighty Gironde River. This elegant resort was virtually flattened in the Second World War, and risen from the rubble is a contemporary, coast town in which I enjoyed pottering about after a welcome swim in the Atlantic Ocean.

While perusing a book shop I encountered Erna. She was a Danish girl from Alborg. I had spotted her at the races. She was far too imbued with the history of the sport to be a 'pit popsey'. This unusual girl took four weeks away from her work and family each year to hitch-hike around the European motor racing scene. Erna had secured a random lift to Royan. From there she was planning to visit Bordeau and Perigueux before aiming for Clermont-Ferrand to see the French Grand Prix. What a sad state of affairs exists in these days that girls such as Erna cannot freely travel to places on their on initiative, without fear for their safety. She joined me for a couple of days until we reached the volcanic landscape of the Auvergne region.

I discovered en route that Erna retained an encyclopaedic memory on the history of motor sport. She guided me through Bordeaux to pay homage to Emile Levassor who, single-handed, in 1895 drove his Panhard-Levassor in the race from Paris to the Gironde capital in 48 hours 45 minutes non-stop! We also meandered along the Bordeaux road circuit where José Froilan Gonzalez won a Formula One race in the 'fifties. I learnt more in the charming town of Perigueux, the regional capital of the Dordogne. In 1898 the Cathedral St Font stood witness to races where the driver de Montaignac rolled his 'Landry et Beyrouc' scrambling around a dusty corner. Both the driver and his mate were killed and are immortalised as the first fatalities in motor racing history.

On several occasions I had listened to people at The Steering Wheel Club talk of the ethereal driving experience. Men like Stirling Moss compared the rhythm of inspired driving to a sexual phenomenon. Innes Ireland was allegedly outstandingly blatant at such a time!

Until we departed Perigueux for Clermont-Ferrand, this spiritual 'oneness' between man and machine had eluded me. Apart from my being in a fairly good mood and impatient to reach the fabled Auvergne circuit there is no accounting for what happened during this journey. As I steered over the N89-E70 in the direction of Brive, I felt a sense of control when we sped along the undulating route. There was little traffic about and I was motoring at a heck of a rate. The fiery sun shimmered over the volcanic landscape. The mirage of 'puddles' filled the road. Everything seemed crystal clear. My reactions and my thinking were totally synchronised. I identified every aroma that wafted through the open side windows — manure, wood smoke, wild flowers, freshly cut grass and oven fresh bread. Gear changes were smooth. I had the braking distances right and yet, in spite of our velocity, the scenery passed by in slow motion. It was a total revelation to be concentrating so well, feeling the rhythm of the car through bends, over humps, across adverse cambers and on blind hill-brows. I was sure there was a sound of music in my head.

Tatty's Vauxhall it might have been, but I doubt if so much joy and kindredness could have been distilled in a Ferrari Berlinetta or a Jaguar 'E'. What made the drive twice as enjoyable was that Erna was also plugged into the sensation. Remember that this was before seat belts had become mandatory. What prompted the senses to click into place simultaneously is hard to define. Racing drivers often find this glorious euphoria. For the first time I had some inkling of what they found on 'cloud nine'. Perhaps Emile Levassor had lent me a guiding hand.

Clermont-Ferrand lies on rising ground in the shadow of the Monts Domes, a region that erupted from ancient volcanic activity. In spite of the considerable industrialisation dominated by the Michelin Tyre Company, the old city has preserved a 17th-century charm. Jackie Stewart's initial observation was more succinct.

'Claremont is supposed to be a health spa. The place is full of old dears whose dinner tables look like chemists' counters. Most hotels are like mausoleums with an air of decreptitude'.

Not everybody would agree with the Scot, but it was against this jaded fabric that the French Grand Prix was run.

After watching the race transporters arrive and park between the cow pats in the transformed paddock grazing fields, and listening to ribald comments vented by the mechanics about their horticultural work area, the prodigious New Zealand columnist Eoin Young and photographers Lynton Money and Michael Cooper joined me for a sight-seeing drive to the extinct volcanoes. As we passed the old craters that encase beautiful trout-filled lakes and foamy waterfalls, their news from England reassured me that Richard was on the mend, but obviously he would be missing this race. At ease, we best viewed the scarped hills from the toll road that wends to the pinnacle of the Puy de Dome.

The five-mile road circuit hugs the rocky escarpment that provides a panorama across the fertile Limagne plain with the city directly below.

Photographically the elevation lent itself to some rare angles, looking straight down upon the cars, especially on the downhill section from the pit area. There are two identical corners on this stretch. Drivers had to be sure of their bearings to avoid an ensuing calamity. As there were so many vantage points from where the onlooker could gaze directly into the cockpit, I was intrigued when Innes Ireland broke down beneath me. Then he clambered onto the rock abutment during practice to extol his observations. He compared the driving skills of his fellow-countrymen Jim Clark and Jackie Stewart.

Clark in the Lotus-Climax appeared effortless when he was going for pole position. Innes then borrowed my telephoto camera, and during the next lap told me to compare Stewart in the BRM. The 'new boy' was driving so much harder than anybody else and was visually much quicker. So the wee Scot must have been losing time on his mentor on the uphill part of the course.

The Lotus driver bagged pole position and in the race claimed victory ahead of Stewart who gained a fighting second place and a tigerish John Surtees who hurled the Ferrari into third position.

When Jackie Stewart won the 1969 French Grand Prix at 'the old biddy's watering hole' he spotted me perched high above the crowd that surrounded his Matra-Ford. It was one of the first occasions on which the winner was presented with a magnum of Moët et Chandon. Suddenly Jackie popped the cork, and I was treated to the very best champagne shower ever. I proudly presented a copy of that picture in colour on behalf of Ford Sport at Brands Hatch after he became the World Champion for the first time in his career in Ken Tyrrell's car.

Historians will note that in 1966 the Grand Prix of 'No Fixed Abode' was held at Reims. I recorded the event, but also returned to Clermont-Ferrand that year for the French Grand Prix du Frankenheimer that was orchestrated by Metro Goldwyn Mayer over eight days.

Apart from earning wads for advising upon camera angles and hamming it up with my fellow photographers as a film extra, I recall this unofficial event for a personal experience. At the end of a day's shoot, John Frankenheimer caught me crammed into a Lotus 33 Climax. It could not have been Jim Clark's because they are considered museum pieces by gentlemen like Lord Montagu of Beaulieu, Tom Wheatcroft of Donington Motor Museum or the Haynes museum at Sparkford, Somerset. The car I occupied must have been the model driven by either Trevor Taylor or Peter Arundell in 1965.

Just before the 'authority' caught me napping, I wondered what natural aptitude men like Moss, Clark, Surtees and Stewart possessed that I obviously lacked. I gripped the red leather steering wheel, located the gear lever, danced over the pedals. I could drive a car. All my faculties were there. I pondered over the area the great creator may have been sparing of when he made me. Did I lack vision, balance, concentration, rhythm, reactions or anticipation? Surely I possessed all these qualities to a varying degree, but which on that list separated me from a champion? That inspired drive and many others along the N89 was proof conclusive that I could put it together. All this was percolating through my mind when Frankenheimer growled 'Well, whaddaya think?'

'F-fantastic, never sat in one before', I stuttered.

'Then do me a favour', smirked the director, 'drive the car back to the garage in Royat for me'.

Stan Collier had listened to all this with a huge grin across his face. 'Well go on then. You write about these drivers who can't pull the skin off a rice pudding. Show Mr Frankenheimer, what you can do'.

A feeling of warmth spread around my nether extremities as I experienced the mixed emotions of keen anticipation and white-knuckled fear. I asked Stan to give me a guided tour of the controls. He showed me the gear change pattern, told me that the engine would stall below 3,500 revs or above 6,500 and advised me not to wrestle the steering as if I were driving a lorry. He then gave me a push, I engaged the clutch and 'bam' I kangaroo'd down the hill, bombed out of my skull in exaltation. The wheels seemed to tower over the cockpit, I was bouncing about and concentrated upon changing up a gear before the needle hit the red zone. I had just about gathered my wits as I turned off the circuit and down the hill into Royat. Pedestrians waved thinking that I was J C and I wished the floor would open up as I popped and banged inside the speed limit to the garage.

Flushed from this surprise experience, I asked a mechanic what kind of speed 4,500 revs was in fourth gear, He reckoned that it was about 110 mph, which compared with Jim Clark's race record in a similar car in 1965 at 90.59 mph which put my effort into perspective and answered all the niggly questions as to why I was not the heir-apparent.

* * *

Beyond the specialist motoring publications, my work was being scrutinised by photographic magazines and the consumer glossies circulated by motor manufacturers like Ford, Vauxhall and British Leyland. While this additional attention provided more grist to the mill, the critical eyes cast by Mum and Dad were still my yardstick. They knew very little about photography, but Mum staggered me in 1965 when she reckoned I was reaching an inspirational peak. Dad felt I wasn't technically perfect. I wondered who had been 'nobbling' their opinions — which I realised were basically right.

I could see a photograph very clearly in my mind and had the ability to translate that image onto film. It was almost second nature to compose the filigree around the hole where the cars would burst into view and complete the photograph. I was a yard or so adrift on critical definition, so I soldiered on trusting that the visual impact concealed the many hours Tom Buckridge at college had spent helping me to master pin-sharp focusing, teaching me how to use depth-of-field with appropriate apertures. I knew that to achieve the acme of success, I had to relate creativity to technical perfection.

By 1968 strange things began to offend my eye. I have mentioned the Bell helmets that effectively de-humanised the driver by masking his face. While I realised that driver and spectator safety was paramount, I questioned whether it was the biblical right of the Grand Prix Drivers' Association to have armco barriers erected. But these damned sheets of steel effectively cut my pictures in half. Gone was the harmony of racing cars etched against natural backgrounds. Time and again I sought backcloths uncluttered by the steel barriers.

I then concluded that visual harassment had always been there in straw bales, earth banks, rubber-retaining tyres and advertising banners. When I worked at circuits in America, I accepted the encroachment of safety appliances and brand-name impedimenta as part of the scene. Their sporting culture was firmly based upon commercial exploitation to a greater degree than in Europe. So in 1968 when Europe went commercial, I became aware of my creativity taking a back seat while I attempted to negotiate commercial terms on technically good photographs. Although I capitalised on the 'required' pictures, it hurt because the essential local ambience was missing. There has come a point where we cannot directly differentiate one circuit from another these days. This annoying aspect was creeping into the game during the late 'sixties. I was horrified about this marching uniformity creeping into our sport, I had slowly to merge the creative and technical lobes of my brain in order to produce good rorty action shots that pleased the eye. It was a mental war which caused despair. I doubt whether within my entire racing career I managed to strike the ideal balance. A strange twist of fate influenced my approach in 1964. By way of a complete change, I accepted an assignment, from Harry Louis, the editor of *Motor Cycle* magazine to compile a montage of pictures that captured the atmosphere of the Japanese Motorcycle Grand Prix at Suzuka. Among other people I travelled with the magazine's race and technical editor, Vic Willoughby, a slight man of boundless knowledge and enthusiasm for motorcycles.

It was a breath of fresh air as we departed London on a British Eagle turbo-propelled flight that would take about 30 hours with fuel stops at Istanbul,

Bombay, Bangkok, Hong Kong and eventually Tokyo. We had plenty of time to ponder the diverse priorities of socialism. Within 48 hours the Soviet leader Nikita Khrushchev was unceremoniously 'retired' by his comrades in The Kremlin. Next day the British electorate booted the capitalist Conservative party from 10 Downing Street. The new Prime Minister was Labour leader Harold Wilson who, upon entering Number 10 for the first time, commented: 'Nice place we've got here' to his wife Mary. We left the affairs of state to the new Government, only momentarily wondering what kind of Britain we would eventually return to.

Upon arrival at Tokyo I received my baggage from the aircraft hold and to my horror, found that my camera case had been crushed. The equipment was scrap metal. I quickly learned a harsh lesson, never again to put cameras in the luggage hold. As it was, my plight was clear: no camera, no pictures, no income! I didn't dare tell Vic of my problem.

Next morning I visited a camera shop in Tokyo's Ginza shopping centre. A polite but startled man ruefully nodded his head, then consigned my wrecked equipment to the waste bin. As I stood appalled, he, with that bland inscrutable expression so typical of the Oriental, lifted a telephone and dialled a number. I overheard one side of a frenetic conversation, then he replaced the receiver and smiled. 'Ten minutes,' he indicated with his fingers. 'Car come, man help you... okay'.

The crowning glory of this animation was that I was chauffeur-driven to the Pentax factory. There I was met by the marketing director who proceeded to conduct me along the production line where a thousand cameras were assembled by men and women within the click of a shutter. My beaming host then took me to lunch — which was a gastronomic experience.

Beautiful girls welcomed us at the entrance which had a highly polished oak wood floor. They beckoned us to sit on cushions while they changed our shoes for a pair of flat-thonged slippers. With a Chaplinesque gait, I shuffled into a private room with my host and sat cross-legged at a very low table. The girls then, according to tradition, washed our hands in piping hot water. All the time they chattered and giggled in high-pitched voices. It was fun. Next a matronly lady came to discuss our meal. I learnt that there are two basic choices. 'Tempura' covers a wide variety of fish foods, while 'Sukiyaki' is primarily made from meats.

While we waited for our meal to be served, the girls in their brightly embroidered kimonos and fat obis with their straight black hair pinned in a bun on top, entertained us with songs and music. Eventually the food was served: dozens of little bowls, some fish, others meat, vegetables, fruit and sauces galore. I cleared my palate with a warm lemon drink which produced expressions of amazement among the girls. It transpired that I was quenching my thirst from the finger bowl!

My cares had been reduced to irrelevance by this gratuitous hospitality. But time was ticking by, I had to join Vic Willoughby for a train out to Nagoya and onward to Hamamatsu where our host Shunzo Suzuki, President of the Suzuki Company, was to welcome us next day.

After the meal, I could appreciate why motorcycle champions like Mike Hailwood, Phil Read and Barry Sheene had queued up to sign for Japanese teams. I was escorted back to the lacquered reception area where a lovely girl bowed low at my presence and then presented me with a big gift-wrapped box. Everybody then clasped their hands, smiled broadly and bowed as I was shown back to the chauffeur-driven car.

On the way to Tokyo, quivering with anticipation, I unwrapped the parcel. To my utter astonishment, therein was a brand-new 35 mm Asahi Pentax camera, a range of lenses and a light meter, Willoughby could not understand my sudden enthusiasm for the Land of the Rising Sun.

The 1964 Tokyo Olympic Games had just reached their grand finale as we arrived in Japan. This seething, industrious country was about to launch itself upon the Western world with all manner of optical, electrical and visual products. In the nicest possible way, Pentax had made me an ambassador for their company. From their point of view, every gift to their Western visitors represented ten off the shelf in the United Kingdom. It was smart public relations, the more so since it occurred at the time of my greatest hour of need.

The party travelled from Tokyo to Nagoya on what was the revolutionary 'Tokiado Express' or Bullet Train as some American colleagues called it. I thought that the train appeared more phallic than ballistic. Thirty years have passed since I made that journey. Apart from being smothered to death in the incomparable luxury and service which one experiences on South Africa's Blue Train, I have not travelled on a railway so efficient as the Tokiado.

It took Japanese Railways ten years to lay the special rail that took a virtually straight line from Tokyo to Osaka. The overhead power gantries became a funnelled blur at something around 230 kph. Although a driver monitored the controls, the entire route was computerised. Each stop was timed precisely for two minutes. At all stations the passengers knew exactly where to stand for swift entry and exit. Heaven helped those with parcels or luggage, although the disabled were given preference above all else.

Once we were on board, it was more like the fuselage of jet airliner. Dual-purpose seats were made to tip so that you faced your fellow passengers or turned your back to them. There was a restaurant car and *en route* waitress service from the buffet. Toilets were always hygienically cleaned, the 'throne' was rather narrow to accommodate voluminous Western backsides. Who cared when hostesses delivered the unreadable daily newspapers, and purveyed fiery drinks and nibbles. There was no class distinction, so everybody enjoyed the same degree of service.

On Grand Prix day, the drive from Nagoya to Suzuka was made simple for the British since Japan observes the left-hand-side rule of the road. Knowing that Japan roughly occupies a similar land mass to the United Kingdom and is grossly over populated by almost 95 million, an air of frantic excitement was created by the deluge of race fans as they wove two-wheeled powered machines between the daily rush hour into Hamamatsu and the congestion building up outside Suzuka. Many benevolent but suicidal riders carried one person on the petrol tank while two more sat side-saddle on the pillion. The kamikaze instinct prevailed as they buzzed crazily through, stationary truck-loads of fans, cars and coaches close to the circuit. The noise of several thousand multi-cylinder eggcups on the buzz was quite excruciating.

I found it incongruous to be welcomed by good old British salacity where ladies armed with brooms and dust-pans got the beady eye from the likes of Mike Hailwood and Phil Read. They seemed integrated within the Japanese teams amid this alien culture. When the team boss stood on ceremony, these two ambassadors of British sport observed all the social etiquettes and displayed their best behaviour.

This magnificent circuit, designed roughly to a figure eight was financed by Honda. As a venue it was way ahead of others in development and safety. The crowd seemed to be 99% male (no wonder the cleaners got the evil British eye) who obediently waved Mr Honda's hats when the host team won a race. Away from Honda's dedicated supporters, the great unwashed out in the boondocks consumed saki, sang the Nippon version of 'Eskimo Nell' and generally rooted for Honda, Suzuki, Kawasaki and Yamaha. Men in blue coveralls and hard hats, all wielding truncheons, maintained the peace. That was the rule of thumb in Japan's chauvinistic society where the female was the subservient specie.

The camera equipment fulfilled its purpose admirably. When I contacted Pentax to voice my appreciation of the loan, the company reassured me that I had full ownership without obligation. So when I returned to Harold Wilson's Britain I made several tests in varied lighting conditions. The 200 mm Takumar telephoto lens was a superb piece of glass, I have enshrined it for posterity.

Unfortunately, the other lenses were not up to the required standard. I spent months plaguing camera suppliers in search of glass that would provide perfect colour resolution because I never used colour-corrective filters. I do not like being spoilt for choice when the action gets hectic. I eventually replaced the original 50 mm lens with a beautifully blued Takumar of a later make. The wide-angle lens was traded in for a Meyer-Optik 30 mm second-hand job that did not distort or fall off in definition at the edges of the frame. I realise that I could later have purchased up-to-date equipment, but by golly, it would take me years to find a lens or lenses that still give me satisfaction. These components will be museum pieces long after I am finished.

As autumn witnessed the curtain down on racing in Europe, I plunged into activities for magazines and enjoyed the social round. That encompassed anything, from the annual Press Trial to the Motor Show test days at Silverstone. A dizzy round of dinners and presentations throughout the country kept me in touch with the fraternity and their local news. At the behest originally of Ray Cunningham at Shell, I indulged a new talent in fronting 'live' promotions at Racing Car Shows. The Pit-Stop Competition was a audience-participation game in which ordinary people could pit their skills at changing four wheels, plugs, top up the oil and clean the windscreen within 45 seconds. Alternative attractions included celebrity interviews when I hosted such names as Eartha Kitt, Kirk Douglas and Dave Lee Travis alongside Graham Hill, Ronnie

Peterson against managers like Colin Chapman and Stuart Turner. On more than one occasion I smashed embargoes by weedling out 'hot news' of new driver signings. In between all the banter I had quizzes, beauty contests and blatant commercials to keep the programme moving. The teams working with me often performed for at least ten hours a day. Apart from hosting shows for Shell and Texaco at the London Olympia Halls, Jackie Stewart enlisted me for a show in conjunction with Rothmans of Pall Mall at the Kelvin Hall in Glasgow.

Living at Rural Park House enabled me to cultivate several friends within the local farming community. They often inveigled me to participate at local agricultural jamborees. In October 1965 I was invited to a Ploughing Match at Home Farm in Eynsford, Kent. Apart from photographing the event for a magazine feature, I acquired first-hand knowledge about the gentle art of ploughing a straight furrow.

My companion was Annette, a New Zealand girl from farming stock on the North Island. She happened to be staying in Gravesend on an extended global holiday with a friend. Annette eventually married a friend of Greta and Denis Hulme's, Bill Cleghorn, who was not only a Justice of the Peace in Rotarua, but he maintained a sheep farm in Ngongotaha. On more than one occasion I have arrived in New Zealand during the antipodean summer when Bill has roped me in to earn some beer money dipping and doping his flock. At Eynsford I was on the final furrows when the farmer stopped me. Judging from the expression of concern on his face something was wrong. He had received a telephone call from Dad saying that Mum had just been admitted into Joyce Green Hospital in Dartford.

Three years previous to this occasion, I was working at Oulton Park when Gregor Grant's secretary Nikki Taylor gave me a similar message. In fact she drove me all the way from Cheshire to Dartford where I met Dad at the hospital. He told me that Mum had just had a 'lady's' operation and she was going to be alright. In the 'sixties medical experts were still coy explaining their diagnosis, but Nikki surmised that Mum must have had a hysterectomy. Had I been more knowledgeable then, I might have questioned that, because I have since learnt that unless circumstances are dire, women do not have emergency operations for such a thing.

Eventually Mum returned to Park House, then typically she returned to work once the doctor had given his clearance. Dad and I kept a wary surveillance on Mum during the following years. She seemed to tire easily and we got concerned over a steady loss of weight.

Working at Brands Hatch was her life's blood, the people kept her going and the Pennington's realised that her obsession kept her happy, but it was taking a toll. In truth, the message at Eynsford was not unexpected. Annette and I immediately drove to Dartford. I harboured a nasty feeling that an epoch was on its last chapter.

A specialist informed Dad that stringent tests were being carried out on Mum. As I stood at her bedside, I was shocked. This was not the mother I saw when I departed from home that morning. She was drifting in and out of consciousness. I felt anger, not anguish. I confronted the specialist in a private room.

'My Mother's got cancer, hasn't she?'

The man was startled at my blatant confrontation. He insisted that the answer would be known only after the tests, then he finally admitted that cancer was a probability. The cruel terminator had no respect for a healthy 56-year-old woman who had never smoked or touched alcohol and had always looked after herself.

Even during the permissive 'sixties smoking and cancer were spoken in the same breath, but few people in the medical profession would actually face up to the issue. The word 'cancer' was swept under the carpet and embroidered with nicer looking patterns. The dark phantom killed its prey by stealth. Just trying to mention it stuck in the craw of everybody's throat.

Dad was oblivious. Where he could see life, there was hope. He clung on to that last shred like a drowning man. Two days later Mum passed peacefully away. With her spirit went a wonderful facet of my life.

Our family was spread about the world. Mum's brother Ron and her sister-in-law Doris had in 1952 emigrated to Australia with their four children. Dad's sister Yvonne and brother-in-law Bill with their son Roger lived in San Francisco. It seemed that only immediate family and friends would attend Mum's funeral at a secluded church in Kingsdown. As it happened Grandad George and Nan came over from Canvey Island. I was delighted to see her troubled sister Margaret and two daughters Anna and Naomi arrive. The Penningtons headed up dozens of members of the motor racing fraternity who had come to pay a final respect. I was proud of the loyalty Mum had gained over the years. Wreaths festooned the graveside from John Webb, Jack Surtees, Mike Hailwood, Tony Lanfranchi and many more from Grovewood Securities and the British Racing and Sports Car Club. After Mum's burial we all returned to Park House for a gathering. I provided the hospitality while Dad was comforted by our relatives. Friends were concerned that I appeared in reasonable spirits. Death in motor racing had taught me to keep a tight reign upon my emotions. I was more shocked than grief-stricken at Mum's passing. Peter Anderson stood by me at this time, but the emotion did come out much later.

In 1987 I was previewing the World Exposition in Brisbane, Australia when I took the opportunity to attend a race meeting at Surfers Paradise. The following day I motored to Highfield near Toowoomba to see my cousin Jennifer, her husband Geoffrey and their family. I was saddened to hear that I had missed Uncle Ron by a matter of weeks. He had died from illness, so Jennie took me to his grave. Over 23 years after Mum's departure, I broke down for the first time in my life. Sitting at Uncle Ron's graveside, everything came to a head. I wept throughout the day. Suddenly Mum was released from my heart with her brother Ron, I could at last start out fresh. The relief was unbelievable.

With Mum's passing, Dad and I knew that our days at Park House were numbered. John Webb's understanding of our situation was both gracious and sympathetic. There was plenty of time to reorientate ourselves. I felt that Dad's enthusiasm for Brands Hatch had been extinguished by our loss. I must confess to being relieved. Attending races every weekend, then returning home to the environment had jaded my enthusiasm for the sport. There was no respite from the continuous thunder. I knew that a change would rekindle my interest.

Just before Easter 1966, Dad and I moved the family home to a smaller dwelling near Meopham. We both felt that a new window of opportunity beckoned.

Throughout 1967 I was aware of strange people in the pits and paddocks of the Grand Prix circuits. These were account executives from multi-national companies looking over the wall at the commercial viability of motor sport. I had taken an academic interest in Bob Walklett's company, Ginetta Cars, whose factory was based at Witham in Essex.

The Ginetta boss had a great friend in journalist Ted Wilkinson, who had offered to compile a folder that could be presented to a company likely to make an investment in a racing team intending to compete in the Le Mans 24-hour race. The G4 model of the Ginetta range had enjoyed unparalleled success during 1967, so Ted wrote glowing comments and backed his statements with photographs. The presentation was then made to a brand manager of John Player & Sons at Nottingham. He in turn enthusiastically put the idea forward to Geoffrey Kent, then Marketing and Sales Director for the Imperial Tobacco Company. Straightaway Kent, himself a motor racing enthusiast, saw great possibilities of brand promotion through motor racing. At that moment, a seed was sown that would change the face of British motor sport.

If John Player & Sons were going to make their début in the sport, the investment would have to be something substantial, and a winner to boot. Ginetta lost the deal, although credit has always been given to Bob Walklett by the Imperial Tobacco Company for introducing the idea.

Kent instructed Timothy Collins and Ken Best of Sales Link Promotions to explore the possibility of going into Formula One racing. The company became aware that Colin Chapman of Team Lotus was in jeopardy, so Collins and Best went to see Chapman to find out if a sponsorship with his Grand Prix team and other formula was viable. The Lotus boss came up with an impressive deal. The Gold Leaf brand name could be incorporated with Team Lotus for his Grand Prix team, Formulas Two and Three, with sports car racing as an option. Kent was impressed, and a meeting was convened between the two key men. 'Gold Leaf Team Lotus' livery was first seen at the Lady Wigram Trophy in the Tasman Series in New Zealand during January 1968.

Motor racing was in business . . .

6

Evacuation in Modesty

THE FLOODGATES of a 'brain-drain' opened during the latter 'sixties. I noticed that some of my qualified friends were leaving Britain to seek golden opportunities in North America. The Labour Government had landed the country with a national debt of billions. For many bright young things the future appeared bleak. Nevertheless, five typists of the Colt Heating and Ventilation Company in Surbiton (where success sprang eternal in Cooper and Brabham country) declared an imaginative 'I'm Backing Britain' campaign. Prime Minister Harold Wilson latched onto the slogan and adopted it as part of his Government policy.

Since premature senility and partial deafness went with my profession, I didn't kid myself of having a brain fit for the drain. However, in order to familiarise myself with motor sport in North America, I departed Britain in 1968 to seek my fortune.

Unlike my pioneering friends who were breaking virgin territory in cities like New York, Montreal and Toronto, I had already travelled extensively in North America. Mind you, being accepted by Americans as a guest is one thing. When they see you move next door, they feel threatened and invite you to join the party before you become competitive.

I had opted for Toronto where I enjoyed a steady friendship with Joan and Jim Clayton. In those days Jim was on the race committee at Mosport Park near Peterborough. Joan had become part of Canadian folklore as a private entrant to Eppie Weitzes. She ran a team for him from 1969 until 1975 in the Canadian Championship series which Eppie won two years consecutively, and in the US road racing series first called the Continental which later became Formula(A)5000, Joan raced Lolas and McLarens. Later she turned her entrepreneurial skills to more charitable avenues by forming 'Windfall' to provide good 'seconds' in clothing for the poor and needy in Toronto.

After establishing a nice homely apartment, I made a bold attempt to capitalise upon my motoring background. I secured a regular job with publisher Alistair MacDonald as an associate editor in his popular magazine *Canadian Motorist*.

This publication was the official organ of the Canadian Automobile Association which had a circulation of 158,000 to its members.

Apart from providing me with a sheet anchor, I had sufficient income to rent an apartment in Admiral Road and pay the bills. Income from freelance writing for British magazines was hoopla money. Having that security made travelling to events across North America much easier.

Since *Canadian Motorist* tested a steady stream of cars from manufacturers, dealerships and whoever else supplied the need, I had no reason to purchase a vehicle of my own. Instead, there were occasions when I could take a car on a test run to a race weekend, provided that I photographed it against a seductive background en route. Within an eight-hour drive of Toronto I could easily reach venues like Milwaukee, Indianapolis, Mosport, Watkins Glen, St Jovite, Mid-Ohio and Elkhart Lake.

Although people in North America speak the common English tongue, their tastes, as I had learned from previous trips, vary considerably from the Eastern Sea Board to the West Coast. In between is the vast cooking pot of America itself. My editor Alex MacDonald not only educated me in the American vernacular and spelling when I wrote features, he also suggested I exchanged the little dumb blonde I wrote at the end of my typewriter, and replaced her with a sophisticated lady with a mansion in St Clair and a ski lodge at Huntsville and a man who resided in a weatherboard house somewhere around Yellowknife on the Great Slave Lake. To accommodate that widespread readership, the very first feature I wrote in the magazine was rewritten nine times before it was judged to be appropriate.

Amazingly, the vast kaleidoscope of North American peoples is reflected in motor sport. I had not long been in England after returning from Japan, and a back-to-back trip across America from Hawaii to New York in 1964, when at the Brands Hatch club house I was introduced to Kas Kastneg. He turned out to be the Competition Manager for Standard Triumph in Gardena, California. He had been at Coventry discussing his plans to race the Triumph TR4As in America. The idea was accepted with open arms by the factory, so Kas started to tool up for the team. The aim was to capitalise upon publicity from class wins to boost sales in America. He sprang the idea of inviting me over so as to chronicle this effort in the British press. Kas had made such a 'flip' remark, I hardly bothered to remember. Anyway, many months later a letter arrived in the post from Mike Cook, Marketing Manager for Standard Triumph in New York. The invitation was simple: I had an air ticket to fly to New York, meet the team, then attend the Sebring 12-hour race as their guest in March 1966.

After I had been warmly greeted by Mike at their Madison Avenue office he talked about the flight to Florida when I interrupted him. I gathered that Sebring was a matter of 1,300 miles or so from New York. So I enquired about the possibility of driving there and back in a TR4A.

'Drive... all the way to Florida... why not fly?' That was the general reaction of my astonished hosts. It was March, bitterly cold outside, and here was this Englishman asking to drive. Cars are a conveyance. We have a nice sporty little tourer, I have four days to reach Sebring before the first practice day. It was an ideal opportunity for pictures, fact-finding and getting to know the product? Besides, I was driving south where — according to newspaper weather reports — the temperature in Miami was a balmy 79° F: couldn't be better.

Mike needed 24 hours to release a fleet car, and provide me a cash budget so that I should be able to depart on the morrow. I used the spare day to re-acquaint myself with Stanley Rosenthall, a respected photographer of motor racing in New York. We had a fresh, bright and invigorating day with his wife Josie amid the foothills around Catskill just north of New York. Stanley shared my ideals in photography, his pictures of cars were a recognised art form across America. The couple were totally un-Americanised. He was abhorred by the 'plastic fantastic' life style. I wondered how they tolerated living on 83rd Street. But then I discovered that many people on Manhattan were like minded.

I meandered along the Eastern Seaboard for three days of touring in the TR4A between New York and Sebring. Driving in America is straightfor-ward, concise, well sign-posted over wide roads which in March were traffic free as I trundled through Philadelphia to the Delaware State. I crossed the Chesapeake Bay by the toll tunnel-bridge. This imaginative 17-mile construc-tion made me wonder at the Euro-Tunnel beneath the English Channel from Folkestone to Calais in France. Surely the French and the English could have burrowed a third of the way across each, then built a bridge in the middle. Crossing Chesapeake Bay was so much more refreshing method of reaching Virginia.

Before arriving in Sebring, I dropped by the dusty Georgetown Speedway to witness figure-eight Derby performed with cars that appeared to have been just hauled off the scrap heap.

The Carolinas were real 'Dukes of Hazard' territory. I even got stopped for speeding between Charleston and Savannah. Now that was fun. It was quite a twisty stretch of road where signs indicated 65 mph and 45 mph on the bends. The road was empty and I was exploiting the TR4A above limits when I spot-ted this Dodge Charger screeching through the corners trying to catch up with me. It was not until I saw the flashing lights that I realised I had been caught by a patrol car.

Where I was holding corners at a steady 70-80 mph he was bumbling, lurching, and wobbling over the road like a demented old rhinoceros. Eventu-ally, along a straight stretch, he gave the Dodge all she had got and finally pulled me up. 'Gee, that was fun!' he exclaimed. 'Where didya get that li'l ole diddy car from?'

In my Oxford English I explained the mission. The officer got very excited, booked me for twenty US dollars, took me to the next burger hut, and pro-ceeded to treat me to a snack with my money! Over the meal, he enthused about Savannah Speedway, then he told me how in 1908 Savannah hosted the Grand Prix of America which was won by Louis Wagner in a Fiat.

I did not realise that Savannah was a black community, so when we arrived on the packed terraces at the speedway, I felt very much that I was the minor-ity white man. Not that I allowed the discrepancy to spoil an evening of great sport. Most drivers in those bangers were white, but when the floodlights for the last race were turned on, they gave a black driver pole position, and we watched him hold onto first place and the spectators yelled the place down until he was nurfed off the oval. I did not join my copper chum in the muted cheering of his demise.

Twelve hours at Sebring seemed pretty harmless stuff after Savannah Speedway. I was glad to record that Kas and his team were weighed down with trophies for the hard-won effort in between the heavy social round.

My journey continued to familiarise me with the American racing scene which I found was roughly controlled by NASCAR and its President, Bill France, the big Virginian. The National Association for Stock Car Auto Racing maintained its headquarters at the Daytona Beach high-speed tri-oval. In the 'sixties the United States Auto Club's primary task was to organise Indycar racing. Then in 1978 Roger Penske and Pat Patrick of USAC formed a breakaway organisation known as CART — Championship Auto Racing Teams.

After Sebring I drove between the two big shrines to motor racing in the United States. It would have been sacrilege to be in Florida and not to pay a visit to the Daytona Beach Speedway. Here was the realisation of cinder ovals like Savannah where I met with Bill France. At huge personal risk, 'Florida's Biggest Buddy' accompanied me for a couple of laps of this amazing bowl in the TR4A. It was not until Bill urged me to stop half-way up one of the steeply banked turns, and then had the last laugh as he watched me heave myself out of the car and attempt to traverse up to the retaining barrier, that I realised how chaps like Richard Petty can tool around there at top speeds over 180 mph.

Unfortunately there was not a meeting on at the time of my visit, but I would have enjoyed seeing those packs of late model stockers 'banging it out' around the tri-oval.

I discovered an entirely different element at Indianapolis where the Hoosier Bowl (formerly known as the Brickyard) is formed by four classic turns that are nothing like as steep as Daytona. I was intrigued to note that during the mid-'sixties Petty had lapped Daytona at 160.63 mph while the record speed at Indianapolis was set by Jim Clark during his victorious year of 1965 at 150.69 mph. That made mincemeat of a very, very, slow lap I made, enjoyed from the elevated cab of a sweeper, of the 2.5-mile oval in 34 minutes!

My historical instinct realised the enormity of this hallowed cathedral in American motor sport history. The roll of honour folds back to 1911 when Ray Harroun drove a Marmon to win at an average speed of 74.59 mph. Littered at each turn was the blood, sweat and tears of great names like Meyer, Schneider, Vukovich, Ward, Foyt and Unser. I regretted that I was not able to witness that historic victory in 1965 when Jim Clark, after three attempts in Colin Chapman's Lotus-Ford, changed the face of Indianapolis forever.

Emotions were still volatile less than a year later when a handful of the 'old stagers' visited the museum with me. Ever since Jack Brabham made his debut in the rear-engined Cooper-Climax in 1961, the days of the traditional front-engined Indycars were numbered. The traditionalists reckoned that the

European invasion had changed America's sacred cow forever. I told them that it cannot be all that bad if 250,000 fans turn up each year to perpetuate Memorial Day in the proper way of Indiana.

I completed my 4,000-mile trip through Canada and returned the car to New York. The only damage was a stoved-in nearside front wing, bent by an errant dog in Kentucky. My steed had behaved itself admirably through hot and cold, snow and dust, rain and shine, and the stories were legion.

I flew back to Indianapolis two months later. Shortly after arriving at the Hoosier Bowl after qualification, I was wandering along the pit lane when Graham Hill sauntered in my direction. His face was a wreath of smiles.

'I've cracked the bastards', he enthused. The remark led me to believe that as a 'rookie' he had claimed pole position in the Lola, a car identical to that which he had been offered at the Cinderella hour alongside his BRM team mate Jackie Stewart: nothing of the sort. In reality he actually started the race on the outside of the fifth row, which was a commendable performance.

What he had 'cracked' was a bastion of the lowest common male morality in the entire United States of America. The focus of Hill's attention from the day he arrived at Indy were the ghastly gents' toilets in the out-of-bounds-to-ladies area known as Gasoline Alley. This den of locked-up garage iniquity where men could be men, unencumbered by female interlopers, was perhaps the most chauvinistic area on earth outside the 'Spot Room' bar in Auckland. When the stakes are high which is invariably the case at Indianapolis — fellows could swear, kick the wall, settle old scores, have a punch-up and, above all else, the mechanics could prepare a car when 'a glimpse of stocking might have meant a half turned screw'.

So why was Graham so pleased with himself?

Well, the alley might have been a domain for 'gents only' but he was disgusted that the water closets had no doors. Graham complained bitterly to the Brickyard authorities. He was a man who preferred to play his one-man band in privacy — not sit on the throne straining at the big base drum with all and sundry stopping by for a chat. Doors were fixed to the thunderboxes in 1966 for the first time in a 49-year racing history. Hill had made his mark upon Indianapolis regardless of what happened on Memorial Day.

The 1966 race became notorious for two reasons: first, there was a monumental accident straight after the start of the race; and second, a complete cock-up occurred when two drivers descended upon victory lane when there hadn't even been a dead heat!

Never in my life have I been witness to such a terrifying and potentially cataclysmic accident. Sixteen racing cars, fully fuelled, ploughed into each other, from which drivers and onlookers survived totally unscathed. Everybody who saw the shunt feared the worst carnage. Visions of Le Mans 1955 when a Mercedes driven by Pierre Levagh had to take monstrous avoiding action around a crowded pit lane in front of the main grandstands, mounted the safety bank and scythed down 70 people, all of whom died instantly.

The saving grace at Indianapolis was the massive retaining fence protecting spectators from the circuit, thus confining the accident to a fairly small area.

Before the race I had been frustrated in trying to decide the best photo-angle for the rolling start. I had the choice of a telephoto shot from high over the spectator terraces overlooking turn one, or I could find a spot inside the crash barrier on the infield beyond the pit lane at the same bend.

I opted for the latter choice because I felt closer to the action. It was a rotten camera angle, a fact I came to terms with as the racing cars performed two warm-up laps behind the pace car. On the third lap, the pace car veered into the pit lane, releasing 33 cars under full acceleration into turn one. Under perfectly normal circumstances this spectacle presents a gut-wrenching sight.

From my view point, it was a screeching sound that alerted me to an errant car. The leaders had already gone through, oblivious of the catastrophe unfolding behind them. Initially, events happened with startling speed. Then the mind adjusted and the awful kaleidoscope shook itself, whereupon each fragment could been seen with stunning clarity. Amid the shattering sounds of tortured rubber, flying debris, metal crunching into metal and gyrating cars, I spotted the London Rowing Club colours on Graham Hill's crash helmet. I focussed my complete attention upon that blue beacon of hope as he steered serenely through the mayhem.

I recalled seeing a film of a deep-ocean racing-yacht as it ploughed through massive ocean swells. There was a visual sensation of now-you-see-it-now-you-don't as the craft rose on the crests, then plummeted to the troughs. This described Graham's progress through the turbulent ocean of metallic chaos. He made it through, untouched and set off to find the leading bunch for a better grid position for the restart of the race.

During the interval when the grisly mess was cleared up, I imagined sixteen drivers sitting in the 'Gents' simultaneously evacuating their bowels with relief. I dare to say that Graham's noble gesture of common decency came not a year to soon for them.

From early days, Cyril Audrey was a timekeeper who won my respect. I was allowed into his hallowed chamber above the main grandstand at Brands Hatch during a ten-lap club race between sixteen cars. He timed each car every lap accurately to within tenths of a second on his watches. He was a respected lap scorer. Cyril took enormous pride in his job wherever he officiated. That was the reason why Colin Chapman enlisted his services for Lotus at Indianapolis.

So when the chequered flag was eventually waved on this beleaguered edition of the 500, Cyril's beaming features confirmed to Chapman and to everyone that Jim Clark had won for the second consecutive year. The fact that Cyril's result conflicted with Lola's number 24 flashing on the illuminated totem of a score board, querying Hill's victory in the Red Ball Special, was tantamount to doubting the divine spirit.

While one section of the pit-lane was bewailing Jackie Stewart's downright bad luck in having to retire with mechanical trouble when he was in the lead literally miles from the finish line, the other half of Lola were a reception committee led by Eric Broadly waiting to welcome the all conquering Hill.

Had Anton Hulman Junior, President and saviour of the Indianapolis

Speedway after the Second World War, made a hash of the final result?

Cyril was adamant that Jim Clark had won for Lotus-Ford. Eric Broadly was equally convinced at the Raceway's result. A small huddle of English writers scrutinised Audrey's lap chart. His case seemed rock solid. So we had the unique situation of seeing two drivers converging upon victory lane. Cyril descended upon the portals of the official timekeepers' and lap scorers' room, and there he remained ensconced for about ten hours, painstakingly pouring over the electronic tapes. Whether he was forced to concede or Cyril admitted to error, the official result stood the test. Besides, Graham Hill (who had remained tight-lipped about the situation), had already dismounted his horse, drunk the holy cow's milk, received the silverware and cashed the winner's cheque. I returned home convinced that Cyril Audrey was the best stop-watcher in the business.

Away from tropical paradises, there can be few places on earth so beautiful as Canada at fall time. The autumn colours can be seen at their most magnificent in the Mont Tremblant region of Quebec where the St Jovite circuit winds an undulating path through the Maple Leaf forests. It was here in September 1966 a new page in North American motor racing history was opened by the first-ever Canadian-American Challenge Cup races for sports cars. The Can-Am Series — as it became known — started at Mont Tremblant, just north-west of Montreal. This baptism by international fire redeemed the circuit for the 1968 Canadian Grand Prix. John Surtees, driving a Lola-Chevrolet won the inaugural event which heralded an era when McLaren's orange Gulf-sponsored wagon train, headed initially by Bruce McLaren, Denis Hulme and later Peter Revson, dominated the series until 1972 when George Follmer stopped the rot for Porsche. Interest in the Can-Am series waxed and waned, possibly because it became such a one-make show, and was suspended in 1975 while a new formula was organised. Within that period, several drivers other than the McLaren team poked their nose into the lucrative Can-Am trough. John Surtees campaigned with Lola, but never got to grips with McLarens again. Then in 1971 Jackie Stewart drove the Carl Haas Lola to third place in the championship that season. Jack Oliver reigned supreme in 1974.

These drivers alternated the Can-Am races with the Grands Prix along a hectic summer schedule. The events were relaxed occasions — plenty of social activity with barbecues and private parties — always amid a rural setting somewhere in Canada or the United States. For the Grand Prix drivers, the Can-Ams were almost a regular busmen's holiday, pretty laid back, in pleasant surroundings, among dedicated and hospitable company.

In 1971 I witnessed Jackie Stewart win the French Grand Prix for Ken Tyrrell at Paul Ricard. The last I saw of him that weekend he was surrounded by a welter of photographers and race fans, all of whom were being sprayed with champagne. Three days later I had flown to America, picked up a hire car and driven to Gainsville. The teams had come to Georgia State for the race at Road Atlanta. As I cruised the streets looking for my hotel, I spotted a familiar figure emerging totally unrecognised from a shop. When I pulled alongside him, the cheerful enquiry came, 'What took you so long?' Jackie Stewart was in town, which illustrated one of the jet-age vagaries of racing on two continents within a short passage of time.

I completed 1966 at the Mexican Grand Prix held over the imaginatively designed autodromo at Mixhuca Magdalena, close to Mexico City's international airport. Michael Kettlewell, a freelance writer, had been sent to report on the race. I had been asked to supply his race report pictures among other assignments. Being totally unaware of the elevation of the city at 7,000 feet above sea level, I was oblivious to the fact that life should be taken easily if one wishes to avoid becoming breathless and exhausted. Ignorance, I can only assume, is a blissful state, because I pursued life vigorously and I did not suffer, while Mike dragged himself about the city wheezing.

A hotch-potch of modern and historic architecture rises within the volcanic plateau poking through the clouds, where the water supply for Mexico City's population has to be pumped from sea level. Occasionally, the demand exceeded the supply. Some mornings I would awake at the hotel overlooking El Reforma, the wide, fifteen-mile-long main street, to take a shower — only to be greeted by a rose that spat, rattled and gurgled — that did everything except provide an invigorating cascade of water. Our supply had been deliberately turned off along our street block, and this produced an amusing side show. Guests in their flowing nighties and negligées, men in pyjamas or boxer shorts, paraded from our hotel across the road to another to complete their ablutions. Virtually nobody complained of this minor hiccup in the system. Men and women enjoyed the informal fashion show of lingerie provided by giggling American tourists.

Attending the autodromo with Jochen Rindt for the first practice session provided quite an eye-opener for me. The entire circuit was surrounded by recruits of the Mexican Army. Each soldier was in Khaki, tin hat and fifty-two studders and fully armed, and they were placed at regular intervals over the safety embankment alongside the circuit. Jochen reckoned that there was a military coup. In fact, this huge battalion was there to protect the race.

While I was wandering the circuit taking photographs, I deliberated over which devil was the most intimidating — a racing car approaching at 170 mph or a Mexican soldier standing at my back with a rifle cocked.

Jack Brabham became the World Champion driver for the third time in his long career, and what made his title all the sweeter was that he achieved the championship in a car — the Brabham-Repco — bearing his own name. The Australian won four races outright, a fact put down to his skill in constructing a 3-litre Grand Prix car while the other teams were dithering over the change of formula from 1.5 litres after 1965. John Surtees, who started the year with Ferrari for whom he won the Belgian race, finished in grand style by winning in Mexico driving a Cooper-Maserati to beat Brabham to second place.

The race was almost stopped because of the overwhelming enthusiasm of the spectators, who — not content with watching from behind the safety fences — stormed the barriers and pushed aside the soldiers to stand right on the curbside as the racing cars bore down upon them. Nothing the officials or the military did to try and put some common sense into their feverous minds would make them move. A horrific catastrophe was imminent. Racing drivers who had retired or pulled off implored the organisers to stop the race.

Surtees being out in front drove accordingly. Being an ex-motorcycle champion, he was accustomed to brushing shoulders with the elements. His team-mate Jochen Rindt thought it was a licence for massacre, but the crazy race ran its course and nobody was hurt, much to everyone's great relief.

I have a great affection for Mexico: the citizens are a poor, resilient race who cope with disasters like floods, earthquakes and subsidence. Historic buildings could be seen gradually sinking into the earth. The taxi service probably reflected their enterprise. A taxi is never full unless the exhaust is scraping along the road. You simply stuck your finger in the air, a cab crammed with people, animals, baggage stopped and it was up to you whether you took pot luck. Having a foreigner in their midst was a good excuse for the other passengers to enjoy a long ride. After all, you would pick up the fare when they all jumped out.

I was introduced to Rosalinda, the lovely well-educated daughter of a popular race official. One night I was invited to their palatial home for dinner. Across the road from the white high-walled mansion were slums where people begged. They seemed to live contentedly cheek-by-jowl in their contrasting life styles.

Next day Rosalinda took me for an excursion in the region of Papantla. There we watched a bull fight and visited a breeder of the best fighting bulls in Mexico. We clambered to the top of an Aztec pyramid, an exercise that found me out. Rosalinda waited patiently at the zenith of the man-made rock pile, while at each terrace I was gasping for air. Friendships of this sort cropped up the world over. Our misguided vanity led some of us to act like modern, worldly gigolos for whom female company was like moths to a light bulb — except that in some cases, our filaments had long since blown. Fun we often had, but true romance rarely flourished. For Rosalinda it was different.

In 1968 a letter arrived in Toronto from Dad. Inside was a note: 'Thought you should deal with this, good luck!' along with a letter post-marked Mexico City. The letter was typed and signed from Rosalinda's father. Apparently I had created much unhappiness after my departure from Mexico over a year ago. His daughter had pined in her love for me. Her father virtually demanded that I should travel to Mexico and fulfil my obligation. I was staggered to say the least. Rosalinda had been wonderful company for my stay in Mexico, but for me it was not love, no matter how rich and influential her father might have been. It was a hard-learned lesson not to dally with alluring Latin maidens.

One Sunday night in early April 1968 after Pierre Elliot Trudeau, himself a motor racing enthusiast, became Canada's Liberal premier in succession to Lester Pearson who had retired, I was walking along Bloor Street West in Toronto. I had just crossed Bathurst Street by 'Honest Ed's' garishly lit general store, and was quietly amused at Ed Mirvish's proclamation 'There's No Place Like This Place, Any Place', when I passed a coffee bar. Coming out was one of the girls who worked at *Canadian Motorist*. We bumped into each other. After initial pleasantries she said 'Sorry about your friend'.

'Friend?' I inquired, 'which friend?'

'You mean you haven't heard Jim Clark is dead?'

That was the first I knew of Jimmy's accident (in a Formula Two race at Hockenheim, Germany). I hugged the unhappy girl good night, then wandered in a maelstrom of emotion back to Admiral Road.

In England the sheer pace of events softened the blow of a driver's death. Here in Toronto on a chill April night, I had few friends, it was past the witching hour and there was no social activity. So I had plenty of time to ponder. I ambled aimlessly north along the wide, cosmopolitan Spadina Road for home.

My girl friend at the time was Jackie Batt, who had flown out with me from England to share my life. She welcomed me at the front door. Her face was drawn, she gripped my arm as we passed neighbours who poked their heads out of doors. It was obvious, from the aroma that 'Shaky', a small-time dealer in grass, had just returned from his monthly trip to Haight-Ashbury in San Francisco with a new consignment. The students were tripping out.

'Hey man, that was bad luck on your friend'.

'Wadda way to go'.

'Fancy meeting God at 150 mph. Wow, a helluva trip!'

Judging from these comments, they had been watching television in their own apartments, smoking grass and having a good time when the news hit the screen. Their inane comments were irreverent. They were not to know how they had touched a raw nerve. I opened our door, pointed Jackie in and slammed it in their faces. Jackie spent a wakeful night as I dwelled about the many times I had spent with Jimmy. I have to admit that work on the magazine next day was a damned chore.

Jimmy's death affected people from all walks of life who were only fleetingly touched by his presence. I engaged genuine concern and admiration for him on many occasions. A few weeks after the tragedy at Hockenheim, Brian Bedford, the actor who played the part of Scott Stoddard in the film 'Grand Prix', headed the cast of a play featured at Ed Mirvish's Royal Alexander Theatre along King Street West in Toronto. Brian and I met up between performances when we took the opportunity to reflect upon the happy experience of working with John Frankenheimer during the summer of 1966.

While Brian Bedford starred alongside the big Hollywood attraction James Garner and the top French heart throb Yves Montand, I knew my place as a film extra. It was Brian who observed the Grand Prix drivers and the effect it had upon his life. His role as Stoddard of the fictitious Jordan Racing Team was stunning. Especially when Frankenheimer directed him to portray some awful gruesome scenes after the character survived a spectacularly set crash in the Monaco Grand Prix. Brian confessed to total awe of the real drivers who risked their all in the quest for victory. At the time we met in Toronto, he explained just how much Jimmy Clark's accident had impinged upon his own conscience. All the more so because 'Grand Prix' was a rare fictional production filmed against a factual background of events. Amidst the shoot it was hard to separate the two when during each race real life incidents occurred when racing drivers were sometimes injured. There were horrified expressions on the faces of Frankenheimer's production team when badly smashed cars were towed back to the pits.

Brian was curious to know how we confronted the tragic circumstances of racing drivers being accidentally killed. I suggested that the drivers knew the risks and equated the rewards and acclaim as ample justification against the possibility of death by their own action. Words that echoed the sentiments felt by Pete Aron the 'other racing driver' played by James Garner.

By chance I reacquainted myself with James Garner at the 1968 Indianapolis 500. He was clearly still enamoured by the whole scene when a similar theme of conversation developed along the pitlane wall. I got the distinct impression that the big movie star placed the Grand Prix drivers at the top of his list of role models when a 'man's doing whadda man's gotta do'. Even Garner buried his ego at the realisation of Jimmy Clark's sacrifice in the name of sport. He admitted that just being 'around those guys' during the production of 'Grand Prix' enhanced certain values within his own life. What John Frankenheimer could never have foreseen in the years ahead, was that 'Grand Prix' has become a precious document recording the sport of that era. Familiar faces, the cars, the circuits, personalities all loom large on the silver screen. It was the first of the 3-litre formula for Grand Prix cars which the Federation Internationale de l'Automobile had initiated to return the 'power and glory' after the punier 1.5-litre Grand Prix cars.

More important still, John must also sadly ponder that most of his 'contracted' Grand Prix drivers, many of whom appeared in the scene at the drivers' meeting shot at Spa-Francorchamps before the 1966 Belgium Grand Prix, are now dead. The impressive roll-call being: Jochen Rindt, Richie Ginther and Joakhim Bonnier in their Cooper-Maserati's. The Scruderia Ferrari driver, Lorenzo Bandini. Mike Spence then drove the Team Lotus BRM. Jack Brabham's team-mate in the Brabham Repco's was Denis Hulme while Graham Hill was then loyal to BRM. Bruce McLaren was branching out himself into racing car construction with the McLaren-Serenissima. So those of us who at the time adopted a puritanical attitude to the sport (including myself) and castigated John Frankenheimer for having the audacity to intrude upon our insular scene, have since swallowed our verbicide whenever the film is repeated on television. His attempt to balance the requirement of Hollywood 'box office' against his pursuit of authenticity by filming against actuality was a gamble that paid off. At heart Frankenheimer became an enthusiast who had a driving need to placate the critical forces from within motor racing. He simply wanted to project a very exciting sport to a greater audience across the world. That he succeeded can only now be measured. Those of us who 'tutted' at his arrogance wish now they had signed the contract with the speaking part royalty clause attached.

The year before he died, Jimmy Clark had tantalised me by mentioning another stab at Indy. I was perplexed by Colin Chapman's decision. After all, the record books stated positively the historic achievements of Team Lotus and Ford Motor Company at the Hoosier Bowl. What else was there left to conquer?

Jim's eyes lit up at this observation and suggested that if I went to Indianapolis in 1968, I would see him whistle around the opposition. Therein was a cryptic clue which I did not notice at the time.

Before Jimmy died at Hockenheim and Mike Spence lost his life testing what the locals called 'the jet-propelled doorstops', it had not occurred to me the 'whistle' was that of the Pratt and Whitney turbine engine placed at the thick end of Colin Chapman's revolutionary wedge shape. Team Lotus intended to bow out of Indianapolis leaving their opponents smarting in the after burn. Unfortunately the best-laid plans turned to ashes and dust.

Upon arrival in Gasoline Ally I encountered Graham Robson, a staff writer for *Autocar* magazine. He had been collating technical data on the Lotus Turbine and informed me that the mood at the Lotus lock-up was grim. I then spotted chief mechanic Dick Scammell in conversation with American driver Joe Leonard, Graham Hill's team-mate for the race. Dick was less than his usual phlegmatic self, but through a mood of dejection he managed to smile a welcome. He told me that Graham was brewing the umpteenth pot of tea, so he invited me to join the crew.

Team Lotus are normally hustle-and-bustle. Chapman kept the troops stirred into action, but not on this occasion. Clearly Colin, Graham and everybody else would have preferred to be basking on a beach in Ibiza rather than being in Indiana. The Lotus boss was still at a very low ebb and this was reflected in the mood of the team.

Never before had I been made so welcome or given so much time of the day by the two great men. If only I had recorded our conversation, which drifted from happier days with Jimmy, to a firm resolve to capitalise upon Graham's morale-boosting wins in the Spanish and the Monaco Grand Prix before coming to America. Graham in a quiet moment confessed that he was determined to win the World Championship for constructors and drivers to bring some light where darkness prevailed. Being at Indianapolis had become to Chapman a necessary evil: his sole motivating factor was to win and to leave the establishment in a quandary as to whether turbo-charged engines could stand up to turbines. That was the sort of grit, incentive and down-right bloody-mindedness that drove Chapman on through this harrowing week.

However, this was not to be. Bobby Unser had his name engraved upon the winner's trophy. Dan landed the Eagle in second place while the Gerhard Special driven by Mel Kenyon was third. The American traditionalists had hijacked the European dream.

After the race I sat down with A J Foyt, a legendary figure at the Brickyard. The Team had all the swagger, volubility and appreciation of the fair sex that J R Ewing oozed in the fictional 'Dallas' soap opera. He surmised that certain people at Indianapolis were gleefully dancing on the Lotus grave. The 'Locust' as they called it, had come, gnawed the greens and left the bowl empty of fun: not a sentiment A J shared, because after years of stagnation, was run between Green Bay, where we stood and chin-wagged, to Madison, another township some 200 miles to the south-west.

For the life of me I cannot recall his name, but this wonderful old chap took me to his home where I met his equally erudite wife. Over three generous glasses of fiery Jack Daniels sour-mash whiskey, I found that these folk knew how to occupy a hot summer's afternoon, which became more fascinating by the minute. Talking about that historic race, the lady bustled into another room and returned dusting down a shoe box full of more sepia photographs of Grandpappy fishing on the lake and all sorts. Suddenly her eyes lit upon two of what appeared to be pen drawings. Her father proved to be quite an artist: the two pictures, with great licence, dramatically illustrated steam-powered relics chuffing along dust roads like highway locomotives.

One of these contraptions named an 'Oshkosh' after the aviation city down by Lake Winnebago, won this trail-blazing event in the hands of Messers Shomer and Farrand, who completed the race within 33 hours 27 minutes at the princely average speed of 6 mph. Patience in those days was a virtue according to the good lady. The incentive to reach Madison in one mechanical piece was rewarded by 5,000 US dollars to the victor. And that's real money, even in these days!

The temptation to pass up the race meeting at Milwaukee in order to spend the weekend covering the 'track' from Green Bay to Madison with my newly-made friends was overwhelming, even for old times' sake. Thanks to Jack Daniels, that fond memory of Green Bay is pickled in my mind for posterity.

By popular consent, the 'Camptown Grand Prix' was elected by the circus as the most appropriate meeting to end the season. Watkins Glen was not always the stage for the climax for the World Championship, but even so, as an *au revoir* to the Grand Prix season, no other place provided a more convivial atmosphere.

The United States Grand Prix (for real) was initially established at Sebring in 1959 when Bruce McLaren stole the march in a Cooper-Climax. Riverside in California then laid out the red carpet for Stirling Moss in Rob Walker's Lotus-Climax with Innes Ireland following the maestro to second place in the works Lotus-Climax in 1960.

From 1961 the event stabilised itself for twenty happy years in the Fingers Lake region of New York State. Lilliputian Watkins Glen may have been, but the big-hearted citizens nursed ambitions beyond their post to keep the race at the southern shore of Lake Seneca. The logistics of accommodating potential crowds of 100,000 each year were horrendous. There was no way that The Glen, or even neighbouring towns like Elmira, Binghamton and Syracuse could supply that number of beds. So it was priorities first, which meant that the teams, officials and marshals had the first choice. The many race fans had to camp within the vicinity: this is the reason why it became known as the Camptown race.

Similar to St Jovite in Quebec, the USGP was held at falltime in October. The Fingers area was mottled in its autumnal cloak of many colours which complemented some of the bohemian and outrageous characters who settled

With Michael Cooper, James Garner and Jack Watson on the *Grand Prix* film set,
Clermont-Ferrand, in 1966.

Photos: Lynton Money.

Alan Whicker makes a point with the author at Brands Hatch during 1966.

Max Le Grand, Eoin Young and Michael Cooper ready for a scene in *Grand Prix* at Clermont-Ferrand, 1966.

Hollywood Film Director, John Frankenheimer, in London for the premier of *Grand Prix* in 1967.

Danger! – Man at work.

Graham Hill gives the eagle eye at Kodak's exhibition of photographs in London, 1966.

(*above*) Sadly, the same day this photograph was taken, Jochen Rindt was killed while qualifying for the Italian Grand Prix at Monza, 1970.

(*right*) Jackie Stewart skeet shooting.

(*below*) Hosting the 1971 Texaco promotion at the London Racing Car Show where Les Leston and Tony Lanfranchi receive their instructions.

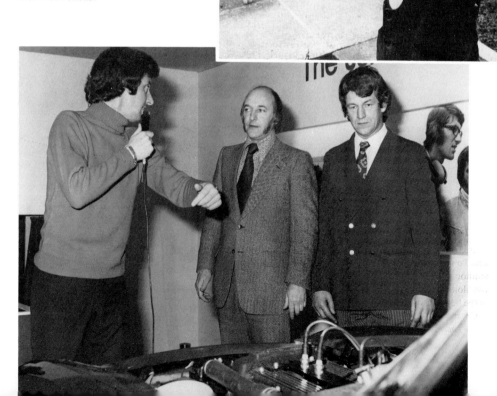

Bob Curl, the Hastings glassfibre fabricator of the Nomad series and the Hesketh-Ford.

Mark König driving the 2-litre V8 BRM-powered Nomad Mark III,
a similar car to that which he drove at Le Mans.

Patrick Depailler
and Tony Rudlin
studiously ignore
the bloke (author)
in the boater
at Crystal Palace.
Photo: Jutta Fausel.

(*above*) Interviewing Geoffrey Kent,
Chairman of John Player & Sons
Nottingham, on the sponsorship
of Team Lotus.

(*right*) Innes Ireland and his mate Davey
dredged the Queen scallops from MV
Kinloch off the cost of North-West
Scotland.

(*below*) Jacky Ickx before a Formula 2
race at Thruxton. *Photo: Fred Taylor.*

Celebrating the Polar Caravans sponsorship of the
1975 Swedish Grand Prix with
Lord Alexander Hesketh and Sven 'Smokey'
Asberg of Scandinavian Raceway.

While enlisted by Swedish publications,
I travelled to races with Ronnie Peterson.

Bertil Holmquist, Chairman of Polar Caravans (*far right*) puts guests to test
in Lapland at 38°F below freezing.

Jackie Stewart reassures Tom Pryce of his pedigree before the French Grand Prix at Dijon-Prenois.

Jacky Ickx makes the classic overtaking manoeuvre in the JPS-Lotus around Niki Lauda's Ferrari on Paddock Bend in the 1974 Race of Champions at Brands Hatch. *Painting: Michael Turner.*

in the camp sites for race weekend. Mingling with the pure enthusiasts were the flower-power people, a strong representation of the heavy mob in the Hell's Angels, dope peddlers, winos, college dropouts, potential blues singers, and all the philanderers from Chattanooga to Cape Cod turned up. It was sweetness and light until the Vikings arrived to taunt the Hell's Angel hard-nippled mollies. Only then did the Watkins Glen constabulary take the truncheons out of their holsters. Providing they could contain these heathens in the canvas village and keep the marauders at bay, a generally liberalised attitude was par for the course. Trouble makers got their come-uppance by being placed under lock and key. Aside from that, a genuine spirit of bonhomie permeated the woodlands every year amid the camp fire smoke.

Cameron Argetsinger was the inspirational force behind the event. He persuaded his fellow citizens that a street race like Monaco would generate free publicity and invite greater tourism to the area when he revealed a plan for a six-mile road race through the streets of Watkins Glen in October 1948. Happy to tolerate the upheaval in order to benefit from extra trade, the Chamber of Commerce positively encouraged the enterprise made by the Sports Car Club of America.

Frank Griswold was a man of substance who raced his Alfa Romeo with such brio that he won both events with consummate ease. Unfortunately, the rest of the field were left to bite his dust when a nasty accident injuring several spectators saw a final curtain prematurely drop on the street circuit. Undaunted, the locals continued to encourage car enthusiasts to assemble at one-make rallies and various gymkhanas until the purpose built circuit was hewn at the top of the hill, and completed by the Watkins Glen Corporation in 1956. Various club and national events were organised by the SCCA until 1961 when the United States Grand Prix had the honeymoon event that turned into a long-standing marriage. Later the race became fragmented between Long Beach, Las Vegas and Detroit: the event was divorced from The Glen because of bankruptcy. Innes Ireland became an integral part of Watkins Glen folklore when he reversed his fortune at Riverside in the Lotus-Climax to beat 'America's favourite President-Elect', Dan Gurney, driving the works Porsche, and Tony Brooks in his BRM. Innes reflected a true 'Glen Man' who loved nature and displayed a child-like mischief. Although the Scotsman never won another race at Watkins Glen, he died in October 1993 knowing that if he had nowhere else to go, a candle burned for him around Fingers Lake.

Graham Hill attained a similar affection in the minds of local folk. After he completed a hat trick of victories in 1963-65, I visited many a home around the area where Graham's picture occupied the mantelpiece alongside Aunt Charlotte and Grampy Tex.

Although Watkins Glen was about 200 miles to the north-west of Manhattan and Lady Liberty, it represented small-town America just as I imagined it without the emotional strife of a 'Peyton Place'. The citizens were open-hearted and although making a buck was the name of the game, they were not blatant money grubbers.

97

I often stayed at nearby Painted Post, supposedly named after an old Indian reservation. One family who put me up had a spare room that was so chocful of motor racing memorabilia that Paul Foulkes-Halbard of Filching Manor would still be there now filling in the gaps of his own book collection.

My arrival at the 10th United States Grand Prix came amid the nationwide ballyhoo of a Presidential election. Although voting was still a month hence, every public establishment in and around Watkins Glen was plastered with Republican and Democratic regalia. 'GO-GO-NIXON' was emblazoned upon walls by supporters of the Republican President-elect who became known when in office as 'Tricky Dicky' — the President even a second-hand car dealer would not trust.

So around this period of the Grand Prix, a punch-drunk electorate escaped to the relative tranquillity of Camptown for a welcome distraction from the campaign. Mind you, the race was fighting for attention on television. The Mexico Olympics were a matter of days away, and it seemed every channel was previewing the games. Had the Grand Prix been a homeless waif, I doubt if the loyal following which The Glen had built up during eight years of continuity would have bothered to make the pilgrimage to anywhere else.

Instead, the roads leading to 'Mecca' were from the early part of the race week, nose-to-tail with big Harley Davidsons weaving between the nippy MG Midgets and bug-eyed Sprites. Later on Jaguar Es vied with Porsche 904s while campers were mobile chicanes weaving around bicyclists towing dogs and wishing that they could get Evangeline on the crossbar instead of her sexy little thumb pulling in Merv, driving a curvaceous Ferrari Dino, down from Long Island for the weekend.

The 'circus' had travelled to The Glen straight from the Canadian Grand Prix at St Jovite, where Denis Hulme in his McLaren-Ford became one of six different drivers to win a race in the same championship season. Quite an extraordinary string of results when you consider that Graham Hill achieved his emotional wish made at Indianapolis to win the World Championship for Lotus and the memory of Jim Clark. He managed only three outright victories — which was incredible.

Between the two races, my girl friend Jackie had returned to England, from a combination of home sickness and necessity. Our romance had foundered with the summer sun while the South-East of England had been saturated by the worst floods since 1953. Her parents' home in Edenbridge was the focus of newspaper attention showing the High Street under several feet of water. I thought that it was appropriate for her to be with her family under our circumstances.

I found myself a 'wayward soul' at The Glen. Chris Amon and John Surtees sensed my feeling of being in limbo and talked at length to me about the new racing scene at home. I had my first sight of things to come at St Jovite when I had to get my tongue around unfamiliar names like Gold Leaf Team Lotus, Yardley-BRM and Brook Bond Tea. The change of culture in Grand Prix racing was made easier to accept after a season exposed to the high-profile commercial exploitation of the sport in America.

Amon was something of a purist, but he realised the financial benefits that came with the commercialisation of motor racing. He assured me that if I returned to the Grand Prix scene, the opportunities to be explored with sponsors were potentially lucrative. Surtees, having been reared against the same background as I had been, realised my sensitivity, but putting things into perspective; I had the choice of going for the big swim or leaving the sport altogether.

The race did a lot to assist my decision. The sight of three British drivers upholding the honour of Queen and Country in the New World was a great inspiration. When you are far from home, in some doubt over your status in life, patriotic fervour plays a big part in destiny. It did the heart a power of good to see Jackie Stewart, Graham Hill and John Surtees romp home in Indian file to claim the top three places in the United States Grand Prix.

The fillip lightened my step that evening when I joined British rally-driver Vic Elford, who was trying his hand at Grand Prix racing, for a walk along the spectacular gorge that emerges at the centre of The Glen. As we watched the foaming rapids and the gushing cascades, Vic looked hard into my eyes and said 'You are more British than a stick of rock'.

As if to drive the last nail into my North American coffin, the British Overseas Airways Corporation then ran a massive advertising campaign which wrenched at the heart strings. The hoardings carried a picture of a British emigré who had returned to England to find his mates in a Tudor Style pub. The slogan was simply 'Nice to see you back Charlie Brown'.

Joan and Jim Clayton, who had become life-long friends, realised the unstoppable force that was at work inside me. They saw me off at Toronto Airport. When I eventually found my feet at home with Dad in Rochester, I drove to my favourite pub. Sure enough old friends were eating, drinking and being merry. When they spotted my beaming face as I waltzed through the door, their reaction was not as I had anticipated:

'What the bloody hell are you doing here?'

7

Other Sporting Distractions

AFTER MY adventure in North America, I woke up to find that Harold Wilson was still presiding over our land. More significantly, the daily newspapers announced that the Conservative Member of Parliament, Mr Edward Heath, leader of Her Majesty's opposition, had appointed a lady as the new shadow Transport Minister. Margaret Thatcher had placed herself firmly on the bottom rung of the ladder to power. Modern history has since recorded Mr Heath's folly in that promotion, with regard to how Mrs Thatcher later superseded him in a leadership battle. Maybe the MP of my birthplace constituency at Bexleyheath recognised a potential leader for the long-term future. The lady had other ideas, such are the machinations of politics.

Politics was a dimension I had noticed creeping into motor racing. I committed the 1969 season to getting my feet back under the table reacquainting myself with colleagues who were convinced that I had 'defected' to Canada forever. Those early days of reorientation indicated that all that Chris Amon had told me in America was true. Business in the way of photography was to be performed for sponsors — which supplemented the still meagre terms that most magazines were still paying.

I also noticed that activities at race meetings had shifted up a cog or two. The atmosphere in the pit lane had a sharper edge. Drivers were more aware of their image and general demeanour. I noticed they had new obligations to sponsors — like photo-calls, buffets with clients, being seen with grubby hands wrapped around the personality girls. Now, these ladies were a decorative addition to the hallowed paddocks in their stilettos, hot pants and sponsor-emblazoned 'T' shirts, purveying anything from free cigarettes to sample perfumes. I enjoyed looking, but preferred the free 'cuppas' dispensed by Brooke-Bond Oxo.

Show business was self-consciously weaving its thread into the hoary fabric of motor racing. This intrusion by stealth was gradually to make a difference in the close relationship which the press had previously enjoyed with the drivers and their teams. At the early stage of the metamorphosis, we could still chat freely to Monsieur Beltoise or have fun on bikes with Jacky Ickx without asking them to consult their diaries, but straws were in the wind.

Throughout 1969-70 most drivers paid a form of lip service to the sponsors. They touched the forelock, smiled broadly and uttered the right com-

100

ments to the President, then slipped away like giggling school boys who had been 'matted' by the Principal. As the seasons rolled on and the gilt turned to gold bars and more numbered Swiss bank accounts were opened, the smirking stopped. The drivers' attitude changed as they rightly became more professional.

Team bosses expressed another point of view on sponsorship. Colin Chapman found it mildly distracting in 1968 when he felt an initial obligation to Gold Leaf by taking time with Geoffrey Kent to explain team aspirations, daily problems and how each hurdle was crossed at a Grand Prix.

Kent soon realised that this consumed Chapman's time when he should be paying 100% attention to the team. Their respective roles were clearly defined. Gold Leaf wanted their brand name to be associated with success in order to maximise upon the publicity. Chapman was left unhindered by the sponsor until the chequered flag, while Gold Leaf busied themselves actively promoting the product. The relationship worked perfectly once those priorities were established in the minds of everybody concerned.

Imperial Tobacco must have been a dream sponsor for Team Lotus. Right from the start of negotiations, Kent reassured Chapman that since he was a racing enthusiast himself there would be good times and bad times. Like a marriage, the partnership between the two companies was intended to be a long-term investment. What was never mentioned, but must have festered in the back of each man's mind, was the ultimate sacrifice.

The courtship was only four months old when Jim Clark died at Hockenheim. Gold Leaf and Team Lotus had barely reached the 'holding hands' stage when the tragedy struck. Colin Chapman confessed that had the sponsor jilted Lotus, it would have been understandable and written off as a fact of life; whereas three years later, when Jochen Rindt died at Monza, the relationship had become firmly established in the public mind as a marriage, the perfect blend for sales promotion. Kent suffered the loss of Jochen Rindt as sorely as did Colin Chapman. But the Board of Directors at Imperial's headquarters in Nottingham were not emotionally involved. The fact that smoking now carried a 'government health warning' made an uncomfortable alliance with a sport that shared an equally lethal outcome. Geoffrey Kent soothed any ruffled feathers and kept his promise to Colin Chapman that the sponsorship would survive, as he originally stated — for better or for worse.

The unhappy outcome was that Jochen Rindt and Gold Leaf Team Lotus became the World Champions for 1970 — a fact that would remain in the record books long after the brand name had been extinguished.

Saddened in the aftermath of Jochen's death, I wandered over to the garages occupied by Team Lotus where the mechanics were going through the motions of packing up. 'Herbie' Blash was Jochen's mechanic. I sat down with him as the distraught man unscrambled his thoughts. Herbie was determined to move from the 'pressure pot' of Grand Prix racing to seek a quieter life in Formula 3. As he reflected upon a glorious year, he pondered the sad fact of preparing Jochen's car throughout the season, and now at this dark hour, his question was 'for what bloody purpose?' The glory days had been snuffed out. As the door closed on Jochen, the time had come prematurely for another door of opportunity to open for Emerson Fittipaldi. I then realised that Colin Chapman's plan was already in place for 1971. By one stroke of fate, a young Brazilian driver had taken on the mantle of number one at Gold Leaf Team Lotus. Few people knew at the time, but Jochen Rindt was intending to retire as the World Champion.

The weekend after the Italian Grand Prix witnessed a phalanx of the British racing press descend upon a National British meeting at Crystal Palace, the circuit closest to the City of London that opened in 1937.

The compact 1.39-mile track in those days ran a ring round the athletics stadium which had slowly been enhancing the prestige of the complex. The circuit had provided some memorable battles, especially in Formula Two racing. In 1964 Jochen Rindt burst upon the scene, thrilling us with his thrusting tail-out skills in a privately entered Ford-of-Austria-sponsored Brabham. He overshadowed the cream of Grand Prix racing drivers that day, and secured a contract with John Cooper. During 1970 Jochen had waged titanic battles against Jackie Stewart which was perpetuated by their outright lap record of 100 mph in the Formula Two race which stood until the circuit closed in 1972.

So perhaps it was divinity that caused the congregation of the motoring press at this fairly innocuous club meeting. When Fleet Street hounds assembled, rumours started to fly about who was going to replace Jochen Rindt at Team Lotus. What became known as the 'silly season' arrived in South-East London with a vengeance. Normally, trying to guess the 'musical chairs' played by team managers as they vie for the services of top drivers is harmless fun which keeps the interest going in the sport during the winter months.

At Crystal Palace, writers speculated upon Colin Chapman's apparent dilemma. Among the more factual rumours circulating was that Imperial Tobacco Company wanted Team Lotus to 'fly the flag' by recruiting an all-British team of drivers after Jochen had retired. Tongues were freely wagging that Chapman might be courting the favours of Jackie Stewart from the talons of Ken Tyrrell's team. In truth Chapman had spent some time quietly trying to persuade the Scot to join Lotus. Emotional and contractual reasons, allied to pure loyalty, meant that Stewart was not up for grabs.

At the time nobody in Fleet Street could possibly have known of these overtures behind the scenes. I was intrigued to see how the fabrications mushroomed into 'fact' from the environs of a beer tent set in the paddock at Crystal Palace. Standing in their midst was David Benson, the motoring correspondent for the *Daily Express*. The dark brown eyes and Cheshire Cat grin remained inscrutably fixed. His colleagues knew that Benson was a 'professional and personal friend' of Jackie Stewart, and realised that the *Daily Express* might have the 'jump' on them in the Monday morning editions. David's gloating appearance was either a bluff or he genuinely had the 'inside story'. Benson would not have the prerogative of breaking any embargo if he did know about Stewart. But — David did have this disconcerting habit of backing known hunches by running an 'I predict: IF STEWART

REFUSES, FITTIPALDI'S IN', which covered a multitude of sins and meant that Benson could say 'I told you so' whichever driver got the Lotus seat. So bearing in mind what I learned in Monza, I was quietly amused by the speculation. 'If Stewart's number one... and Chapman wants an all-British team... who is around?' John Miles was already at Lotus... could be him... Nah, great test driver... couldn't drive out of a paper bag... must be Jack Oliver... what about Derek Bell?... pull the other one son... I go for Peter Gethin. And so it went round in ever-decreasing circles.

As it turned out, Emerson Fittipaldi would run alongside the Swede, Reine Wissell.

On odd occasions during 1969 I had seen the Brazilian drive in the Formula Three Lombank Championship, which he won with comparative ease. In a rugged Brazilian way, he was a handsome young man, his face framed by a mane of black hair and long side boards. What caught the attention of the girls was his dark, deep-set brown eyes which lit up when he raised his brow and smiled at them.

Emerson was already accounted for by Marie-Helène, a typical effervescent, cross-bred European-Brazilian girl who had shining blue eyes, lots of bounce and a wicked sense of fun. Often she would spot me and run up to chatter on about the most outrageous topics. On one occasion at Brands Hatch we talked about Emerson's early days in Brazil when he raced Karts and Formula Vee. I asked Marie-Helène to what extent his ability shone above his competitors. Her eyes widened, the pupils dilated and she uttered words to the effect that before Emerson became Kart Champion, he raced soapboxes when he was young and was the fastest because he had the biggest rocks! I remember studying the toes of my shoes and attempting to stifle a great urge to laugh out loud.

Marie Helène gaped at me perplexed, wondering why I was shaking, fit to burst. Still she went on about the big rocks as tears welled up in my eyes and streamed down my face. She rattled on about the downhill races in soapboxes and how Emerson added to his inertia and top speed by piling big rocks onto his chariot. Limp from laughter, I surmised that regardless of his 'rocks', clearly Emerson was not wanting in virility. Nor were Marie-Helène's basic instincts lacking, come to that.

Fittipaldi made his Grand Prix debut at Brands Hatch in 1970 when he drove a Lotus-Ford 49. It was an inauspicious introduction to the highest echelon, but he was among the points two weeks later at Hockenheim when he came fourth in the German Grand Prix. What the race boffins in the canvas pub at Crystal Palace could not possibly have anticipated was the Brazilian's outright victory in the United States Grand Prix exactly a month after Jochen Rindt's death. If Colin Chapman had contemplated his retirement from the sport, Emerson delivered a tonic at Watkins Glen to soothe a heart that had been shot to smithereens.

Chapman's amazing ability to spot the latent-champion qualities in young pretenders, then to design and build a racing car to complement the talent was legendary. Innes Ireland's boisterous ability provided Team Lotus with their very first Grand Prix victory at Watkins Glen in 1961. Racing's accident-prone Houdini found himself in the wilderness shortly after his finest hour: Chapman had been blinded by Jim Clark's ability, so we would never know to what heights Innes might have risen under the Lotus Chief's military regime. When Clark's star disappeared from the galaxy, Chapman scouted around the ranks which — apart from promising men like Jack Oliver, Richard Attwood, Piers Courage and Vic Elford — lacked a real spitfire. In consequence he chose the well-proven abilities of Graham Hill who had previously won his stripes with Lotus in 1958. In spite of being a near 'ancien pilote', Hill delivered the worldly goods in 1968. Jochen Rindt responded to the beckoning call to support Hill for 1969 with the enticing promise of a championship-winning car the following year. With Jochen's demise came Emerson Fittipaldi, who could have been partnered by Ronnie Peterson. He had already conceded to the expansive new March team. Instead, Peterson's compatriot Reine Wissell grabbed the second Lotus seat with open arms, relegating 'super-Swede' as Ronnie became known, to the role of bridesmaid.

I questioned Colin Chapman about his clairvoyant powers in his choice of new young drivers. His reply was succinct: 'Effortless speed' as apportioned to Jim Clark and Emerson Fittipaldi or 'animal competitiveness' of the sort reflected in Jochen Rindt and Ronnie Peterson. Chapman reckoned that a tiger could be tamed, whereas a tortoise could never be tweaked. So where did Graham Hill and his 1978 World Champion Mario Andretti fit into this scenario? Chapman smiled: 'Occasionally grit determination and a great dollop of mechanical sympathy can succeed.' The Lotus boss should know. From 1963 when Team Lotus achieved its first World Championship, he captured the title seven times.

In March 1974 I was working in Sweden when I had a call at my digs in Stockholm. Tommy Peterson invited me to his family home in Orebro on the way through to Gothenburg to catch the Swedish Lloyd flag ship *Saga* for home.

Tommy was the complete opposite to brother Ronnie. He had dark, receding hair and chunky features, loved to dress in leather and relished a good time. Each year of the short-lived Swedish Grand Prix at Anderstorp, it became as inevitable as the midnight sun that I would end up at the High Chaparall Hotel knocking back the Class 3s alcoholic beer with Tommy. So it was a pleasure to visit Tommy on home ground for a change. Orebro is a fairly typical Swedish township, very conservative. The centre with its market square is dominated by the church while the symmetrical estates and blocks of apartments stand in the shadow of a massive water tower. Bengt Peterson ran a bakery from which he made a modest fortune. Tommy often helped father Bengt in the bakery, otherwise the time was his own.

The Peterson's home was modern and typically functional. The wooden torps in the forests where Sweden's cottage industries flourish probably feel more cosy to the stranger than the more sanitised brick-built homes. Swedes are not pretentious. A table is to eat from. A chair is to sit upon. A television is to watch. A bed is for sleeping in, they do not yearn for other encumbrances. So the Peterson's house — while warm, welcoming and spotlessly clean — was not what an Englishman would term a castle. After Tommy greeted me, he appeared embarrassed when I exercised the intrinsically British trait of wishing to 'nose' about the family dwelling. He gave me a conducted tour, opening every door — even Ronnie's bedroom — when I noticed that there was one room bypassed. 'What's in there Tom?' I asked. He paused as Swedes are apt to do. 'The family silver' he ventured. Tommy cautiously opened the door of a darkened room, flicked on the light and there, low and behold, was the 'family silver'. Tommy had already shown me six trophies which he himself had won in various competitions, but nothing prepared me for the vast array that confronted me in Ronnie's trophy room. The magnitude of sporting prowess can never be truly realised by figures and statistics printed in regimental columns. Only when you view shelves weighed down by shimmering silver-ware, towering trophies, figurines set upon onyx, numerous plaques, silver plates and effigies can you grasp a person's achievement. Trophy rooms at football clubs, cricket clubs and swimming clubs invariably represent a team effort. Motor racing is a mechanical team effort, which depends upon the ability of the driver to win races.

After examining each trophy I ventured to Tommy that he must be proud of brother Ronnie's achievements. He shuffled his feet, shrugged his shoulders and sighed. I suddenly felt uncomfortable because I had reduced myself to yet another 'rubber-necker' who had gone to Bengt's palace to view the crown jewels. He murmured at being pleased for Ronnie, but I felt that I had dug a trench of embarrassment between us. So I slapped Tom on the back and suggested that we went to a dive bar in town for a session of Class 3s. His cloud of inferiority lifted immediately. I was talking a language he understood. Ever since that day, Tommy has represented six hard-won little trophies, and I admire him just as much for them, and for his yen to be his own man.

Motor racing in Scandinavia was slow to find ground — literally. In a land where two-thirds is under snow or permafrost for at least six months of the year, laying a road circuit north of the line between Stockholm and Oslo was totally impracticable. Arable and grazing lands are at a premium either because the base is solid granite or else because vast areas are covered in conifer forests. The rest is swamp land, hardly the foundation upon which to place a venue. Anderstorp is the exception to the rule. Consequently, racing circuits, like golf courses, were considered a low priority when such land could be farmed.

This probably explains why rallying became the number one motor sport in the Nordic countries before racing found a foothold. Norway was the exception again. Small club rallies were organised provided that the conservationists did not see forest tracks being churned into a glutinous mire. However, boisterous enthusiasts had new found acres during the winter months upon which to map out 'circuits' for ice racing. I watched a meeting at Fluberg just outside Oslo and was thoroughly entertained by a full programme of Formula Vee and saloon car racing. On another occasion I attended a meeting at Lyksele in Sweden, a venue in Lapland where daylight hours during midwinter are restricted to about three under grey skies. Thousands of race hungry fans drove through darkened hours to reach the lake where a 25-race programme of Formula Vee, saloon and motorcycle races were rattled through before dark.

International ice racing occurred in Sweden during 1947. The venue was mapped over a frozen lake at Rommehed and was heralded as 'The Swedish Winter Grand Prix'. Power-sliding over the unfamiliar surface and having enormous fun were Reg Parnell and George Abecassis who dominated the meeting in their ERAs. It should be explained that the opposition were stranded on board a freighter carrying their cars which had become ice locked.

Sporting to the nth degree, Parnell and company agreed to stay in Sweden for another week, by which time the other competitors had their cars. Another meeting was hastily organised over Lake Vallentuna and Reg still ran away with the spoils, winning races at average speeds of up to 68 mph. Later on Karlskoga set the trend for race circuits followed by other venues like Knutstorp, Mantorp Park and Kinnekul. During the incredibly short seasons, these circuits became the breeding ground for such drivers as Reine Wissell, Ronnie Peterson, Torsten Palm and Ulf Norinder. Rallying, however, was still considered the people's sport and over the years Sweden introduced such larger-than-life characters as Carl-Magnus Skogh, Erik Carlsson and Tom Trana. Each of them won enormous credit for Saab and Volvo by annihilating all-comers on the RAC Rally of Great Britain in the 1960-70s. At home most of them went broadside to work along dirt roads, while snow and ice were milk and butter to them, reducing our forest tracks to a pleasant run in the country.

Finland also produced its fair share of 'silent heroes' who relished the loose surfaces and enabled drivers of Timo Makinen's ilk to blaze trails for other 'Flying Finns' like Simo Lampinen and Hannu Mikkola.

Joakim Bonnier, the multi-lingual Viking, became the President of the Grand Prix Drivers' Association because he was the only bloke who could make sense of the pot-pourri of nationalities racing then. The moody Swede had his days like the Kentish 100 race for Formula Two at Brands Hatch when he diced on equal terms with Stirling Moss, both driving Porsches. Finland, notoriously shy and unforthcoming as a nation, thrust Leo Kinunen into long-distance racing with distinction and he was followed by Keke Rosberg who in 1982 found himself World Champion in a Williams-Ford.

Many people had the suspicion that Reine Wissell stole the march on Ronnie Peterson when he signed for Team Lotus in 1970. In terms of driving ability, the final judgment often came down on the side of Ronnie when final speed and tenacity came into the frame. Reine, on his day, was virtually equal and probably the more consistent of the two drivers. Sweden couldn't care less, after Bjorn Borg had set tennis alight — having the prospect of two young drivers pitching their skills against the world was a double-headed bonus. Initially, the fable was not written that way.

Max *M*osley, Alan *R*ees, Graham *C*oaker and Robin *H*erd were the powers-that-be who exploded into Grand Prix motor racing from nowhere in 1970.

106

Apart from running two 'works' cars for Chris Amon and Jo Siffert, MARCH — as the embryonic team became know (by taking the initials of the founder directors) — also made a sale of two cars to Ken Tyrrell who viewed the deal as an interim bargain while he developed his own Tyrrell-Ford for Jackie Stewart and Johnny Servoz-Gavin. Rees had spotted a similar raw potential in Ronnie that he had recognised in Jochen Rindt years earlier. Rather than let the Swede find his way into the hands of opponents, Rees suggested to his fellow Directors that it might be money in the bank to have Peterson's signature as well, as a medium-term investment.

When the 1970 season got under way, a patient little voice enquired 'What about me?' Peterson was not content to kick his heels, so the yawning gap in March's already stretched resources was adequately bridged by Colin Crabbe, a 'bunterish' vintage-car enthusiast and prolific salesman. By emblazoning 'Antique Automobiles' over a spare March-Ford which was duly painted maroon and yellow as Crabbe's colour's, the unlikely combination made their first faltering miles into the Grand Prix arena.

I was first introduced to Colin Crabbe at the Dutch Grand Prix: we had dinner with Max Mosley in Zandvoort. A plan evolved that I would attend a few races with Antique Automobiles to get the inside story of Ronnie's first season in World Championship motor racing, then feed back the good news to Sweden through my various media outlets.

From Colin's point of view, it was a heck of a weekend to get his feet wet in top-class motor racing. Jochen Rindt's victory was totally overshadowed by the horrible death of Piers Courage. Only eighteen days previously, Bruce McLaren was killed at Goodwood while he was testing his Can-Am McLaren. Fate played a tragic hand when Bruce's memorial service was held at St Paul's Cathedral in London the day before Piers's funeral at St Mary's Church at Shenfield in Essex.

Throughout this ordeal, Colin and I were lunching over the prospect of Ronnie racing in the French Grand Prix at Clermont-Ferrand. It was akin to some ghastly black farce. Colin realised that I knew my way around the European circuits and suggested that we travelled together. Clearly Colin and I were like-minded in that we enjoyed the open road and stopping at likely beauty spots for a meal or an over-night stay. Racing on such a slim budget reflected badly on Ronnie who strove with all his might to produce a result, or even to finish in the points. Ronnie finished the season with nothing on the board whereas Reine scored a commendable third place in the United States Grand Prix.

My reports to Sweden were almost a parody and comparable to Nigel Dempster's column in the *Daily Mail*. I remember penning after the British Grand Prix at Brands Hatch, that I had driven Ronnie to play in a cricket match at Merstham Hatch. I had taken loan of a Silver Shadow from Rolls-Royce at the behest of Dennis Miller-Williams, their starchy but dry-humoured Director of Public Relations. Colin had filled a wicker hamper with numerous tasty nibbles and bottles of champagne while I found a cricket bat and some balls to help Ronnie to initiate himself into the noble English game

107

before joining the Grand Prix Drivers' team against the Lord Taverners. Quite what Ronnie's manager Sveneric Erikson made of this from his Malmo office I do not know, but Colin thought the farrago was an enormous hoot. Ronnie Peterson may never have become a World Champion, but the team at his Buckinghamshire homestead would have welcomed him onto their green.

* * *

Throughout 1973 my friends in motor racing sensed a 'distracted' person. More pointedly, Bernard Cahier and his wife Joan who together acted as 'mine hosts' for Goodyear, suggested that I was becoming a sports writer and that motor racing was just part of a overall theme. They could have been right, because throughout the year I had been telling them of observations I had been making over the wall.

I had also entered 'phase two' of my approach to photography. Creative pictures were not sufficient to enable me to make a proper income. It was worrying me, so to make up for lost ground, I pondered the advice of a new face on the scene, Nigel Snowden, a very accomplished all-round photographer from Australia. He made no bones of the fact that he attended other sports outside the motor racing season. It sounded like the answer to my problem. Perhaps I had been wasting my time seeking sharper definition to my pictures. All natural inspiration had flown out of the window. While the quality of my photographs was now virtually perfect, they lacked sparkle and spontaneity because I was being paid to follow the brief of graphic designers and art editors with big companies. The trouble was that what was suitable for a client was a complete anathema to a magazine. While I paid lip service on these commercially-orientated briefs, inside I was retaliating because my imagination was on 'hold' — the very mention of personal ideas was frowned upon. I resented this approach. After all, I had been attending the scene for many years, and felt in a strong position to contribute a wealth of ideas and experience. In the end, I got bored rigid with the racket and longed for magazines who would give me a new lease of life. *Car* magazine had moved on to other pastures, but Reuben Archer of *Fast Car* came along, and his approach was like a breath of fresh air in a very stale climate.

During 1973, I found that solace raised its pretty head in a string of girl friends. I shared meaningless shallow relationships with a masseuse, then with the boss of a Mayfair escort agency, with a Lincolnshire farmer's daughter and with a handful of nubile beauties whom I met playing volley ball and badminton with the Eureka Naturist Club at Fawkham. Going to the midsummer ball in birthday suits was novel. Imagine asking a lady for a foxtrot, a quickstep or a breaststroke! Jiving in the buff is one thing. Performing a smoochy last waltz while holding my partner at a distance indicated that I had really returned to the fundamentals of life.

Back in the office I was getting the occasional request for 'mixed company' to be used on the covers of motor racing magazines. *Bilsport* started off this theme when they asked for a picture of Jo Siffert and Brian Redman posed with their Porsches around a 'leggy' girl. *Motor Racing* magazine were slightly more demure. They talked of a photograph of Jacky Ickx in close-up profile looking into the eyes of an attractive girl. Circulation was either hitting rock bottom or else the message which I had been repeating time and again had at last got through to some fusty editors.

One of the allurements of Grand Prix racing from my early days was the various 'families' one constantly met over the years. There was a continuity at some circuits like Monaco, Spa, Zandvoort, Monza and Watkins Glen. When I set out upon the circuits a wide-eyed and bushy-tailed 'freshman' in my twenties, dating local girls was a novel and pleasant distraction although it has to be admitted that in sparsely populated venues like Spa, the drivers attracted the 'top draw' while the minions got the 'quality seconds'. As I got older, my priorities changed very subtly. Not only did I find the 'pit-popsies' blossomed into ladies of fond regard, but long-standing friendships remained after they had married and in some cases reared families.

This subject was born with some regret by Mum, who according to Dad cherished a wish to see her only son settled and married before her demise. With the kind of life-style I had adopted at 25 years of age, that crossroad in life would have been impossible to fulfil. I think that deep in her heart Mum probably knew that, and was relieved that no damsel was put through such an emotional wringer.

Aside from the racing, during the early 'seventies I was honoured to be made the President of the Dartford and District Motor Club. Apart from taking the Chair at the AGM I invited distinguished guest speakers like Stirling Moss, Stuart Turner and Jackie Stewart to enlighten us. For such a rural, youthful and enthusiastic club, we maintained a quality in guests that was the envy of practically every association in Kent. I took part in a couple of club rallies and treasure hunts with motoring writer Sue Baker as my navigator. I got the distinct impression that Sue thought I was a better photographer than a driver. Quite honestly, I had no reason to be sullen, but to alleviate this creeping apathy between races, I became engrossed with other pastimes. Graham Hill took me along to a Pro-Am Golf tournament in Gravesend. I remember that he introduced me to Tony Jacklin, the one-time Open and US Champion. Apart from arriving in a chauffeur-driven limousine, Tony managed a round of 68 on a golf course he had never played on before. After the match, I found Tony to be extremely affable despite bitter disappointment after being pipped at the 18th flag in the 1972 Open Golf Championship by a marauding Lee Trevino. Tony had come to within a whisker of winning his second Open Championship title. His reaction to such a set-back surprised me. I told him that racing drivers tended to shrug these things off, and maybe he should try the same attitude — which showed my complete ignorance of the niceties in golf. Since that day the royal and ancient game changed from being an elitist sport to being a pastime with which I could readily identify.

In between the French Grand Prix at Paul Ricard which was won by Ronnie Peterson in the JPS Lotus-Ford, I went to see another Swedish star who was giving the tennis world something to talk about at the Wimbledon Lawn

Tennis Championships, before moving on to Silverstone. I sat mesmerised by a titanic battle fought between Britain's Roger Taylor and Sweden's pubescent idol Bjorn Borg. In blistering sunshine, Taylor beat the blond teeny-bopper and I found patriotic strings in my heart that had never been plucked.

Another heart-rending exercise I became involved in that summer was with a New Zealand girl, Sandra Bluett who was determined to swim across the English Channel. Captain John Hayes of New Romney introduced me to this tough lady from 'down-under' and invited me to join him aboard his escort boat when he deemed the weather and tides were right for her attempt.

Never in my life have I seen a human being suffer so much to complete a monstrous ideal. Captain Hayes, who had supported many a channel swim in the past' was a tough tar. Sandra had steadily progressed to about mid-channel when she started to cry with back pains. The Captain hustled me below deck and told me to ignore her pleadings. I thought he was a wretched man. After much wailing, we heard the rhythmic splish-splosh of her stroke. Then she would pause and plead for redemption. According to Captain Hayes, he recognised a point when his swimmer was no longer going through the agonies of completing a swim. Sandra was really suffering, so we went on deck and took a long hard look into her anguished eyes. A human spirit had been broken, so we hauled her out. Damn it all, she had swum further than most people walk in a day, but that kind of sentiment means nothing, especially when you have to return forlornly to the harbour at Folkestone a fallen heroine. That is the toughest sport I have ever witnessed.

I had an insurance broker who lived in Gravesend. He was mad about power-boat racing. Eddie Fraser served me well for several years before I learnt that he was the Class Six British Champion. Once the cat was out of the bag, he invited me to join the officials' boat offshore to watch a race out of Brighton. Eddie won his class hands down. Unfortunately, I was embarrassingly sea-sick aboard the gin palace, and on the calmest of days — that took a lot of explaining to Eddie.

Brighton became the focus of my attention again when the third division team Brighton and Hove Albion rocked the soccer establishment by enlisting the services of Brian Clough and Peter Taylor. I first saw the 'Seagulls' play under the explosive new management in a home match against York City. Never in my life had I stood on the terraces and heard the tribal war cry of 'Sea-gu-lls' rendered alongside the choral bellow of 'You'll Never Walk Alone' vented from the North Terrace. All too soon I learned what I had missed in my youth at Bexleyheath & Welling FC.

Just when I thought that motor racing fans were by comparison a tranquil lot, I was disproved at Brands Hatch in 1976 when the British Grand Prix vocally erupted after a first lap shunt on Paddock Bend between Clay Regazzoni and James Hunt. The Royal Automobile Club threatened to disqualify Hunt and his Marlboro-McLaren-Ford. The injustice to the paying public was felt as 75,000 enraged fans roared disapproval and got their star turn reinstated when the grid formed up for a re-start of the race. Soccer fans often voice their mutual disapproval of bad decisions by the referee, but I do not think a red card could be withdrawn under the same circumstances.

As I am a fierce patriot and a royalist, the wedding of HRH The Princess Anne to Captain Mark Phillips provided an occasion when I stood all night outside Westminster Abbey to witness the pomp and circumstance. I had not indulged in these simple pleasures as a lad. It was as if 1973 rekindled a lost boyhood that had been completely stifled by Brands Hatch.

These diversions had refreshed my outlook upon life. By the end of the 1973 season, I viewed motor racing through a broader spectrum. I had proved to myself that tunnel vision can be a danger to mental health.

Right at the twilight end of 1973, I took a long-standing friend, Pat Harman, for a drink at a local in Meopham. Pat had gone from making shirts in Mayfair to becoming the 'knicker lady' when she started a job with Janet Reger, a brand leader at the time in ladies' unmentionables. After a pleasant evening enlightening me upon the lingerie industry, Pat took me to a girl-friend's house for a night-cap before we parted to go our different ways. The village of Vigo is spread over the escarpment of the North Downs. Here at a homely town house I was introduced to Pamela Easterbrook.

An oft-told anecdote relates that I never actually 'courted' Pam, but simply loved her upon meeting and never got around to going 'home'!

Six years later following this unusual prelude, we were happily married in May 1979. I walked into my relationship with Pam in 1973 when a campaign was launched by the Argentine government to regain the sovereignty of the Falkland Islands from Britain. At the time I was curious as to why the Argentineans were bothering to claim territory off our shores. So when I got geographically orientated, I was dumbfounded to discover that this minor British Colony was in fact 8,000 miles away from the 'mother country' in the South Atlantic Ocean, and not somewhere off the Atlantic coast of Scotland as I had mistakenly imagined.

A few years after the Falkland Islands were invaded in 1982, I had the occasion to fly there out of RAF Brize Norton to realise why Margaret Thatcher, the Prime Minister of the time, had gone to so much trouble to defending the colony which was closer — much closer — to the predator. After the 18-hour flight aboard the RAF Tri-Star, I was shattered to land amid a way of British life hither to completely forgotten. I was still on British soil, met by British people who were living according to all the codes of Crown, Government and work practice as if I hadn't moved an inch off Lands End. Only then did I realise what all the fuss was about in 1982. I was travelling across Russia from Moscow to Khabarovsk by the Trans-Siberian Express when the Falklands issue brewed up. We had stopped for a few days at Irkutsk, the fur-trading centre in the middle of Siberia. Imagine my astonishment when I was watching the Russian Television News with my KGB Lady companion Tanya, when pictures of our troops in combat training flashed upon the screen from HMS Hermes.

Suddenly my thoughts turned to Pam, home and everything I cherished. All the more so when Tanya looked bewildered at the sight of battleships, P&O cruise ships and the QE II, shown steaming south with daggers drawn. She could not understand what a right-wing Government was doing sailing so far to rescue a pile of rocks from a right-wing junta. I have to admit that the whole episode appeared farcical from this distance. However, I patiently explained to my fully-paid-up Communist Party member that Britain still had colonies spread about the world. When big bullies tried to impose themselves upon the dependents, we had to retaliate. Tanya smarted at the implication of my remark — the Russians had at the time become interlopers in Afghanistan!

From an emotional point of view I had met Pam after her previous marriage had broken up. She was left to fend for a very special son — Stuart. When I first saw Stuart he was still babyish, full of life and rolling around on the floor. His cheerful nature did not betray a child who had suffered brain damage. This lovely, blond boy who responded to attention with a grin had, in fact, suffered the worst possible case of cerebral palsy. His body was wracked by spasms of involuntary movement. Stuart had no control over his arms, legs, speech or natural bodily functions. I had not noticed this upon first sight. I simply saw him as a baby coming to terms with the world. Then Pam explained his impediment to me in detail, and I found myself involved in the disturbing world of disablement. My first natural reaction was — how on earth am I going to deal with this? The answer was simple, I had to try to accept Stuart as he was and not how I thought he should be. My initial faltering steps into his world were perhaps harder than anything I had ever had to accept in my life. But over the weeks, months and years, coming to terms with Stuart, I discovered areas of my own character hitherto unexplored. Any personal problems I nursed evaporated as I helped Pam feed him, change his clothes, attend to his toilet and put him to bed. What initial resentment I felt that Stuart might drive a wedge between Pam and me disappeared in the fullness of time.

We tried desperately to seek for Stuart the best possible treatment in terms of physiotherapy, caring attention and some form of rehabilitation. When I moved in with Pam, she was running Stuart regularly up to Great Ormond Street Hospital in London for treatment. We searched the country for a residential home. Our journeys took us to the Lake District, we saw an institution in Bristol that horrified us and eventually we found temporary sanctuary for him at a Peto Unit in Billingshurst, Sussex.

At around this period I had come to know the Welsh racing driver Tom Pryce and his wife Nella. We became close friends. What made our relationship so much easier was Tom's genuine concern for Stuart. He accepted his disabilities, but felt helpless at not being able to assist him in anyway. Others of our friends were equally sympathetic, like Bob Curl who made a special table-seat for Stuart to eat from and play with toys on. Morris Nuffield Nunn (better known as Mo) of Team Ensign always put us up when we visited them in the Midlands. The British Kart Champion Chris Merlin and his wife then, Chris, were hospitable beyond the call. We no longer felt inadequate to the situation within the fraternity, and that was very important to our future.

8

Patriotic Bears

IF MY personal life had been completely turned topsy-turvy with my faith in human nature restored, then 1974 also went some way to rekindling my interest in motor racing. I had baulked at the commercialism of our sport because it took the essential fun out of life. Then 'Bruin Bear' came along, virgin white, incorruptible, with a big smile upon his face, and announced that motor racing was a joyous, honey-coated sport to behold.

All those months of keeping 'mum' about a brand-new Formula One racing car that was taking shape in Hastings could be wildly exploded. Hesketh Racing had been carefully incubating their new offspring: the galloping white charger with James Hunt handling the reins was ready to take on the world.

The aristocratic patron inspired a British flag waving spirit of patriotism within his team of unlikely individuals. Bruin Bear was played by Lord Alexander Hesketh who lived in the family Northamptonshire pile at Easton Neston which encompassed the horse racecourse outside Towcester.

My role as historian and photographic observer for the April International Trophy meeting at Silverstone on behalf of *Fast Car* magazine had been enlisted by Bubbles Horsley, the Hesketh team manager. I was ably abetted by 'Chicken' the Bear's appointed photographer. Our hero was James, known within the team as 'The Shunt', while 'Harv' was in reality Doctor Harvey Postlethwaite, the man who designed the Hesketh-Ford racing vehicle.

The important supporting cast of transient race mechanics included 'Beaky' one time member of Team Lotus, properly known as David Sims. Then Dave Buller who deputised for Malcolm Gregory and Mike Avery who between them drove the racing car transporter. The bearded court jester Willy Rushton, Sir Walter the pourer of Moët et Chandon fame, Tank Engine the guzzler and Bob the Body Curl who all did their best to take this congregation of sporting automobilists seriously.

Upon arrival at the team marquee I had pinned ceremoniously upon my breast pocket a badge heralding the 'Back British Bears Campaign' and straight away I felt at home.

As thousands of expectant race fans infiltrated the pits to get a close up of a potential new hero and his team, the air reverberated to the sound of a helicopter ferrying in his Lordship's many friends. Wandering like a lead-footed ballerina amid this organised chaos was Harv, puzzling away at his pocket calculator. He had been known to short-circuit his theories through computers, and he wished that such a mechanical brain was available.

On race morning a ten-minute practice period gave the mechanics an opportunity to see if the midnight oil was working properly. It was not timed, so The Shunt's pole position on the grid was sacrosanct. Just before the car was fired up in the garage, a maid appeared with a tray full of teas and cakes. Behind her, Sir Walter and Chicken arrived to make a thoroughly uninformed inspection, bleary eyes were rubbed and a couple of pictures were taken before they retreated to a champagne breakfast in the marquee. During the high-speed limbering session James hit a hare. Bob the Body inspected the blood-spattered body work and performed a quick fibre-glass job.

A cloud of despondent confusion hovered over the black Imperial Weed pit. Ronnie Peterson had problems with wing settings, tyres and engine mountings. This news sent Tank Engine into a fit of the giggles as he blurted to all and sundry that lunch and drinkie-poos were ready. Over a bottle of Dom Perignon and a plate of lobster, I nattered to John Woodington, (one-time BRSCC Marshal) now working at B S Fabrications, who constructed the Hesketh chassis.

'They're hard task masters this lot', he muttered, 'Harv sends down a drawing of a wishbone, he wants it just so, no mucking. Otherwise you get it back until it's bloody right. Mind you, we don't mind working to such fine degrees. You gets yer money if yer deliver the goods. It all boils down to detail. Harv is a stickler, so are Lotus, but March are different. Depends upon the value a designer puts on his job.'

Willie Rushton butted in pleading to be absolutely ignorant of this 'confounded noisy sport'. His sort of chassis is curved, with spongy front suspension and a rear end that over-steers a bit. As for that girl James — 'what a revver!' Suddenly the flap into the marquee parted, and The Shunt made his entrance, steaming profusely and leering at the tea maid. Decked in orange racing overalls, the debonair blond looked the part, but as Rushton enquired: 'is that highly mobile sex symbol capable of winning this race for Bruin Bear?'

Bubbles was quick to steer James away from the champers and cigars and out of the clutches of any willing bird. Instead he dragged his driver over to Le Patron for a big high-powered talk-in. 'God, they look serious', cackled Chicken.

After lunch, the virgin white Hesketh-Ford, ('About the only virgin in these pits', mumbled Willie) was pushed into the assembly area by Beaky and a load of helpers. As the car stood proud, Colin Chapman sidled up, looked at the tyres and grinned: 'No way Firestones will win today'. A thousand eyes glared at the Lotus boss as he added the aside 'I hope'. Clearly, the opposition were shaken by Hesketh's meteoric rise among the ranks.

The dramatic start was too much for Rushton, he slid down the garage wall, bottle of champers in hand. The Union Jack was dropped by Don Truman, Ronnie was suspended by wheel spin and enough smoke to please JPS. The

Shunt shot off the line like a bitch on heat, then came to a grinding halt. The cause was clutch slip. Bruin Bear hardly dared to look, as the raging mob swarmed by his beloved steed like locusts. The Shunt rammed the gear lever into first, broke the nob in his hand, and then with a huge shot of adrenalin, roared off in pursuit of the hounds. Jochen Mass in a Surtees-Ford led into Copse Corner. The German was adroitly put in his place by a snarling Peterson. The big question in Bruin's mind was: 'Will James have time to catch the Weed?'

The gap between The Shunt and Ronnie was diminishing at an astonishing rate. The girl called James declared that she was almost wetting herself in excitement. His progress was heart-stopping. Tank Engine passed out. By lap 28 James was right behind Ronnie. It was a back-tingling sight as the Hesketh dived on the inside of the Imperial Weed at Woodcote. The girl called James was saturated. Le Patron hardly dared watch the black-and-white minstrel show. He sniffed a daffodil in his breast pocket. Rushton was revived by Chicken while Beaky, who had seen it all before, stood po-faced with the signal board. Ronald could only sit there in the black box, as he watched the gleaming white charger disappear into the distance. All manner of sun worship, crossing of hearts, fiddling with rosary beads, begging forgiveness and a new pair of knickers was promised for the girl called James, if The Shunt brought the unlikely dream to reality.

Then in one magic moment of ecstasy James burst into view and took the chequered flag, to a thunderous roar from the multitude in the grandstands. David had slain Goliath. Saint George had killed the dragon. Bubbles almost suffocated Bruin Bear. The Aristocrat had vanquished the Imperial Weed.

Observing a Formula One race can rarely be said to provoke hilarity. But at Silverstone my sides were aching from laughter. This incredible Whitehall-like farce continued into the evening back at Easton Neston after one hell of a thrash in the tattered marquee. A motley collection of souls wended their way up the driveway where pheasants preened and cows mooed into the sunset. I ran fingers through my hair and tried to present a veneer of respectability befitting an English stately home.

I tottered into Hesketh Towers, peered into the Pink Room, where my ears were attacked by 'Bulls-eye' Sykes giving a rendition of:

'The Ballad to Hesketh Racing...'

> *We all wear jackets of red, white and blue*
> *There's one for me and there's one for you.*
> *How did they do it, how do they do?*
> *To me it looks completely cuckoo*
> *How did they start, how did they begin?*
> *'Cos Hesketh Racing has scored a great win . . .*

My eardrums could take only so much, so I ventured into the Blue Room where James was trying to inform Mark McKormack in Cleveland of his victory. There was a moment of reflection: never before had so much lunacy, in so short a time, conquered so much intellect. Through these desperately short-sighted rose-coloured spectacles, motor racing the Hesketh way seemed the best way to go.

* * *

As Jackie Stewart's racing career with Ken Tyrrell came to a premature end when he achieved his third World Championship title after his team-mate François Cevert was killed during practice for the 1973 United States Grand Prix at Watkins Glen, the door was left open for every opportunist to claim the Scot's illustrious crown.

The 1974 world championship trail was disconcerting in that seven different drivers won a Grand Prix. Nobody seemed to have a clear advantage. Ronnie Peterson won the Monaco, French and Italian races. Argentina's Carlos Reutemann claimed the South African, Austrian and American events. While between them Niki Lauda, Jody Scheckter, Denis Hulme and Clay Regazzoni won the rest. Much to everybody's surprise, the season came to an end with the newly crowned World Champion in Emerson Fittipaldi driving the Marlboro McLaren-Ford. He seemed to surface from nowhere with victories in Brazil, Belgium and Canada!

Only in 1975 did the convergence of two great forces become apparent. James Hunt and Niki Lauda were clearly on course for a major explosion of their driving talents. Such were the eruptions in 1976 when Hunt drove the McLaren and Lauda had the Ferrari, the fall out produced some of the most controversial but exciting season's of racing for many a year.

James Hunt was determined to make his mark right from early days in Hastings, when he deeply gouged his name on the boarding school wall. His impact upon motor racing was equally conspicuous. Not that he won any of the British Formula Three Championships, unlike Bev Bond, Tony Trimmer and Roger Williamson — who, by sheer consistency, plugged away to take the honours. Mind you, not many became real Grand Prix drivers. I have gleaned every championship table of the early 'seventies and there is not so much as a mention of James Hunt in the first three of any championship. He won a Grovewood Award which was considered a kiss of death, but then a driver doesn't get branded 'Hunt-the-Shunt' without qualified reason.

Speaking to his competitors at the time, I noted a similar theme of conversation: 'Hunt!!! bloody fast, but off his perishing nut', and that was stating the obvious politely. So was it unremitting velocity that caused him constantly to deviate from the straight and narrow course?

Again the fire brands spoke of James to an echo — it was a question of elbow room. The pent-up energy of a driver at the drop of the starter's flag must have caused such a rush of blood that it affected his judgment. Trimmer reckoned that if there was not a gap to allow him to overtake an opponent then he would turn a half-inch into a yard. Even without a half-inch, James would merrily drop wheels into the dirt and barge through. Invariably such hectic full-blooded determination ended up as a modern work of steaming art in the earth bank. Times without number James would disentangle himself from yet another wrecked car, shake his fists, rant and rave, then a half-hour later he'd be kicking the garage door to pulp for his own stupidity. This side of his character remained with James throughout his Grand Prix career and was not consistent with the behaviour of a lover of budgerigars. Why on earth he went for gaps that patently never existed was beyond the fathoming of most team managers. James never recognised a door slammed in his face. 'The bastard cut me up', he would bitterly complain about what is considered a perfectly legitimate manoeuvre in motor racing, better described as 'narrowing the approach to a corner'.

When James Hunt did maintain a cool disposition and keep it on the island, he won races. Even then he appeared totally amazed at his accomplishment. James would swear with a hand on his heart that he had not driven any differently from his normal way of driving.

In spite of his public-school boy petulance, I savour an abiding personal memory of James Hunt. As a stoney-broke Formula Three driver he approached me in the pavilion bar at Brands Hatch after a meeting and asked to borrow a 'fiver' for a round of drinks. I did not question his integrity — James had the money. Several years passed. After he had retired from racing to join Murray Walker in the BBC Television 'Grand Prix', commentary box, we performed an 'Evening with James Hunt' at the Congress Theatre in Eastbourne. Cutting it fine before we were due to appear on stage, James burst into my dressing room about five minutes before we faced the audience. Full of profuse apologies about being 'better late than never' he thrust a crumpled envelope into my hand. I left it unopened on the dressing-room table, not realising that I had misinterpreted his sorrow. After the show, we sank a few beers before we departed for home. Only then did I open the envelope. Inside was a crinkled, mint-fresh £5 note and signed across it — 'Sorry so long, James'.

Pit boxen are the 'fast forward' service bays on a racing circuit. They bear a similarity to that red light district in Amsterdam where a man can legitimately tell his other half that he is doing some 'window shopping'. Such was the death of 'pit popsies' at one time, when Innes Ireland led, and eventually won, the Tourist Trophy at Goodwood in the British Racing Partnership Ferrari Berlinetta, he would rumble along the pit lane for refuelling and a wheel change. While he was slowing down, Innes would cast an eye along the pit counters. He was perusing the delectation, looking for a juicy morsel with whom to celebrate his victory that night!

Pits across the world come in various shapes and sizes. Some are adequate to the job, others are totally unsuited. Circuit designers contrived 'pokey' little stables with a cobbled paddock like those at Zandvoort where the pits seemed to be wedged into the most cramped plot on the circuit. Those at Nürburgring were even worse, and a potential death trap when fires broke out. Many team managers who doubted whether their driver had spotted the pit signals had a second bite at the cherry, by getting the lad to hang the board out on the return straight after the North Turn.

At Le Mans there was an incongruous situation where 'guests' could be wining and dining in the hospitality boxes right above the team service area. So while favoured clients sipped Chateau du Barrail lounging over the sill, on occasion they would be treated to 'flambé à la Matra' or something equally indigestible when tired hands made a hash of the well-rehearsed refuelling routines.

At circuits that have grown from nothing over a period of time like Brands Hatch, modern facilities have had to be designed into a ready-made layout. Room had to be found to erect the original old breeze-block boxen between the top and bottom straights. It is a wonder that nobody keeled over in those draughty hell-holes. Later on, after much whinging by the GPDA and the Constructors Association, newly-appointed pits and lock-up garages were constructed facing over a much wider service road with parking at the rear for the transporters. In order to accommodate the extra facilities, the bottom straight was modified. But even this edifice fell into disfavour, so during the winter of 1993-4, £2.5 million was spent on yet another complex.

Before the days of 'S' bends to slow down cars making their 'entrée', the 'austfarht' from 'sling-shot' alley was left open for the suicidal getaways made after servicing. Years ago, a car would simply screech onto the circuit from where it was standing, scattering photographers, mechanics, girls and officials in its wake — which might explain why the most ambitious girls gravitated to the area. Apart from being where the action was, when a race was over a bachelor driver who won, lost or simply retired with his big end gone, was easy prey to a pair of flashing eyes.

As racing became more politically convoluted and contrived, the 'crumpet' had to be rationed to legitimate driver relationships. Gone were the days when a girl could saunter into the shrines, a stop watch dangling from her pretty neck and — without so much as a 'pit pass' — be allowed to decorate a counter.

I first met Niki Lauda in the pits at Brands Hatch. It was during practice for the traditional August Bank Holiday Formula Two meeting. Niki in 1971 had secured a 'sponsored' drive with the works March Formula Two team to support Ronnie Peterson. Practice had finished. I had joined Ronnie with his girl friend Barbro and we sat on a vacant counter to watch Niki at a distance thrash out details about his car with Robin Herd and the mechanics. The headstrong Austrian was patently unhappy as he stalked over to us. It was probably not an appropriate moment for Lauda to make my acquaintance, but Ronnie introduced me to Niki. He turned, shot me a glare that would have killed, nodded his head, gave a toothy smirk, sniffed and promptly went back to collar Robin Herd.

Ronnie intimated that his team-mate was 'bloody crazy' and briefly explained that Niki was literally racing 'on tick' (read as sponsorship for March's benefit) from Erste Oesterreichische Spar-Casse, a big Austrian bank. It was a deal based upon advertising and promotion which tied Niki up with £20,000 in case he cooked his goose. I defended Niki and told Ronnie that there stood a man with confidence in his own ability.

118

My working relationship with Lauda may have got off to a tenuous start. Various writers had told me that he was arrogant, self-opinionated, abrupt, ill-mannered — all qualities that did not betray a strict upbringing. But now that Niki had kicked over the traces, I recognised natural rebellion to everything his parents stood for in pride and etiquette.

The young Austrian was anxious to make a few short cuts up the ladder. Impatient to hoist himself into the top echelon, Niki made a deal with his bank to 'buy' himself into the March Grand Prix team. Financial Director Max Mosley probably thought that every Easter egg had a yolk of gold. Unfortunately for Niki, 'Old Lauda' as Grandpa was known, pulled the rug from under his grandson. The father-figure had influence in financial circles around Vienna and he quietly stopped the deal. This left Niki in a state of high dudgeon.

Fired with ambition to furnace-like heat, Lauda set up another line of credit with Raiffeisenkasse Bank, secured his Formula One drive with March and departed the Bicester works stony broke, but impatient for instant success. Lauda's emphatic belief in himself paid dividends, however, this did not make it any easier to get to know him. Lauda and I could be likened to the diverse poles of a magnetic field. I was advised by the Austrian writer Heinz Pruller that beneath Niki's dour features and darting blue eyes, beat a heart of an emotionally sensitive man. My colleague reminded me of Jochen Rindt and how I eventually forged a marvellous understanding with his 'ne'er-do-care' attitude to life. Heinz advised patience before I prejudged the new Austrian hero. Unfortunately, I never did get on terms with Lauda, but oddly enough when Niki graduated to Formula One with Marlboro BRM in 1973, he would spot me taking notes and without being prompted would wander up and brake into a stilted conversation about the state of his game. I assumed that he wanted to get his story correctly on record.

At Monaco in 1974 Niki tore me off a strip. Contrary to belief, it was not true that I had misquoted him. During practice when he secured pole position, he spied me walking down Mirabeau, past the Tip-Top Bar. Niki lunged upon me in the crowded pit area with an incredulous expression on his face. He asked me how long I had been in the sport. I told Lauda since before he was born. The incredulity turned to stark amazement. He then told me to set a better example. What crime of passion had I committed? Apparently, he was on a flying lap, the Ferrari twitched through the Casino Square and hit the hump on the exit before plunging down Mirabeau. Just where the cars go 'tippy-toey' over the bump, Lauda noticed this 'bloody lunatic' walking down the hill with his back to the traffic. Yours sincerely had committed the cardinal sin of all photographers, and he rightly berated me.

After admitting the error of my ways, I pointed out that it was impossible to walk the Monaco circuit facing the traffic. He was right, and I was honest enough to admit that the artist Michael Turner and I had been pinned to a wall by an errant car in the same area many years previously. This statement fuelled Lauda's concern still more. He reckoned that I must be 'thick' not to have learnt the lesson. Point taken. However, I did wonder how a driver on a scorching lap found the time to register a minion like me being a naughty boy? I guess that's why Niki Lauda is a brilliant racing driver and I am just a photographer. It was a pity he retired from that race with ignition trouble, so he was in no mood for conversation.

Six months before the old breeze block pits at Brands Hatch were bull-dozed to build the new complex, a huge controversy broke out during the British Grand Prix which revealed a chink in Lauda's tactical armour.

Britain during race week was in a state of paranoia. Visiting writers congregating in the press room for the first day of practice at Brands Hatch voiced genuine concern and fear about what was wrenching our green and pleasant land apart. Nowhere was safe. People from the world over arriving for the Grand Prix were glad to get out of London and into the many country hotels and pubs in Kent. IRA terrorists had breached high security and bombed the Palace of Westminster. There had been explosions in Manchester and Birmingham. A person unfortunately died in a fire that blasted the Tower of London.

The atmosphere at Brands Hatch seemed unreal. It was akin to the race being held upon a battle field. The attacks dominated all conversation until practice finally burst into life. Lauda swept all before him to be on pole position. Ferrari were quietly confident of a successful result. Then on race morning police and sniffer dogs were rampant in the main grandstand. A bomb scare had scorched down the telephone lines. It turned out to be a sick joke, but nobody could rest until the all clear was given. Instead, domestic upheaval was quickly overtaken by an equally dramatic race. The John Player Grand Prix as the national British event became known, was perhaps overshadowed by outside events. Who knows, but my belief was the Royal Automobile Club would rather have been anywhere but Brands Hatch that afternoon.

Rob Walker is renowned within motor racing circles for his fine qualities as the perfect English gentleman. At the British Grand Prix he officiated in 1974 as a member of the RAC Competitions Committee. After years as a private entrant in Grand Prix motor racing, Rob of all people probably knew the nitty-gritty more than most of his colleagues. After the race I was in the Ferrari enclosure with him and a very despondent Niki Lauda who had seen first victory, then a chance of any championship points snatched from his grasp. In the opinion of Rob Walker, the RAC had made 'a bloody cock-up'.

Nobody could have foreseen the chapter of events that was to unfold after Lauda made a copybook start. He hurled his Ferrari into a formidable lead ahead of Jody Scheckter's Elf-Tyrrell-Ford. That was the position until 20 laps from the end of a 75-lap race.

Brands Hatch had a reputation for engendering the raw basic competitive instincts of a racing driver. Whether it was the natural amphitheatre of the old club circuit with its close proximity to thousands or the nature of the entire circuit, I do not know. But drivers did admit that there was a special kind of mentality inspired at Brands Hatch which rarely surfaced at any other venue.

Whatever provoked drivers to display a 'devilish' side of their skill it affected Lauda that day. On lap 25 the Austrian established a new outright lap record for the Grand Prix circuit at 1 min 21.1 secs with a speed of 117.63 mph. Acoustically, I knew Brands Hatch so well that when something abnormal happened on the circuit, I 'sensed' an incident before it became apparent on the lap chart.

Hans Stuck's March went out of control at Dingle Dell. I remember turning to a colleague and commenting upon a bang somewhere in the country. Stuck survived a heavy crash which had sprayed the road with fragments of bodywork and metal. From that moment the race was somewhat spoilt by an abnormal number of punctures. Drivers who managed to nurse their cars around to the pits caused a great deal of activity in the narrow service road.

For reasons I don't recall, I had elected to watch this race from the vicinity of the pit area, which — in view of what happened later in the race — was a fortuitous decision. Clay Regazzoni, Lauda's team-mate, had weaved his way into second place when he became a casualty of Stuck's misdemeanour. So Scheckter was back in business ready to threaten the Ferrari. On lap 55 it dawned upon Lauda that he, too, had fallen victim of the March bug. His right rear tyre was slowly deflating, not with any suddenness, but the car was handling strangely in left-hand corners and it presented Lauda with a problem. Four-second wheel changes were still an exercise to be aimed at in the future. A pit stop at this crucial stage in the race with the lead in question would be instant suicide. At this time the gap between the Ferrari and the Tyrrell was around nine seconds. A few laps went by and Lauda calculated that he could survive to pick up second position. Scheckter had got the message and he started to pile on the pressure. The South African had blown Lauda's plan.

Realising that all was not well with the race leader, I marched along to the Ferrari pit to have a front seat upon the unfolding drama. Remember, these were the days before drivers enjoyed radio contact with their team managers. So Ferrari's design manager Mauro Forghieri looked a mite perplexed. Lauda had worked hard for his lead and now it was dwindling away for no apparent reason... that is, until ten laps from the end of the race. Only then did it become noticeable from the sidelines that the Ferrari had a tyre problem. Forghieri ordered his pit crew to be ready. Still Scheckter bore down relentlessly on the Ferrari, which was handling like a drunken juggernaut.

By now the crowd was becoming quite vocal. Ferrari fans, well aware of a new champion apparent in Lauda after his victories at Jarama, Zandvoort and possibly at Brands Hatch, were waving him on. While supporters of Tyrrell sensed blood, and being a British built car, shrieked Scheckter on to even more inspired planes. Now we would learn if Lauda's growing ability as a tactician was vulnerable.

My obsession with the 'pits of the world' was about to realise a finale of Cecil B de Mille proportions. I could hardly believe that the epic was being staged at the 'home' theatre. Brands habituées had long known the overcrowded pit lane. In order to control the many hangers-on who, as the final curtain was nigh, gathered in the area which constituted the exit road onto the circuit, marshals pulled a rope across the road to stop eager well-wishers from flooding the track when the chequered flag was dropped — a phenomenon of Brands Hatch for as long as I could recollect.

On this occasion with five laps of the race to go, this motley collection assembled, forcing the marshals to cast the rope and even to link arms. The deputy Clerk of the Course decided that he should move the course car onto the pit lane amid the photographers and dolly birds. With the race now at its crucial stage, the pit road was effectively blocked and thus preventing any race car from making a rapid exit.

A frantic Forghieri was unrestrained with Latin rage. On the one hand Lauda seemed doomed to self elimination. On the other hand, even if the chief were able to service the Ferrari, with the pit exit blocked by a human wall, he was onto a loser anyway. Maybe Lauda knew something Forghieri didn't know.

The desperate Austrian could see that the offending tyre was now chunking. His valiant effort to preserve his lead was all over as the blue Tyrrell loomed larger in his mirrors. Forghieri had leapt onto the pit wall in his concern that Lauda had not stopped. Then with one lap to go, the Ferrari hobbled into the pits. A lightning wheel-change was made and Lauda screamed off, praying that the human wall would part as he approached it at around 100 mph.

At that moment the situation was not only potentially lethal, it was downright madness. Surely Lauda must realise that the game was up. Either that, or there was going to be a mass slaughter.

Within an inkling, Lauda to his horror realised that the course car was also in his path. He freely admitted afterwards that he would have charged the human barrier and prayed for a parting of the ways. Then, from nowhere, a marshal appeared with a red flag. He stood in front of the crowd madly waving it, with a ferocious Ferrari hurtling down upon him. Lauda literally stood on the brakes. He released his safety harness and leapt out of the car. Black with rage he stalked off to the Ferrari pit.

No wonder Rob Walker looked on, his head nodding in shame. The RAC had created an unholy mess of our prestige race. There was no room for denial that the RAC, Britain's leading organisation for motorists, had, in the eyes of the world, created a pathetic situation out of gross incompetence. The marshals were simply doing a job, no doubt under instruction.

The start line and pit lane marshals were commended by the teams on this occasion, for keeping the service road relatively free of photographers during such a hectic race. When Lauda eventually regained his composure, he openly admitted to the fault in his sterling effort to nurse the Ferrari to a finish, and the danger he presented to his competitors and himself.

Niki showed considerable folly in ignoring the pleadings of his team manager to make a pit stop within ten laps of the flag. He was tactically in the wrong to take a chance.

The perspective of a race leader is entirely different to that of a placeman. Lauda desperately wanted to win the race which is entirely different to defending one of the first six places to claim World Championship points. At the latter stage of the Grand Prix, Lauda the racing driver honestly felt that a handful of points was better than nothing. He seemed to pay no heed to the added danger his crippled Ferrari presented to his opponents, let alone to himself. Lauda is paid to drive, and to win — or at the very least do his best. That was his attitude, and the devil take the hindmost.

On the other hand, the driver can have that decision taken out of his hands by the race officials. In my opinion the Clerk of the Course should have ordered Lauda to be black-flagged at least ten laps from the end. That would have thrown the rule book at Lauda and forced him to enter the pits, wheels would have been changed and a lot of blushes would have been spared. To my knowledge, Niki Lauda has firmly drawn a curtain over the 1974 British Grand Prix. When I spoke to him a year or so later, he was man enough to admit that Brands Hatch had taught him a lesson as a tactician. I think this was shown through the rest of the Austrian driver's career.

As for the Royal Automobile Club, well — they blundered on in their own sweet way. After announcing that Lauda had finished on paper in ninth place, they reassessed the 'almighty cock-up' and finally awarded him fifth place. As it turned out in 1974, the result had no effect upon Emerson Fittipaldi's World Championship. Had the outcome been closer, the RAC might have been crucified.

* * *

Fishing is not my favourite pastime. That's possibly because I have a short fuse on patience. Therefore, how I have come to accumulate friends who find satisfaction standing for umpteen hours on river banks dangling a line is baffling.

My kind of fisherman was Denis Hulme. In New Zealand we would lower his power boat into Lake Rotoiti, chug out to a promising spot, then troll lines for rainbow trout. On one occasion we had been wallowing in the late afternoon sun for an hour or so when Denis quietly suggested that I pulled the lines off the stern. I noticed that he closed the lid of a wicker hamper basket that was creaking with half a dozen fish. A lake warden pulled an outboard dinghy alongside. Denis exchanged pleasantries. I watched the eye of the warden focus upon the wicker basket Denis was now sitting upon. The chap was no fool, but eventually he went away looking extremely perplexed.

'Bit dodgy, that', grinned Denis, 'could have lost my licence if he'd caught us trolling.'

In Britain Davy Watton was to angling what Barbara Woodhouse was to dogs. This bearded gnome-like man from Broadstairs gave me a severe rap across the knuckles when I reiterated my fishing experiences with Denis Hulme. He marched me off to the glassy waters of Bayham Abbey trout fishery near Tunbridge Wells. There Davy educated me in the gentle art of casting a line and playing the fish into the net. Unfortunately, those lessons did not prevent other 'fishermen' from corrupting my best intentions.

My one-time karting friend Chris Merlin and his family lived at 'Mountain

Ash' a splendid old house that stood proud of the estuaries of the rivers Esk, Irt and Mite at Ravenglass in Cumbria.

Merlin's idea of recreation on a summer afternoon was to take a plastic milk container, put a whiff of petrol inside, then play cat'n'mouse against the 'beckies'. Chris blasted salmon to the water surface by detonating the bottle from a battery, then stunning the fish. He would wade in and pick up the fish. I never considered this as fair game. What made the adrenalin pump was performing this barbaric mission just beyond the ear-shot of the warden. We crawled along river banks amid the long grass and rushes on our stomachs. Then at a given moment a dull 'thump' would hit the water and, while I kept watch, Chris would pick his crop.

One year when Pam, Stuart and I enjoyed the Merlin's hospitality at Christmas, I telephoned Innes Ireland who then lived at Borgue, near Kirkcudbright. The gregarious Scot immediately invited us to visit his baronial pile close to the River Dee. Chris and I drove across the border for a hilarious afternoon sampling Ireland's select blends of Scotch whisky. Before we departed, Innes pulled me aside and suggested that I join him for a fishing trip early in the New Year. Addled with bonhomie, I agreed, and two months later I made the trek from Kent to Kirkcudbright, not knowing what the devil I had let myself in for. I met Innes on the quayside where I was flabbergasted to learn that I was about to crew the motor fishing vessel '*Kinloch*' for a month of piracy way north on Loch Ewe. I telephoned Pam to explain that my weekend of fishing was going to be slightly longer than anticipated!

The dual roles of Innes Ireland as a racing driver and of me as a racing photographer ran parallel in the 'sixties when Innes was not being hospitalised. He retired from the commercialised climate of Grand Prix racing, then dallied awhile as the sports editor of *Autocar*. He soon tired of being manacled to a desk so he went freelance as the Grand Prix correspondent for the American magazine *Road & Track*. Even this fresh air job was not enough to placate Ireland's lively spirit. So he quietly returned to the bosom of the mother country by moving back home to Kirkcudbright in Dumfries and Galloway. There he and his then wife, Edna, re-established themselves at Senwick House overlooking the River Dee. Innes then invested much of his race earnings in a small fleet of three fishing trawlers.

Unbeknown to me, *Kinloch* had been fitted out to dredge the Queen Scallop — or 'Queenie' as the trade call this crustation. I was to play deck hand, drinking partner and late-night chin-wagger to the Captain and his first mate, wee Davy, a lad of 17 years whose dialect was so strong that I could barely understand him!

Scotsmen at the best of times are a tough breed — the further north you travel, the more so. This lily-livered Sassenach realised on this bleak day in February 1976 that the going was intended to be rough and that my character was about to be re-shaped. It was then that I discovered another side to Innes Ireland. Being couped up on *Kinloch* for a month, working up to sixteen hours a day, was compensated for by enjoying the company of a natural character and survivor. We chugged our worthy little vessel around the Mull of

Galloway to Girvan where Innes had arranged for our victualling. We then pointed the 37-foot trawler upon the first leg of a journey through the Inner Hebrides. Our trip to Loch Ewe, a bite out of the hide of Wester Ross, was calculated by Innes to take two days. What I thought was going to be a 'jolly' in fact turned out to be a fascinating military-style operation. Innes had to steer a course by compass, echo-sounder and radar over turbulent waters. I cooked breakfast as we rounded the Mull of Kintyre. The subject of Paul McCartney's romantic ballad bore no resemblance to the grey, fog-laden scene of the North Channel.

The steady plod north to approach the Sound of Jura was less a hazard in our small craft once we reached the protection of Islay Isle. Mind you, the currents that run in this area are incredibly strong, and these made the diesel motor labour until the tide changed and we coasted along with the flow.

For me this formidable rampart of North-West Scotland was a whole new scene. We spied crofters' cottages, and Innes cursed the regimented reforestation. Trees, he protested, grew haphazardly and they should be replanted in the same way to maintain the natural effect. Already I was finding a man who cared very much for his heritage. I pondered about his handsome, rugged features as he stood at the wheel and contemplated the passing scenery. The Innes the entire world knew to be a fun-loving, party-going, devilish racing driver seemed far from this cynical character, who — though content with his lot in the wide open spaces — seemed embittered that racing had not fully rewarded his skills. But then as the sun burned away the mists, his spirit rose and suddenly there was a 'good-to-be-alive' feeling in the air.

Our overnight stop brought us alongside Tobermory on the Isle of Mull. No sooner had we tied *Kinloch* securely, than Innes was off hot-foot to a local pub. The proprietor was somewhat taken aback when Innes suggested that we embark upon a whisky-tasting of 72 blends behind the bar. For five convivial hours which became more raucous as the night went on, we waded through the selection. I hasten to add that I probably came to a grinding halt after sampling about twelve blends. Innes was still trying to decide upon the best fire, tingle and taste long after closing hours. Then dawned the realisation that this little lot had to be paid for, and Innes confessed to not having a penny on his person. I elected to leave him propping up the bar while I went to *Kinloch* and got his cheque book. Our host was none to pleased about receiving a cheque for £52 from a stranger three parts gone in the wind. However Innes with great deliberation signed the transaction and the proprietor gazed at the cheque very carefully — when a realisation shone in his eyes. He had been puzzled the whole evening over the familiar face, and when he read the signature, the publican straight away stated his intention to frame the cheque. As the skipper and I wended our way back to the boat, Innes gave a broad grin and said 'Not a bad evening on the house — Eh lad'. The cheque was never cashed.

Bearing in mind that this fishing trip happened a few years after Innes had retired from racing, I was constantly amazed at the long memories of people in the Highlands and Islands. Apart from being a boisterous man in the best of company, Innes Ireland bore a name that provoked twin reactions. Women revered his character while most men bluntly commented upon 'that no-good mad man'.

A gentleman whom I encountered in the general store at Tobermory next morning obviously had some knowledge of motor racing. 'That's Innes Ireland', he said, eyebrows raised in amazement, 'it's a crying shame how the famous fall from grace. Fancy, today the poor lad is a trawler man'. He continued nodding his head with incredulity and went on: 'Nay, but if Innes had employed himself like wee Jimmy or Jackie, he wouldn'a be a lacky now'.

Once we had slunk out of Tobermory before sunrise, we had breakfast, then wee Davy and I cast aside our cumbersome oil skins and set to work on the foredeck, sorting out the dredging nets and checking over the winches and pulleys. Innes was in the wheel-house nursing a hammer-like head and attempting to steer a course through the Sound of Sleat that separates the Isle of Skye from the Scottish mainland. It was a wintry sun that welcomed us at the Kyle of Lochalsh. The air was clear as crystal. Unshaven, bedraggled, but hearty, we searched the labyrinth of narrow streets for the village store. Local inhabitants stepped aside as the 'wild bunch' raided shops for newspapers, magazines, favoured butterscotch sweeties for Davy, bottles of hooch and razor blades. For me, the buccaneering spirit was fast becoming attractive. Innes rolled back with several calor-gas bottles for the galley stove. Not far from the boat a buxom woman recognised the skipper and went into an uncharacteristic embrace. Momentarily taken aback, Innes relished the attack of an elderly female admirer, who he later described as having boobs the size of Zeppelin Airships! Over a coffee on board *Kinloch*, Innes admitted that he would have merrily suffocated to death in her embrace — had she been 30 years closer to pubescence.

I got a distinct impression that Innes Ireland, bygone celebrity, was somewhat bemused by these occasional flashes of recognition. He openly bathed in the limelight at racing circuits, but away from the melée, meandering around in his home ground, so to speak, upset his composure. Mind you, signing cheques to settle pub bills showed a conscious awareness of who he was, and he took full advantage of the situation.

After the Kyle, we started to travel through parts of Scotland that roused the true Pict in Innes. In the background of the ghostly reaches of Loch Torridon, capped in snow were the oldest hills on earth. Beinn Alligin, Beinn Liathach and Beinn Eighe stood pink and gaunt and looked like images rather than weathered uplands. For Innes the impressive backcloth was the root of his heritage. Away from the bustle of city life and the stress of a cosmetic world, he stood on the stern of *Kinloch*, and peered with longing at the fluctuating grandeur.

The Atlantic Ocean forcibly trespassed upon our sheltered voyage. An opening between the northernmost promontory of Skye and the Isle of Harris exposed us to the full welter of the open sea. Here other trawlers could be seen bobbing on the horizon. Innes elected to drop the dredge nets in order to test the machinery. We weren't in prime 'Queenie' water yet, but tea was the offing and sweetmeats were to be savoured. We hauled in the nets as *Kinloch* turned to starboard at the estuary to Loch Ewe. The dredge was sparse, but fruitful. As we dropped anchor, the sun set upon the jagged Beinn o' Chais- gein Beag. This background was to be 'home' for a month.

Over that period we worked industriously. Our days of toil varied from eight hours up to twelve of back-breaking effort. Often local trawler men would venture alongside and issue threats. We were accused of poaching the water, taking their living and told in no uncertain manner to bog off back home. Innes argued adamantly that he had every right to fish their waters, and that they should get off their bloody backsides and join him if they felt that strongly. None of the locals from Aultbea took on the challenge. Their traw- lers idled in the tiny harbour while we gleefully dredged the scallop beds clean.

We dropped anchor each night in the lee of the Isle of Ewe, away from the twinkling lights of Aultbea. One night BBC Radio News crackled the announcement that Iceland had broken off relations with Britain over the cod war. At this statement Innes's face beamed. He identified our own mission and grinned: 'That's it, by the time we leave, Aultbea will have declared war on us'.

One day, after six hours of the hardest manual labour I had ever exper- ienced, Innes logged 63 bags of prime scallops. We were loaded to the gun- wales. The time had come to venture ashore to unload onto a lorry. Our catch had to be driven to the fish farm in Kirkcudbright. Within 24 hours those suc- culent meats would be served in the best restaurants in London, Paris and New York.

With no interference from militant locals, the catch was transferred and on its way south by three in the morning. We were all tired out of our brains. Davy dropped exhausted in his bunk. Innes saw no point in cooking a meal. Instead, he took a whisky bottle and we sat down contented with our labours. By that time three weeks had passed. It was Innes who commented that not once had we mentioned, let alone talked about, motor racing. From the blue he fired the question which I had been avoiding over the past year or so — 'Why the hell did I still work at the races if I was not content?'

Bobbing about in that early dawn, my body aching, my mind numb and longing for sleep, I was suddenly shot back in to reality. I confessed to Innes that the scene had changed and was no longer enjoyable. I admitted going through the motions at races and, under still heavier interrogation, I owned up to myself that motor racing had not been my 'choice' but merely a subject in which I had become involved because when I was a boy there seemed to be no alternative. Had I realised a choice earlier in life, I might well have taken to travel writing and photography rather than sport. I had been afraid to make the plunge into an unknown field. The whisky had me talking openly to Innes as I had never done before. For me, that pleasant night of solitary confine- ment with a true friend, was a slow dawning of discontent. On other nights of the remaining week on Loch Ewe, I often turned the tables. I was curious to learn from Innes how he saw his own legacy in motor racing.

It appeared that over the years Innes had been subject to so many terrifying shunts that he made James Hunt appear an apprentice car-breaker by comparison. Often I had witnessed his arrival at the pits on foot to face a menacing team manager while Innes approached with his knowing expression 'Who me?' written all across his face.

There were times when he was subject to mechanical failure. There were other times when he made a down-right miscalculation and suffered horrendous injuries. The crashes Innes was able to walk away from were treated with disdain as mere punctuations. The full stops were the 'thunderous nasties' that damned well hurt and hospitalised Innes. He became familiar with so many nurses that it was a miracle he didn't marry one!

Those horrible 'bang-ups' as Innes described the write-offs, led him to identify himself with cats and their nine lives. Innes never gave a toss about danger or the punishment to his body and the never-ending repair he had to suffer. But he admitted quietly in retrospect that each accident took its toll upon his constitution. He privately felt that each bang was a life gone and that one day the great reaper would eventually snuff him out before his natural term. Innes hoped fervently that he would be romantically entwined with a woman whom he loved passionately when the last call came.

I firmly believe that such a finale is the dying dream of every red-blooded male. For Innes to have popped his clogs at the exquisite moment of orgasm would have provided his epitaph — 'He died in the last flush of old age'.

His thoughts upon his own destiny were remarkably prophetic. Innes died in peace from a heart attack. The ninth life was not wasted amid a tangle of metal and fibre glass. When we did talk of some of his many friends who had lost their lives in action, Innes became quite weepy. He very much admired Mike Hawthorn and Peter Collins and was deeply affected by the loss of Alan Stacey at Spa on that tragic weekend which also took Chris Bristow. He reckoned that both young drivers had the guts and determination to make champions, but Innes was quite emotional about Stacey who overcame disability to drive. Archie Scott-Brown was another driver who, although he had one useful hand, by sheer grit launched himself into motor racing against all medical advice. Innes revelled in men who overcame physical abnormalities to achieve success. Innes would love to have seen a man like Douglas Bader, the war-time Royal Air Force pilot who surmounted the loss of both legs to fly again, sit in a racing car. He was convinced that Bader had the 'right stuff' to make a bloody good racing driver.

Looking back over the crop who clambered into Grand Prix racing after he retired, Innes reckoned that only a handful of them got his blood coursing. He enjoyed watching Jochen Rindt and Ronnie Peterson even though he misunderstood their respective life styles. Tom Pryce, the brilliant young Welsh driver who never realised his prime, won a special place in the Scotsman's heart.

I noted that each of these drivers was of the 'tigerish' breed — all arms and elbows, foot firmly on the noise, backside waving in the wind. Did he identify with the 'all-or-nothing' brigade? Spirit was the essential quality which Innes

(*above*) James Hunt was a popular
Brands Hatch exponent.

(*left*) Angela and John Webb, the management
of Brands Hatch, receive the 1982 FOCA
award for the best organised Grand Prix
of the Year.

(*below* Niki Lauda gets the Goodyear
low-down at the 1974 Italian Grand Prix.
Photo: Jutta Fausel.

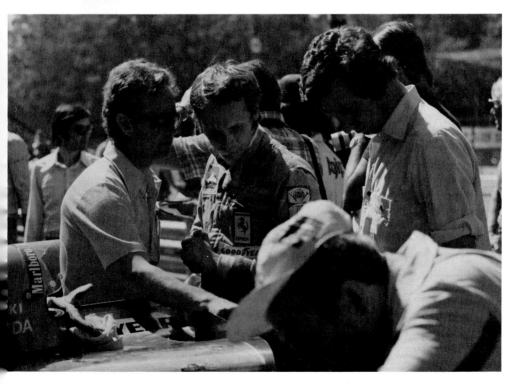

I wonder if this was the 30 hp
Wolseley that my Austrian
acquaintance photographed
at the 1902 Bexhill races?

Two great British racers –
Hon C S Rolls in the Mors and
Charles Jarrott with his
Panhard – await a practice
run before the Bexhill Races
in 1902.

Mr Alfred Harmsworth in the 15 hp New Orleans and Mr C Gregson's 12 hp Gladiator
await the light tourist car race.

admired in a driver, and he loved to stand on a fast bend and see such drivers hurtling through at eleven-tenths, in effect tossing the text-book out of the cock-pit. No racing school could teach that sort of style, he reckoned.

Of those drivers who perhaps fell a tenth or so below that bench mark, Innes thoroughly enjoyed watching Jacky Ickx on a good day. He was convinced that Ickx was the one driver in modern history who should have been a World Champion and probably the best the sport would have had as a gracious sporting ambassador. Next was James Hunt in whom Innes found a kinship — not for his innate ability to wrap up racing cars, but for pulling the best crumpet in town and still managing to conserve sufficient energy to become a World Champion. The rest Innes clearly disregarded as a bunch who could not drive a push-chair.

I certainly encountered another facet of the complex nature of Innes Ireland whom until this trip I had known only as a rather exuberant racing driver. I discovered another man who possessed a monumental capacity for sheer hard work. Whereas the average fisherman might consider a twelve-hour day quite sufficient, Innes drove himself, along with Davy and myself, to work sixteen-hour days. When my back ached and my hands were cut, blistered and calloused, I could have hated his guts and created a mutiny. But he inspired enormous loyalty and repaid such effort handsomely. In spite of his natural durability, I often felt that one word would create a situation whereby his natural mischief would have bubbled to the surface.

On the last night of our pirating mission, Innes cast caution to the wind: we hove alongside at Aultbea and joined our warring friends in the pub for a session. I sampled the local mix of Guinness and black-currant. Innes was on the whiskies and started to stir the opposition by challenging them to balance glasses on their head and knock back a shot. By the close of the evening, the locals were eating out of his hand. The vagabonds had committed their dastardly deed and could return with honour next season.

If those four weeks with Innes Ireland in Scotland had served a purpose for me, the slightly flabby photographer who went north of the wall returned a toughened character who had been made to face up to his own future. Innes, if nothing else, had pointed out the crossroads in my life. The time to decide upon a new direction was fast looming.

9

Verging upon Fame

STUART BEING so totally dependent upon Pam and me meant that we had two options when I travelled to races. Throughout the early days of our relationship, I attended meetings abroad regardless. But I was able to provide treats. One treat that was always refreshing was a day out when the three of us went to Lydden Hill where the real grass roots of club racing were alive and kicking. The Kent circuit, just outside Dover, was very reminiscent of Brands Hatch during the 'fifties — all ham pies, doughnuts and ginger beer affably served from a catering hut. Lovely!

Apart from a handful of Formula Ford and Formula Three drivers who had raised a modicum of sponsorship from a local publican or car dealer, competitors at Lydden raced on shoe-string budgets at their own expense.

Because Stuart was bound to a wheelchair, Lydden Hill was an ideal venue to take him where officialdom showed a more lenient attitude and was helpful in allowing him to mingle among the racers in the paddock. We could push him safely around and catch up with friends like Folkestone's proverbial 'Rear-lieutenant' Roger Hurst, who gained national notoriety from being the keenest and most enthusiastic tail-ender more times than he actually won races! Then we rooted for Lennie Marchant, the glass fibre fabricator from Hastings. He and Bob Curl occasionally shared a Formula Ford. It was in this unsullied atmosphere that Pam became enamoured with motor racing. I couldn't accuse her of being a groupie who hitched her star onto mine as the provider of a meal ticket to the Grands Prix. But it was good for me that she enjoyed the camaraderie at club level.

When Pam's parents were confident enough to handle Stuart and care for him for short terms, Pam and I felt able to venture further afield. We attended the late Graham Hill Trophy meeting at Silverstone in April 1976. At the recommendation of Bob Curl, we stayed with Mr and Mrs Tyrrell, a farming family who worked Silverstone Fields. The weekend was so pleasant and relaxed that I wondered why it had taken me so long to find their haven of horticultural peace so close to the circuit. What luxury to lie in bed each morning, listening to the distant thunder of snarled traffic jammed along the Towcester road. Having breakfast with the farmer and his family as practice started was taking liberties to the nth degree. Silverstone took on a completely different complexion when we were able to stay with the Tyrrells.

The meeting served to remind me of how Graham Hill had retired from driving to manage his own racing team. The height of irony was that after so many years at the wheel he should have died in November 1975 in a flying accident.

For the life of me I cannot recall when I actually heard the news of a Piper Aztec light aircraft that had crashed in dark, fog-laden hours on the Arkley Golf Course when the plane was on its final approach to the airfield at Elstree. When Graham's death registered, I felt absolutely nothing, and yet I had known Graham Hill since those early days when he attended the racing school at Brands Hatch. Pam, I know, wondered at my rather po-faced attitude to his death. *Autosport* printed a colour picture of Graham on the front cover of the magazine as a tribute to him. Tony Brise who died in the same accident was contracted to drive the Embassy-Hill Formula One car which they had spent that fateful day testing at Paul Ricard in the South of France.

I remember purchasing that issue of *Autosport* and spending many long moments gazing at the photograph, trying to analyse my feelings. Graham appeared indestructible, and yet I felt a sensation of relief. I lingered over the familiar moustache, the long greying hair and the piercing eyes. I did not feel sorrow for Graham. That magnificent face had lived a thousand lives. I felt that Graham was reaching a compromise with life. Racing had so long been the energy, now it was spent. He would have to content himself in a supporting role, living in the reflected glory of his driver Tony Brise. After being so long the star turn, Graham was ill-suited to the chores of being a team manager. It bruised his ego. I felt that he should have retired completely from motor racing and taken a place in public life.

Tony's potential died with Graham, which was sad — Tony was realising his niche. Graham had provided the ideal role model for youngsters. Anything less would have tarnished a perfect career. I felt for Bette, his wife, and their children as I looked at that photograph. It is always those who are left behind who suffer the most in these circumstances. Graham had spotted latent star quality in Tony Brise and quickly signed him with Embassy-Hill. Tony along with other members of the team like Ray Brimble, Andy Smallman, Terry Richards and Tony Alcocks also died with the legendary man. Tom and Nella Pryce urged me to visit Tony's wife Janet at their home in Old Bexley. It was strange under the sombre circumstances to return to my familiar childhood roots. Not that Old Bexley had changed much, because I soon discovered the Brises home without stopping to ask directions to the road. I found Janet at home alone, still silent in her grief. Her face wore the vacant expression of a person in deep mourning. Janet, a very attractive young woman, was surprised to see me. After a warm embrace, the emotion burst out as we sat in the lounge. I had not known the Brises very well, but as Janet dabbed the tears from her eyes she unselfishly wondered at how Nella Pryce would cope in the future, knowing that the birthday of her good friend fell upon the very day Tony had died. Ironically, much later when time had healed the emotional wounds, the two girls created Pryce & Brise Antiques, a business that dealt with 18th and 19th Century glass, furniture and decorative items from a shop in south-west London. After the initial shock of my unexpected arrival in Old Bexley, Janet made a pot of tea. It was then she broached her concern for Bette Hill and the children at their home in Shenley. It was a strange encounter in a place I had known so well, and yet on that day I felt that I was an interloper upon a very private grief.

At Silverstone I met with Bette and was struck at how being made a widow changed a person in appearance. It was a heck of an ordeal for Bette, finding herself in an atmosphere she knew so well, where everybody was so kind and understanding. Somehow, the big hole left in her life was magnified as she visited the teams, knowing that the empty garage was set aside out of respect for Graham.

I muttered platitudes to Bette, then she brightened as she asked if I could rummage around in my photo-library for any spare photographs of Graham to add to a collection she was making. As if that day was not solemn enough, I had been requested by *Bilsport* to arrange an interview with Gunnar Nilsson, the promising Swedish driver who had been struck down by cancer. Somehow, I could have easily have walked away from motor racing there and then, my mood was so depressed. But Pam's enthusiasm to witness her first Formula One was such that we, of course, stayed at Silverstone. Apart from odd moments, I have no recollection of that Sunday at all.

If my enthusiasm for motor racing was on the wane, Pam (having experienced the sight and sound of 'real racing' for the first time) was keen for more. Pam is an intelligent lady, whose opinion over the years I have learnt to respect. If I had ever doubted feminine intuition, I found this valuable asset in a woman aplenty in Pam. She reckoned that I was foolish to consider retiring from the sport — not just for her new form of recreation, although it was clear that she gained much enjoyment from being involved. But she reckoned that I should remain in the bosom of the 'Grand Prix' family because it was the subject which I knew best.

However, Pam also respected that I had other fields of endeavour to conquer. So while the going was good, Pam ensured that she was in tow for some of the European assignations.

A sign of change came in two distinct decisions during the summer of 1976. Firstly, we had a hankering to move from Kent and to seek a new home somewhere along the south coast of England. The second turning point came when Pam spotted an advertisement in the *Sunday Telegraph*, Chay Blyth and his partner Robert James were looking for a crew to work his ketch *Great Britain II* in the 1977-78 Whitbread Round-the-World Race. Was my beloved lady trying to make a point? Whatever was in the back of her mind, I took the first opportunity in three years of our knowing each other to arrange for Pam to travel abroad with me. Bertil Scanell of Scandinavian Raceway invited us to be his personal guests at the Swedish Grand Prix to assist with publicity.

We sailed on Swedish Lloyd's good ship *Saga* from Tilbury to Gothenburg. It was a short but romantic voyage of 36 hours across the North Sea when we enjoyed the luxury of a twin first-class cabin and meals at the Captain's table. I treated this trip as a busman's holiday. Volvo in Gothenburg had kindly offered to provide us with an estate car, so we took a leisurely drive through the back lanes of Jonkoping to the small village of Gnosjo where Bertil had arranged for us to stay with Stig and Janeth at their home near Anderstorp.

Before attending the practice for the Grand Prix, we decided to spend a 'free day' in Karlskrona, the historic port on the Baltic coast. After exploring the gracious old town, we went boating and swimming before relishing a late lunch in a restaurant that overlooked the tall ship *Jarramas* tied alongside in the natural harbour. Swedish summers may not generate the fiery heat associated with the mediterranean climate, but this did not detract from the romance and enjoyment of my walk along the waterfront with Pam. At last, for the first time in our co-habitation, I was actually 'courting' the lady of my life.

To be honest, I could have remained in Karlskrona for a week, but we returned to Anderstorp for a Royal reception presided over by HRH Prince Bertil in the Sportshallen. Our host was a real motor racing enthusiast, who at this time lent his position and name to the Swedish Grand Prix which was under governmental threat as a 'dangerous sport'.

After this formal occasion, we then sped through forest roads under the glow of the midnight sun to join Mo and Sylvia Nunn for dinner at the High Chaparral Hotel. Over a typically bland Swedish meal, Mo suggested that Pam and I should travel to the Grand Prix with Team Ensign in exchange for some public relations. At this time Team Ensign were not setting the world alight with a string of victories. But I had a great deal of admiration for Mo and his small Midland team, so I mulled over an idea. I could attend races with different teams to secure the 'inside story' of each Grand Prix from the viewpoint of either the driver, the sponsor, the team manager or the mechanics. It was a package which I felt confident would attract the attention of editors. So Mo suggested that we attend the Dutch Grand Prix with Team Ensign. I promised him a reply at the British Grand Prix. As further encouragement, there was a glint in Mo's eye at this invitation. Little did I know, but the cheeky Cannock Chaser was hatching a plot to lure Jacky Ickx into the team.

Up to the point of the Swedish Grand Prix, the 1976 season had been dominated by Ferrari, especially Niki Lauda — who had won the Grand Prix at Interlagos, Kyalami, Zolder and Monaco. James Hunt, in a quest to seek the World Championship had signed for Marlboro-McLaren. His chances of securing the title looked extremely slim at Anderstorp. Apart from a very controversial victory at Jarama, the Woking team were down on their luck. Although Sweden was not a portent of events to come, it provided a race that went against the norm. The 'swamp circuit' favoured the Tyrrell-Ford. They had scored a one-two in 1974 when Jody Scheckter and Patrick Depailler made a clean sweep, and who would have guessed that a revolutionary six wheeled design inspired by Derek Gardener would supply a repeat performance? Nobody could see the wisdom of having four front wheels, but Anderstorp was the proof of the pudding.

After the race I drove a red-hot typewriter at the local offices of *Varnomo Nyether*, the regional newspaper that had enlisted my services each year as their 'Grand Prix Correspondent' for race week. *Bilsport* had a deadline, having held two pages for me for their July issue. I had a feature for *Cars and Car Conversions* on Bo Emmanuelsson, the bearded Viking who drove angry American sedans in the national saloon car championships. I was sending photographs back to England for the British Grand Prix programme and had one other column to write for *Bil* the Norwegian tabloid. Later on I joined the editorial staff of *Bilsport* for dinner at the ranch.

All my best laid-plans to whisk Pam off to Norway for a week's break almost came undone in the Swedish forests. Outside the High Chaparral stood a single fuel pump which I engaged to fill the Volvo in anticipation of the run from Anderstorp to Oslo. I had poured a couple of litres into the cavernous tank when a man came running out of his hut screeching at me to stop. It was just as well — I was filling up with diesel, something a normally aspirated petrol car chokes upon. So I drove like a demented creature around the car park in order to mix what remained in the tank before venturing forth into the twilight zone. Fortunately, my desperate zig-zagging worked and the hardy Volvo engine gulped the last few litres without a hiccup!

Next day, Pam and I drove north into Norway. We had the facility of a friend's holiday home in Fredrikstad which overlooks the rocky shores of the Skagerrak, In those days Norway was considered far too expensive for all but the most well-heeled British holidaymaker, which explained why the handful of people among the rock pools and coves were either natives or richly endowed Swedes.

The sun was warm enough to bathe nude, so we frolicked with the honey-coloured Scandinavians in the refreshing sea. We also discovered one of the best Chinese restaurants north of the Great Wall.

All too soon we had to wend our way back to Oslo where I had arranged to meet with Jon Winding-Sorensen, the editor of *Bil* newspaper. We enjoyed occasional 'pay-day' conversations during the course of a year at the charming old-fashioned Theatre Café on Karl Johangaten. Jon played out a set ritual which was typically Norwegian. We indulged a form of high-calorie tea which was composed of huge creamy buns and cakes, a samovar of tea liberally punctuated with fiery toasts taken with schnapps — a most enjoyable and heart-warming ritual in the cold winter months, but not something I savoured so much in the warm days of high summer. Nevertheless, only after this habitual bloatation did Jon, almost as an afterthought, empty his pockets of crinkly kroner notes by way of my payment. Since a litre of beer was then around £4.00 and my remuneration was commensurate with the Norwegian cost of living, as his British correspondent I did well, the more so since he never bothered to count the money so I invariably ended up with a tidy percentage of 'interest', full of glutinous confectionery and a mellow mood after toasting our working relationship on numerous occasions. This aspect of my work served to provide an insight into the minds of various nationalities.

For me, Norway was enigmatic when it came to affairs of motor sport.

Various provincial clubs organised rallies amid the tremendous forest regions that abound the country. There was winter ice racing while that larger-than-life Oslonian, Tom Cornelissun annually promoted and organised the racing car show. Every motoring event was invariably over-subscribed by eager competitors while exhibitions were crammed with fans heaving to acquire pictures of Grand Prix drivers and bolt-on goodies and moon over the rare sight of a Formula One car on display.

Jon's little tabloid was avidly read the entire length of the geographically slim-line country. In 1977 plans were revealed of a racing circuit in the Ostfold region to the south-east of Oslo. I visited the location, talked with the circuit designers and then broke the exciting story across the Scandinavian motoring press... all to no avail.

Until this day, Norway has still not placated the rampant enthusiasm for motor racing. I assume that during the 'seventies while Sweden ventured where the Norwegians feared to tread, they did not bother. At the time, a great deal of political upheaval was created in Norway when the Government was forced to resign after a national referendum voted against Norway joining the European Economic Community.

I half wondered whether Norwegian politics suffered a similar *malaise* to that in Sweden. I found a clue when I encountered Peter Ronningen, the Chairman of the Norwegian Winter Olympic Committee who placed the successful bid to secure the 1994 International Winter Olympics in Lillehammer. He told me that Norway was convinced that there is no business like 'snow' business. Peter was a motoring enthusiast himself and a gentleman farmer.

Until Sweden was forced to succumb to Governmental pressure in banning the Grand Prix after 1978, Finland and Denmark upheld the great sporting traditions with rallying in Finland along with purpose-built car-racing circuits at Haemmenlinna and Keimola. One of Finland's early racing heroes in the 'fifties was Nina Rindt's father, Kurt Lincoln, who drove in Formula Two and sports car races.

Long before the Latin verb which translated means 'I roll' made Volvo a worldwide name in car manufacturing, Denmark claimed a historic first during 1886 when Hammel designed a horseless carriage to commute between home and work. The contraption was pieced together by Hans Urban Johansen, an employee at Albert Hammel's engineering factory. The Hammel was powered by a two-cylinder, four-stroke engine that worked up a maximum speed of 6 mph. No wonder that it never went into production. It became known in Denmark as the 'lazyman's walker'. It was reliable enough to finish the 1954 London to Brighton Run.

* * *

The early 'seventies witnessed a certain amount of upheaval in my life. Dad had married a woman he met on the emotional 'rebound' of my mother's death. He introduced me to the lady when she came to visit us at Meopham. Straight away I had an uneasy feeling about the friendship. But it was not for me to intrude upon Dad's life. I should have been thankful that he might possibly spend the rest of his days in happiness. He married the lady and they moved to Rochester while I was living in Canada.

When I returned home I found that my new base was in Rochester. Although I harboured many a fond memory of the famous Medway town from my days there as a student, returning to the fortified city with its splendid castle and sprawling cathedral was not totally happy for me.

I did not relish the prospect of my step-mother. We clashed in personality and to add salt to the wound, I could see that Dad was not blissfully wed, either. So when everything came to a crashing conclusion, Dad found a small residence at West Kingsdown within earshot of Brands Hatch again.

At that stage I was still fancy-free, but during our short stay in Rochester I did become involved in a medium that had intrigued me. Harold Rogers opened BBC Radio Medway in Chatham during 1970. I saw the opportunity to get my feet wet in broadcasting, working alongside such polished professionals as Simon Dee and Jimmy Mac.

In between attending Grand Prix and Can-Am races during 1971 I trickled down to the studios in Chatham High Street, regularly to perform my own music programmes, make featurettes for the Breakfast Show and spend Saturday afternoons acting as Aunt Sally to the famous Mr Dee whose overwhelming vanity had been his downfall. I actually got on well with Simon and enjoyed our bouts of banter on the air when steadily I strengthened my spot and gave him a hard time. The caustic wit swapped between us may have been listened to by only one man and his proverbial dog, but it gave me invaluable experience for the future.

The funny thing about this 'hidden profession' was that Simon never knew that I was gallivanting around the world covering races. He assumed that I was like him, a lay-about, who sunned himself during the week and arrived at BBC Radio Medway to earn a crust. One week of appalling weather in July 1971, I returned from a Can-Am race in America, baked to a frazzle after five days of sunshine at temperatures reaching 100°F, and that really wound Mr Dee up. He looked extremely pale by comparison and voiced his jealousy on the air.

Back at West Kingsdown, we were akin to one side of a bookend. 'Red's Hostelry for Racing Drivers' was situated on the west side of the village along the A20 main London to Maidstone arterial road while we propped up the east side. A permanent resident at Red's was Tony Trimmer who embellished his racing career when he claimed an infamous win in the Formula Three race that was prelude to the Monaco Grand Prix in 1970. Tony's name then joined the list of illustrious Monaco winners who had thrust through the junior ranks to be spotted by the Grand Prix elite. Names like Jackie Stewart, Jean-Pierre Beltoise and Ronnie Peterson had been etched by the engraver on the famous trophy.

Under an avalanche of publicity Tony Trimmer returned to Red's modest accommodation, a real local hero. We fully expected that he would be reaping a 'down payment' on a mock tudor pile when Formula One team managers beat a path to the door. In reality, the level-headed Trimmer waited and fretted. Oh the telephone rang endlessly for a week with calls of congratulation from long-forgotten friends and colleagues in the racing game. But the familiar voices of John Cooper, Ken Tyrrell and Colin Chapman did not come humming down the line beckoning him for a test drive in a Grand Prix car. Instead all kinds of obscure calls from second-raters and notorious moonlighters filled his diary.

Tony and I met a month or so after Monaco to discuss where he had gone wrong. It was a tricky question, the more so since my managerial and diplomatic skills are practically nil. But I did pass on the suggestion that he should have trekked to Mahomet because mountains rarely move to offer a minion a favoured test drive. Tony sheepishly admitted that he should have struck while the iron was hot. As history will state, Tony Trimmer never carved a niche within the Grand Prix circus, which I thought was a shame. I consider that he was cast from the same dependable mould as drivers like Derek Bell and Derek Warwick — fast and reliable, a driver who at his best could hoodwink all of his opponents. Tony was plunged into the same pool as Alan Rollinson, Mike Beuttler, Bev Bond and Andy Sutcliffe, all potentially great British drivers who got overlooked when the dazzling talents of Emerson Fittipaldi and Jody Scheckter blitzed the scene. No wonder our 'maybe men' got disgruntled, and in many cases it was not for the want of trying. Money was beginning to speak, the day of the rent-a-drive was on the horizon.

There was another time when I happened to drop by Red's for a chat. She was a direct forthright woman who stood no nonsense from the lodgers. Red's acid tongue had licked many a wayward lad into shape. On this occasion she went on and on about a new resident she had begrudgingly taken in from Ruthin in Wales. Tom Pryce, who was the son of a police officer, had decided to make the bold move from within the bosom of the Welsh Hills, to pursue his astrological dream in the South-East of England. Red encouraged me to seek Tom, a pale streak of shyness who spent countless hours of solitary confinement in his bedroom. The lanky boy whose large soulful eyes peeked from beneath a cascade of dark hair greeted me with a ready, deeply etched grin. Red was right — Tom could barely string two words together in conversation, but those eyes betrayed a look of inner determination. The reticent Trimmer was by contrast positively gregarious!

I next saw Tom at Brands Hatch, driving a Motor Racing Stables single-seater. Chief Instructor Tony Lanfranchi was in the observation tower casting a critical eye upon the new-comer. The flamboyant Yorkshire tutor reckoned that Pryce showed a 'bit of spirit' at the wheel. It remained to be seen how his colours would shine in battle.

Geoffrey Clarke, the Managing Director of Motor Racing Stables, had capitalised upon many hundreds of pupils being processed through the school. I wondered if he had ear-marked a potential world champion. At that time, Clarke admitted that some hot-shoes had been spotted, but there was nobody they truly felt the company could invest in as a Formula One potential. Apparently, Tom Pryce was just another promising 'goer'. But they did keep a weather eye on the Welsh lad. Regrettably, I lost track of Tom for a while as I fulfilled commitments and continued to travel abroad to races. Now and then I read that he won occasional races. The armchair pundits started to type favourable comments upon their Remingtons.

On Good Friday in 1974, by way of a change I attended an international motorcycle meeting at Brands Hatch where a 'match' had been devised between top riders from Britain against a team from the United States. It was the sort of meeting when a great feeling of patriotism buoyed the crowd behind the national team.

Among the thousands creating the carnival atmosphere was Red, who was also relishing the change. Away from the house she was relaxed and talkative. To my surprise she told me of Tom's rise and said that Token, a privately entered Formula One team, were taking an interest in him. Naturally, my ears pricked up at this marvellous news. Then Red changed her tune slightly when she went on to say that she hoped his chances were not weakened by 'some bird' he was seeing regularly. This note of sarcasm was the first time I became aware of Nella. She lived with her family somewhere along the narrow undulating lanes in deepest Otford, hardly a stone's throw from West Kingsdown.

Much later on, after I had met with Nella, when Lady Diana Spencer hit the headlines with her courtship with HRH The Prince of Wales, I was struck by the amazing similarity in appearance between the two girls. It was obvious that Tom's natural shyness had been replaced by a quiet confidence that had undoubtedly grown with the progress of his racing. As he surged through the ranks of motor racing, pretty girls had taken note of the wistful Welshman. Judging from Red's comments, Tom was truly smitten. That day I watched the motorcycles with a heightened anticipation, and a resolve that I must contact Tom Pryce again.

During the 1974 season I had been assigned by *Fast Car* to attend the Grand Prix as their feature writer and columnist. In June I motored to Northampton to visit Alan Rees who had left March to become the team manager of the newly-established UOP Shadow racing team. Alan was the 'AR' in March when it was established by Robin Herd, Max Mosley and Graham Coaker in 1969. In his new position with Shadow, Alan was forever scrutinising the lower echelons of the sport looking for latent driving potential. His particularly sensitive antennae tuned in to Tom Pryce during the Belgian Grand Prix at Nivelles. There Tom was making the best fist he could with the Token-Ford. Alan zeroed upon the glimmer of an uncut diamond.

My meeting with Alan came just a week or so before the French Grand Prix moved on to yet another venue at the minuscule circuit of Dijon-Prenois.

The perpetually sullen features of the man who can safely lay claim to having encouraged the latent abilities of Jochen Rindt and Ronnie Peterson convulsed into a smile as we mulled over his most recent signing into the UOP Shadow team. Alan had done a deal with Chris Meek of Token Racing to release Tom Pryce so that he could sign a Shadow contract. At the very next race in Holland, Tom had set the racing world upon its ear with some blistering laps around Zandvoort during qualification. So the prospect of travelling with Shadow to the French Grand Prix had real significance. Rumour had it that Shadow's number one, French driver Jean-Pierre Jarier, felt that his nose had been disjointed by Tom's meteoric appearance in the team. Alan clearly relished giving the Frenchman something to stir his rancour, a feeling strengthened by the fact Tom was a chip off his own Welsh heritage.

Naturally, I was intrigued to learn how Tom attracted Alan's discerning eye, and wondered how Tony was overlooked after his Monaco win during 1970.

Rees posed a scenario. If I had the choice of Tony Trimmer and Ronnie Peterson, whom would I go for? I evaded the question and pursued the tack of encouraging British drivers, Alan pulled a familiar 'Punch' expression upon his recollection of Trimmer and conceded that he was a 'metronomic' driver, like many journeymen of the Derek Bell and Brian Redman ilk who ticked over reliably enough, but lacked the vital spark. Alan during his hey-day in Formula Two racing was a polished professional racing driver who drove well-prepared cars for Winkleman Racing, but like the metronomes, never stirred the blood. Perhaps this was the deciding factor in Rees's case — he was attracted to the animal aggression displayed by Rindt and Peterson. By that token, Tom Pryce was another red dragon, breathing fire and brimstone — and he was Welsh which must have added to the patriotic fervour.

I travelled with Geoff Chamberlain in the UOP Shadow transporter from Southampton to Le Havre. We rolled into Dijon-Prenois paddock in indian file with BRM and Embassy Racing team wagons. After Geoff had parked the monstrous Ford tractor-trailer, I was welcomed by a genial American who apologised for his hacking cough. Ben Williams was the International Racing Director for Universal Oil Products. On this initial encounter I was not so much concerned about his team, more for the general health of the man who co-ordinated an ambitious worldwide racing programme. Ben pointed to the blue haze that hung over Dijon and bundled me into the UOP motor home, glad to be out of the exhaust pollution. Over a beer, Ben cleared his tubes sufficiently to explain UOP's relationship with Don Nicholls and his Advanced Vehicle Systems — namely Shadow, which started in 1971 when the vast Chicago-based oil company invested in Can-Am racing. UOP were racing toward cleaner air with a new lead-free-fuel which their chemical division had concocted. It was a unique sponsorship in that UOP were not a consumer company loud-hailing a product. They entered motor sport as a mobile, public laboratory for the process development of the fuel which would ultimately be consumed by passenger cars — and in so doing, would help cure Ben's violent throat.

At Dijon Alan was looking to Jarier for a good result in front of his 'home' crowd. The French driver knew Dijon-Prenois well. The circuit was just over two miles and it contained a Scalextric type of back section. Considering that the host country boasted such magnificent road circuits as Rouen, Clermont-Ferrand and even neighbourly Reims, having the premier event at Dijon was a complete anathema to most racing teams.

Tom had been granted the services of Roger Silman and Paul Pimlott as his mechanics. Both men were spiritually down in the dumps after suffering the death earlier in the year of Peter Revson, who lost his life while testing at Kyalami. Roger confessed that if Tom qualified anywhere on the front six rows he would be 'chuffed' to bits. So imagine the ripple of contained excitement along the Shadow pitwall when Tom recorded a time that placed him on the front row of the grid beside Niki Lauda's Ferrari!

Over lunch, Tom was completely nonplussed by all the fuss. Then a report filtered into the motor home that flag marshals on post eight around the back of the course had reported that Tom's car was seen using more of the curbs and infield than was thought prudent!

Rees leered at Tony Southgate, the car's designer, and cursed the 'bloody frogs'. Tom confessed that he had allowed the car to drift over one curb with two wheels because Tony advised him that the car could take the punishment. It did not matter because Tom thought that he could equal the time over a modified line. Jean-Pierre was looking more than sheepish. This sort of come-uppance can rot a driver's confidence, especially on his home circuit.

During the final period of qualification, Alan had the unique emotion of seeing one protégé in Ronnie Peterson driving the John Player Special Lotus-Ford knock Tom from his perch onto the second row next to Clay Regazzoni's Ferrari.

The cook at the Hotel du Jura, where most of the Shadow team were staying in Dijon, had become accustomed to boiling Tom a three minute egg each morning. Alan's wife Debbie looked at me with raised eyebrows when Tom refused his treat in preference to a cup of tea. That Sunday morning he was mentally grappling with his achievement. Nella had no way of quelling his apprehension. I took the cue to sit with him in a quiet corner of the restaurant. The large doleful eyes stared deeply into my own.

'I want to go home', he whispered, 'I didn't think it would be like this'. The retiring young Welshman I had first encountered in West Kingsdown had retreated into his shell. Here was a rare insight into the mind of a driver coming to terms with his immeasurable ability. Quite honestly, at this nerve-wracking juncture, Tom had no comprehension of his skill and could not fathom why he could joust with men who were still his heroes. He invented all manner of excuses for Lauda and Peterson as if he wanted to evade the glorious reality. First, it was that the Ferrari must have qualified on a full fuel load. Then maybe they had the wrong tyres on. I quietly placed a hand on his shoulder and reassured him that his achievements were attained by his own merit. He looked aghast that I had not provided some sane excuse to release the horrible anguish. All that Tom needed to do was to nurse himself quietly into Formula One, find his level and given time he would have the beating of his opponents. Jackie Stewart indicated an understanding of Tom's predicament in being the 'rookie' at the head of the grid. 'I know just how you feel. Just play it cool, Tom; don't let the others fluster you. If you make a slow start, pullover, let them go past — there is no shame in that. Then you have the entire race to take your chances. You could finish in the first six'.

Tom looked at the World Champion, grinned broadly, said 'thanks' and indicated that he wanted me to join him in the motor home. 'Bloody hell', grinned Tom, 'Fancy Jackie Stewart talking to me like that. I reckon that was great'. It was fascinating to see that Tom had no knowledge that he was already one of the ten fastest men in the world. To have an object lesson from the man himself meant far more to him than anything else at that moment.

On the grid Tom looked cool as a cucumber, although he was far more concerned with the water temperature needle which was in the red. He was so preoccupied with this and keeping one eye on the flag that he forgot to note his revs. When the flag dropped, the Shadow lurched forward, the Cosworth coughed, then Tom felt he was hit twice. Fittipaldi's Marlboro-McLaren elbowed through on the inside which knocked Tom straight into James Hunt's Hesketh. Jarier had wisely hung back from all this drama. He lost places, but cruised through the race to finish in twelfth place.

Alan later sat down with Tom, who was forced to retire on the first lap, and reassured his driver that the weekend's work was well done. All that he had to learn now was to forget the instruments and just keep an eye on the rev-counter. The car would have cooled down in the race.

After a battle royal with Lauda's Ferrari, Ronnie Peterson won the race — which brought a glimmer to Alan's eyes. Ben was at first filled with disappointment. Later that night he informed us that his cars had won the Can-Am race: a small tonic, because he never coughed again all evening!

Tom secured his spurs with racing's elite at the German Grand Prix on the Nürburgring with a sixth place — his best in 1974, plus a single championship point. That single digit did not reflect the true impact he had made that season

Then early in 1975 came the Welshman's red-letter day. Tom won the Race of Champions for Formula One cars at Brands Hatch in front of John Watson's Surtees-Ford and the JPS-Lotus-Ford driven by Ronnie Peterson. The local boy had 'come good' and provided a rare excuse for all his mentors at Brands like Tony Lanfranchi, Syd Fox, Tony Trimmer and the Directors of Motor Racing Stables to push the boat out and virtually sink it in overwhelming delight while they claimed the 'schooling' of a future World Champion. The only person absent from this rumbustious occasion was Tom. He had quietly slipped away to Otford for a more sober evening with Nella, his wife-to-be.

Having scaled such a peak, one would have imagined that Tom could turn the other cheek upon the world. Not Tom — vanity and conceit were foreign to his nature. Next day I called into Red's with a sheaf of national British newspapers emblazoned with stories and pictures of a 'new star'. Red pointed up the stairs, indicating that 'his nibs' was still coccooned in slumberland while she was cursing to high heaven because the telephone hadn't stopped ringing all the morning. I found Tom in his room. The curtains were tightly drawn, there were no lights on and he was just lying there hardly daring to rise. He castigated me for tossing the newspapers on his bed. Instead of being exultant, Tom was traumatised by his first taste of fame. If Red thought Tony

Trimmer's Formula Three win at Monaco posed a blatant intrusion upon the privacy of her household, having a Formula One lodger was a declaration of outright war. It was perhaps fortunate for Red's peace of mind (give me a regular Formula Ford nobody any day) that Tom made Nella an honest woman and they invested his mounting income in a secluded period house nestled amid trees near Ightham in Kent.

Apart from his coup in the Race of Champions for UOP Shadow, Tom had a jittery start to his Grand Prix season in 1975. Eventually, he showed sufficient form against the more nimble McLaren, Ferrari and Tyrrell-Fords by accumulating eight points from the Belgian, Dutch, German, Austrian and Italian Grand Prixs.

In spite of his busy schedule of races and testing, Pam and I saw a lot of the newly-wed couple. They often turned up with a cheery. 'What's New' at our house in Vigo for a morning 'cuppa' and enjoyed Pam's home-cooked evening meals. Away from the ballyhoo, Tom relaxed completely. For intrinsically Welsh reasons, he was immensely proud of his new-found status. He had proved that a lad from the hills could succeed, given the platform to show his undoubted ability. His fervent hope was that 'his doings' inspired more of his countrymen who saw very little beyond a rugby ball, Glamorgan Cricket Club and Max Boyce. Apart from that, we rarely discussed motor racing.

At this early stage of the nuptials, Nella picked Pam's brain on the co-ordination of draperies against furnishings while Tom and I talked about subjects ranging from photography to Stuart's well being. In June that year we indicated that a move was afoot, and that Pam and I were scouring the south coast for a home overlooking the sea. Tom and Nella often spent days at Hastings, meandering along the promenade and exploring the Fire Hills. We had a feeling that had it not been for the congested A21 coast road, they might have considered a place in East Sussex.

As a character study, I was fascinated to witness the gradual metamorphosis of Tom Pryce. Marriage clearly suited him and Nella provided the important sheet anchor to his nomadic life-style in racing. Nella had a cultured upbringing, her emotions were strongly disciplined. But in off-guard moments, I detected a concern for Tom's survival in a sport which she privately thought was damned idiotic. In spite of that opinion, she did nothing to change the man she loved.

The young man who cowered in the glare of triumph in the Race of Champions became totally at home with his new-found status. The world treated him well and he was level-headed enough to see through all the 'bull-shit' of celebrity that attended the Grand Prix driver. In this respect Tom Pryce, private citizen, could accept the plaudits at a race meeting, and still walk virtually unnoticed along the High Street. He enjoyed the best of both worlds. When I informed him in 1976 that I was considering the idea of becoming a member of the crew on a deep-ocean racing yacht in the 1977-78 Whitbread Round-the-World Race, he looked incredulous. 'You must be mad, you'll kill yourself.'

Such words of wisdom uttered by a racing driver smacked of contradiction.

10

Goodbye Brands – Hello Bexhill

BRITAIN WAS sweltering through the furnace-like summer of 1976 when the British Grand Prix graced the brown and parched undulations of Brands Hatch. The severity of those long hot days had prompted the Government to publish a Drought Bill informing the bronzed population how to ration water over the hottest period, apparently, in 250 years.

On the same July weekend, Her Majesty The Queen declared the official entrée to the Summer Olympic Games in Montreal. Fortunately for the Royal Automobile Club, race fans thought twice about staying at home to watch television and cheer on the British Olympians. Instead, they trusted the torrid weather conditions and festooned acres of farmland surrounding the Kent circuit with a patchwork of tents and caravans. Watkins Glen had never witnessed 'camp-town' of such proportions. Amid sauna-like temperatures the great perspiring British public and a goodly selection of Europeans arrived scantily clad, billy-cans full, ready for a weekend of sport.

Since Brands Hatch was to be my last 'working' British Grand Prix, I took the opportunity on the Thursday before the meeting to amble around the entire circuit to savour the pre-race atmosphere. The huge temporary grandstands of scaffolding were already in place and numbered. Flags and bunting were being ceremoniously hoisted. I watched the man titivate the curbstones with fresh paint while another fellow went over the white lines to outline the circuit for the umpteenth time. The last bristles of the burnt grass on the club circuit were being mown as I walked under the bridge onto the Grand Prix circuit.

I helped to peg out canvas advertising banners at Hawthorn Bend. In the hot conditions a mobile road sprinkler was damping down the road surface. The BBC were positioning their television cameras on platforms and towers ready to transmit to a nationwide audience and far beyond.

All the way round the circuit, deep gouges on the road were tell-tale evidence of horrendous accidents. Black tyre marks described lurid excursions by errant cars. In the hollows of Paddock Bend, Pilgrim's Drop and Dingle Dell, a multi-coloured strip of under-bellies had been scraped where cars had bottomed out — a terrifying reminder of 1971 when a Formula One race was held in honour of Jackie Stewart's second World Championship, In a hectic race Jo Siffert's Yardley-BRM went out of control on the approach to Haw-

143

thorn Bend, I stood paralysed as the car slew out of high-speed control and crashed heavily into the bank in front of me. The BRM had turned upside down, Seppi was trapped in a blazing inferno from which he never survived. The haunting image of Jo's pyre against the background of his fellow competitors who had pulled up in their racing cars behind a marshals red flag on Pilgrims Drop, helpless witnesses to Jo's sacrifice, had a devastating effect upon me.

Away from that poignant spot, activity abounded over the spectator enclosures as caterers erected ice cream kiosks and marquee bars, jacked up mobile burger joints, souvenir shops and temporary toilet facilities. The prelude to the Grand Prix on the 'home circuit' always awakened the senses, none the more so than in 1976. It was not quite the case of 'goodbye to all that', but I felt a sensation of tranquillity mixed with a feeling of relief. I had made the decision to get off the merry-go-round while the music remained jaunty and the ride as enjoyable as ever.

The priorities of motor racing had, during my career, changed from fairly carefree to a growing attitude of responsibility. Safety had come to dictate the camera angles and spoil the view. I had no complaints, only that progress for me had eaten into an inspiration born at the time of *Genevieve*. The constant relationship I shared with the course and flag marshals was still strong. I wanted to depart after this last British Grand Prix with inspired work which the faithful Pentax had recorded during my career. The marshals were to grant me that final gesture by allowing me to pitch-up in restricted territory. I vowed that every shot was going to be a masterpiece. Brands Hatch had rarely looked so attractive decked out in its Sunday best. The portent to my turning a new leaf came after weeks spent with Pam viewing many likely properties in coast towns like Folkestone, Rye, Hastings and Eastbourne. We finally settled our choice in Bexhill-on-Sea only days before the Grand Prix.

An atmosphere of reckless abandonment echoed about Brands Hatch throughout the two days of qualification before 'Mad Sunday' dawned. The tribal instinct more familiar to soccer matches communicated itself between the packed terraces of the natural amphitheatre and the seething industry constricted within the crowded pit lane and Formula One Paddock shoe-horned onto the infield. Rarely had I witnessed such a barbarous passion in British motor sport. This was sixteen years before Nigel-Mansell-mania. Such volatile enthusiasm was expressed at San Marino and certainly in the Monza cauldron. But at Brands Hatch, where the only known war cry was 'lick your pencils girls' until 1976, the Kent circuit had been a venue of rectitude. The crowd were braying for British domination as pole position was tensely fought out between Niki Lauda's Ferrari and our Adonis gladiator James Hunt in the Marlboro McLaren-Ford. The Austrian claimed the sweaty honour, which left a feeling amid the pulsating throng of 'wait and see' when true battle commenced.

A salivating press had drummed up a fierce patriotic fervour, Hunt was the catalyst, while Lauda was depicted as the prancing interloper.

During the practice days I had quietly spoken with the start-line marshals about photographing the start of the Grand Prix from the gantry which then over-hung the grid. Officially, I knew that such a facility was absolutely prohibited, which made the request all the more compulsive from my point of view. Practically every camera angle at Brands Hatch had been exploited. Nevertheless, I had the nod-and-wink from the gentlemen marshalling the area. They would allow me to mount the steps as the cars bellowed off to complete the warming-up lap.

So much drama surrounds the start of a Grand Prix that my unofficial move would have gone unnoticed by the RAC hierarchy. But as history has eloquently stated, the 1976 British Grand Prix provided a two-act drama of cataclysmic proportions. Act One witnessed the howling pack catapult off the start line with Lauda a nose in front. I secured some tremendous pictures and was scuttling down the gantry steps when I caught the eye of Dean Delamont, who in the role of Julius Caesar presided over the meeting, I was braced for an admonition when a greater priority distracted the emperor's attention.

The scene became chaos at the approach to Paddock Bend, when everybody wrote their own variation of the theme, Photographic evidence suggested that Regazzoni's Ferrari stepped out of line and effectively slammed an iron door against Hunt's McLaren which in turn launched James into precarious orbit. The outcome produced stultified panic in the race committee's watch-tower. Before the dust had settled and the blue tyre smoke had cleared, James had landed amid a sea of red flags, effectively stopping the race — for what reason only the powers-that-be could judge. Within the time that it took for Lauda to complete his first lap, the road was clear of debris. Only the air was rife with unsporting indignation as drivers, team managers and Uncle Tom Cobley descended upon the RAC Race Committee demanding an explanation.

Amidst the bureaucratic mayhem, Hunt steadily trundled an ailing McLaren along the Bottom Straight to retire behind the pits. The crowd of some 80,000 could hardly believe their good fortune. Act Two was being hurriedly programmed, thus providing Hunt with another bite of the cherry... but that was before Mr Delamont and his courtiers had their say in the proceedings. The McLaren team had substituted Hunt's race car for a spare; but according to the ten commandments, such sleight of hand was forbidden. So officially James was out of the re-started race

Oh woe is the tainted memory of my last working British Grand Prix when race commentator Anthony Marsh announced this early demise of the star. The collective vocal reaction by the indignant crowd who had paid honest cash to see James Hunt trounce the opposition was overwhelming. Fists flayed the air. If 'people power' was going to have a bearing upon the event, then each and every one of the aggrieved fans chanted an ever louder chorus: 'WE WANT HUNT'. It worked. Dean Delamont and his incapable men were verbally bludgeoned into reinstating Hunt's position in the race. While the RAC bowed to public opinion, their collective attitude was 'so be it' — we'll disqualify Hunt should he win or end up in the championship points'.

When Marsh made the papal statement over the public address, a massive cheer for justice reverberated around the Kentish hills. By now I had wandered up to another vantage point at Druids Hill Bend where I felt the power of the masses rain upon me in a sea of sound and jubilant faces.

As every record book amply illustrated, James Hunt sprayed the winner's champagne over the photographers from the victory rostrum. He was then disqualified from the result which could have spoilt his World Championship chances that season. Niki Lauda was hailed the new winner of the second Brands Hatch farce. The famous Whitehall Theatre in London could not have staged a greater laughing stock. But around the corner in Pall Mall, the Royal Automobile Club were now the acknowledged impresarios for orchestrating gigantic cock-ups!

That evening Pam and I joined Mo and Sylvia Nunn for dinner at the Tollgate Hotel near Gravesend. Mo thought that the whole event was a huge hoot. He understood my embarrassment and sadness that the home race had not emerged as a classic event, which I would have preferred as a lasting memory of the circuit closest to my heart. So I drew a curtain over the comic opera as we relished the prospect of attending the Dutch Grand Prix with Team Ensign and working alongside Jacky Ickx. When Mo offered transport, Pam and I declined gracefully. We had decided that when in Holland we would go 'dutch' on our journey to Zandvoort.

* * *

Pam and I had spent the summer of 1976 enjoying house-hunting expeditions along the coast of Kent and East Sussex. There was a wild moment when we wistfully considered a move to Cumbria. That idea was knocked upon the head when I discovered that Pam was very much a 'townee' who enjoyed the bustle of life about her. Until then, my options of choice had been wide open until we narrowed the area down to the coast. At least once a week, we would drive to places like Folkestone, Rye and Eastbourne, loaded down with estate agents paraphernalia and gandering around what sounded suitable to our price. All this was extremely new and untried territory for me, Pam found it unbelievable that I had reached the grand age of 36 years and had never so much as taken a sniff at the housing market and all the pit-falls of entering into such transactions. So during our explorations I was very much the 'passenger' peering about places and accepting them on a purely aesthetic premise rather than delving into the practicalities of living in such places.

One day Pam dropped me in Bexhill-on-Sea while she went and examined some houses in Hastings. Bear in mind that this was during the blazing hot summer, so no sooner had Pam driven off, I sat down and contemplated all around me while looking out to the sea. On those balmy days, the thought of finding somewhere overlooking the coast was extremely seductive. However, common sense had to prevail, so I turned my head and faced upon the elegant parade of Marine Mansions that overlooked the De La Warr Parade. To my astonishment I spotted several estate agent's boards proclaiming that certain properties were on the market, Almost without thinking, I instinctively felt that I had found 'home'. Straight away I sought the agent concerned, and gained access to a variety of apartments — some lofty and very much the rich man's hidey-hole, others small, cosy which just fitted the bill. One in particular was 21 Carlton Court which had unaccountably stood empty for some considerable time. I couldn't believe that such a delightful little eyrie had not won somebody's heart. Mind you, it was totally impractical. There was no lift and in order to reach the third floor, one had to mount 58 steps! My dream was shattered when I considered Stuart's disability, and so I discounted the probability that Pam would even give it a second look.

When we were reunited, she was utterly fed-up. Her visit to Hastings had been fruitless, so I casually murmured the idyllic little escape route at the top of the stairs. I must have struck a nerve. She ignored the inconvenience of the stairs, and we looked around the lounge and kitchen overlooking the sandy shore line and the Good Lord Rocks. The bathroom was ample for our needs, the spare bedroom functional and the main bedroom ample for us with its view of the Gullivers' Bowling Greens. Just to indicate how unpredictable this chosen lady of mine could be, she smiled approval and my heart sang.

Come August, my mind was so preoccupied with all things domestic that I set aside the German and Austrian Grands Prix without so much as looking over my shoulder. We had at last found a little home of our choice. At this late stage in life, I was blissfully happy. Of course we had to mull over the immediate priorities for Stuart whose life since I had known him was being cast between places like Great Ormond Street Hospital in London and various homes and hospitals in our endeavour to improve his quality of life. East Sussex had an ample choice of special schools and homes where he could seek proper treatment and physiotherapy to meet with his needs at this stage.

His long-term future was of greater concern. But as I said to Pam, once we got Stuart established within the local system, then surely by some onward-going theme, his needs within the community would be set for the rest of his life. We realised that Number 21 was somewhat impractical, but did not allow this to colour our new choice of home.

Before we moved from Vigo, there came a point where Pam reckoned that it would be advisable to meet with her parents, Hilda and Alan Larkin who lived in the commuter belt at Petts Wood, Kent. Alan had spent most of his life gainfully employed at the Danish Bacon Company, working from their offices in Cowcross Street, London. Hilda was enlisted by Stanley Gibbons, the international philatelists based in London's Strand. They were a solid couple who courted and married when the vows honestly meant something. Without question, they accepted our co-habitation and provided Pam and me with considerable understanding and support. After her first broken marriage and the sad development of Stuart, the Larkins, I believe, were content to see their daughter happy as we attempted to start life afresh in Bexhill. Next we had to seek the approval of Dad. Several months had passed since I had strayed from our common home in West Kingsdown. Although I was still using it as my postal address, after moving in with Pam I rarely mentioned my whereabouts, although I felt sure that Dad had surmised I had found somebody to live and share a form of domestic life with. It was difficult. On the one hand Dad — and, of course, Mum — had brought me up to study the 'family values' of marriage, while the idea of couples living together and even rearing children were definitely beyond their ken.

One evening I drove to West Kingsdown and gradually informed Dad about Pam, about where I had been living and about our future plans. Dad didn't actually broach the subject of marriage, having just suffered the break-down of his second relationship. He probably thought that co-habiting wasn't such a bad idea. However, I asked him to visit us at Vigo for dinner one even-ing, and he was thrilled. Now the ice had been broken on all sides to a vary-ing degree. Rather selfishly, I felt more at ease with myself and with Pam. Although we had survived the permissive 'sixties, I still felt awkward as I attempted to inform parents born just after the turn of the century, what co-habiting was all about. Fortunately, they could see Pam and I were obviously in love, that we cared for Stuart and were all but married at that stage. We felt that everybody was content to allow the relationship to take a natural course without exerting any pressure upon us to 'do the right thing'. By the time we had decided upon our abode in Bexhill, the town house in Vigo had been sold. Pam was blessed with a good brain, and she reckoned that we had a bet-ter bargaining lever when it came to purchasing another property with the cash-in-hand. So when the time approached for us to relinquish the house in Vigo, I hired a truck and we physically moved the furniture into temporary storage in Hastings while the deal on Number 21 went through. During that two-month limbo, we 'lodged' with Alan and Hilda. This was a period that could have made or broken a beautiful love affair. In reality, it was an inter-lude during which I was versed by Alan on the vagaries of buying-and-selling property.

Throughout this time, certain colleagues in motor racing had wondered about my whereabouts. When I politely informed them of my plans, gasps of disbelief were forthcoming. They had only known me as a gallivanting bache-lor and surmised that I would return to my pleasure seeking tendencies when my attention focussed back on motor sport. They grossly under estimated my love for Pam and my yearning to turn over a new leaf.

There was a single previous occasion when I visited Bexhill. A page in a fusty diary mentions a day when during the summer of 1957 a coach-load of us from Medway College went for a treat to Hastings. Blond, blue-eyed Penny of the dress department was the light of my 17-year-old life. She must have found me a dreadful bore not wishing to patronise the candy floss, the slot machines and the fair ground attractions on Hastings Pier. Instead we spent the entire day strolling along the beach to Bexhill and back. Lovely Penny remained a discreet distance from me after that trudge and frankly, in my mature years, I can't say that I blamed her!

Bexhill grew from the little Saxon village of 'Bexle'. The 'Old Town' remains perched at the summit of Upper Sea Road where St Peter's Church marks the location on the skyline. The original Manor House was owned until 1963 by Sir Leicester Harmsworth, a member of the Northcliffe family whose forefather, Alfred Harmsworth, had founded Associated Newspapers.

Two other items of Bexhill's recent past had served to maintain in my mind an awareness of the place before we moved there. I was a dedicated fan of BBC Radio's 'Goon Show' which starred Harry Secombe, Peter Sellers and Spike Milligan. The post-Second World War programme was a pastiche of British humour at its most zany. Since then I have read many books written by Gunner Spike Milligan 954024 who for some misguided reason put the blame upon William the Conqueror, joined the 56th Heavy Regiment of the Royal Artillery who were posted to Bexhill during the summer months shortly after war broke out.

Some of the 'old buffers' still emerge for the annual reunion when elaborate yarns of the war are colourfully embellished in bars and clubs along the promenade. Their eyes twinkle when they recalled the WVS Forces recreation centre on the apex of Sea Road and Cantelupe. Local girls were often 'chatted up' and coerced with Woodbine fags offered in Players packets and promises of romps in haystacks in fields between Sidley and Ninfield.

There was categorically no truth in the malicious rumours that the regiment got so bored at night that they raced anything on wheels along the De La Warr Parade after dark without lights on. Spike spent twelve years trying to persuade HRH The Prince of Wales to be a guest at one of the reunions in the Manor Barn. Against enormous odds, The Goons' most staunch royal fan arrived in Bexhill for a private men only knees-up as the guest of honour in 1989!

While we were betwixt and between abodes, I often put up at Bob Curl's newly acquired house in Brede, a small village outside Hastings. On one of my 'sorties' to Bexhill to measure up Number 21 and dust it down, Bob blithely reminded me of Frank Nichols the founder of Elva Cars. I was aware that Elva's roots were in Bexhill but had not cottoned on to the fact that Frank was a true Bexhillian, the fourth child in a production line of seven Nicholette's. His father was 'Pop' Nichols who made a living as the Longley's van driver, delivering goods for the large family store that stretched along the east side of Devonshire Road.

Shortly after Prime Minister Neville Chamberlain announced that 'Britain is now at war with Germany' in September 1939, Frank was called up and recruited to the Territorials. The Army posted him to serve at El Alamein then later he was wounded in action outside Benghazi. He suffered semi-paralysis for almost two years before making a gutsy recovery. Along with thousands who survived, Frank was demobbed in 1945 to be welcomed back home by his girlfriend, Joy. The couple married a year later and they set up home in Bexhill.

Frank ploughed his army gratuity into a small garage at Pevensey before moving into a workshop on London Road, Bexhill. For six years he accumulated money in the murky waters of the second-hand car market during which time he pursued a growing enthusiasm for motor racing — nothing too serious, but he pottered around some 'clubbies' with a Lotus 6, and accounted for himself quite well.

Another local fanatic was Mike Chapman, who was then labelled the 'inventive jackdaw' because he collected car parts from which he built road Specials to order. Frank spotted potential and asked Mike to make a 'Chapman Sports Motor'. The CSM bore a remarkable similarity to the Lotus 6. Colin Chapman's cars were the trail blazers in their class, and realising some opposition appear on the scene, he accused Frank for blatantly copying the model.

Ever since I had known Frank in the 'sixties, he was rarely without his cloth cap, which epitomised his barrow-boy mentality. The demeanour was totally at odds with Bexhill's rather cultivated and sometimes pompous ambience among the opulent residents. One minute he would give you an affectionate hug, then in a trice the mood would swing to a 'full nelson'. So when Colin Chapman kicked up a stink, Frank delivered a verbal upper-cut and told the Lotus boss to 'get bloody stuffed'. After that stinging riposte, any acrimony between Lotus and Frank was decided on the circuits in competition. In this mood, he seriously considered starting production of his own kit cars from the London Road garage behind the fish and chip shop.

Throughout 1954 the CSM with more 'mods and tweaks' was deemed the fastest 1100 cc sports racing car in Britain. Frank sold the 'beasty' in order to start his own business.

The brothers Murphy were old muckers with Frank. One day while in the Windsor Café, Frank cast about for a suitable name to christen a new marque. Between them they conjured up the name 'Elva' — a dogs' dinner of the French phrase 'elle va' which, roughly translated, meant 'she goes'. Whether there was a sexual innuendo, Frank would not say. Anyway, the name Elva evolved, Frank liked the 'ring' and another round of teas was ordered to celebrate the birth of a new car company.

Frank with his small workforce knuckled down to assemble the first Elva sports racing car which was powered by a highly modified Ford 100E engine. With Peter Gammon at the wheel, the car won the 12-lap, 1200 cc Sports Car Race at the 1955 Easter Monday meeting at Brands Hatch. The Bexhill firm slowly flourished in Gammon's reflected glory, which prompted Frank to sign Robbie Mackenzie-Low, another young firebrand, who went to Aintree in May 1955 and scored there as well. The works Elva 1100s were virtually unstoppable that season with eight wins, eight second places and seven thirds from a total of 29 events. Part of that tally was achieved by Stuart Lewis-Evans, a future Grand Prix star who joined the team midway through the season. Frank had struck gold.

Frank's days as a racing driver were numbered when he suffered a freakish accident while he was testing a works Elva at Brands Hatch in 1956. He had omitted to fasten the two front screws and leather straps which secured the bonnet. As a result, while he was lapping the Kent circuit, the bonnet flew over and cracked Frank on the head. Whether he was wearing the infamous cloth cap or a crash helmet, until this day Frank swears that amnesia blotted his memory.

Around the winter time of 1956-57 when the feel-good factor mushroomed across America after Republican President Eisenhower won through to a second term with a greater portion of the vote over the Democrat candidate Adlai Stevenson than in 1952, Frank had a call from his buddy Walter Dickson. The American car dealer encouraged him to look across the Atlantic for a fertile market for Elva road-going sports cars.

Coincidentally, the political climate changed in Britain when Sir Anthony Eden resigned as the Conservative Prime Minister, weakened by his handling of the Suez Crisis. The Queen then sent for Harold Macmillan. Straight away, the new leader, who later said: 'You've never had it so good', saw the post-Suez repairs to Anglo-American relations as his first priority. In view of this move, Frank determined that Elva should get a foot in the door of prosperity.

In early 1957, Archie Scott-Brown, the amazing one-handed racing driver, introduced Frank to a graduate engineer — Peter Nott — who was immediately enlisted to join the design section. Peter was an ex-public-school boy who went to Cambridge to obtain his degree. He initially worked at Rootes in Coventry where he met up with Michael Parkes (who later drove for Ferrari) and Tim Fry. One of Peter's first jobs with Frank was to work on the original concept of the two-seater Elva Courier. Sketches of a simple design were sent to America for Dickson to approve a car for 'racy' enthusiasts to enjoy on the road and even at the circuits. Frank and Peter originated from socially divergent family backgrounds, a fact that often caused tempestuous arguments when in most cases they emerged unscathed and happy to reach a compromise on ideas. Tim Fry styled the body, and many alternatives were made by Bob Curl and Arthur Rotham before Frank gave the nod of approval.

As the development on the Courier progressed, the workshop in London Road bulged with activity while the racing division was moved to nearby premises behind the York Hotel adjacent to the main company. Believe it or not, the fish and chip shop was at this juncture subsidising the factory, much to Frank's relief. Then in July 1958 the aluminium-bodied prototype Courier was shipped to Continental Motors in Washington DC. Various people tested it and *Road & Track* magazine published a favourable report which caused Frank's normally pensive features to break out into a huge smile of satisfaction. As Frank admitted, his baby was made for robust customers who have cast-iron-bums which might have rusted because early models leaked like a 'perishin' colander'.

Elva had the prospect of becoming a major employer in Bexhill, which prompted Frank to approach Bexhill Town Hall for more premises. The town fathers were utterly indifferent to his appeal — which was perhaps not unexpected. They had quashed an application to develop a full Grand Prix circuit outside the resort during the early 'fifties.

So Elva eventually moved to a site in Hastings. Around this time, Bill Meace became the General Manager of Elva, and with his arrival Bexhill's part in the history of the company was reflected in the day when the police arrived to investigate the disappearance of a special cylinder-head from the store. It turned out to be a false alarm, because Ron Veness had fitted it to his car for testing. Nevertheless, another employee of a more dubious nature, got the wind up because he had secreted an almost complete Courier in his garden shed. The lad took fright at the police. He tore out of the works, opened the shed and promptly dumped his ill-gotten booty into the sea off Bexhill!

* * *

Between frequent trips to Bexhill, I caught up with writing and dispatching features to the publications who knew nothing of my future plans. There was solitary days when I witnessed other sporting phenomena. I travelled to Sunningdale to watch the Professional Ladies Golf Tournament. This was an enlightening initiation when I felt that I was the proverbial square peg watching ladies attempting to putt little white balls down tiny holes. A mood of chauvinism welled up in me at the sight of these delightfully-dressed butterflies partaking of a game that is ungainly enough for men to play.

On another occasion I had access to the members enclosure at the Oval cricket ground to blanch at England being defeated by a first innings West Indies total of 687 in the final test match of the 1976 series. Little seems to have changed over the passing years. I did attend the Oval in the vain hope of seeing a classic day's play: not that I was disappointed, but the recurring theme in Test Match Cricket seems that whenever I go to watch England, they collapse, which might explain why I prefer to watch Test Matches on television.

I enjoyed playing the occasional game of cricket and often participated in charity matches on behalf of the Church of England Children's Society. Even at this village-green level my ability was not truly appreciated. I was hopeless in the field. My bowling (according to Mike Deness, the Kent bowler) was better adapted to petanque. As for batting, I never stayed at the crease long enough to find my true forté. But placed behind the wicket, I became a man possessed. Experts often commented that goalkeepers and wicketkeepers were spoken of in the same breath — they were bloody masochists. Maybe the next Grand Prix would prove them right!

11

She Married the Chauffeur

LIVING WITH the Larkins was no problem. They sensed that Pam might welcome a break when I spoke of the possibility that she could join me for the Dutch Grand Prix. To take the responsibility of Stuart for a long weekend was quite a step away from baby-sitting for a few hours during an evening. But Hilda and Alan felt equal to the task, so with a great sense of release, we motored across to Harwich to catch a ferry bound for the Hook of Holland.

We left the car at the Harwich ferry terminal and travelled lightly because we had decided upon a madcap idea of cycling from the Hook to Zandvoort. Having studied maps that detailed cycle tracks, I had estimated a journey of about 40 miles. Pam reckoned she could cope with that distance in view of the flat terrain of Holland. Since the torrid summer heat still hung over us, a bicycle ride for two seemed an ideal way to explore the Dutch coastline.

After a dreamy North Sea crossing, we arrived at the Hook, stepped ashore and immediately started to explore the bicycle hire shops. Rents varied amazingly between shops and between the choice of model. We opted for a couple of fixed-wheel, sit-up-and-beg jobs. Once we were mounted astride these bone-shakers, I reckoned that Zandvoort was around four hours away. According to the 'relief' maps of Holland, nothing more than a pimple on a Dutchman's backside would intrude upon our progress. What was not indicated, was the sand dunes sculpted by the elements. When you have mentally adjusted yourself to an 'easy ride', a dune of some 100 foot altitude presents a breath-taking challenge to limb and spirit.

After four fairly leisurely hours, we had circumnavigated that unpronounceable Dutch resort 'Scheveningen' and wearily rolled into Katwijk-ann-Zee. My backside had been rubbed raw by the wire-sprung saddle. I had to grin and bear it. I guessed that Pam must have been suffering some discomfort, but if 'im up front' showed signs of flagging I should never get her to move another inch. As it was, the poor woman was periodically asking how far we had to go. Either I had grossly underestimated the distance, or the sand dunes, combined with the humidity, were knackering us. The expedition, though cultural and delightful, had become a test of endurance.

'Not far now', I reassured my wilting rose as dusk dropped its curtain with embarrassing rapidity upon another scorching day. At one point we had completely missed the knee-high sign-posts along the cycle path, and found ourselves weaving a devilish line between fast-moving traffic along an auto-route! That fazed Pam completely. I had a feeling that she had lost confidence either in my judgment or in the scale of the maps.

We tottered into Zandvoort seven hours after departing the Hook, in a mixed state of exhaustion and exaltation. It was after dark although the town was en fête with illuminations and the Grand Prix atmosphere. We eventually discovered the Hotel Keur where we wheeled our steeds into the hotel lobby and, at that moment of relief, vowed never to ride the damned things again. Our Dutch host enquired how far we had cycled. Pam breathlessly informed him of our marathon from the Hook. The poor man was astonished. He reckoned that we had travelled some 70 miles, and offhandedly informed us that no self-respecting Dutch person would attempt such a journey.

We limped into the dining room to find Sylvia and Mo Nunn at the entrails of their evening meal. The Team Ensign management were speechless at our gargantuan ordeal. Mo's pixie-like features radiated a sarcastic smile before he reminded us that after the race we would have to repeat the entire episode again. Sylvia chastised us both for wreaking such havoc upon Pam. Love's sweet charity got short shrift that night.

However, the aches and pains were soothed when Jacky Ickx joined us. He expressed delight and admiration at our expedition. As a former motorcycle trialist and competitor in the harrowing Paris-Dakar Rally, Ickx knew something about enduring pain and relentless sand dunes. In fact throughout the Grand Prix, I had a hard time keeping him off my bike. He insisted upon borrowing it to avoid the traffic jams to and from the circuit.

Throughout my period in motor sport, Jacky Ickx was the one driver I was able to identify with. There was much more to the enigmatic young Belgian besides motor racing. His initial introduction to the sport came when his parents purchased a Zundapp trials motorcycle. His virtuosity as a 'plodder' did not go unnoticed by the German factory who signed him for his services when he was seventeen years of age. By 1963 Jacky was the Belgian motorcycle trials champion.

'Mud plugging' demands special skills to traverse impossible-looking sections up near-vertical earth banks, along stone-based river beds and over rocky scree. A good rider must possess stamina, a high degree of balance and great mechanical feel to plod a motorcycle through such elements without even so much as a 'dab' with either foot. The secret of such an exercise is finger-light throttle control. Buried deep in the psyche of such riders is a streak of obstinacy and a talent for adapting to sometimes atrocious conditions.

Not all these finely tuned qualities are required to become a top Grand Prix driver. However, Ickx created a record in long-distance racing with six wins at the Le Mans 24-hours plus many outright victories in other World Sports Car Championship races. His achievements were placed against his 'plodder's' mentality.

When it came to the highly competitive 'sprints' of Grand Prix racing, Jacky by his own admission reckoned that how well he performed depended upon his calculation in the given conditions. He claimed the highest honours for both Ferrari and Lotus in Grand Prix racing, but his ability to 'mix it' was always open to question. When Ickx did place a tyre where angels fear to spin, his improvised passing manoeuvres were so audacious they became legendary. No witness will forget the classic race when in diabolical weather conditions during the 1974 Race of Champions at Brands Hatch, he overtook Niki Lauda's Ferrari around the outside of Paddock Bend. Jacky disregarded the build-up of rubber and grit off the racing line. He utilised the rough surface as 'glue'. Anybody else would have flown off such a treacherous tarmac. But Jacky's 'plod' instinct took Lauda so completely by surprise that the move upset his rhythm for the remainder of the race — which Ickx gleefully won.

His motorcycle background undoubtedly influenced his attitude when the Grand Prix Drivers' Association judged the Nürburgring and Spa-Francorchamps to be dangerous for drivers and spectator safety. Jacky's pedantic opinion served to alienate him from many of his fellow-drivers who thought that he harboured a death wish, which in fact was quite to the contrary. Rarely has there been a more intelligent driver because Ickx reckoned that racing was a calculated risk regardless of how safe a circuit was contrived to be.

In the past I had enjoyed a thoroughly professional understanding with Jacky Ickx. At Zandvoort his reserved manner evaporated as we relaxed and enjoyed each other's company within the sporting atmosphere of Team Ensign.

I knew Mo Nunn when he was a polished Formula Three driver cast in Alan Rees's metronomic mould. He ran Team Ensign from its headquarters on the Queens Industrial Estate in Chasetown amid what is jokingly known as the 'Black Country'. Although managed on a tight shoe-string, Team Ensign always arrived to race on the appointed hour at each Grand Prix. Often Nunn's little clique was snubbed by the big boys. Mo's car always had to qualify in order to race. If by chance he didn't make the line, then he would still wait in case another journeyman had a shunt and his driver could replace the vacant spot on the grid.

When Mo arrived at Zandvoort with Jacky Ickx on a lead, the pit lane had to sit up and take notice. Either Mo had printed a load of filthy lucre or Ickx needed his head examined. Outside of Ferrari, Lotus and McLaren, the second division like Surtees, Shadow and March were incredulous at Nunn's little coup.

At this stage in the World Championship, Lauda had unfortunately been put out of the reckoning after a 'fire-ball' shunt at the German Grand Prix which all but made him celestial. Amazingly, the plucky Austrian driver was back in harness at the Italian Grand Prix two months after being given the last rites. So while Lauda was hospitalised, James Hunt and Marlboro McLaren were in the fresh air.

Nobody knew what was the inducement for Jacky to consider Team Ensign. According to Mo Nunn, he simply contacted the Belgian driver with the suggestion. Ickx had no commitment to race in Formula One at the time. The offer was accepted in the spirit in which it was given. Mo had the car, Ickx had the ability. The free spirit responded to a gentleman's agreement that had no strings apart from a share of prize money and bonuses should Jacky finish the race in the points. Jacky's motive was not just to come along for the ride. He was intrigued to discover the areas of difference between the big works teams and a beautifully prepared car like the Ensign. While mega-bucks obviously spoke when it came to winning races, where were the short-comings of the Ensign as against say the McLaren? Would it be inherent in the design of a car, in the power unit, in the choice of tyres, braking or even in the driver! Jacky set himself a realistic target to attain a good position on the grid and to race for a finish in the highest possible place. Only then would he be able to feed-back to Mo exactly where the Ensign was wanting.

Although I was 'on business' at the Dutch Grand Prix, for me there was an end-of-term mood. The pure joy of working with a small privately-entered team reflected all the most pleasurable aspects of the sport. There was none of the beady-eyed, stony-faced attitude around Mo Nunn that was prevalent within the McLaren and Ferrari pits. By virtue of his position, Mo was part of the political structure of Grand Prix racing, but his minority of one fought its corner when the Ministerial heavyweights trespassed upon his constituency. Enlisting the services of Jacky Ickx had certainly moved Mo's bench-mark, at least for that weekend in Zandvoort. Team Ensign posed more than just a peripheral threat. We relished in the discomfort of our bigger rivals.

Sylvia generally administered us 'free-loaders' into fulfilling small obliga-tions. Pam was delegated the job of caterer, a task that required the making of sandwiches in the rear of the transporter. Team Ensign were a major sponsor away from the luxury of a motor home. So crates of soft drink were piled among the tool boxes and greek columns of alloy wheels. At some time dur-ing meal preparation Jacky hoisted himself into the transporter, his eyes sparkling with wicked mischief as he proceeded to undress and change into his racing gear while Pam, trying to butter the crusty baguettes, studiously ignored him. As the mechanics tried to forage about in their many boxes of spares, writers from a multitude of countries huffily demanded an audience with Jacky. Many were curious to know why he had joined Team Ensign when more illustrious équipes would always offer him a home.

With typical good humour, Ickx's sensuous lips parted in a smile when he parried the queries with a diplomatic calm as he struggled into his fireproof underwear. For Pam, the entire charade proved hilarious the more so when the hard-pressed mechanics of those 'illustrious' teams dropped by and sensed the frivolous mood. Wistful expressions spread over the faces of the Ferrari mechanics who still showed Jacky Ickx great affection even though he hadn't driven for them since 1973.

Practice and grid positions were incidental to my story. Suffice it to men-tion that Ronnie Peterson drove against the grain with those teams in cham-pionship contention when he secured pole position for March-Ford. I got the impression that James Hunt was a pawn to his own hype being a major distraction. If he was going to make any impression upon Lauda's monumental championship lead, he had to score points while the Austrian was enduring a miraculous recovery from his holocaust at the Nürburgring. Ferrari were speculating out loud upon Niki driving at Monza. Whether this rumour was instigated by the Italians to get Hunt and McLaren geed-up was open to speculation at the time. But it certainly concentrated James who at the end of the day claimed a valuable victory over Clay Regazzoni's Ferrari with Tom Pryce in a fighting third place for UOP Shadow. In view of events to come at the Italian Grand Prix and beyond, Niki Lauda made a heroic return to centre stage just six weeks after being embalmed like an Egyptian mummy. Ronnie Peterson vindicated his sudden resurgence at Zandvoort by winning the Italian Grand Prix for March, thus leaving the door to the championship open for both Lauda and Hunt. The climax to the explosive 1976 season saw James Hunt become the World Champion driver by a whisker in torrential rain at the Japanese Grand Prix from which Lauda conceded to discretion rather than valour.

At Zandvoort, Jacky didn't place Ensign among the points, but his overall assessment of the car was of greater value to Mo Nunn than a victory would have been.

Apart from adjusting the Ensign to Zandvoort's idiosyncrasies, Ickx often tucked the car into the slip-stream of faster opponents powered by the Cosworth-Ford in order to relate the discrepancy of speed between the Ensign and say the McLaren or the March. Jacky eulogised happily to Mo about the Ensign's handling on corners and compared it favourably with any other car he had driven. Not much was lost in the braking area and the car sat down nicely under hard acceleration. Mo realised, of course, that McLaren had the superior engine — which accounted for the legs it had on the Ensign out of corners and at top speed along the straight. Apart from those known facts, Jacky reckoned that he could stay within sniffing distance of Hunt along the undulating fast curves in the country. Mo's frustration was that if he could secure the well-tweaked Ford engine which McLaren had, his car might be extremely competitive. It was a scenario which, under Ford's contractual agreements with possible championship contenders, would be hard to prove.

The days when under-financed private entrants could take on the mighty works teams unfortunately went with Rob Walker and Lord Alexander Hesketh. Sponsors rarely backed a 'hunch': only proven winners could retain the favours of commercially motivated companies.

After the 'seventies, the climate became more favourable when sponsors realised the growing exposure achieved by worldwide television coverage. Even midfield runners fighting their own private races would catch the attention of an imaginative producer.

For the vast majority of onlookers at Zandvoort, Team Ensign's appearance was a non-event. My opinion differed in that we had by far the most pleasurable and constructive weekend when proceedings were viewed through Mo's eyes. He then had a yardstick of his ability and that of the Ensign-Ford.

The realisation barely sank in at the time, but the 1976 Dutch Grand Prix at

Zandvoort was my last race in any official capacity. It was appropriate then that I bade *au revoir* to John Hugenholtz, the circuit designer who had inspired Zandvoort and many others across the world. I had known John since 1961 when we first met and he had kept a fatherly eye on me ever since. I could not have wished for a happier ending among friends, observing Jacky Ickx whose attitude ran parallel to my own ideals. Ironically Pam's enjoyment of the sport had been kindled as my flame was extinguished. In time to come, I could appreciate that this probably wrankled with her, and rightly so. After all she had enjoyed a unique sight into an exciting and colourful world. Now all that was going to change.

We cycled back to the Hook of Holland on my birthday in almost half the time it had taken us to reach Zandvoort. As we sailed into Harwich the headline news was that rain had stopped play at Lord's cricket ground for fifteen minutes. The huge crowd had apparently gone into a frenzy of delight. Spectators danced in the puddles. That short sharp shower had signalled that the drought was in its smouldering embers. Thousands of people, especially in the South-West of England had gone without water that day. Denis Howell was created the 'Minister of Drought' so at the celebration of my 36th birthday I downed a few beers after we returned to Petts Wood.

* * *

Gifted with a glance into life's rear-view mirror, I made two major commitments in 1976 that would influence the rest of my life. One was very positive, the second without real anticipation.

Cutting new ground by moving to Bexhill-on-Sea was a positive statement of starting afresh by moving away from previous associations. Secondly, I firmly closed the door upon one career, and created a hiatus which I filled by volunteering to crew on the illustrious ketch *Great Britain II* in the 1977-78 Whitbread-Round-the-World Race. With my income drastically reduced and moving house before reorientating my career, seeking a life upon the ocean wave was extremely self-indulgent. I should have dove-tailed motor racing with my ambition to travel and find a career on television. I felt a strong urge to place a buffer between the two parts of my working life. Sailing was not a forte. In fact prior to meeting with Chay Blyth and Robert James among many other aspiring crew persons at the Seymour Hall in London to be assessed, I had never even set foot upon a dinghy. Chay reassured me that I was the best possible candidate for the job in that I had no preconceived ideas about how to sail, and that he would personally train me.

Over the years I had noted Chay's amazing heroics upon the great oceans, and upon meeting the man at a celebrity race at Brands Hatch, revered him as one of life's modern role figures. For him to suggest that I was fit and able enough to crew on *Great Britain II* was for me tantamount to blowing away a few myth's and legends.

Anyway, our fine skipper Rob had chartered *Great Britain II* from Chay Blyth's company Supersail to complete the race. The £64,000 charter fee was to be split equally between the sixteen crew members. So I had let myself in for £4,000 of self-imposed isolation over eight months in the 'Grand Prix' class of deep-ocean racing. I did not have that much spare cash. Nevertheless, everybody was hell-bent upon committing me to this outrageous whim. Very soon after moving into Bexhill, we explored various ways of raising the money. What a way to start a new life!

Contrary to the more flamboyant neighbours Eastbourne and Hastings, the shrinking violet of Bexhill, situated roughly half way between them, has long created for itself the aloof attitude of being a 'residential resort'. The rather featureless three-mile promenade stretches from the Cooden end to the west-side of the town along to the elegant De La Warr Parade at the east-side. The parade rises up to Galley Hill where, during the war, Spike Milligan manned an O.P. just in front of the now demolished fisherman's cottages. According to Spike there did not seem to be a war in Bexhill. It was a wonderful 'shirts off' posting in the summer.

Only since the early 'nineties have the recalcitrant father's in the Town Hall shown some reaction to the hue and cry of the Chamber of Commerce and the small band of hoteliers, all of whom were slowly going broke from lack of seasonal trade. What hurt the Chamber more was that Eastbourne and Hastings had for years creamed off trade from Bexhill. It was inevitable that the resort languished as a backwater totally dependent upon local trade and passers-by who took the trouble to turn off the A259.

Admittedly during the summer months, especially over weekends and the long school holidays, the promenade and beaches were dappled by hundreds of day visitors. Most of them were picnickers, and very few patronised the local shops. They came, they saw, then returned home reinvigorated from the fresh breezes. Residents took an alternative view to the traders and hoteliers. Their opinion was that Bexhill was perfect as a resort for retirement, with all the niceties of living by the coast without the kiss-me-quick and the candy-floss brigade — just the sort of haven where burnt-out captains of industry could drop anchor. Bexhill's appeal was its relative solitude, and it was a handy place to get about shops and enlist some personal service.

A standing joke among comedians who appear at the Congress Theatre, Eastbourne, is that Bexhill is the cemetery with lights where 'old fogies' tra-velled from London by train on a single ticket, because most of them would not live long enough to make the return journey!

Over the years Bexhill has developed a widely known reputation for the discrepancy between its youth and its elderly residents in their driving habits. Strangers arriving in the town notice the 'Bexhill Driver' a mile off. They curse the erratic behaviour of local motorists who drive at snail's pace in the middle of the road and park where their fancy takes them. There are some spirited ladies who can be heard to floor the accelerator until the engine is screaming, then drop the clutch. Richard Attwood did a fair impersonation of a Bexhill Driver by kangarooing along in a series of burps, screeches and farts, sounding like a euphonium being played with a constricted wind-pipe. The same ladies are known to brake upon a sixpence either to chat with a friend or to allow the neighbours 'tabby' to cross the road. Because longevity is rampant in Bexhill, there is a very high proportion of middle-range, low-mileage motor cars on the second-hand market, most of which are in pristine condition. Potential customers have to check the brakes and clutch thoroughly before trading in their cars for some amazing bargains that have been wheeled into the dealers after the passing of another 'decrepit pilot'.

Shortly after our move to Bexhill, friends from afar waxed curious as to why we chose to reside in such a 'dead-'n'-alive' place. I don't study astrology, but months later I encountered a local clairvoyant who told me: 'Ours is not to reason why, we must accept that destiny meant it to be'. Just how fate plays her deft hand was forcibly shown when less than a week after our removal, I was nosing about in the shopping centre. Towards the southern end of Sackville Road is the De La Warr Pavilion which was built during 1933-35. The building represented such a landmark in the history of British architecture that it was formally opened by the Duke and Duchess of York (who later became King George VI and Queen Elizabeth.) Since that royal occasion, some local opinion has deemed the theatre-cum-conference centre a 'bloody monstrosity'. The futuristic façade made the establishment appear something like a beached cruise liner after the storm. I am sure that the German architect Erich Mendelssohn would rotate in his grave if he realised that the revolutionary welded-steel-framed building, the first ever constructed in Britain, was spoken in the same breath as the *Titanic*. The on-going non-conformists wish that it would suffer the same fate of the stricken ocean liner. Whether you like the shoe-box design or loathe it, the pavilion today is deeply entrenched within Bexhill's community life as a rendezvous to eat, drink and be entertained.

Like so many parts of the promenade where one feels that town planning was perhaps decided during a session of one-over-the-eight, the De La Warr Pavilion presents a strong, angular presence which dominates over the hotchpotch of Victorian and Edwardian buildings. Mixed with this cosmopolitan aspect is a touch of colonial reminiscence derived from when Lieutenant-Colonel Henry Lane, a veteran of the Indian Mutiny, became the Father of Local Government in Bexhill. Later on, The Maharaja of Cooch Behar frequented the resort where he found a perfect retreat from duties of state.

On this particular morning, I got around to perusing the 'What's On' in the foyer of the pavilion when a very familiar voice jovially bellowed from behind: 'What the devil is Max Le Grand doing here?' Straight away I recalled first hearing this clear voice over the public address system at the Snetterton 3-hour race in 1959. I turned to find the familiar rumpled figure of Lawrie Webber grinning at me from beneath a shock of wavy, unkempt hair. When I informed the open-handed commentator that Pam and I had moved into the area, he immediately pronounced us insane!

Although he is naturally gregarious, Lawrie has quietly woven himself into the tapestry of motor racing, working upon his own innovative ideas. His links with the sport originated in 1946 when John Cooper enlisted his considerable mechanical ability to help construct and develop the half-litre, rear-

Mr Muir deputised for Mr Alfred Harmsworth in his Mercedes here on the start line at Bexhill, 1902.

Mr Clay's 'Wind-cutter' at Bexhill in 1902.

The 1902 Concours d'Elégance after the Bexhill Races.

On the start line at Bexhill a Napier (S.F. Edge?) and a Daimler ready for the off.

All race prepared at Bexhill – a Darracq (No. 18) and Vinot-Deguingand (No. 27).

Another Napier on the streets of Bexhill in 1902.

engined Cooper double-knocker Norton-powered racing cars, the sort I was weaned upon at Brands Hatch.

Later, my ebullient chum moved into Paul Emery's little workshop. Paul made his name constructing and racing front-engined 500 cc single-seaters. He got extremely ambitious around the time when Lawrie loomed in the shed door, trying to piece together a Formula One car. The Emeryson-Alta set a new 'Ladies' record at Shelsey Walsh Hill Climb in 1957 when Roberta Cowell, after a sex change from being ex-POW Bob Cowell, blasted up the hill in 40.14 seconds. Miss Cowell must have been the only person to improve her own time set some years previously when she was a gentleman!

Lawrie inspired the idea of fitting disc brakes onto a Formula One racing car, thus setting the pattern which all the other teams followed. He became a great 'mucker' with Willie Griffiths, an equally adroit mechanic and they tooled about with Paddy Gaston for sometime at club meetings. Gaston's ambition had limited horizons, so Lawrie eventually ended up in Bourne where he developed the revolutionary Rover-BRM gas-turbine sports cars. The first turbine-propelled car was driven by Graham Hill and Ritchie Ginther at Le Mans in 1963. Because the Automobile Club de l'Ouest could not match the power unit with a normally aspirated car, it ran a solo time trial. Hill and Ginther screamed around for the 24-hours and under normal circumstances would have been classified to have finished eighth overall. Lawrie continued to experiment with the Rover-BRM which appeared again considerably modified at Le Mans in 1965. On that occasion Hill was partnered by his Grand Prix team-mate Jackie Stewart when they finished on level terms in tenth place. I think Lawrie found that era with BRM to be one of the most productive in his career.

Apart from my occasionally hearing his dulcet tones at odd Snetterton club meetings, our paths rarely crossed. Now, many years later, I found him living in Bexhill with his wife Valerie, (a pianoforte teacher), and his daughters. So he had to be daft into the bargain for living in this neck of human decay. Naturally, Lawrie edged me into the pavilion bar for what turned out to be a pleasurable session. It went without saying that he pointedly enquired why the hell I had chosen to shack up in Bexhill. When I informed him that it was to enable me to escape from the long tendrils of motor racing, he laughed long and loudly.

'That's what *you* think, mate', he grinned, 'before long you'll find yourself right back in the thick of it here, mark my words.'

* * *

My commitment to the Round-The-World Yacht Race was made absolute when I paid a £400 deposit to secure my berth. The media across the South of England had a field day proclaiming: 'Bexhill man will sail round-the-world, has no money, never sailed before, declares *Great Britain II* will win race'. Through my writer's eye, I also found the entire saga incredibly far-fetched. Within Bexhill there were believers like Derek Last, a small local industrialist who volunteered to form a committee — the Bexhill Round the World Appeal — to raise my portion of the charter fee. Much as I appreciated the public-spiritedness of the man, common sense told me that the situation was getting ludicrous because there were certain elements who thought I had moved into Bexhill in order to sponge upon the goodwill of the population.

Nevertheless, the fund raisers were local traders and businessmen like Bill Hampshire, then Manager of the Midland Bank. Lawrie Webber felt an allegiance while Ron Storkey of the Bexhill Club added weight and provided a rendezvous for meetings. Ivor Brampton was a wealthy businessman from Cooden who became Mayor of Bexhill at this time. We were a motley lot, enthusiastically tossing in ideas to raise the cash. The idea was to publicise Bexhill through my worldwide exploits in the ports o'call which were being made by the racing yachts along the 27,000-mile passage, at Cape Town, Auckland and Rio de Janeiro. Whether this was to be a glory trail or whether I would sink to oblivion in Davy Jones's locker didn't bear contemplating. The upshot was that I went on a training sail with Chay Blyth to the Channel Islands. The living legend declared me fit to sail and I was elected to join the crew of *Great Britain II* for the Fastnet Race. This was to have been my one and only race 'in anger' which was aborted just off the Bishop Rock Lighthouse when we were becalmed for 24 hours. Skipper Rob James thought that our next priority was to head back to Portsmouth to prepare for the 'big event' which was only weeks away.

In spite of the enormous efforts made by the bounty hunting-committee, I still had to appeal for an overdraft at the bank to top-up a short-fall. To my eternal relief, and thanks to Pam, I was in the race. The net priority was to learn something about Bexhill-on-Sea so that I could extol its virtues abroad.

I buckled down to absorb some of the history by visiting the local museum in Egerton Road. I plagued the library and fingered the files of the local newspaper, the *Bexhill Observer*, and even got my nose into fusty archive material in the Town Hall.

My very first intimation that something untoward was afoot resulted from my seeing a photograph in the museum. It depicted turn-of-the-century automobilists apparently in combat apparel, driving at some considerable velocity along the De La Warr Parade. The picture was hung under the cryptic heading 'The First Bexhill Races'. Struck dumb with disbelief, I wondered if Lawrie Webber's prophetic remark was about to haunt me. Had fate by some amazing coincidence pre-destined me to make this discovery? Until that moment of realisation, I had absolutely no clue about Bexhill playing host to the very 'first motor races in England'. And yet there was the evidence set graphically before me of motor car racing along the very stretch of road over which we looked from Number 21. Until then, I had thought that Brooklands was the true spiritual home of early motor racing in the United Kingdom.

Perhaps it was just as well that the main focus of my attention was upon all things nautical. The sleeping dog and its true significance within motor history was allowed to lie. I vowed that upon my return from the yacht race I would delve into this little-known aspect of motor sport. I wanted to know more about the Bexhill Races, and to substantiate that mellowing photograph in the museum.

The beginning of 1977 started off with a riot of promotional activities on the radio and Southern Television loud-hailing my ambition to become a 'Jolly Jack Tar'. In February, Chay Blyth arrived on the doorstep to endorse my candidature as a crewman on *Great Britain II* along with fifteen other people, including a single female, Diana Thomas-Ellam whose parents lived in Eastbourne. By way of a break, Pam and I then escaped for a week at Chris Merlin's house in Ravenglass.

Shortly after arriving in Cumbria, I sat on the front doorstep of the Merlin's house, 'Mountain Ash', and watched the tide off the Irish Sea fill the Esk river bed in front of their garden. The air was quite warm for mid-winter. I allowed my mind to sink into a limbo. I gradually became aware of a figure standing over me in the front doorway. It was Pam. Upon turning I gestured for her to join me, when I noticed that her face was contorted into a grimace. She was stifling tears. Naturally, I was concerned about there being something wrong. Pam is by nature a transparently honest lady. She wears her heart on her sleeve. Whatever the crisis looming now, she was either reticent, or unable to release the burden. Pam just stood there, gazing squarely at me, her eyes reddening as tears welled up and her face turned a darker shade of crimson. 'Tom's dead', she said.

Her entire body started to convulse as the emotion fought for release. Fast returning from my mental limbo, I had barely understood what Pam had actually said. I recall thinking, or saying, something stupid like: 'Tom — Tom who? What are you talking about?' Realising that this was such an idiotic statement, I tried to bite my tongue before it tumbled out. It dawned on me with startling clarity that she was referring to Tom Pryce. That same weekend, the South African Grand Prix was launching a new season of World Championship races. I automatically realised that it as the final day of qualification before the race at Kyalami on the Sunday. I had not been away from the scene long enough to realise all that was going on those many thousands of miles away. After I had comforted Pam, she told me how the news of Tom's untimely death had been flashed on a radio bulletin.

As we hugged each other, I could no longer shrug off another racing driver's misfortune. There in the Lake District, emotions felt raw. What made Tom's accident all the more tangible was the awareness that for the first time, somebody I dearly loved was also affected. That really hurt, probably more than I cared to admit at the time.

Later on, the Merlins and their dogs joined us for a walk to the grounds of Muncaster Castle. Chris glanced at me and realised that all the old bravado and excuses that racing drivers died having the last laugh, meant nothing. Tom and Nella had become more than just friends. We'd shared our hopes and ambitions with each other. Pam felt a need to 'do something', but I resisted her natural reaction. Nella was in South Africa. There was nothing we could do but just share our thoughts. For the first time, I had the overwhelming sense of relief that I was out of the sport. A week or so later, Pam and I attended Tom's grave in Otford. It was sad to admit that motor racing had provided enormous pleasure, but Tom's death had finally brought the curtain down. Whether an encore was due, I did not know.

* * *

The Whitbread Round-the-World Race drifted slowly into history along with eight months of beating, running, surfing, broaching and simply idling in the doldrums. Whether I made a valid contribution to our glorious victory in the overall line honours is open to question. Frankly, there were ghastly moments when sheer terror transfixed me to the bunk. Living cheek-by-jowl with sixteen other strangers who ranged from a police cadet to the Marketing Director of Esso Petroleum — a Baronet, the Right Honourable Quentin Wallop — and the ex-secretary to the Chairman of Plessey was something of a social comment upon the British class structure. But our Skipper Robert James, a wiry, fair-skinned, sandy-haired, be-freckled man, taught us from his previous experience of ocean racing, about interlocking human relationships and working as members of a team.

We had started out from *HMS Vernon* in Portsmouth, the laughing stock of the entire fleet of fifteen yachts. Nobody — Robin Knox-Johnston, Leslie Williams, Clare Francis, John Rigdeway or French legend Eric Tabarly — gave us a hope in hell. So after the cannon was fired to start the race from Southsea Fort, we cast our inferiority-complexes overboard, and under Rob's inspired guidance, welded ourselves into some semblance of order. It was pure purgatory learning to sail in these horrendous conditions. Rob must have examined his own sanity at times. In the end his wisdom and naked guts won us through. To complete such a punishing exercise taught us all about the basic animal instincts of human nature. Rarely have I felt so vulnerable to other people. That was the same for each of us. Deprived of privacy, we learnt to respect the 'quiet moments' we all sought in 'hidey holes' found in the sail wardrobe, or the engine room and secured behind the retaining blinds of our bunks. Above all else we learnt not only to live with one female on board, but Diana won the respect of the entire crew for her attitude under what must have been exceptionally trying circumstances.

Perhaps more chastening for each of us was the voyage of inner discovery. I cannot admit to be thoroughly enamoured with the man I faced up to at sea. Being tossed about the oceans in the most diabolical conditions of extreme heat, cold, damp and saturation while living at a perpetual 45° angle on a beat exposed every human frailty. On only a handful of occasions did I call upon strengths which I never realised existed. When all was said and done, I knew exactly where the barriers of my psyche were in terms of fear, competitiveness, stamina, tolerance, adaptability and good humour.

One 'civilian' to our effort who provided a pillar of strength in New Zealand was Denis Hulme. The ex-World Champion met me off *Great Britain II* shortly after we came alongside Marsden Wharf in Auckland. Denis sensed that I was a demoralised being. I had reached the half-way stop riddled with doubt whether I was capable of complementing the overall crew effort. At sea, I was fighting for survival with one hand and working the boat with the other. The actual race was hardly a priority. It was a nightmare.

Denis patiently listened to my anguish while we lounged in hot sulphur pools, trawled for trout and simply relaxed in the garden. His conclusion was so crystal clear that I wondered why I had not thought about it myself. Denis suggested that I turned my priorities on their head. He told me to think race — boat — self, in that order. It worked. My entire mental attitude changed almost immediately. Rob and the crew noticed a difference along the Southern Ocean to Cape Horn. Conditions were awful for everybody, but the spirit of 'gung-ho' coursed through us all. We bombed into Rio just 35 minutes ahead of *Heath's Condor* skippered on that leg by Leslie Williams after 7,500 miles of incredible racing.

Quite by chance I ran into Ronnie and Barbro Peterson in Rio. They were astonished at my about-turn in life. I shall never forget Ronnie's expression as he gazed about the yacht. I sensed a new-found respect from my Grand Prix driver friend. We shook hands on a bet that *Great Britain II* would win the race on outright handicap into Portsmouth — a wager that set the rest of the crew up for the last slog home.

Strangely, Pam never held fear for my welfare at sea. She dreaded those periods at each port o'call in Cape Town, Auckland and Rio de Janeiro when she thought that I was prone to every temptation available. People later told me of their puzzlement, how she was full of the joys of spring when we started each new leg of the race.

What was still more curious upon my return home was that I settled straight back into the domestic routine. After the initial pleasure of our being together again, she cursed me for cramping her space at Number 21 where I got under her feet. She had to purchase more food, more toilet rolls, wash and iron twice as much clothing and make room in the bed for me! Having a new Cape Horner about the house was more added work. All those people in Bexhill who had driven her mad saying 'He won't be long now' could have taken a running jump until she got back into the 'couple mode'.

Grand Prix drivers like Graham Hill can bathe in their glory for as long as they live. Skippers of deep-ocean racing yachts sometimes become legendary figures like Chay Blyth. The 'winch fodder' are 'ten-day heroes' around their vicinity. The after-glow of achievement soon loses its rosy hue when the mundane daily chores of life take over. Earning the honest crust urgently became a priority. Before the press cuttings turned at the corners and radio or television lost their immediate interest I took the plunge when David Haigh, the editor of *Scene South-East* invited me to recall tales of derring-do on the regional programme at the studio in Dover.

After the live interview, David asked as to what the heck I did for a living? 'I'm looking for work' I retorted, 'give me a break on your programme'.

Breaking into television as an inexperienced presenter did not just happen. But David Haigh was equal to my brass neck and promised a studio audition. A year later after much prodding and poking with programme planners and middle management at Southern Television, I was assigned to a 'pilot film' on rock climbing at Eridge in Kent. Usually these botched reels of film are consigned to the bin. Imagine my joy when David viewed it, and transmitted the item that evening! I was given a rolling contract which lasted until Southern Television lost its franchise.

Just before that lucky break, the *Daily Mail* sportswriter Ian Wooldridge made a tantalising challenge. The wager was simple: a group of individuals had to work their various ways around the world on just £50 within 30 days and with no pre-arranged fixes, no visas, no cadging off sugar daddies abroad and no freebie airline tickets. The emphasis was upon the individual's audacity and enterprise.

The concept was outrageous, but with £500 reward for those who completed the task, the gauntlet was picked up. Pam, who by now was resigned to this foot-loose co-habiter, accepted yet another month's leave of absence, six months after I had completed the yacht race!

Having sailed around the world, I had a unique perspective upon our habitat. The good earth was not just sixty hours circumnavigation by jet airliner, but a vast horizon that had taken 134 days on *Great Britain II*. I was not daunted by working a passage, which was a straightforward operation. The real challenge was the business of 'working' each ticket. Judith Chalmers, a lady of some considerable worldly experience in holiday travel for television, was present at the start in London. She tried to find out my plan of attack. When I informed her that no such thing had entered my head, Judith fixed me with a circumspective expression on her lovely open face, then wished me 'good luck'.

In fact I had spun Judith a tiny white lie. Dennis Miller-Williams, the lugubrious public-relations officer for Rolls-Royce in Mayfair, had kindly arranged a chauffeur-driven Silver Shadow for my departure at the starting gun. It was a glorious way to go nowhere in particular. In fact the chauffeur's expression was a Rembrandt: as we drove along the Victoria Embankment he half-turned his head to ask our destination. When I said that I hadn't a clue and that he should drive on until I had perused a shoal of airline schedules, the poor man must have felt like a spare part made redundant. Eventually, I decided to try my luck at London-Gatwick Airport, which on a Sunday afternoon did not sound very promising.

My errant passage wended via Los Angeles, Hawaii, over the equator to New Zealand and Australia, then on to India and thence straight back to London. Because of inspiring other adventurers, misfits, drug-runners and freeloaders, I cannot possibly reiterate the methods by which I wangled my way into a wide variety of 'jobs' to raise the air fares. There were numerous occasions when I had the threat of eviction and deportation hanging over my head. I will acknowledge a debt of gratitude to the New Zealand Consul in Los Angeles for bailing me out. Then Sir Dove-Myer Robinson, who was at that time the autocratic Mayor of Auckland, set me up as his chauffeur. A dismissive Sydneysider customs man turned a blind eye, and a carpet-seller on the water-front market of Bombay provided the one leg up which I needed to complete the exercise. Between these illustrious far-flung gentlemen I just about kept inside international law. I actually completed the circumnavigation inside 27 days and returned to London's Fleet Street with a £63 profit for my exertions!

After two circuits of the world within twelve months, my considerations turned to 'us'. Pam and I had lived together for five years. We were man and wife in all but name. I cared for Stuart's welfare as if he were my own son. Since we had moved to Bexhill, his daily needs in terms of physiotherapy and education had been allocated at Glynde Gap School for the Disabled nearby. There had been occasions when Pam had spoken of our future. She wondered out loud about having a child of our own. I realised that in view of Stuart, Pam felt a basic need to produce a perfectly-formed offspring. Having already feathered our nest in Bexhill, the feeling was growing within myself to perpetuate the family line. So marriage seemed the next logical move in our lives.

I had been reticent about undertaking such a commitment. Stuart was the original stumbling block, but I had learnt to cope with him and felt able to accept his disabilities with gusto. I suffered a partly selfish feeling of 'losing liberty'. At the age of 39 years, I had grown accustomed to opting for each new experience. In spite of this juxtaposition, and after I had been eight months away on the yacht race, Pam and I were still together. Either she was stark staring mad to put up with me, or I had found a special lady.

At around this period of emotional adjustment, I had taken on a spare-time job, taxi driving, to boost the household funds. One day I was delivering a fare to Hastings station, when the dawning suddenly appeared crystal clear. After the customer's departure, I switched off the radio contact with Thomas Taxi's based in St Leonards, then drove home. I proposed to Pam on the spot and felt a sensation of enormous relief upon her acceptance.

The story of our marriage could so easily have ended up with 'The Bride Married the Chauffeur'. I had borrowed a lovely vintage Rolls-Royce from Dermot Bambridge, an old motoring chum who lived in nearby Pevensey Bay. He had kindly agreed to be our driver, resplendent in his chauffeur's uniform. When our great day dawned on Friday 25 May, we were awakened by the telephone. It was Dermot's wife profusely apologising: her hubby was struck down with the lurgie. She told me that I could collect the Rolls if I could name another driver. So at the appointed hour, I donned the chauffeur's cap and drove Pam with Pat Harman, her lady in attendance, to the Hastings Registrar's Office.

We arrived in splendid gear-crashing style to see all our relatives and friends present and correct. As I braked to a shuddering halt adjacent to the registrar's office doors, a reporter from the *Evening Argus* sidled up and through the corner of his mouth suggested that I perform another lap around the block because the groom had not arrived! Picture the demented man's face when I jauntily told him not to worry, got out of the Rolls and proceeded to escort Pam on my arm into the ceremony. He must have envisaged the scoop of a lifetime.

Everybody attempted to guess where in the world I was going to whisk Pam to for our honeymoon. Wild rumours spread of tropical paradises that varied from the Seychelles to Bermuda. In fact, we opted for a down-to earth break at a delightful old farmhouse just across the Ipswich-to-Norwich railway line off the A12 at Yoxford in Suffolk. Having lived in a state of 'marriage' for so long, it seemed daft spending hard earned-cash escaping to the far ends of the earth. What was the point when romance continued to blossom among the farm animals?

Virtually every week I was recording television items spread over the South-East of England that provided first hand excitement and stimulus. Hundreds of sports clubs across the region found a shop window to promote their membership and show their skills. I was the poor man's John Noakes attempting everything head first, placing my faith and well-being in the hands of the experts. Only once did I come a 'cropper' and that was when Gordon Jackson, one-time British motorcycle trials champion, invited me to try my hand at his sport near Canada Heights at Swanley in Kent. I was attempting to follow Gordon down some stone steps into a sunken garden. To perform this shot, I had to exercise the minimum of throttle control. Needless to say, I got slightly exuberant and went flying over the handlebars. The motorcycle landed on top of me at the bottom of the steps. My face was badly cut and I suffered multiple fractures of the left wrist. The story finished up in St Mary's Hospital at Sidcup with me doing a piece to camera, saying that this foolish soul would try motorcycle trials again at a later date!

In between 'shoots' I dabbled in writing and giving public talks to various clubs and associations. I also spent odd times frequenting The Bexhill Club where I met an assortment of local retired gentry and business people. On one particular morning I happened by for a coffee, when I walked into a fairly heated debate at the bar upon the claim that Bexhill was the very first resort in the United Kingdom to allow mixed bathing in the sea. It transpired that the decreptitudes arguing the toss over this juicy morsel of history were club members and a number of visiting guests from Brighton.

The interlopers insisted that The Prince Regent had hosted parties on the beach at Brighton during the 18th Century, when ladies coyly frolicked in the waves with ardent gentlemen. Local fishermen and their buxom wives apparently stood waist deep in the sea, driving a wedge between the sexes at the slightest suspicion of 'hanky-panky'. Some of these hardy boatmen, in the name of defending their fishing grounds, were often witnessed outside mobile 'bathing machines' awaiting unsuspecting occupants about to wade into the water. These sadistic 'minders of the peace' were known as dippers when a bather thrust open his changing-room door, the dippers submerged him for what were known as 'health reasons'.

Even if The Prince Regent swam too far out to sea or looked to be in pursuit of a damsel, he was wrestled unceremoniously back to the shallows, which did not sound like 'approved' mixed bathing to me.

So when the Bexhillians fought their corner, they confidently quoted guide books published in 1896 which stated that Bexhill was the premier seaside resort around the entire coast of Great Britain to publicly allow mixed bathing without restrictive practices. Men, women and children all swam off the level sands at low tide. In high summer mixed bathing became a real feature of the resort. What an incongruous sight it must have been to see the gentlemen picnicking on the beach wearing straw boaters and blazers, with their ladies over dressed in broad-brimmed hats, long skirts and tight bodices, then in their midst, men and women cavorting out of bathing huts in 'scanty' swim suits and charging into the sea giggling and screaming at their new-found freedom.

So with great respect to Brightelmstone (as it was known in The Prince Regent's time), this onerous debate remains open to the jury's verdict.

I scanned newspapers of the time that are kept on file in Bexhill library for information about mixed bathing. I was found wanting. Instead I turned up pages of news about 'The Races' in the sepia-toned editions of the *Bexhill Observer*.

On the very day when Muhammed Ali, the ex-World Heavyweight Champion Boxer, announced his retirement from the ring, I telephoned *Motor Sport* magazine, which incorporates the *Brooklands Gazette*. On only one previous occasion had I been introduced to William Boddy, the founder-editor. He portrayed a rather aloof somewhat diffident man, who was and is very highly respected as a historian on all matters appertaining to veteran and vintage motor cars.

I had made a solitary encounter with Mr Boddy along the Madeira Drive at the conclusion of another London-to-Brighton Veteran Car run. So I did not feel on a friendly conversational par enough to 'phone and say 'Hello Bill, I've uncovered this story on The Bexhill Races. Bexhill claims to be the first home of English sporting motorists. Would you care for some copy?' Knowing of Mr Boddy's close affiliation to Brooklands, I was in a quandary. Would he appreciate a carefully researched synopsis of events leading up to the first races along the De La Warr Parade in 1902? As it happened, I did not get to speak with Bill Boddy. One of his minions indicated that I might send the story on a speculative basis — nothing was said about commission. I needed a carrot to make the donkey work so I contacted Michael Bowler, then the editor of *Thoroughbred and Classic Cars* magazine. He confessed to being totally ignorant of Bexhill's story. The more I talked, the more I felt Michael's curiosity grew. He became eager enough to ask that the griff be sent along with photographic evidence and any other paraphernalia.

The donkey could now go to work . . .

12

Bexhill in Context

TO FULLY realise Bexhill's history, there are two clearly defined eras which today are two visual tiers. The upper part on the 'Holy Hill' is the real Old Town of Bexle which slowly mushroomed after King Offa of Mercia's charter granted land upon which St Peter's Church was built in 772AD. The gist of that charter can be read on the wall of the arch between the tower and the nave. Then by contrast with the actual social structure, the lower marsh of Bexhill, facing the sea became the aristocratic part of the area while upper Bexhill was populated by those who worked the land and started the brickmaking kilns. Old Bexhill was retained by the church until 1561 when Queen Elizabeth I acquired the Manor of Bexhill from the See of Chichester along with seven others in the diocese. Nine years later The Queen granted the Manor to Thomas, son of Sir Richard Sackville. Thus started an association which is recognised by the name of Sackville Road and the famous hotel of the same name on the sea front. Even before these happenings, life roamed this part of the coastline.

When a local schoolgirl recently paddled along the seashore during a very low tide, she spotted evidence of early habitation from some 130 million years ago. A giant footprint was discovered at the waterline adjacent to the Angling Club. Biologists determined that the massive impression was made by the prehistoric Iguanodon, a creature that walked upon its hind legs and stood to the height of 45 feet. It was preceded by the smaller Scelidosaurus by some 45 million years. Bexhill came of age in 1846 when the London to Brighton & South Coast Company opened its railway between Lewes and Bulverhythe, a lovely little rural line that wended through fields and glades within the parish. The station was ordered by the Earl to be situated at the bottom of the hill on the seaward side of the sprawling De La Warr estate.

The growth of what became known as Bexhill-on-Sea from the marshy south side of the railway was decided when the 7th Earl De La Warr commissioned John Webb, a reputable builder and contractor from South London, to construct a sea defence and a broad, curving promenade from Galley Hill westwards along the shore to what is now Sea Road. After surveying the task, Webb quoted his terms at £34,000 to complete the job, a sum considered to be worth a king's ransom in those days. Clearly not impressed by this substantial figure, the Earl struck a bargain with Webb by offering him the bogland to the west of Sea Road in part payment for the sea wall. Webb was a far-sighted man who, after squelching around in the glutinous acres, astutely accepted the apparently unpromising land.

By 1883 the sea was controlled beyond a sturdy wall behind which a sweeping esplanade for constitutionalists and bicyclists to enjoy without encumbrance. From there on sections of land were avidly developed under the auspices of the Earl De La Warr. A matter of three years later, John Webb reached a gentleman's agreement with the 7th Earl to lay a western promenade as part of his plan to develop an area which became the Egerton Park Estate. He then built roads that appeared more like causeways reaching inland, akin to ribs off the sternum, from what is now the West Parade and the Marina, where residential properties and shops stand today.

Less than 100 years separated Bexhill's hey-day from the time when Pam and I moved to Number 21. The uninterrupted view across the channel to the Sovereign Lighthouse that stands nine miles offshore over the shoals to warn shipping away from danger, did not exist at the turn of the century. On dark winter nights, the De La Warr Parade is a still a place where a man and his dog might be seen in the dazzling Sovereign beam that flashes past every twelve seconds. If I looked to the south-west from our lounge window, where the Kursaal, half-theatre, half-pier, once stood, there now stands the Bexhill Sailing Club. The bandstand that attracted hundreds on Sunday afternoons is now a convenient rain shelter. Both landmarks stood inside the ornamental gates to the De La Warr estate. By craning my neck to look east, I would just about have spotted the ornate ironwork of the Cycle Chalet opposite the Sackville Hotel. This amazing little emporium with its clock-tower was where bicycles could be hired by those who wished to pedal sedately along the cycle way.

All these novel architectural trinkets that made Bexhill 'the place to go' for London socialites are now gone. When Carlton Court was a complete house amid the most elegant terrace overlooking Sussex-by-the-Sea, I would have enjoyed the best possible view of the mixed bathing. I can just imagine some gentlemen residents of yore, sitting upon their balconies with 'vision enhancers' akimbo as they watched the daring damsels dabble in the sea.

It appears sacrilege to call the Manor House in Old Bexhill a 'barn' when the place was the medieval seat of the Bishops of Chichester. In truth the Manor was purchased from its last occupants during the mid-sixties by the Bexhill Corporation for the sum of £23,000 and then systematically demolished. Some of the foundations remain like the buttress and a trefoil-headed window standing along with some outhouses and the tranquil wall garden.

In the 18th Century the Dorset family converted the rambling old house into a hunting lodge from where they entertained sporting guests on wild-fowl shoots across the marshes. Then the Brook family adapted it into a farm house, to which the place was entirely unsuited. The real potential of the Manor was realised again by Gilbert George Reginald, Viscount Cantelupe, son to the Earl De La Warr, when in 1891 he commanded alterations. Here was a young man blessed with enterprise, vision, audacity and the important connections in exalted places to realise his ambitions for Bexhill-on-Sea. He required a desirable residence for guests — even members of royal families. Work commenced upon the original part of the house where he greatly enhanced and lightened the drawing room with a lovely bay window. In one outhouse was maintained a gas-driven engine that generated electricity for lighting and a specially rigged telephone for direct communication between The Manor and the estate buildings along the sea front.

Viscount Cantelupe succeeded as the 8th Earl De La Warr when his father died in January 1896. Before then he had dedicated himself to local government. The Corporation recognised his entrepreneurial skills. When Colonel Henry Lane passed on in 1895, Cantelupe was immediately voted into the Chairmanship of the town's first Urban Council. In the midst of his rise to local government power, The Viscount became wedded to Muriel, daughter to the 1st Baron Brassey of Normanhurst. The couple reared their only son, Herbert Brassey Sackville, in 1900. Two years later the marriage foundered in divorce. There was a whiff of scandal which caused the Borough to overlook his candidature for mayor. The Earl did take office for two years — two momentous years for Bexhill, when the horseless carriage fired the Earl's imagination.

Bexhill citizens reckoned that something special was going on when the Viscount had a private cricket pitch rolled out where in 1894 he treated the local sloggers to a match against the full South African touring team. Even larger crowds witnessed the local XI getting beaten by the Australian test team two years later. The Viscount had proven his pedigree, and the public thirsted for other momentous sporting occasions.

There is room for wonderment at what the true Bexhillians up in Old Town made of this astonishing rate of expansion both socially and architecturally. The 'purty luttle missus' daughters of the working families, often wandered down Sea Lane (as Upper Sea Road was known) Upon reaching the promenade these teenage girls stood and stared in amazement at the distinguished visiting gentry as they breathed the ozone while escorting their ladies dressed in their extravagant city finery.

While the farmers harvested corn in the summer, they must have examined the intelligence of the 'Lunnen city gents' who purchased large sections of marshy land for prestige property development. One day two bowler-hatted gentlemen appeared along the road sitting aboard a carriage that breathed steam, rattled and made an 'ell of a racket. That De Dion Bouton was the subject of talk for ages. It was in 1896 when the Emancipation Act recognised a class of light locomotive of up to three tons. From that time onwards the man with the flag who walked precariously ahead of the horseless carriages was made redundant. The automobilist was given his head, at least within the highway speed limit of 12 mph.

I look back now and remember little indicators when I was deeply involved in motor racing, that probably pointed to my on-going association with the sport, no matter how many times I deviated from the main theme of my life. A typical example was that day in 1968 when I stopped at Green

Bay, Wisconsin. I had absolutely no previous knowledge of the place, and yet from all the towns I could have chosen, the brakes went on there. To this day I have no logical explanation for drawing a halt on the start line of the very first race for mechanically-propelled vehicles in the world.

Since my departure from motor sport, my travels have brought me into contact with folk and artifacts which, no matter how tenuous, have been inextricably woven into the fabric of motor sport. The oddity is that once I had embarked upon the journey into the history of Bexhill and its chapter within the context of motor racing history, some trails evaporated. I was invariably beaten to the post by the 'great reaper' before encountering frail segments of the human puzzle who had first-hand knowledge of events gone by.

Long before men competed against each other in automobiles, genuine pioneers and great inventors tried to equate a form of generated power to the wheel. One such revolutionary was Richard Trevithick, a notable Cornishman and a brilliant engineer who created in Cambourne ripples with the magnitude of the Atlantic rollers. He mounted one of his non-condensing, high-pressure steam engines on a rolling chassis transported by cartwheels. At this early stage in the evolution of the motor car, the term 'automobile' had not been coined. Imagine the astonishment and then euphoria among the small band of locals as Trevithick created history before their eyes,when he audaciously invited seven of them to join him on a 'run' to the crest of Cambourne Beacon. What rammed Trevithick's invention home to any spy was that the power of his carriage enabled him to ascend rather than to make a 'flat run'. That was confidence in his own engineering ability. He motored to the top at 2.5 mph. Had not the contraption been weighed down by delirious passengers, he might have reached thrice the speed!

That momentous celebration was on Christmas Eve in 1801. In the New Year Trevithick was fired with still greater inspiration. He next created a working relationship with Andrew Vivian, a coach builder, and between them they refined the steam carriage. All the mechanical components were forged in Cornwall. Then, after meticulous assembly, Trevithick sailed with the carriage to London where the chassis and engine were fitted with a stylish body in 1803. The finished product was duly christened the 'Celebrated London Carriage'. Sceptical would-be investors were nonplussed by this new mode of transportation as they trundled along streets at 10 mph with Trevithick mastering control at the tiller. There were favourable comments upon the 'smooth' ride in comparison to the discomfort of the jerky horse-drawn carriage. In spite of the encouraging verdict made by the city gentlemen, no 'backer' was prepared to place money where his mouth was, so the steam carriage was taken to pieces.

Across the world other engineers like Oliver Evans, who was hailed by Americans as the second 'James Watt' made self-motivated steam-driven conveyances. A Czechoslovak known only as M Bozek wheeled out a steam 'Phaeton' which unfortunately suffered from an 'inadequate boiler', a common gremlin at that time.

Meanwhile, in England the first signs of internally combustible power were

173

being exploited by Samuel Brown in 1824. This first carriage was driven by an adaptation of this patent gas vacuum unit which was fuelled on a smoky coal gas. Brown tested his vehicle by mounting the long gradient of Shooters Hill to the South-East of London, trailing clouds of noxious fumes. Modern environmentalists would have nipped Brown's steed in the bud, since his idea was a portent of things to come. As it was, the ratio of cost-to-power was calculated to be uneconomical, so after a tirade of damnation and confounded blasting, London preserved its clean air when the principle, though proved effective, was abandoned.

Many a fabricator laid claim to have invented the automobile, but none came closer than Siegfried Markus. This jovial Austrian engineer was reported to have made experiments with atmospheric gas engines mounted in a hand-cart around 1864. Apparently, there was proof in print around the time of the Paris Exposition in 1900 that the Markus 'car' built in 1875 was on show. Close examination at the time revealed a historical error. The vehicle concerned was constructed by Marky, Bronovsky and Schulz at a small workshop in Adamsthal during 1889. Poor Siegfried never had his achievement carved in stone!

Instead Karl Benz of Mannheim, Germany, wears the mantle of the inventor who probably manufactured the first four-stroke gas unit set within a tricycle made for two. The Benz Tricar showed enormous potential. The first-ever 'car sale' was negotiated in 1887 when he sold a model to Emile Roger, a Paris-based engineer. Roger was so impressed that he applied for, and was granted sole agency rights in France for Benz. Thus was launched the motor car which established the industry upon the world.

Contrary to popular assumption, Gottlieb Daimler, the baker's son from Schorndorf who combined forces with Wilhelm Maybach to build the first high-revolution petrol engine in 1883, never worked with Benz in his own lifetime. The merger between Daimler and Benz took place some years later. However, in 1901 Daimler, while he still had strength, delivered a high-performance car which he named 'Mercedes' after his daughter, to Emile Jellinek, the Consul-General of the Austro-Hungarian Empire based in Nice. Jellinek was reputedly an avid sporting motorist, who was alleged to have entered his 5.9-litre thundering white charger in the speed trials run along the Promenade des Anglais.

Earl De La Warr almost became obsessional in his crusade to place Bexhill on the map as a fashionable resort. He made 'official visits' to the Côte d'Azur where he fraternised among many British aristocrats who wintered there on the basis of 'being seen to be seen' in places like Monte Carlo and Nice. He was receptive to ideas that related to Bexhill.

In 1901 he joined a party amid the huge crowds that flowed into Nice for the Speed Trials which had become a regular feature. Immediately, the Earl was captivated by the vision of so many motor cars assembled along the Promenade des Anglais. He relished the jovial enthusiasm of the French and noted that the British joined in the fun. Ladies were dressed in their 'Sunday best' and gentlemen wore more casual sporting apparel. Apart from the animated chatter, the contagious atmosphere of 'joie-de-vivre' was like an electric current buzzing along the avenues and on the beach. Nice was 'en-fête' for the trials with flags and bunting. As the Earl watched the cars chase along the course, he posed himself a question. Could such a festival of speed be transported to Bexhill? Would the English respond to such a spectacle with the same unbridled ecstasy as the French? These and many other queries ran through the Earl's mind as he envisaged the De La Warr Parade, Bexhill, being revered in the same glowing terms as the Promenade des Anglais in Nice. The common denominator would be the sporting automobilists. What fun — what a coup!

Earl De La Warr had a staunch ally in The Honourable John Scott Montagu MP, who accompanied him to the Côte d'Azur in February 1902. The politician realised the prestige value of such an event for tourism, trade and the hoteliers. If Bexhill could hoodwink other coastal resorts like Hastings, Eastbourne and even Brighton, by hosting the very first motor races in England, the electorate would reflect favourably upon him in the wake of such glory. Any thought of racing automobilists being loud, uncouth and anti-social by the nature of the machines they drove, was viewed as a small penance by contrast with the ultimate prize.

Raymond Mays became the 'God-Father' of ERA after he had polished his reputation as a driver behind the wheel of the successful voiturettes, especially as a leading exponent of the hill climb. After the Second World War BRM also gained from his experience. I recall a conversation Raymond had with the Monegasque driver Louis Chiron when he attended a Monaco Grand Prix in his paternal right as a member of Les Ancien Pilotes Association. They discovered both had met with a latter day Selwyn Edge, better known as S F Edge the unremitting, hot-tempered, British driver who became the British team captain after a heroic victory driving a six-cylinder Napier in the 1902 Gordon Bennett Trophy. Chiron argued that Edge won that race by default because Eliot Zborowski sawing at the wheel of his German Mercedes, was given penalties. So S F and the all-British Napier were declared the winners. Mays had nothing to say about that, but turned the subject to compare small traits of character between Edge and a certain G Hill who became World Champion driver in 1962 in a BRM.

Displaying his renowned passion, Chiron agreed the similarity did not stop at the sharp brown eyes and bristling moustache. The great Monegasque driver was convinced that Latin blood was stirred into the volatile Edge character. While Graham was also known to be fiery, the modern racing chevalier was at his most intimidating when the familiar face turned crimson as he 'simmered'. Both men eventually retired from the sport to administer the running of their own cars. Edge proved to be the more astute businessman.

S F was constantly in pursuit of velocity linked with reliability in his cars, and persisted in cajoling the engineers at Napier onto greater efforts in the search for performance. The relationship with Montagu Napier began when S F wheeled his 1897 Panhard-Levassor into the small Lambeth workshop to have the tiller replaced with a proper steering wheel, a 'mod' that greatly improved Edge's control of the car. Even then Edge was already selling imported cars. With a going concern, it made sense to take over the production of Napier. S F was the works driver, so any success he had in racing was sure to boost sales. Apart from Napier, S F was also the Managing Director of De Dion Bouton Great Britain Limited, and played one business off against the other. Commercial sponsorship was already rife before the millennium!

Before the first races at Bexhill, Edge had a growing affiliation with the resort. This was recognised in 1954 after Mrs S F Edge, (widowed after her husband's death in 1940), suggested an idea to the Veteran Car Club of Great Britain. She still lived at 10 Jameson Road in Bexhill, so the place was a constant shrine to Selwyn's memory. The S F Edge Trophy Meeting came to pass with the Jubilee Speed Trials.

Returning to those origins, Earl De La Warr sought encouragement for his racing ambition from Edge who happily agreed to give his racing Napier a few bursts along the parade. S F gave an enthusiastic nod of approval to the latent 'course' while local onlookers nudged each other in keen anticipation of events to come.

* * *

What is that indefinable charge that raises the sporting rascal in any red-blooded British motorist in France? Can it be the funnelling effect created by those regiments of trees that line many of the routes nationales? Perhaps cresting a rise to surge down ten miles of straight undulating road stretching towards infinity. Maybe it's the deserted D roads that cause a rush of blood as we bomb through the one-horse village of Vibrac at least 60 clicks over the limit, scattering poultry, clucking protest in our wake. Or does the answer lie in the strange British quirk for driving on the 'wrong side of the road'?

As a member of the generation twice removed from the pioneering days of road racing in France, I wonder at driving in those endurance events. The mind boggles at the hours navigating those bone-shakers along dust-roads lined with avid spectators. Were they 'he-men' or utter maniacs and were their riding mechanics brainless rock apes? Pioneering requires a dollop of masochism and downright cussedness to 'improve the breed'.

If we use maternity as a metaphor, motor sport went into labour in France, and in those early days fed from her generous bosom to grow into the sport we know today. The roads that criss-crossed France to meet with frontiers of other countries like Spain, the Benelux and the old Austro-Hungarian Empire, gave rein to the full potential of the motor car whereas the British initially treated the horseless carriage with disdain. After all, how on earth could a man possibly control a vehicle that lacked the obedience of man's constant friend. No matter how much the 'converted' preached of adequate brakes, reliable steering and a control over that combustible power, the Red Flag Act was enforced in 1865. Every 'road locomotive' as they were called, was required to have three persons in attendance: one to stoke the blazing boiler, a second person to pilot the carriage while a third man was required by law to walk ahead of the vehicle brandishing a red flag to warn oncoming traffic and pacify restive horses. Such a ridiculous regulation was framed to emasculate the adventuresome motorist by restricting him to a maximum speed of 4 mph on the open highway and 2 mph through built-up areas. A man running ahead could not endure a distance of any consequence. Besides, the cumbersome law was so flagrantly abused that legalised motoring came into being with the Emancipation Act in 1896, and the country went barmy from there on in its new-found liberty. Only then did a really competitive spirit rise in the breast of British motorists wishing to prove their worth abroad.

The gap between the traditionalists (who preferred the horse and carriage) and the motorist widened until common sense prevailed that journeys could be performed within almost half the time by using the horseless carriage. Drivers would set forth from London to, say Brighton, behind the carriage and team. By the time friends had galloped to their destination, the motorists had been refreshed and rested and had become impatient for the horse-drawn vehicles arrival. In France such piffling wagers between the different kinds of horse power meant nothing. Full-blooded inter-city racing was the rage.

Commercially speaking, witnesses to the mad-cap chases were greatly influenced by the outcome of these events. Cars that were unreliable stood out like sore thumbs, whereas strong, fast machines driven with zest to victory caught the eye of enthusiasts with substance. Each race created a growing clamour for the automobile of proven quality. There was prestige at stake and it was not just production quantity at the bottom line. National pride was being called into question as well.

If the mushrooming motor industry in France, Britain and Germany needed any more impetus beyond racing, then the opportunities sprang eternal on the dawn of the Twentieth Century. At that time, Britain's imperial powers, whether cherished or otherwise by colonies, were stretched around the world. Queen Victoria died fully believing that she reigned over an Empire that had one heart, one head, one language and a single policy. Truculent members like South Africa were regally struck from any official reference. Besides, a bloody skirmish the Boer War turned out to be, it was still regarded as good for trade. As Britain wildly celebrated the Twentieth Century, level-headed businessmen like Lawrence who had acquired the British licence to produce Daimlers and Frederick Lanchester had ensured that his models were rolling off his Birmingham production line in 1900 to reap the rewards of optimism.

The Daimler Wagonette had long trumpeted the six-horse power vehicle as being 'the sportsman's choice' — valiant hype that did not stem the flow from across the channel of the De Dion Bouton range, which during 1900 sold over 1,500 voiturettes. That far exceeded the combined production of Daimler, Wolseley and Lanchester. Such was the proliferation of vehicles upon the grossly inadequate British road system that one of the games people played was trying to identify the manufacturer. Many people were then illiterate, so when they could not pronounce a foreign name, they bastardised the terminology. Edge blanched at his De Dions being referred to as 'Ding-Dongs'. Owners of the Begot-Mazurie must have squirmed in embarrassment when youths shouted from the roadside: 'There goes a Bag o'Misery'. Other parodies rolled off the tongue when the Hispano-Suiza became laughingly known as the 'Banana Squeezer'. The best of the uncouth references, I believe, was 'I-shot-a-flash-Sheeny' — a rare beast that was one of the first to develop four-wheel braking properly — addressed as the 'Isotta-fraschini'.

While most of the cars being raced were instantly recognisable by the fans, patriotic identification fed fervour in 1900 when the organisers of the Gordon Bennett Trophy imposed the first national racing colours on the teams. Spectators could now recognise their team because the French cars were blue, the German cars were in virgin white and the Belgians adopted a dazzling yellow. Continentals fought for the favoured green. Debate was settled when Charles Jarrott received the green from the organisers of the 1901 Paris-Berlin race. British Racing Green remained the national colour until it disappeared under a welter of corporate advertising impedimenta in 1968.

Early organised competition in Britain was of a restrained nature. There were no great road races — a few picnic tours that was all, until a 325-yard hill-climb run was cordoned off at Petersham Hill in June 1899. There was a sprint meeting cobbled together on a public road outside Colchester a week later. Nobody had a clue about who was driving what, but some wag in a Delahaye could have made a name for himself when he 'scorched' the course at an average speed of 27 mph to record the fastest time of the day — but he omitted to deliver his entry form! Compared with the hairy-chested competition on the Continent, Britain did nothing much to stir the corpuscles until the Thousand-Mile Trail that was organised by the Automobile Club in 1900.

To digress, without a doubt one of the most influential authorities in early motor sport was the Automobile Club de France. This pillar of rectitude was established as Spring blossomed over Paris in 1896 by the Comte de Dion. The Club was instrumental in providing the ground rules — such as they were — for road racing. This sparked off a 'clone' shortly afterwards in Britain where vested interests attempted to raise a banner in the so-called national interest as a governing body. There was a certain H J Lawson, a Victorian 'whizz-kid' with dubious commercial interests in motor cars, who instigated the 'Motor Car Club'. Several astute cronies smelt a rat as it became obvious that this Lawson chap was endeavouring to monopolise the British motor trade. Nobody was party to such 'goings on', so a rebel group was formed within to scotch Lawson's commercially-orientated ploy. Thus the Automobile Club of Great Britain and Ireland was formed in 1897. The same committee of sporting gentlemen were granted the 'Royal' prerogative in 1907 by Edward VII. The same club remains today as the Royal Automobile Club, which still presides over British interests in motor sport and general motoring.

While feeling its way, the newly-formed committee, having out flanked Lawson, set out the basic aspirations of the Club. They realised the glamour of racing in France, but having just emancipated the carriage, their priority for the motor car during its period of teething troubles was to organise trials intended to prove reliability. These events would be unlike the London to Brighton Run which was neither a race nor a trial, but something of a 'hooly' for the self indulgent. The club set itself publicly to demonstrate the real capabilities of this novel means of locomotion. Important data had in some way to be accumulated by way of endurance runs, test trials and speed events, or sprints. This was cracking new ground for the British sporting motorist, although it was probably laughable to those 'speedsters' across the channel.

The Automobile Club got its feet wet in the competitive arena by stealth. News of racing motorists being involved in horrendous accidents in the road races in France was not helpful to the image which the club wanted to adopt from the outset. Cries of an irresponsible attitude were imagined within the Mother of Parliaments.

Around this time, interest in the motor car had reached fever pitch. If two cars were seen beating it down the local high street, folk would gather and cheer them on. Any event was given coverage in the newspapers and in the specialist press that was out of all proportion to what really went on — a fact which did not go unnoticed by the Earl De La Warr, who noted the column yards, not inches, that were devoted to the first One Thousand Miles Trial.

Those who have witnessed the assembly for the annual London-to-Brighton Veteran Car Run at Hyde Park Corner will have some inkling of the terrific atmosphere that must have filled the air along the shore of the Serpentine that April morning whereas the sight of so many veteran cars penned into a single area is novel to us modern motorists, imagine the almost 'manic' enthusiasm generated by hundreds of automobilists ready for the 'off' in 1900. Perhaps the collective and distinguishable sounds of various cars that ranged from Lanchesters to the ubiquitous De Dion Boutons and the nippy Panhards — anything from a regal Benz to the Barriere tricycle and the Leitner dog-karts — found favour with the milling crowds who not only relished the sights, but listened in amazement to the symphony of wheezes, hisses, pops and bangs that echoed amid the guttural roar of the European thoroughbreds. This was to be the first demonstration across the country that the motor car could perform all the manoeuvres and functions which each manufacturer claimed for its steed. Drivers of varying skill then had the opportunity to show the hordes of onlookers who lined the route that the motor car was a carriage without a horse, and was now the only alternative mode of transport. As the trial departed from London, with it went the finalé of the early belt-drive, and in came the motor car as it has evolved today.

Mr Alfred Harmsworth lived in a baronial pile near Reading. Those who stopped for lunch and mechanical inspection noted that some of the 'tiddlers' had already expired. Full of nourishment and fine wine, the bonhomie could not be doused by torrential rain as the motorists splashed over the wet tram lines in Bristol where they made the first night stop.

Drivers, unable to curb their competitive, spirit exchanged outrageous tales of 'races' along the narrow roads out of sight of law enforcement officers. The bedraggled, but indefatigable gladiators and their wives or lady friends pushed on north through Birmingham and Manchester. They spent a fourth night at Kendal. On one visit to the Merlins in Cumbria I met with an elderly gentleman who had witnessed this 'unbelievable mob of pioneers' arriving in the Cumberland town, many looking more like Scott of the Antarctic than like heroes of the mechanical age. Without the protection of windscreens the motorists were warmly wrapped up in huge fur coats with gaiters to match. The gentlemen looked more like Lappish deer herdsmen while some of the ladies donned masks and fine lace veils to protect their complexions from stones, dust and the roaring wind. Allweathers of New Burlington Street, London must have done a roaring trade in ladies' leather motor clothes.

Drivers had nursed their cars up to Dunmail Raise, to Keswick and onward to Carlisle. Many an epic struggle was chronicled in the local press. Some cars gave up the ghost in a cloud of steam. Still, a goodly number of erstwhile motorists, determined to complete the course come-what-may, wended their passage through huge crowds in Edinburgh as they entered the cavernous overnight halt inside Waverley Market.

Scottish writers and photographers waxed lyrical at the sight of these robust vehicles that had survived this far along this amazing odyssey. Photographers were seen almost literally swinging from the rafters to attain high viewpoints to secure full-frame pictures of this unique assemblage. Whatever the Automobile Club's data-gathering reason for this mechanical trial, romance with the motor car was evoked as the local people eavesdropped upon stories swapped by the motorists of audacious driving to combat the weather, Scotland's undulating countryside and the hundreds who lined the roads, totally unaware of the dangers of errant cars. Amazing tales of fortitude emerged as one driver told how his car's steering came adrift, so he steered by dragging his boot along the ground. Even more horrifying was the man whose brakes were so worn the car would not hold on a gradient. So he became distinguished as having attained the record speed going backwards!

Whether these heroes and their heroines were becoming blasé about the trial or were simply adapting to their circumstances, regardless of numerous mechanical maladies, they learned to improvise in order to keep going. A tremendous spirit grew out of the event, whereby fellow motorists would stop to aid the afflicted and those who suffered an accident. In spite of the hardships the general consensus was that the return route south to London seemed nothing like as strenuous as the struggle going north. The road from Edinburgh was traced through Newcastle-Upon-Tyne, Leeds, Sheffield, Lincoln, Newport Pagnell and onward to Whitehall along the way the survivors had to compete in the first successful sprint meeting held in Britain.

The Duke of Portland had generously allowed a course to be arranged for a flying-start mile in the grounds of Welbeck Park. Since the road was not quite level, the average speed of each competitor was taken from a return run. At the end of the meeting, the Honourable Charles Rolls was posted as the outright winner with a two-way average speed of 37.63 mph driving a 12 hp Panhard.

The first '1,000' was undoubtedly the most successful event run by the Automobile Club at the time. There were 48 registered finishers. Only minor injuries were incurred by some reckless motorists.

The horseless carriage had arrived . . .

13

A Sackville of Cylinders

DURING HIS visits to the South of France, Earl De La Warr became increasingly aware that competing members of the Automobile Club had made recommendations to the committee for a competition, similar to the Nice Speed Trials, to be run in Britain. After S F Edge had completed his surreptitious reconnoitre along the level parade in 1901, the Earl instructed his agents to prepare a rock solid proposal favourably indicating that Bexhill-on-Sea was a prospective venue for such a speed event.

Certain other members of the British aristocracy in the land were also seeking the prestigious coup of hosting the very first races in the kingdom. Lord Suffield had posted an unexpected bid outlining the basis of a track at Cromer in Norfolk. The impetuous Duke of Portland who had banned motor cars from his estate at Welbeck Park after the Thousand Mile Trial, also awoke to the opportunity. He experienced a near miss after the sprint meeting in 1900 when an automobilist caused him to tumble from his bicycle. The Duke eventually swallowed his bruised pride. The Park continued to be a popular sprint venue for many years. The nobleman rashly assumed that the Automobile Club would look no further than his proven course.

The philosophy developed by the Automobile Club was that such an event would provide a terrific impetus to the fledgling British motor industry. Competing in front of an avid public, the performance of the competitors, class distinctions and the overall fastest time of the day would provide the best possible stage from which manufacturers could reap car sales. The multitude would also be able to compare British-made cars in direct competition with the best from France and Germany.

Earl De La Warr agreed with the club's keenness to arouse to greater heights the public enthusiasm for the emerging sport in Britain. In so doing, the host to such a huge attraction with all the attendant publicity would reflect favourably influence upon trade and commerce, boost tourism and have the hoteliers rubbing their hands in keen anticipation of more 'bums-in-beds'.

Nothing was taken for granted when the Automobile Club approached Earl De La Warr with the proposal that Bexhill might possibly feature the race meeting. There were ulterior motives for the Club's suggestion. A big plus in Bexhill's favour was its close proximity to Channel ports whereby foreign competitors could gain easy access to the venue.

This priority excluded the facility at Welbeck Park. The Cromer overture was quite as attractive as Bexhill but this failed because Cromer was too remote. So on a blustery March day in 1902 a small delegation from the Automobile Club drove from Whitehall Court down to Sussex-by-the-Sea to test Bexhill's capability.

Their intention was to negotiate with the Earl's agents a private mile-long track along the road that ran parallel with the De La Warr Parade. At the time of the inspection, only half of the road to the eastern extremity of the estate was complete. The club required a downhill 'run in' for flying starts, and suggested that the road should be extended to the crest of Galley Hill. Without a moment's hesitation, the Earl agreed to the request and to the suggested removal of his beloved ornamental entrance gates in the observance of safety on meeting days. It is worth recording that two completely independent foot and hand braking systems had not become mandatory until 1903. Four-wheel brakes were not even compulsory hence the reason for a suitable braking area after the finish line in which drivers could bring their steeds to a halt at the end of the course.

Living over the shop at Brands Hatch, I had, over the years, come to realise just how militant local residents whose property backed onto the circuit could be. Unscrupulous estate agents allegedly showed prospective purchasers around houses when there was no activity on the circuit. After such people had moved into their newly acquired habitat, some families were rudely awakened by Formula cars roaring beyond the trained ivy and tall trees at the bottom of the garden.

While noise abatement societies did not exist in 1902, Earl De La Warr must have been conscious of a simmering minority of Bexhill citizens who would not take kindly to their peace being shattered.

I can only surmise that such disturbed persons in Marine Mansions, and private residences along from the Sackville Hotel and off-shoots from the Parade like Brassey and Middlesex roads, took refuge at Bridge Parties held in secluded Cooden or Little Common, just as the mature majority of Monte Carlo residents still escape the bedlam of the Monaco Grand Prix in the peace havens along the cornice above the Principality.

While the odd protester kicked doors behind drawn curtains, I imagine that living at the dawn of the new millennium must have been an intoxicating experience. As Bexhill busied itself preparing for its Grand Prix, Britain's first submarine was being launched at Barrow-in-Furness. The very first newspaper to be printed in mid-Atlantic was distributed to passengers on board Cunard's liner *Etruria* . Today a newspaper is gone with the chips, but imagine the excitement on that ship at being able to read news from Blighty, over a thousand miles from Land's End. The passengers probably learned that Thomas Edison had invented the new electrical storage battery. What an incredible contribution he made to the smooth running of the motor car — even today. All fantastic stuff, and still there were eccentric ladies like Mrs Anne Taylor who desperately sought worldwide fame by hurling herself down Niagara Falls in a barrel to reap rewards that would pay her mortgage.

This thrilled the condescending onlooker. I wonder if Guglielmo Marconi added to Mrs Taylor's notoriety when he transmitted signals from Cornwall to Newfoundland, thus establishing the first signs of worldwide wireless communications. Amid this intoxicating era of evolution, it went almost unnoticed that Marcel Renault claimed a scintillating victory in the first Páris-Vienna race driving a car of his own manufacture. News editors then must have wondered which way to turn as invention burst upon the world virtually every day. Perhaps the only earth-shattering news which 'held the front page' broke when the US President, William McKinley, died after an assassination attempt by Polish anarchist Leon Czolgosz. Nothing much seems to have changed in the New World since!

Against this background of rampant progress, Serpollet had set a new motor car speed record of 74.5 mph at Nice, Bexhill had been partly transformed into a race course. Local supporters of the project took their daily constitutional along the east promenade and came to know every yard of the newly-laid non-slip gravel road intimately. The 'track' as it became known, had been surfaced from the brow of Galley Hill where it ran parallel with the original golf course, and descended 160 yards over the start line onto the measured kilometre. Two fairly gentle curves featured in the length before the original cycle track finished on a line directly below Number 21 Marine Mansions. Had I been born another generation or so earlier, I would have savoured a completely unencumbered view from our eyrie.

It was estimated that the gradient at Galley Hill was an ideal one-in-twelve, sufficient to enable cars to cough up a fair head of steam before hitting the timed section. One 'fly in the ointment' was the distance from the finish line to the estate gateposts — some 260 yards. The indefatigable Edge blasted his Napier along the course, crossed the line and literally 'stood on the brakes' to get the errant car drawn up short of the four brick-based columns, two of which formed the imperial arch with the De La Warr coat-of-arms in the centre of the road. One failure or slight deviation, and S F could have demolished himself, the car or the Earl's beloved boundary posts. Nobody seemed perturbed, least of all Selwyn Francis who reckoned that if two powerful cars arrived simultaneously in the braking area, providing that the entrances were clear, including the arch, the drivers would find somewhere to go. As it turned out the problem had got magnified out of all proportion. The officials of the Automobile Club declared themselves well satisfied with Bexhill's track after side-by-side test runs during May 1902. In fact, the august gentlemen envisaged that the course would be operational for many years hence.

Shortly after moving to Bexhill in October 1976, I became curious about a dark, forbidding, red-brick hulk at the east end of Knole Road. The opulent building had witnessed better days, and had fallen into neglect for reasons which I did not know at the time. On impulse one Sunday morning I strolled from Number 21 past the towering edifice and pushed a side door off Middlesex Road to enter it.

I was horrified to stand within the decaying skeleton of a former glory. Windows had not just been smashed — vandals had pushed entire frames out from their mountings. So apart from being dark and dingy, there was a draught which blustered around the portals. Plaster had fallen from the ceiling, rising damp mouldered on the walls. There was a vaulted reception hall to the north façade alongside which I imagined horse-drawn carriages drew up. As I peered about the decrepitude, a door opened and a man I recognised to be our postman beamed a warm welcome. I told him of my nosiness. 'Oh, that's alright', he grinned, 'I live here!' I was aghast to learn that other souls also inhabited flats dotted about the various floors of the building.

He invited me into his abode through a heavy wooden door. Inside was a postman's castle, all cosy, welcoming and full of one man's happy life. His home was hard to equate with the desolation beyond his front door... and this was chintzy Bexhill!

Over a cup of tea I asked him what on earth this elegant fallen lady was at the time of her prime? The postman's face adopted an expression to that of a jilted lover. 'It's sad to relate' he murmured, 'but I live in the former Sackville Hotel'.

Had there been a 'star' award, the one-time opulence I gazed upon would not have warranted a three-four-or even a five-star rating. Such was the reputation of the hotel at the turn of the twentieth century, people along Piccadilly, London before the Bexhill Races had only to mention a long weekend on the south coast, and the Sackville name would have turned the heads of eaves-dropping gentry.

Without a doubt, when the 7th Earl De La Warr financed the building during 1888 on land which was part of Arthur Sawyer Brook's farm, he must have demanded 'simply the best' — the same credo required by the Sarkies Brothers when they opened Raffles Hotel in Singapore during November 1899 — and my, how the two hotels bore a similarity with that 'home-from-home' ambience. The basis of the Sackville was curious in that it was originally a row of four dwellings incorporated into the hotel.

The newly-constructed west side of the complex was built of brick made at the local works in Sidley, and laid in a Queen Anne style, with a tower at the southwest corner. This landmark rose from the base to summit with a turret and flagstaff at the pinnacle. London architect Graham Awdry was briefed to attach the hotel directly onto the four houses. It was planned to merge everything eventually into a single unit, including the Earl's residence overlooking Bolbrooke Road. All-in-one, the twinned establishment stretched across the entire block. Later on the views from the top floor took in the entire panorama of the original cycle track which later became the race course. By the simple expedient of knocking through arches, the two separate buildings became one, with connecting corridors and stairways. The overall appearance of this grafting operation was novel. It presented the hotel wing as a four-floor facility, the façade of which matched the original three-story dwellings. Today the entire building is a cleverly married block of equal levels.

The Sackville Hotel was officially opened by the 7th Earl in July 1890 with pomp, panache and politically correct guests. They travelled from London by train and locally by trolley-bus and mingled amid the towering palms and bamboo trees that festooned the reception area and the dining room. The effect of luxuriant comfort with not a penny spared had the very important persons agog. While the manager of London's Tivoli Restaurant compared initial impressions with Bexhill's station master, a lady correspondent from *Vanity Fair* compared notes with the London editor of the *New York Herald*. Anyone not totally enamoured with the Sackville was stunned into appreciative silence by the gastronomic delight set before them on tables embellished by huge spreads of white lilies. The Earl had spared nothing on the menu which included juicy morsels like *Saumon Bouillé* and *Sauce Cardinale* followed by *Patés de Pigeons de Bordeaux* or *Jambon D'York en Bellevue*. The entremets offered *Gelées Macédoine de Fruits au Champagne*, and those represented a small fraction of the total choice! This fine repast occupied four hours in its digestion and the excesses were washed down by the finest selection of wines which Mr Hardwicke, the hotel manager, could secure from France.

The tone had been set, so the Earl's son, Viscount Cantelupe remained in residence to welcome guests. For two years he entertained lavishly before moving to the Manor House in 1892. Once the Sackville had become established as a 'growing concern' the De La Warr family disposed of the property in 1897 to Frederick's Hotels Limited, who then owned it for sixty years.

At the outbreak of the Second World War in 1939, there was a large-scale evacuation of Bexhill — a signal for Brigadier A C Critchley to commandeer the west wing of the Sackville in order to train Royal Air Force recruits who probably could not believe their luck at being posted to such a luxurious billet. It was miles better than Gunner Spike Milligan had on top of Galley Hill where he manned the mighty Spandau to little effect at a blue horizon clear of any enemy attack — a boring duty since Bexhill saw no real action until 1942, when the town centre was damaged by a 'tip-and-run' raid.

The hotel was mopped up after the war and returned partly to a forlorn splendour. Notable signatures in the visitors' book showed Charles Chaplin, Anna Neagle and Anthony Eden escaped the madding crowds there, but sadly (in spite of such patronage), the Sackville gently sagged into decline. The hotel was traded several times after 1957 before its closure was forced by an austere economic climate. After 1963 the good times became an echo when the adjoining rooms were converted into apartments. Since the day when I met my postman, the Sackville has been refurbished. Now its occupants enjoy their twilight years in a style reminiscent to the 'good old days'.

When it had been established that the races were a definite fixture for the 1902 Whitsuntide weekend, word soon buzzed around motoring circles in London, Paris and even persons in Brussels were enthused about making the trip into history. The Automobile Club were quick to advertise the Sackville as the official headquarters for the meeting. So the committee block reserved many of the readily vacant rooms, and those remaining were provided for racing members on a first-come-first-served basis.

Guests who managed to secure a south facing suite had a fine view of the coast-line over the Cycle Chalet. The ornate building that stood along the original cycle track, was commandeered by the timekeepers, while VIPs had access to view the races from the balcony. Here the electronic telegraph board was situated to inform the spectators of each race time and average speed.

The sea during the latter end of May was a bearable temperature for a dip, so there was a special path from the Sackville to the beach where leather-skinned individuals could change in the hotel's bathing machines and plunge straight into the water. Many of the 'softies' with their wives-mistresses-girlfriends, were observed leaving the hotel by the Middlesex Road door to stroll furtively along Knole Road to the Bexhill Hydro, a health spa which was directly next door to where I lived! On learning this, my mind boggled at the goings-on at this apparently well-supervised establishment which was dedicated to rude health. There were vapour and hot-air boxes and separate treatment rooms for tannic, iodine and electric baths.

Throughout May 1902, gaggles of motorists would arrive in Bexhill to try their paces along the new course. Early in the month a run was organised between Crystal Palace and Brighton. Heavy rain deterred many of the motor-ists who had entered, so a motley bunch of bedraggled drivers and saturated passengers trickled into Brighton on the Saturday. S F Edge, who had missed the main congregation in London, arrived in Brighton on Sunday in his 75 hp Napier to join the diminished few. After a sociable day by the sea on Sunday, a decision was made that before daybreak on Monday, those who had already posted their entries for the races were to drive along the coast road to Bexhill for some 'unofficial practice'. A wide disparity of vehicles ranging from an 8 hp New Orleans to a 60 hp Mors, similar to the 1901 model run in the Paris-Berlin race, wended past Eastbourne at sunrise. Bexhill residents had not even stirred as the Honourable C S Rolls blasted down from Galley Hill with Edge's Napier in tow a length or so behind. The competitive spirit was such that both drivers raced back'n'forth several times. By the time the two mis-chievous pilots had settled their private wager, hotel guests at the Sackville had parted their curtains. Dressed only in night shirts and nighties, they were hanging out of opened windows to cheer the cars on to greater speeds.

According to Mark Mayhew's suspect timing, the Hon C S Rolls had made the fastest trips along the course. Edge explained that his Napier was not then in full racing trim, but he estimated that the fastest time of the day could be in the region of 42 seconds over the kilometre, a speed of approximately 52 mph. The two racers concluded that the run down to the start line from Galley Hill might need to be extended, because neither car had reached full racing speed where the timed section was supposed to start.

By the time that a sleepy policeman was reported to have arrived at the scene on a bicycle to witness the fuss, the two drivers and their cronies, wear-ing 'What us?' expressions, had parked their vehicles in Bolbrooke Road and were having breakfast in the hotel!

Leon Serpollet was the main topic of conversation wherever automobilists gathered. His record-breaking run in Nice just one month before the Bexhill Races could not have been better timed. The British were curious to see what had jokingly been described as the steam-propelled 'Easter Egg' because of the Serpollet's ovoid aerodynamics. Seated within this projectile, Serpollet had shot along the Promenade des Anglais in 29.8 seconds to set a world record for the flying kilometre.

Its miraculous speed caused spectators along the Nice course to ebb in astonishment as it approached them. Then as the Serpollet 'whooshed' past them they flowed back into the car's slip-stream to see the finish. British competitors present like Baron Henri de Rothschild, Charles Jarrott and S F Edge realised that the shorter run-up at Bexhill protected Serpollet's record in England.

Nevertheless, after Nice, an English enthusiast Mr W L Creyke, purchased Leon Serpollet's 'Easter Egg' which led the Brits to believe that the Frenchman's teeth had been drawn. Serpollet fell back on his earlier white-painted steam car in which he placed greater faith for Bexhill. Since Mr Creyke had not 'cracked' the 'Easter Egg', he still promised to enter it at Bexhill, thus providing Serpollet with a second option. No wonder that the British drivers had clandestine practice forays at Bexhill. Somebody had to hold a candle to Leon Serpollet by fair means or foul. A steeper ramp at the top of Galley Hill was requested to help drivers to achieve that extra inertia.

* * *

Strange but in spite of the enormous success and prestige attained by French cars in endurance road races and speed trials, the French Government found the growing sport to be élitest and a complete anathema to the state of the economy. They did not appreciate that the sport was creating a demand which in turn boosted the industry. Instead, they penalised the motorist by enforcing car registration for vehicles capable of more than 20 mph. The Government hoped that this would create a double-edged sword in that it would cut down traffic and make the roads safer for pedestrians and for horse-drawn carriages.

On the subject of safety, the Automobile Club de France had not framed regulations that concerned the physical well-being of chauffeurs and their passengers. They raced through towns and villages where only a modicum of protection was offered against unyielding lamp standards, corners of buildings and obstinate trees. Apart from cloth caps, goggles and long leather coats, the competitors were unprotected against a high-speed 'prang'. Many of the routes were barely marshalled, and junctions and cross-roads lacked police control. Since it was unlikely that anybody would make a reconnaissance of a course that could be up to 700 miles, each pilot drove at every corner and hill-brow totally 'blind'. So great were the dust clouds that experienced drivers steered by the tree-tops along the road. There was not a pace note in sight, since passengers were mechanics, not navigators.

Charles Jarrott summed up his chosen sport admirably by likening it to 'chasing unobtainable horizons during an earth tremor which has awakened you from a deep sleep.' Speed was the cross which every driver was happy to bear in his flight to victory. Whether the cars were controllable was another question in this unexplored territory where every yard was an adventure. At the end of each 'Paris-to-Somewhere', casualties were legion, and fatalities a matter of fact.

A bankrupt Government deluded itself into believing that the road races were a passing fad. But as the sport grew with each new development, they sat on the fence awaiting the first fatal accident that involved spectators. The clamps would then be applied to road racing with a vengeance. Jarrott described the horrors of charging through villages and small towns where walls of people separated only at the very last second in order to allow his huge rampant Panhard through. A monstrous carnage was waiting to happen.

During those early years a roll-call of brave and often reckless drivers began to grow. This included names like Marcel Renault and Leslie Porter. Then M Tourand smashed into a crowd at Angoulême killing his mechanic and a soldier. This was almost the last straw to break the camel's back.

Despite the apparently precarious state, road racing continued to thrive in France. The ACF proved beyond doubt that competing in the 1901 Paris-Berlin race assisted manufacturers in the development of power units and their reliability was of benefit to the showroom touring car. Drivers had developed such a mechanical feel that they could nurse a car to finish. This was graphically illustrated when, after the finish in Berlin, Henri Fournier went to claim a famous victory in his Mors — fired-up to head the post-race parade only to grind to a halt with the drive chain broken.

As if to placate President Loubet's supposedly intransigent governmental attitude, the ACF introduced 1,000 kg weight limit upon the big cars which placed a curb upon the size and power output of an engine. This was an attempt to prevent manufacturers from going 'speed mad' and point them down the road of reliability. Overwhelming power was still the winning formula in the heavy car class, but it was amazing how the more nimble lighter vehicles were able to keep up with the monsters on twisty sections of road.

After the Paris-Berlin Race, the Government sanctioned the 1902 Circuit du Nord Race, the very first event specifically organised for propaganda purposes. The 'alcohol race' as it was advertised by the French Ministry of Agriculture, served to promote this national product as a fuel which competitors had by regulation to use in their cars.

Drivers of the 'hybrid' cars found the top-end performance was blunted, some drivers poured a gallon of alcohol on board to be sure that they had sufficient to get far enough down the road to enable them to fill up with petrol. The race was heralded a success. No spectators suffered because they were amply warned of cars approaching when marshals detonated 'bombs', Maurice Farman was judged the outright winner, he averaged 44.8 mph for the 537-mile course driving his Panhard, presumably on the pure alcohol fuel, Marcellin's 24 hp Darracq was first in the light-car category at an average speed of 41.2 mph. The relatively narrow margin between the classes on this occasion created a stir in that only 3.6 mph separated the two cars, but on the road that represented quite a distance.

I had keenly perused a wonderfully descriptive report by H Walter Staner, editor of *The Autocar* of his experience in being a passenger to a racer, which he compared to being on the footplate of a locomotive train at full steam. He had never felt such a sensation of speed so intensely as when he sat beside Leon Serpollet in the 'Easter Egg' at Bexhill. Until they reached the middle of the course, the pace was unremarkable, probably fifty miles per hour. Then the car seemed to increase in speed, and before the finish line was reached he felt certain that well over one mile a minute had been accomplished. It was estimated that the Serpollet reached the end of the course travelling at 70 mph. This practice run for the benefit of the press won huge favour. Mr Staner with his colleague Mr Roger Wallace did some quick calculations: upon the reckoning that they had completed the kilometre in around 42 seconds they must have averaged 54 mph or thereabouts.

14

In Praise of Riding Mechanics

I TRIED to imagine the absolute ecstasy which that created in the mind of such an authority who had seen the motor car evolve, but had never before been driven with such gusto. By contrast with the modern idiom, it might have compared with a blast around the Nürburgring as passenger with Stirling Moss in the works Aston Martin.

Mad keen to get just a tingle of that sensation evoked in Mr Staner's breast, and remembering Charles Jarrott's stirring insight, I persuaded Paul Foulkes-Halbard, the owner and curator of Filching Manor Motor Museum near Eastbourne, to unearth his white Mercedes 70 and give me a blast to Bexhill and back. Paul's attitude towards modern motoring stirs the soul as a wooden spoon would a bowl of porridge. His entire appearance and social demeanour is cast-off from the Edwardian era, where you feel he would have been better at home. Beneath Paul's mood of sarcasm and outright belligerence there is heart that loves nothing more than mucking about with pensioned-off automobiles and their restoration to their former mechanical good health. Once that job is completed, the affair is consummated behind the wheel, man-handling the beasts into a re-enactment of their true ferocity.

Paul needed no second asking to push out his beautifully presented 1904 Mercedes, which came to him as a pile of junk boxed up on a quayside in Buenos Aires. Today, it is the sole survivor of its type and model. While he cossets the Mercedes decked out in traditional white livery in the museum, Paul believes that a motor car is there for the driving, and is capable of giving this almost extinct animal a good hiding to clear the cob-webs.

As he donned the appropriate leather helmet, lowered the split-lens goggles over his forehead, and he wound the hand starter, the blue eyes sparkled. The car grumbled into life. It was stripped of mud-guards and any kind of protection from the elements, so I was in for a treat of 'macho-motoring' at its best. Seated some four-foot-something above terra firma, I felt a vulnerability — not that I was particularly concerned as we trundled from Jevington. The high-mounted steering wheel and any other loose appendage 'shimmied' even at a steady 30 mph to the A259 Pevensey Marsh Road. Various bugs and fragments of grit peppered my face as tears welled up in my eyes from the wind. Once we had cast off the restrictions of Westham, the open marsh road invited Paul to call on the horses. At around 1,000 rpm this unruly white charger would be getting into its stride at 60 mph. Impatient with modern motorists, Paul hauled the Mercedes into the glory lane and dared any oncomer to stand his corner. Suddenly the brute force was unleashed, other drivers glanced in their rear-view mirrors and straight away reverently hugged the curb as we ducked and wove a hair-raising pattern along the road.

I could barely keep my eyes open, such was the blast upon my face. I was gasping for breath, the Mercedes was providing a vibro-massage of incomparable sensuality. So this explained why riding mechanics perished with a grin on their faces! The hedgerows wavered by as if in a heat haze. The marsh road was a relatively smooth, modern mettled road. When we did hit a ridge or a sunken garden, it jarred, but nothing like as bad as Jarrott suffered. Paul re-asserted his grip on the wheel, then bellowed above the wind's roar: 'Reckon we're doing about 75 mph'. No bobby would stop this monster in a mile of cemeteries.

At such a speed the Mercedes — being top heavy — felt precarious. A deviation from the norm would produce a sensation akin to Blondin wobbling on the tight rope over the Niagara Falls. The shimmering front wheels looked as if they were of narrow gauge like bicycle wheels. The big old head-lights vibrated on the mountings fit to fall and yet in spite of the shimmy-shakes Paul sat resolute. God help any stray dog, charging bull, witless chicken and all the other extraneous life that stood in the way of the 'real racers' of yesteryear.

I remembered reading of Charron splattering a big St Bernard, which managed to jam the Panhard's steering gear. Undeterred, Charron charged across the road, aviated a ditch, scraped a cleeve between two trees before taking a bow facing arse-about-face.

While I had every faith in Paul's ability to wrestle this bucking bronco, heaven only knew what would be our epitaph should he have lost control. Nasty etchings gleaned from mellowed books filled my mind of crews thumping trees and curbs at a healthy rate, and being tossed to the road like cannon fodder. As we tenuously teetered around a climbing left-hand curve by the old Northeye Prison where Bertrand Gachot served at Her Majesty's pleasure, a flock of geese looked every way but ours and threatened to find out why the chicken crossed the road. 'Dinner's up!' yelled Paul going straight for the neck of a gangling ganders. Thank goodness those stupid birds dispersed. The twelve-mile ride left me shaken, but incredibly exhilarated.

My admiration for those heroes of yesteryear was ten-fold. How they suffered 700 miles of such torment over unmettled roads remains beyond comprehension. But I declare that Paul's Mercedes 70 is a great motor car. Unfortunately, my experience merely served to romanticise those pioneering open road races. In view of what happened in 1903 when everybody's nightmare came true because the French Government put the kybosh on endurance events. President Loubet's cabinet had put a strangle-hold on motor sport, having rejected the 'Week of Speed' in Pau and stopped the Nice-Salon race. In a zealous mood the ACF retaliated against the authority to put man and machine through even more formidable paces.

The Paris-Madrid is now viewed in motor racing history as a watershed.

Fearing the worst the club cunningly decided to seek favour with King Alfonso of Spain, who was a renowned motor sporting enthusiast. The plan was to work the route from Madrid back to Paris. The frontier crossing was indicated over the Guadarrama mountains on a rough track comparable with the formidable Alburg Pass traversed during the Paris-Vienna race in 1902.

King Alfonso, probably in the dark on the French political ramifications, had unwittingly been used to twist the arm of President Loubet. After great deliberation and shrugging of shoulders, the ACF was begrudgingly given the thumbs up to continue plotting the route from the Spanish border back to Paris. No record indicates how many cars started out from Paris for Bordeaux, but as they hurtled south-west that day, garbled reports were telegraphed to Paris of terrifying accidents. The numbers of dead and maimed rose with each passing hour. Later reports suggest that the 'hundreds' of injured was highly exaggerated. Since there was no method of separating the truth from plain scare-mongering, the French authorities acted without hesitation and told the ACF to stop the race immediately at Bordeaux.

A massive hue and cry echoed in the Gironde capital. Protests by drivers about a 'chicken-hearted parliament' compounded the cry that Loubet was a Dracula figure who sucked the life-blood from motor racing. Reviewing the event with distant hindsight, one feels that the clamp was inevitable and probably served a timely lesson to the ACF to get its house in order if motor sport was to continue in France.

The Government suggested 'round races' similar to the Circuit des Ardennes which provided a perfect example. It was properly policed so that the crowds were allowed to view from specifically controlled enclosures.

The first car to arrive in Bordeaux was the massive 11.2-litre 70 hp Mors driven by the shy Frenchman, Fernand Gabriel, whose date of birth was never made known. How this diffident character could produce such an epic performance was remarkable. He had left Paris in 82nd place. Gabriel's strategy was simple: he sped along wide, open roads and drove with care through built-up areas. In spite of this stop-go tactic he averaged 65.3 mph along a beautifully controlled race, managing to avoid careless spectators and scared animals and to steer past wreckages.

Another competitor was Louis Renault, who with his brother Marcel recognised that the best way to indoctrinate people with the idea of their marque was to race — and race to win. By attempting to fulfil that ideal, Marcel was instantly killed when his 30 hp Renault careered headlong into a tree on the side of a narrow street in the rustic village of Coune-Verac. A man and his wife from the house opposite dashed to aid the stricken crew. Marcel's riding mechanic survived the 'bang'.

Louis raced on ahead oblivious of his brother's death. Renault finished first in the light-car class and second on the road behind Gabriel. After being told of Marcel's loss, Louis Renault immediately withdrew his cars from racing for the remainder of the season. The era of open road racing had drawn to an ignominious close. A new dawn had come to pass.

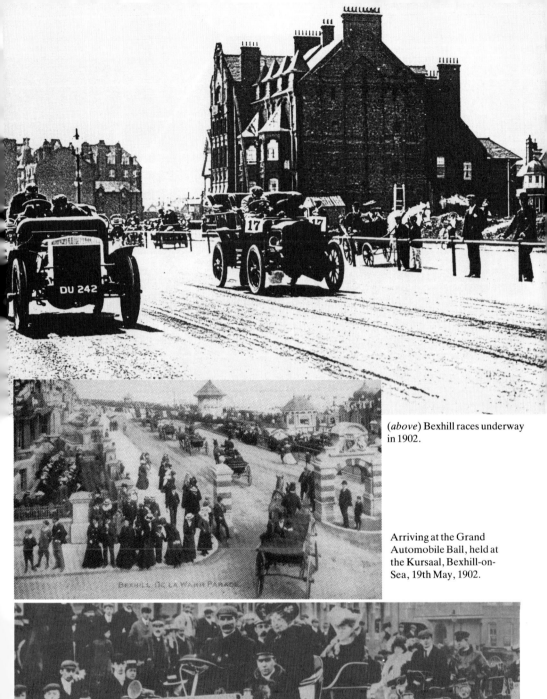

(*above*) Bexhill races underway in 1902.

Arriving at the Grand Automobile Ball, held at the Kursaal, Bexhill-on-Sea, 19th May, 1902.

S F Edge at the wheel of his Napier in Bexhill, 1902.

Some of the Bexhill 100 Committee headed by Brian Hazell (front far right) at the unveiling of the obelisks in September 1994. *Photo: Don Bostel.*

Raymond Baxter makes the opening speech at Bexhill's unveiling of the commemorative obelisks by Ivor Brampton in his uniform as the Deputy Lieutenant of Sussex. *Photo: Don Bostel.*

Project Volta by St Richard's School in Bexhill set a new world record for electric-powered under 500 kg cars, attaining 106.746 mph in September 1993. *Photo: Tony Hillyard.*

The author in Senna's McLaren at Bexhill, with his old chum, Neil Trundle. *Photo: Don Bostel.*

The Bexhill 100 Festival of Motoring is held each May to celebrate Bexhill-on-Sea as the venue of the first organised motor races in Great Britain where, on Whit Monday in 1902, participants from home and from across the Channel took part, while crowds of spectators, literally in their thousands, witnessed these first unique races on British soil.

* * *

The sobering events of 1903 were of course beyond the build-up to the Bexhill Races. No two moods could have been more extreme. We can only wonder what might have afflicted the Automobile Club had they delayed their meeting until 1903. That speculation will do nothing to dull the pride of John Russell. He is the only Bexhillian whom I found to be in possession of a small silver medallion, proof that his grandfather, Louis Russell, actually participated in the Bexhill Races.

Russells is the one family business in Bexhill that spans three generations from the days when the reins were laid dormant and horse power was steered by a tiller until today. Now the garage stands upon the original site on London Road. That sort of continuity serves to intrigue, because it could spell stagnation or inspire progress. I found that something of both camps had been maintained today. So I wondered what Louis Russell would make of his garage if grandson John were able to conduct him over the premises. He would find the building virtually unchanged. Only progress has revamped the façade.

It is quite possible that, if grandpa Louis mounted the stairs to his office from where his son Alan inherited the concern and where John rules the roost today, he would recognise some of the original furnishing. After the 'glitz' of the modern showroom, the three Russell generations were concertinaed into Louis Russell's original office. This showed no disrespect to John, but it merely reflected that the grandson was like his forebear — a rare traditionalist born with foresight.

Since John is the last male in the family line and his daughter has shown a disinclination to continue the family business in preference to riding (rather than driving) the family continuity will no doubt be swept out by the new broom.

Louis Russell began as a small engineer in Bexhill during 1896, the same year that the Emancipation Act was enforced. It would be wrong to say that Louis opened his business as a 'garage' since the definition means a house where cars are repaired. He may have tinkered in a small way with the automobile, but this genial industrious man capitalised upon small day-to-day domestic repairs and the maintenance of bicycles. Louis was known locally as the 'Jack-of-all-Trades'.

Then a day came when a physically handicapped gentleman visited Louis with the specific request for a customised invalid carriage. So Louis set-to and cobbled together a machine from all spare parts stored at his workshop. Eminently satisfied with his new perambulator, the man was able to propel himself to 'shoots' on the marsh.

Then by chance an Indian Prince darkened his door step. His Royal Highness required several water pumps to fill his swimming pool from the sea. These two sophisticated tasks gave Louis confidence to adapt a Merryweather Steamer into Bexhill's first fire engine to complement the local ambulance service which his company also ran. In consequence, Russell became known as 'Bexhill's Father of the Fire Brigade' which made him a prominent member of the town's social services.

Around the period leading up to the races, Louis Renault and brother Marcel were building motor cars in a shed at Billancourt. Destiny played a hand and the two Louis met at the Bexhill Races to form an alliance which remains as the longest-standing Renault agency in Britain.

The welter of national and regional publicity that started with a trickle in March 1902 steadily gathered momentum and became a raging torrent with the advent of May. Every single press release was published virtually verbatim in the national broadsheets and certainly the Sussex regional and local newspapers donated plenty of editorial space.

As the readership devoured the information, public conversation became dominated by 'The Races'. This was Derby Day and the Cheltenham Gold Cup rolled into one, and the hard-worked press office at the Automobile Club struggled to supply a voracious demand from newspapers throughout the country and the specialist motor magazines.

The Earl De La Warr publicly feigned modest surprise at the fanatical interest. Behind closed doors at the Manor House he was euphoric and confessed that Bexhill had become the epicentre of the motoring world. He could be excused such an extravagant remark, but even in his wildest dreams the Earl had grossly underestimated the importance of playing host to the first motor races in the land. If there was a sign of opposition among citizens to the onslaught upon their secluded community, any resistance would surely be overwhelmed. As it was, practically everybody seemed to be surfing upon this great wave of opportunity.

Weekenders who habitually travelled from London and the home counties to the larger and better-established resorts like Bournemouth, Bognor Regis and Brighton, created outlandish reasons not to visit relatives and friends in order to satisfy their curiosity about this 'up-start' Bexhill. Worse still 'day trippers' who went by train to Eastbourne and Hasting, were to the chagrin of the respective authorities, being enticed to dally awhile along the race track.

Many returned to their favoured watering holes, uttering aloud at the fuss over a stretch of road where a lot of people were showing off their noisy motor cars. Clearly, not everybody was enamoured with the prospect of the most historic cavalcade of the century. Perhaps they had not cottoned on to the fact that all the ballyhoo was about an impending event and not just a huge publicity stunt to draw visitors to Bexhill.

Naturally, the Earl would have contradicted this opinion. He was magnanimous enough to realise that the races would benefit the entire area along both ends of the coast. There were not enough hotels to accommodate the extraneous visitor aside from the 'right people' who were directly involved with the proceedings. A small section of Bexhill's working population in Sidley caught a snort of elitism. Or to quote more bluntly: 'a downright toffee-nosed lot were coming to town'.

The Earl being sensitive to the true Bexhillians' mood, pointed out that this was a temporary aberration, and assured them that in the wake of the event the entire town would prosper from people visiting regardless of their social distinction. While the press concentrated upon all aspects concerning the build-up to the Whitsuntide weekend, there was speculative gossip on the social scene as well. Chit-chat centred upon who were the distinguished guests of the Earl and Lady De La Warr staying at the Manor House. 'Stringers' — better known as 'sneaking informers' — were retained by the London newspapers to discover the guest list at the Sackville and other hotels in the town. Society columnists were having a field day as snippets of information were filtered back to the editorial desks.

News of a more substantial nature from the Automobile Club revealed that Mr Alfred Harmsworth had purchased the 40 hp Mercedes driven by Werner on the La Turbie hill climb and the Nice Speed Trials where it claimed a gutsy second place. After the car had been on display at the Club's motor show in London's Agricultural Hall, Mr Harmsworth stripped it down in preparation for Bexhill.

Perhaps the most potent headline came after the Club had deliberated long and hard and decided that it was safe for vehicles to race side-by-side. Thereby the winner of each heat would go forward. Provision had also been made in the hastily written regulations to avoid the absurdity of touring cars racing against automobiles designed for competition. The specialist press, like *Autocar*, applauded such a ruling as sensible, and would ensure a true spectacle for the public. Unlike Nice when cars ran singly and the competitive spirit was measured against the clock. Walter Staner summed up by stating: 'There will therefore be exciting finishes as well as racing speeds'.

In anticipation of a huge influx from London to Bexhill, the London Borough and South Coast Railway Company advertised special trains. The interesting comment upon this move was to avoid the traffic and parking problems during the race weekend. Crowds attending the entire meeting were estimated to be around the 20-25,000 mark. In reality over 35,000 people crammed into Bexhill, stretching every convenience and facility to its uttermost. Fears that Bexhill, a town of 13,000 inhabitants, would grind to a halt from congestion, were not well founded. It was just as well that a large continental entourage was dissipated because the 'Circuit du Nord' happened over the same weekend.

There was some cause for concern in Piccadilly when Mr Roger Wallace KC took the chair at a meeting to read a telegraph received from representatives of the ACF. He read the content, which suggested that the Bexhill meeting should be postponed! Club officials around the table were dumbfounded by this outrageous request. Then Mr Wallace read on to find that Continental chauffeurs were prevented from competing at Bexhill because it coincided with the 'Ministerial Alcohol Race'. The telegraph went on to ask if the races could be postponed until another weekend.

This blatant effrontery caused the committee to consult with Charles Jarrott who was entered in both events. He saw no conflict of interests. After recording a splendid second place driving his Panhard in the Circuit du Nord, he drove through the night to Dieppe for the Newhaven ferry on a rainy Sunday.

That same evening Jarrott was safely ensconced in the Sackville and fresh to race on the Monday.

Confident of Jarrott's opinion, the French plea was politely treated with the disdain it deserved. Amazingly enough, although this sensational news was released to the media, most newspapers gave it barely a column-inch, which was about the length of its importance. Privately, to show goodwill, the club promised to consider another meeting at Bexhill later in 1902.

In spite of this opportunism, a goodly number of foreigners continued to make advance bookings at hotels in Eastbourne and Hastings, which were at last benefiting from the 'over spill' of the gravy train.

It is interesting to reflect upon this trail-blazing meeting because almost everybody was in a learning process. Methods of organising such an event were learnt from Nice and adjusted to the new circumstances. But the Automobile Club were well aware of having to 'educate' the spectators into watching this brand new sport in comparative safety.

More was needed than the mandatory sign warning spectators that 'Motor Racing is Dangerous'. So regulations were composed and published in Bexhill newspapers for the public's welfare. Since very few onlookers would have a clue what 75 mph meant — most of whom had never witnessed such velocity. So it was forthrightly mentioned that the racing automobilists would be driving outside the law, exploring the ultimate power of their cars. Under these 'open' conditions, the competitor has total right-of-way on the track. It was strongly advised that, in view of the unfamiliar speeds attained, people should at all costs avoid crossing the road while racing was in progress.

Regarding actual spectating facilities, nobody was allowed on the course from the De La Warr Gates to Galley Hill on Whit-Monday without a ticket. Chairs on the north side were hired out for one old shilling, while chairs on the south side had to be booked. What many people found difficult to believe was the instruction for the police to prohibit the use of any camera, photo or cinematography apparatus without a special permit.

Spectators were also told that a gun was to be fired as each vehicle left the starting point on Galley Hill and that there would be another shot at the finish line. These explosions would enable amateur timekeepers to record the times of chosen racers to obtain an approximate idea of the relative speeds before the official times were posted.

As a visual indication of the winner of each heat, if the car on the side nearest the sea won, a green flag was shown. If the car on the north side won, then a yellow flag was waved. For the shortsighted, seats could be obtained at the finishing point for two shillings each: fantastic value to witness the very first 'Chariots of Fire'.

Marshalling the entire event meant that the Automobile Club and the Earl depended upon many willing volunteers. Fortunately, people were falling over themselves to be given a task, and it was not just to get a good view of the races. This role was undoubtedly filled by the Honorary Observers, carefully chosen officials who were strategically placed at one-hundred-yard intervals on the track side of the spectators' fence. What was given to be a task of seeing 'fair play' and controlling the crowd turned these men into paragons of courage — not because they were the first in line of defence should a car lose control, but because they had to stand their ground for most of the day in spite of being unmercifully harangued and abused by the spectators behind who insisted that these intransigent officials were obscuring their view.

Each one of the twenty two men placed on either side of the course had to report back to the judges any competitor who crossed the central line or impeded the fair passage of his opponent. All the observers were allocated a pea-whistle which they enthusiastically blew to create a high-pitched wave of sound down the length of the track, which became almost continuous as the faster cars whisked past them. The fanfare served a dual purpose in that it warned irresponsible members of the public hastily to vault the fence to safety and it alerted the timekeepers and judges in the Cycle Chalet of another race approaching its climax.

By the end of proceedings, the cacophony of different combustive sounds and the compulsory whistling had caused certain members of the public to attend the St John's Ambulance Brigade first-aid marquee for antidotes to relieve chronic headaches and to soothe eyes that were smarting from the unaccustomed fumes and flying grit.

While admission charges were made for special enclosures along the Sackville end of the course, the Earl De La Warr in tandem with the Automobile Club informed the general public that they were at liberty to watch proceedings over the weekend from the golf course on Galley Hill and both sides of the course up to Bolbrooke Road free, gratis, and for nothing. Perhaps even more important from the parochial standpoint, the Earl went to enormous lengths in the press to assure all citizens that the most extravagant function in Bexhill to date had cost the local authorities nothing. By contrast, the Municipality of Nice now had to donate Five Hundred Guineas to the Automobile Club de France in order to secure the annual speed trials for the resort.

One can only guess at the horse trading that must have developed in France. Not only were the Mediterranean towns and resorts vying for the limelight, but the health spas and towns set within wine regions probably perked up a deal to ensure that the ACF noticed their charms. A place like Nice was no doubt aware of such bidding and continually kept the situation under review. There would come a time when the disruption and cost outweighed the profit and the benefit.

The 'Fathers of Power' at Piccadilly were determined to attract a top-quality entry represented by most of the great pioneering sports motorists from Britain and the Continent. In spite of the unfortunate clash of dates with the Circuit du Nord, the committee worked upon the assumption that generous prize monies and handsome trophies would lure great names across the Channel for their prestigious event. Baron Henri de Rothschild without formal invitation did not hesitate to post his entry in late April after becoming the fastest motorist in the World, Leon Serpollet and his charming wife received a gracious invitation personally from the Earl De La Warr as the star

197

attraction soon after the Nice Speed Trials. Louis Renault, who had enjoyed many great wins in the voiturette light-car class between 1899-1903, and his brother Marcel were also 'select entries'. Other slightly lesser mortals, until they also claimed fame, were Fernand Gabriel, the enigmatic winner of the aborted Paris-Madrid race and Maurice Farman, the Francophile from England who claimed a famous victory in the Alcohol Race that very weekend. He was urgently persuaded by Charles Jarrott to follow him on that inspiring night-time dash from Paris to Dieppe by the light of a small acetylene lamp.

A concerted effort was made by the committee to elicit trophies and cash prizes from their influential members and friends within the three remaining months to organise the Bexhill Races. Even in 1902 daggers were drawn in Fleet Street between the *Daily Mail* and the *Daily Express*. Like so many evolutionary things of the time 1896 was the year marked out when Alfred Harmsworth formed Associated Newspapers to publish the *Daily Mail* and he was not slow in offering the most coveted prize: 'The *Daily Mail* 100-Guinea Challenge Cup' which was presented to the fastest car weighing under 1,000 kilograms, irrespective of whether the car was driven by steam, electricity, petrol or other motive power. There was a carrot to encourage the donkey in that the flying kilometre had to be covered within 40 seconds, or 55.9 mph.

The *Daily Express* had no real option but to present 'The *Daily Express* 50-Guinea Challenge Cup' to the winner of the Special Class. Also keen to boost readership through making a contribution, *The Car Illustrated* magazine inaugurated a '25-Guinea Cup' for the winner of Class A. A similar prize appeared from another source *The Country Gentleman* magazine. Realising the commercial gain of being associated with such an historic event, many Sussex-based companies and distinguished individuals offered prizes. The most notable trophy on offer locally was 'The De La Warr 30-Guinea Cup' to be presented to the winner of Class C. Mr Mark Mayhew, the Vice-Chairman of the Automobile Club and Chairman of the Races Committee, presented 'The Mark Mayhew 25-Guinea Purse' along with a Club Medal to the fastest of the cars to win Class H of the Speed Section and the Special Class for big racers. 'The Pape 25-Guinea Cup', presented by Mr E J Pape of Moor Hall, Bexhill, went to the fastest car in the Tourist Section irrespective of class.

* * *

In April 1902, there were two unrelated events which were newsworthy. Magistrates in Glasgow had kicked up a storm when it was ruled that men must replace barmaids in all licensed premises. Within days of this apparently chauvinistic injustice against women trying to scrape a living, when Sauchiehall Street echoed to cries of protest by scorned barmaids, Mr Bradney Williams of the Bexhill Motor Company along with his retained engineer Mr E Harris and Councillor Mr H Brooke, modestly embarked upon their own great Glasgow-to-Bexhill drive aboard a 8 hp Argyll light car with a tonneau to seat four. The Argyll was a newly-designed car patented by the Hozier Engineering Company at Bridgeton, for which the Bexhill Motor Company had just secured the agency for Bexhill and the surrounding area. In order to launch sales in Bexhill and capitalise upon the races, Mr Williams had planned his reliability run for maximum impact.

Apart from this laudable enterprise, Mr Williams wished to confound once and for all the doubters that the motor car was capable of travelling over long distances without countless hitches and troubles. He also wanted to prove to himself and Councillor Brooke that a light, low-priced car could be easily handled.

Before they left Glasgow to the barmaids screeching blue murder and threatening to castrate any magistrate stupid enough to walk down Sauchie-hall Street, Mr Williams completed the business agreement with Argyll and then proceeded to start the 492-mile run from the Hozier works. They got lost twice within 30 miles of Glasgow before finding the broad well-surfaced road to Carlisle.

There was a fuel stop at Abington because they had used more petrol than anticipated attempting to extricate themselves from the crawling labyrinth of roads out of Glasgow. In spite of his wisdom and worldliness, Councillor Brooke was not a proven navigator by nature. Nevertheless, while fuel consumption for the journey had gone to the wind, the Councillor was displaying an almost boyish enthusiasm for this momentous adventure. According to Mr Harris, who was feeling a mite redundant because the Argyll was behaving so well, the run through Lockerbie to Gretna Green, where they crossed into England by the Garrieston Bridge, was almost soporific. Since the main road was so well maintained, they completed a measured mile between the 52-53 milestones outside Glasgow in a time of 2 minutes 20 seconds.

Harris at last came into his own between Carlisle and Kendal where they made their first night stop. Having filled up with petrol in Carlisle and topped up the water, Williams pulled the car to the side of the road near Penrith to oil the clutch. The intrepid travellers completed 140 trouble-free miles, even surmounting the dreaded Shap Fell in gathering darkness in fine style. Far more dangerous was the 14-mile descent in pouring rain and total darkness. Sometimes Harris had to walk in front of the car to save the brakes by leaning heavily on the bonnet to stop the car running away. They reached Kendal safely within ten hours.

The Argyll had acquitted itself well along the first day's run, so after Kendal it was no surprise to find niggling little gremlins creeping in to keep Harris thoroughly involved. At this stage in the evolution of the motor car, there were no comprehensive 'hand books' to instruct the intrepid trio on the mechanical foibles of the Argyll. What printed information was to hand, proved to be almost incomprehensible to the average person. Harris cleaned the spark plug, but still the engine continued to misfire. A lose lead was detected on the electric connectors and the replacement cured the annoying loss of power. Right as rain, they chuntered onward through Lancaster, Preston and to Manchester.

At Chorley they missed another junction. The air went blue and Harris cringed at his mistake. Williams made a 'U' turn then shot back on to the road for Wigan. Surprisingly enough, it was not raining over Manchester. Brooke dispensed with his great-coat and helmet as they crossed the swing bridge over the ship canal in warm sunshine.

Although it was only day two of the run, the Councillor was already impressed with the Argyll's stamina, his approval marked by an almost permanent grin on his weather-beaten face, hitherto, even Bradney Williams was forever commenting upon how trouble-free the endurance test was turning out to be. Harris preferred to keep two superstitious fingers crossed. His only comment was that as a trial of unsurpassed endeavour, the exercise was turning into an incredible non-event. Any thoughts of relating to a hair-raising adventure evaporated into trivial incidents like getting lost, or being stopped by 'hitch-hikers'. Just outside Trentham two men flaged them down. They were not going anywhere, but were simply curious enough to kill the cat. One of the audacious potters even asked if he could 'give it a drive'.

The closest the Argyll came to a premature abolition happened when a rampant horse inadvertently trotted into their path from a side turning. Then in fright of the car the beast reared upon its hind legs and unceremoniously deposited its lady rider on to the road. Midlanders were not accustomed to having to look and listen for the 'teuf-teuf' of motor car on their approach as this incident showed.

The incident happened just outside Lichfield, and Councillor Brooke was not sure whether the stricken woman was more startled by her steed's alarming behaviour or at the prospect of three hearty men running to her rescue!

Since Mr Williams' careful calculations for the entire run had been 'thwarted' by the later-than-anticipated departure from Glasgow and the numerous excursions down wrong turnings, when they cruised into Warwick it was back to the drawing board. By a unanimous vote, they elected to skirt London by a westerly route, rather than chance a faltering clutch through the busy city.

Their second day's run from Kendal to Warwick was an astonishing 175 miles in 10 hours 13 minutes, not accounting for stops and deviations.

The overall speed limit on all roads during the early 1900s was 12 mph so the threesome had to keep a weather eye open for law enforcement officers. Harris had estimated that motoring along stretches of 'plain going' the Argyll had reached speeds of around 48 mph. The boys-in-blue would have had a field day had they known that the Argyll had averaged 15.4 mph along the entire journey!

Oddly enough, the third and final day's run from Warwick to Bexhill proved to be the most troublesome. Although the car suffered a slipping clutch which they remedied at Henley-on-Thames, the remainder of this 'Bexhill-or-Bust jaunt suffered more from human frailty than from anything else. By now limbs were aching, nethers were sore and their eyes smarted. With the air persistently blowing in their faces, thirst was the plague of all three men. The inevitable part of that cycle meant that more stops to answer the call of nature and the replenishment of flasks — more than had been calculated in their original schedule.

Harris thought that the most emotionally draining effect was the sheer frustration from making a nonsense of their 'misguided maps'. Navigational errors played havoc with their run south of London. A real blight upon their morale occurred at Chertsey when another missed turning caused them one heck of a detour that ruined the calculated fuel consumption for the leg. They had to stop again to 'tank-up' wasting yet more precious time. If that was not enough aggravation, then tempers became still more frayed as gloom gathered over Godstone. Road conditions became fearful and were compounded by thick fog in the valleys and incessant rain over the hills. On top of this, they got lost and the accumulator packed up. Harris exchanged it for a new one by the light of a gas lamp somewhere near Blindley Heath. As visibility slowed them to a crawl, Bennett offered to get off the car at each cross roads to read the road signs carefully against the map. Now that they were within striking distance of Bexhill, none of the men wanted to prolong the agony.

They motored slowly into Bexhill at 1 am on the fourth day. It was bucketing with rain, the streets were awash and not a soul stood along the curb to wave them in. Originally, they had planned to bowl into Bexhill at the noon hour for the benefit of the press and to let the attendant crowds witness a truly magnificent little motor car finish in a burst of glory through the De La Warr Gates and over the pukka 'race finish line'. In reality the gentleman of the press were in slumberland. Williams, Brooke and Harris faced the media as heroes later the same day.

The Argyll had completed the 492-mile marathon within 32 hours at an average speed of 15.4 mph. Still spattered with mud and grime, Harris was amazed that he had not had to change a single wheel from a puncture. A goodly crowd of onlookers cast intense scrutiny over the car, and word had it, that two orders for replicas were placed before dusk. The tour had been justified on that score alone. So the infernal detours and the unreadable misguided maps were quickly forgotten.

Williams had proved conclusively his point that the Argyll had the heart of a lion and the stamina of an ox. He reckoned that the experience had been 'one of the most pleasant of my life'.

Ultimately Bradney Williams probably created more mileage and goodwill for Bexhill Motor Company in terms of business than he would have done had he competed in the 1,000-Mile Trial. The Argyll had made a pure undiluted statement. Old-fashioned folk who still regarded the motor car with fear and trembling, were the first to raise their hats to the three travel-worn motorists for their bold endeavour. Not so many 'doubting Thomases' regarded the snorting conveyance as an obnoxious novelty. In Sussex, as if proof were needed, the development of travel by motor car had been fulfilled. The Argyll's run had proved to prospective buyers that the light whiz-mobiles were dependable as a mode of transport. From that day onwards, the horse was put out to grass, and the Argyll remained in the motor business until 1931.

That night they toasted Glasgow's absent barmaids in the Sackville Hotel .

15

Ignore the Imperious Police

PROSPECT FOR Bexhill's future could not have appeared rosier than in May 1902. The Races had seemed to dominate everything, but since the town had been cast into sharp focus, two other parochial landmarks in Bexhill's History were also magnified out of all proportion.

Firstly, Bexhill was granted a charter of incorporation by King Edward VII during the year of his coronation. And secondly, the new borough was elevated again shortly after the races, by the grand opening of The London, Brighton and South Coast Railway's new terminus at Bexhill West which joined the London-Hastings line at Crowhurst. Unfortunately because the new four-mile stretch of line had proved to be a greater under-taking for the contractors Price and Reeves than was initially envisaged, the branch line into Bexhill was not opened in time for the races.

As the Chairman of the Urban Council and the Incorporation Committee, the 8th Earl was by far the most influential figure in Bexhill up to this time. He, of course, realised that after May 1902, there would be a major shift in the balance of power as local leadership took office. In spite of this sway, the De La Warr family and the Earl's Brassey maintained the prestige of social leadership in Bexhill. Their continuing presence ensured that the flourishing town enjoyed a standing far beyond its station. So the transition from a practically insignificant village-on-the-hill to a popular health resort, in terms of profile, now was compared with Brighton, Eastbourne and Hastings.

The official incorporation ceremony took place two days before the Whitsuntide races. Bexhill was abuzz. The reception of the Charter Proclamation proved to be an outstanding day in Bexhill's history. Early on Wednesday morning, a deputation which included Mr R B Gaby and Mr J D Achison, travelled by train to London-Victoria to witness Bexhill's Deputy Provisional Mayor, Mr Daniel Mayer, receive the charter.

While these formalities were going on in London, Earl De La Warr, the Charter Mayor, had been driven from the Manor House to Bexhill Station by Bradney Williams in the now famous Argyll motor car, restored to pristine condition for the auspicious occasion.

Upon returning from London, the deputation was greeted by huge flag-waving crowds that lined the streets of Bexhill. A rare and intoxicating atmosphere of civic pride filled the air as the Mounted Police headed the procession led by the Band of the 2nd Cinque Ports Royal Garrison Artillery Volunteers. VIPs and many civic dignitaries from towns all over Sussex followed, swamped by the wildly cheering crowds. Only in 1935, when the Duke and Duchess of York went to Bexhill to open the De La Warr Pavilion, had such a state of euphoria since been known. The sensation bubbled to the surface again in 1966 when Queen Elizabeth II and the Duke of Edinburgh made their first official visit to Bexhill. But elderly citizens who recall the three occasions, believe that 'Charter Day' was the happiest of them all.

The rear guard of the huge procession was the ubiquitous Argyll with the Charter and Deputy Mayors waving boisterously and shaking hands with anybody who could reach them. A tiny but significant piece of history was made by that drive to the Town Hall. It was the very first time that a Proclamation Charter had been officially conveyed by a motor car. What an appropriate coup for the town.

Early arrivals for the race meeting must have wondered if all their coronations had come at once. There was a sumptuous banquet at the Kursaal followed at twilight by an illuminated outdoor fete and fireworks display in Egerton Park. As the crowds dispersed after an uproarious night, the many automobiles crowding into the town served as a reminder that 'The Big One' was still to come.

If Bexhill citizens had not already been fanned into an inferno of excitement by the Charter of Incorporation, the *Daily Mail* fuelled speculation on the possibility that the King might attend the races.

There was no official confirmation or denial from Buckingham Palace of such a rumour. However, another more substantial piece of news reached Bradney Williams at the Bexhill Motor Company where he was animatedly talking to passers-by about his epic run from Scotland. Apparently, the barmaids' dispute in Glasgow had gone to the Court of Appeal and they had won a reprieve which overturned the ban on female bar staff. The reason for the ban in the first place had been clouded by obscure legal jargon, but the move was to maintain good order, morality and propriety on licensed premises. One sanctimonious landlord had stated that barmaids were exposed to improper language, sexual innuendo and after hours had been known to be 'set-upon' and raped — allegations which for the most part, were denied by the ladies concerned. The magistrates claimed that the ban on the barmaids was really taken to defend susceptible young men — and old men, from the temptations of the flesh — a pitiful example of justice, and the successful appeal had Bradney Williams rejoicing, with an aside that some Bexhill public houses should also take note!

Logistical problems loomed large during the week or so before the races. The Sackville Hotel was pronounced 'full' after Mr A Woolfe, the Frederick Hotel's manager, revealed that all the rooms had been applied for three times over, and applications were coming in at the rate of fifty a day. Mr J Glover, manager of the Kursaal and local tourism officer, substantiated this enviable claim and recorded that all accommodation in Bexhill was fully engaged. Persons of substance had happily accepted bed-and-breakfast boarding in order to be 'on the scene' rather than 'camp out' at Eastbourne or Hastings.

The new-born enthusiasts of motor racing who travelled to Bexhill by train or even by bicycle, were prepared to 'slum it' in shop doorways, stables, hay-lofts and sleep open on the beach

Before a racing wheel had been turned in anger, the town's prestige had grown inestimably. Apart from the valuable publicity accrued from the races, Mr Glover at the Cinderella hour woke up to the fact that the town's prestige was not being upheld and people needed something permanent to remind them where the races first happened. He hit upon the idea of a Bexhill Town Cup, and felt that it was inappropriate that the Earl De La Warr should be prompted to inscribe Bexhill Town upon the handsome cup which he was presenting.

Now that the Urban Council was a rudderless ship and the new corporation was not to be installed before November 1902, somebody had to take the initiative to seek subscribers for such a trophy. Within 24 hours of the suggestion being announced in the local press, cash contributions were made at the Kursaal by local traders and private citizens which ranged from five shillings to £2 2s 0d. A telegraph was sent to the Automobile Club stating that Bexhill Town wished to contribute a 25-Guinea Wish Cup to celebrate the first meeting at the resort. In 1904 this was replaced by a Rose Bowl.

Members of Parliament who were dedicated automobilists were caught in a quandary. A suggestion across party lines had been to inaugurate a 'House of Commons 40-Guinea Challenge Cup'. While certain of Lord Sainsbury's Tory Government members were all for rewarding endeavour in the races, this provoked disagreement with the opposing parties. They felt that the motor industry should deserve a bouquet. Politically, this was recognised by all parties as a sensible move. After all, not all the electorate would be racing mad, whereas the average person would agree to rewarding enterprise.

The initial idea promoted by socialist thinking, was to judge the most 'practical peoples' automobile'. The Tories objected, stating that this would not include the wide range of cars expected at Bexhill. Besides such an accolade could be victory for a foreign car manufacturer, and would do nothing to promote the fledgling British motor industry. A compromise was attained upon a 'pride of ownership', thus realising a Concours d'Elegance, or to put in English, a competition for the 'Best-Looking Turn Out' — the outstanding qualities of a car, regardless of value, being: (a) Elegance of design, (b) finish and appointments, (c) comfort of the car, and (d) smartness combined with suitability of dress of occupants. There was one stipulation: this was not a fancy dress parade — cars could *not* be decorated with flowers or ribbons. Such filigree was considered too 'twee for such a robust weekend. These rules were generally acceptable to all parties. The competition was judged by a balanced committee of non-competing members of the Automobile Club, citizens of Bexhill selected by the Earl and cross-party members of Parliament.

Quite what in the way of entertainment for this 'combustious weekend' was considered as appropriate had the Director of Entertainments at Bexhill in a quandary. All the rage was the American 'Cake Walk' dance. Isadora Duncan was 'wowing' audiences, but was considered to be too risqué, while the 'curved and coy' routines of the fabulous Gibson Girls troupe might have created a lust of unimaginable proportions for discreet Bexhill. Instead a policy of 'middle-of-the-road' attractions suitable for all ages and classes was considered appropriate. After all, playing Brighton at its own game was simply 'not on'. So it fell to the Jeanne Douste Opera Company to keep the masses entranced for the three days preceding Whitsuntide. On the Sunday, what was described as a 'startling innovation' featuring 'A Church Parade Band' — was in fact the De La Warr Orchestra — weather permitting would play outside the bandstand by the Kursaal.

Cynics might well scoff, but in those days His Majesty's Army Band played church parade music at St James's Palace every Sunday morning, so Bexhill was responding to umpteen requests for a similar performance.

The real fun was being stored up for The Automobile Club Ball at the Kursaal. A battalion of workmen from Goodyers of Regent Street, London would work through Sunday night to decorate all the ornate arches with pink flowers. Since the Earl and the club were at pains to remove any false impression that only 'Pink Domino's' would be admitted to the after-race ball: they stated the function was also open to full evening dress. There would be prizes for the most outrageous fancy dress and dominoes. Obviously the 'letting-down-of-hair' would be after the regal supper.

In their collective wisdom, the Automobile Club committee had requested the availability of fuel in Bexhill together with the price per gallon from all garages. Only three known replies were forthcoming. The De La Warr Cycling Boulevard and Motor Depot were full to the gunwales with Pratt's motorspirit at 1/3d per gallon. They had garage storage and a cleaning service, both at 1/- each.

Spring Brothers in Station Road were prepared to sell petrol in six-gallon quantities at 1/- per gallon — no deals. One gallon would go at 1/1d and they had 200 gallons stock. Lastly, Bexhill Motor Company would charge 1/1d per gallon to competitors garaging their cars and 1/4d to passers-by. Oil and spark plugs were also on offer. Russells did not sell fuel in 1902, but they had shelves of accumulators, lamps, tyres and oil with reliable expertise to hand. The clamour for garage space by competitors created quite a 'black market' once all the properly accredited establishments were declared 'full'. Anybody with a spare stable, barn, outhouse or even a shed was pounced upon, duly beaten down from charging extortionate rents like 'two bob' a night, and promised rides in kind.

Having secured a number of beautiful motor cars upon their property, locals would chat to neighbours and roll off illustrious accomplishments. The most unlikely inhabitants made outlandish statements such as having 'the actual Renault old Louis won the voiturette class in the Paris-Berlin last year'. Walter Mitty emerged from every corner — and what harmless fun it must have been!

Every organisation has a 'work-horse' and the role of work-horse fell upon the broad shoulders of Mr Claude Johnson, the Secretary to the Automobile Club. He was a perfectly affable man who could turn authoritarian when the situation demanded a strong arm.

He was meticulous and patient with the endless queries that deluged him as the event drew near. When the time came to move everything from Piccadilly to Bexhill, the committee were all hands on deck, but it was Mr Johnson who supervised the transport of paperwork, trophies, banners and the room allocations at the Sackville.

Among the numerous tasks to be completed before race day, one of the most testing was to find a company, or set of trusted timekeepers to record each race. Mr Johnson had observed the timing apparatus at the Nice Speed Trials. Some 'finnicky' competitors often questioned its reliability if a time was posted which they reckoned was 'slow'. On the other hand, all was peace and goodwill if 'optimistic' times were recorded. Competitors beamed at the bonus by the 'slip of the hand'. Claude Johnson spoke with several time-piece manufacturers and organisers of athletics meetings to get an overall opinion as to the most appropriate method of timekeeping. After all, these records would be carved in stone as historical fact, apart from being the 'bench-mark' for racers in the immediate future.

After considerable deliberation, he followed up a suggestion to contact Colonel Crompton, the founding Director of the electrical firm, Crompton and Parkinson. The Colonel, an entrepreneur to his finger-tips, spotted a window for displaying his precision equipment. He accepted the invitation to supply a specially devised system of time-recording for Bexhill. Colonel Crompton, along with several of his boffins, visited the Bexhill course to size up the job-in-hand.

Throughout the week before the races, the finished product, a spaghetti of electrical wire spanned the length of the measured kilometre. These connected his elaborate telephone and timing equipment between the race headquarters, the Cycle Chalet and a posting at Galley Hill. Crompton was aware of electrical failures, so he backed up any shortcomings within his apparatus with an entourage of bicyclists who pounded between the three points of vital communication.

As it happened there were some 'short circuits' on race day when scattered showers drowned elements within the system, but in the end, Colonel Crompton produced results that were not too seriously questioned. The entire network was based upon a threadbare billiard table from the Sackville, which was set within the doorway of the Chalet with 'guards' on patrol outside the door to ensure no 'funny-goings-on'. Colonel Crompton was elected as the timing referee in the Chalet along with Harry J Swindly, who was Honorary Official timekeeper for the Automobile Club. He supervised F T Bidilake and E R Shipton (the official timekeepers) who took times throughout at the start and finish and were able therefore to make good the failures of the electrical equipment when the rain wreaked its havoc. The gentleman actually responsible for the operation of the timing gear were Mr Manville at the start and Mr Lyons Sampson at the finish line. Between them these men worked prodig-

iously for eight long hours, come rain or shine, to produce as accurate a result
it was possible to do at that time.

Although the race starters were all members of the club, S F Edge volunteered his services between races to supplement J E Sutton, Rees Jefferies and
C Lewis. It was common sense to have an experienced 'racer' in their midst
because Edge understood the mechanical niceties of holding a motor car too
long on a slope when under starters orders. The Clerks of the Course were
appropriately the Earl De La Warr and Mr Mark Mayhew of the Automobile
Club. They were greatly relieved that S F was such a willing hand at this crucial stage, and gave confidence to the other competitors. Standing by to
observe fair play were Mr A F P Bird and Mr Boverton Redwood.

If there was any alarm or despondency spread during the week prior to the
races, it was voiced by lovers of the horse and carriage and other so-called
'backward-thinking people'.

Having been bludgeoned for weeks at the prospect of Bexhill being turned
into a 'speedsters paradise' where policemen smiled benevolently upon the
motorist who at the races would have *carte-blanche* permission to break the
laws of the land, the voice of the minority was to be heard. The vociferous
few forecast that accidents of such horrendous proportions many drivers
would be killed or maimed. They portrayed a human carnage of inestimable
numbers should a car run out of control at high speed and plunge into the
crowd. The press paid surprisingly small lip-service to the feelings of these
people. Instead the general consensus on motor racing was overwhelmingly
positive. National newspapers carried such glowing comments:

'Is it possible to find any sport which for pure excitement can be compared to autocar racing?' — *Daily Express*.'
'Automobilists from all parts of the world are waiting with keen anticipation the
results of the Bexhill Races.' — *The Pall Mall Gazette*.
'Some sensational speeds are expected and it is more than likely that the world's
record will be broken.' — *Daily Mail*.'
'The race between Baron Henri de Rothschild and Mr Alfred Harmsworth in their
respective Mercedes could witness the battle of the century.' — *The Globe*.

Such flights of fancy being penned by some of fleet Street's more sober jour-
nalists buoyed by this wave of enthusiasm, were claimed by old hacks as
dreams born from the bottom of a tankard, which should be treated as the
froth of escapism.

* * *

It was the Friday before Whitsuntide, torrents of rain had been falling all day
when a motley bunch of rugged individuals motored into Bexhill from London. To all intents and purposes they appeared for all the world as if they had
just completed the Peking-Paris in a monsoon, let alone a rather damp drive
from the capital.

As the first batch of club members motored along the De La Warr Parade, they heartily punched the air, and after they had drawn up outside the Sack-ville Hotel, three cheers rang out of the dismal conditions. Nothing was going to dampen the spirit of anyone on this historic weekend.

Their cars were caked in mud while the occupants appeared more like the heroes of Kazan than able motorists from Piccadilly. Nothing seemed to deter the bedraggled lady passengers (and drivers) who seemed to thrive upon their pioneering spirit without caring a jot for vanity. The rooster tails of muck which had been thrown up by the wheels had covered everybody in grime. Those wearing goggles raised them and they looked more like the Black and White Minstrels than like pilots of the new world conveyance.

Roads at the turn of the century were made either of cobblestones, a rolled asphalt aggregate or compacted earth compilation, mixed with either crushed rock or brick for better drainage. Any other surface could be likened to a farm track.

The bicycle created a demand for smoother roads. More to the point, it was necessary to keep cyclists off the pavements where they disturbed pedes-trians. Surfaces of natural rock asphalt were laid in and around towns while portland cement was applied to the pavements. It had long been a grouse of 'road users' that pedestrians had better surfaces to walk upon, whereas those who were horse drawn or motorised had to contend with a rough ride. In the event of rain some surfaces became a glutinous morass. Huge pot-holes broke many an axle, and wheels often collapsed. The arterial roads that connected large conurbations like Birmingham, Bristol and Manchester with London were very well maintained as Bradney Williams would testify. But he would also assert that any deviation from the beaten track would turn a pleasant drive into a complete lottery.

Around the transitory period when horse drawn carriages were still preva-lent, but the motor car was still finding its wheels, drivers in the Home Coun-ties had to remain vigilant. Many a proud motorist had his ego 'punctured' while driving his lady love because tyre failures were the bane of his life. Bursts were frequently the cause of running over blacksmiths' nails which had worked loose from horse shoes and littered the highways and byways. The life expectancy of a new set of tyres fitted on the average light car driven at 20 mph was estimated at 2,000 miles, driving with care. Big cars like the Mors, Rapier and Benz would chew through rubber at the rate of a set of tyres for every 1,000 miles. In 1901 Alfred Harmsworth owned four cars. None of them had done more than 3,000 miles before he had to consider the many cuts and punctures and put them in for a tyre service. Four new sets of tyres cost Mr Harmsworth £450! But the newspaper magnate was no slouch at the wheel.

The quality of pneumatic rubber was so poor, that when George Lanchester personally delivered one of his cars to Rudyard Kipling, he suffered 21 punc-tures along the 200-mile journey from Birmingham to Rottingdean near Brighton. Tedious though the continuous repairs were, Lanchester reckoned that it was still worthwhile to develop the tyre, because solid rubber examples made for a rough ride. Kipling never did learn why his Lanchester was hours later than the expected time of arrival. The term 'running in' could be no excuse, the expression had not been coined in those days.

After a hot bath and a change of clothes, everybody went outside the Sackville to witness Earl De La Warr together with Mr Mark Mayhew, Chairman of the races committee and Head Marshall of the Course, mount the Sackville tower. Their respective duties were firstly to raise the Union Jack, then to unfurl the banner for the Automobile Club of Great Britain & Ireland. Amid cheers the party below cracked open some bottles of champagne to toast the King and the success of the first races to be held in his kingdom.

While these jollifications were going on, a couple of enthusiasts from Ghent, Belgium, arrived unannounced to watch the proceedings. They had crossed the Channel to Dover on a whim and driven their 10 hp Ricard to Bexhill fully expecting to walk into available accommodation. They had already approached the receptionists at the Marine Hotel, York House, Hotel Riposo and the Metropole — to be sadly informed that every room was booked. Undaunted, they entered the Sackville where Mr Theodore Chambers was at the reception desk when he overheard the couple being regretfully told that the 'house was full'. Mr Chambers had booked a double room and two singles for his party through the Club, and he graciously offered the Belgian pair his available double room for one night. The gesture was much appreciated — it set the tone for the weekend.

Nobody knew what happened to the couple after Mr Chamber's good turn, but no doubt they returned to Ghent with a favourable impression of Bexhill.

Saturday was a day of assemblage, meeting, greeting, eating, drinking and meandering the streets of Bexhill to view the mass of motor cars that littered every curbside, back street, and available parking space in yards and forecourts. Visitors jostled with local citizens who were anxious to complete their weekend shopping. The entire town reverberated to the hum, hiss, chug and rattle of machinery. Toxic exhaust fumes filled the air, perfume to the hundreds of onlookers who cocked an ear upon the outlandish experiences being recounted by motorists who had journeyed from the far corners of the country.

Along the parade, competitors were stretching the legs of the touring class, while testing their cars and familiarising themselves with the course. It was a right old free-for-all. Idle strollers were being blasted by the cyclonic disturbance caused by motorists whisking past them. Even now, eternal optimists were approaching Claude Johnson for a late entry into the races. Many were disappointed to find that the list had long been closed and that even the reserves were over subscribed. Most of them spent the afternoon exploring the narrow lanes over the marsh between Pevensey and Hurstmonceux. They encountered other happy automobilists. Everybody waved at everyone else, some almost losing control when more exuberant motorists faced them head-on around blind bends. No accidents were reported and good humour filled the air.

Drivers approaching Bexhill from London, Surrey and Kent told of persecution by the police around the Uckfield area. Officers-of-the-Law had leapt out of hedgerows to wave speeding motorists down and put themselves at risk in so doing. Some of the big cars were belting along at 50-60 mph, well over the mandatory 12 mph limit. The police had arranged a system of signals enabling them to prove whether or not that cars were travelling through Uckfield within the law. But the sheer weight of numbers was unprecedented. It was almost impossible to observe the speed limit through the village since it was approached by way of a steep hill.

While the light cars did their utmost to adhere to the law, Napiers, Daimlers and Panhards were blasting through, honking their horns, ringing bells and generally bellowing at everyone insight. One Edwin Midgley in his race-prepared Napier was halted by 'a suicidal officer' who stood his ground south of Uckfield and flagged down the indignant racer. The officer promptly summoned Mr Midgley with a speeding fine of £1-0-0d plus costs!

The dreaded 'blue paper' summons to attend court meant another tiresome journey for the offending drivers, some of whom were distinguished club members. There was small wonder that the respective rural constabularies could not heed the attitude taken by the Bexhill police. Their brief was to 'turn-a-blind-eye' to those driving with some verve — only motorists blatantly speeding and causing danger to others should be hauled up. This was a fair enough code in view of the extenuating conditions. Under any other circumstances, the respective drives of Charles Jarrott and the Honourable C S Rolls from Paris to Bexhill after the Circuit du Nord, would have gone into the books as 'heroic'. As it happened, in spite of crossing the Channel at two widely differing ports, they plunged into Bexhill within 3 hours of each other.

Rolls decided to take the immense 60 hp Mors on the ferry from Calais to Dover. The entire drive was performed in abysmal weather which did not reduce the speed at which the cumbersome Mors was driven.

After unloading at Dover, Rolls continued the relentless pace along the winding coast road over Romney and Walland Marshes. If a policeman had been fool-hardy enough to apprehend Rolls, the officer would not have stood a chance. As it was, Rolls motored through villages like Dymchurch, Brookland and Icklesham, flat out, 'side slipping' or oversteering, through bends with tremendous panache hurling up a huge plume of spray in his wake. Stray dogs yelped in panic, cats zapped across the road, their tenth life in their paws. Rural inhabitants either stared in amazement or were doused by the 'raving lunatic' as he roared onto Hastings. Rolls throttled back as he motored sedately through Glynde Gap into Bexhill. Suddenly from the pitch dark, he was apprehended by a policeman who issued him with a summons, not for his 60 miles of rapid progress, but for his driving without lights!

In order to create their own interest in the races, the general public were notably showing signs of allegiance either to a particular make of car or to a driver. Wherever British and French enthusiasts crossed paths, the French echoed the name 'Serpollet' time and again. The locals, partly in ignorance and confusion responded with the chant of 'Napier, Napier', while others rooted for 'Selly Edge, Selly Edge'. It did not matter a toot because everybody was entering into the spirit of the occasion.

While the French were far more familiar with motor racing, for the British supporter Bexhill presented a blank board about a new sport which they could draw their own conclusions. They fast came to terms with the machinations of the automobile. Every opportunity was taken to acquire knowledge. Amid a deluge late on Saturday afternoon, a racing Darracq freshly arrived from France pulled up in Devonshire Road. A terrible din was being emitted from the nether region, which prompted a crowd to gather in order to see 'what was up.' The driver was Fernand Gabriel, not yet famous for winning the Paris-Bordeaux section of the aborted Madrid race in 1903. The moustachioed driver sat unconcernedly while his mechanic fiddled about with spanners and wrenches. Every twiddle and turn was clinically observed by the crush of people. Then the mechanic stood up, grinned at the crowd, raised a damp leather cap and mounted the car.

Gabriel opened the throttle, and they shot off. Not all pre-race scrutineering had been confined to Bexhill. Since there was not yet a goods yard at Bexhill, many competitors had visited the weighbridge at the L & N W Railway Company's yard near Brompton Road station in London on Friday, to record their motor car's unladen weight. On Saturday, the remainder tootled over to St Leonards where, at West Marina station, the same formality presented the crowds with the amusing sight of motor cars being steered in-and-out among the heaps of coal and cattle trucks in order to reach the weighbridge.

* * *

What has been most striking as I have turned over the stones that built up the Bexhill Races, is the vivacity of description. While perusing umpteen national and local publications, I found that most writers were literally hunting for words to enable them adequately to express the sights and sounds of a totally new experience. What a fantastic privilege they enjoyed to be on the ground floor of the history of motor racing. In attempting to analyse how a first-time observer seeks to register his opinion and observations, I have found myself grasping at straws.

Had I never seen a motor car before, let alone a vehicle travelling up to 75 mph how would I comprehend such speed when all I could relate to was the pace of a horse breaking into a gallop or a locomotive running at full steam.

That sensation cannot be compared with taking a person to witness his first-ever motor race at, say, the British Grand Prix. Such a person has already been preconditioned to speed, whether to an express train or to a jet airliner upon take off. One such occasion, I was accompanied to a Grand Prix by a person with completely new eyes. In this case the overall speed did not impress him nor the deafening sound, the colour and the excitement. That person was totally numbed by the entire experience. Only days later when he had recovered his senses did he start to appreciate certain aspects of the race. In this particular case the start of the Grand Prix — with its narrow margins for error and those first frenetic laps — had made the greatest impact. Because that person had no real allegiance, no emotional tug or the first clue to unravel the confusion of pit stops, cars being lapped or cars simply going missing from mechanical failure or accident, it became a mish-mash and appeared extremely processional. Motor racing either serves to stimulate the senses or is an ear-splitting din that bores the uninitiated rigid.

Spectators and those observing the Bexhill Races in 1902 were for the most part, witnessing a totally new sport which was actually being born on their doorsteps. These virginal minds might have read about those inter-city races in France, and gazed at the photographs transfixed. But they could not imagine the speed, noise and mayhem generated by the magnificent men in the motorised machines. Not a soul had jaundiced eyes. No ears had been attacked by the roar. They could not relate to the speed of the motor cars racing past them.

Nothing illustrated this ignorance of the fact more than the police patrolling the feed roads into Bexhill. They were caught completely by surprise at the velocity of offending vehicles. No officer could pull up a motorist and with conviction accuse him of breaking the speed limit by 55 mph. He would not have known what that speed meant. All he saw was a motor car being driven by an irresponsible individual that was travelling like a 'bullet from a gun'.

I imagine that Sunday in Bexhill must have been a truly fascinating experience for everybody concerned. It was no better penned than by the correspondent of the *Bexhill-on-Sea Observer* from which I quote:

> The scene on the Bexhill Front was one of the greatest animation. Thousands of people congregated in expectation of a full dress rehearsal, and they were not disappointed. At the Bexhill Motor Company's depot in Sackville Road, crowds of people gathered to watch the cars as they came up to lubricate. In the mews at the back of The Sackville Hotel dozens of cars had found a shelter, the coach houses being full of them. Early in the morning the 'motor grooms' were hard at work examining the machinery and polishing and shining parts, while others removed pounds of mud which had been accumulated on the journey down.
>
> By eleven o'clock, the course was filled with scores of cars flying up and down the De La Warr Parade, along the Marina and in and out of the little side streets of the town. The drivers looked as if they had known the place all their lives. Some of the powerful racers appeared later, sweeping by with the rattle of a Maxim, filling the spectators with awe and admiration. French automobilists, who were in a strong force, distinguished themselves with their terrific speed, curves and corners being turned without the application of the brake. Exclamations of amazement were frequently heard as to the wonderful control exercised over the cars, which seemed more quickly responsive to the steering gear than a horse to the rein, and it began to dawn on those who had predicted a number of accidents, and a busy time for the local undertakers, that when a motor car is driven by an expert the possibility of danger to the public is exceedingly small. The most serious event to be chronicled is the smashing of a terrier dog opposite the Sackville, when the wheels of a car passed over the beast's body. The canine inquisitor was not killed outright, though removed in a damaged condition from the course. The prophets of calamity were completely mistaken, because nothing of any note took place during the weekend to mar the meeting. To the credit of the animal world, it must be said that the horses of Bexhill, probably well accustomed to their strange rivals by now, took

very little notice of the whizzing vehicles. It was noticed that a lady riding mistress did not hesitate to take her charges along the De La Warr Parade when the entire roadway was alive with cars. Among the most notable motors to be seen was S F Edge's famous English-made 75 brake-horse-power Napier, which holds the world's records for 1,000 miles and 100 miles.

For the benefit of those who do not understand the term 'brake horse power', it may be explained that 'horse power' is a French phrase of registration, but it is of exceedingly elastic quantity. Whereas 'brake horse power' is a fixed unit of capacity, which might explain why French vehicles of a nominal capacity beat English automobiles of an apparently greater capacity.

Bexhillians were fast educating themselves into automobilism, by Sunday evening they knew a Panhard from a Mors and a Mors from a Napier. They could tell which were Mr Serpollet's cars and which of those belonged to the Honourable C S Rolls. They were also making a serious attempt to understand the intricacies of the new national sport. A week or so ago, few of them could tell the back from the front end of a motor car. A contemporary remarks that those who did not know a Panhard from a Mors after being at the races a little time would have been confined as a 'blithering block head'. It may not have been so bad as that, but there was certainly a very marked and noticeable interest taken in the cars by everybody who was out and about.

Although it was windy and at times cloudy, the sun shone brilliantly throughout Sunday, licking up the mud and water from the overnight rain. At noon on the Sabbath the first concert took place at The Kursaal, in which the handsome collection of cups and prizes for the races were on display. The afternoon witnessed still more 'practice sessions' when the motorists were obviously bent upon keeping their cars in good form. Some of them were turning from Sea Road and negotiated the De La Warr gates with half a breath of fresh air between their wheels and the piers. The French motorists especially managed to judge gaps and distances with uncanny accuracy. They drive to a much finer degree and with great gusto, whereas the English drivers lack the, same confidence and slow right down to filter through the gates and around turnings. Only automobilists of the calibre of Charles Jarrott, The Hon C S Rolls and S F Edge, who with the considerable experience of racing on the continent, show anything like the same high speed skills when driving around Bexhill!'

Just to read these first-hand observations by a local reporter evokes a unique inspiration of a man grappling with unaccustomed oils with which to paint a pristine canvas.

Sunday evening bore witness to the kind of revelry normally associated with fair-grounds, Bexhill's streets were choc-a-block with motor cars, giving the town the atmosphere of being the entire centre of automobilism throughout the kingdom, which indeed it was at that moment. Every hotel bar, every public house was crammed with happy people knocking back alcohol as if they were at Alexandria in the desert heat. Every ribald song rang out in Devonshire Square where a man with his accordion accompanied a hundred or so men and women who danced to his tune. Mr James Coward pushed his Mustel Organ from the Kursaal to various street corners to enliven the evening. As darkness fell upon the beach, screams and yells could be heard from the sea as Frenchmen and their ladies bathed and cavorted amid the waves.

After various evening meals, beaming 'gentlemen' rose from hotel dining tables with a 'purty luttle muss' on their arms, and would retreat 'upstairs and next door' where heaven only knows what went on. Bexhill at midnight was 'the place to be' even though a workforce were still putting out seats in the parade gardens which served as the enclosure for VIPs and the course was still being marked out with tape. A blackboard in the Sackville Hotel starkly announced: 'FIRST RACES AT 10 am DUE TO VAST ENTRY.'

This meant that those on day trips from London for the advertised 2 pm start were going to miss the initial historic runs, such was the popularity of the event. As the pubs closed, hundreds of figures huddled into shops, doorways and many more slept rough on the beach.

It was going to be that sort of night!

16

Sensations of Speed

ALTHOUGH ONLY three months had passed in gestation, The Bexhill Races, according to Claude Johnson, had undergone an elephantine period of pregnancy. The otherwise painful hours of labour had, in fact been remarkably trouble-free. Now that Whitsuntide had arrived — and what should have been a joyous birth at dawn, was in fact a grey, threatening day with voluminous clouds scudding across the sky — for anything but the strongest spirits, a dampener of a start. Not on your life — every soul who had already arrived in Bexhill, whether they huddled in a shop doorway or lay spread-eagled with a damsel of no fixed relationship at the Metropol, was determined not to let a shower or two extinguish the sense of occasion. The only prospect to be daunted was a racer looking to enhance his reputation with a record-breaking run to put Leon Serpollet in his place.

As a regiment of black rain clouds marched up the Channel from the southwest and dumped their buckets of discontent upon the hallowed course, depression among the organising officials turned to joy as the first groups of hardy spectators began to assemble over Galley Hill and along the course before breakfast. Although sorely tried, the local enthusiasts dedicated to claiming the best vantage points before the day trippers teemed down from London, may have felt like drowned rats, but nothing short of outright war would have shifted them. Their patience in the face of the diabolical elements was unexpectedly rewarded when S F Edge on his Napier 'race-tested' the course with Charles Jarrott and his Panhard. If nothing else had happened that day, the sight and sound of those two speedsters 'giving their all' filled the onlookers' goblets to the brim. Very soon the formality of testing track conditions was overtaken by two extremely competitive spirits. On one magic run between showers, both cars tore down from Galley Hill side-by-side, bucking, slithering, teasing and roaring together through the curves in a fashion which nobody else would witness that day.

The two Great British sporting motorists reported their opinion of the course to Earl De La Warr and Mr Mark Mayhew saying that races between two big cars side by side, while desirable, would be a danger to the public if anybody lost control. The Earl and his colleague, being extremely aware of the risk of any adverse publicity respected their conclusion — caused a heavy sigh of relief from Superintendent Elphinstone and his massive retinue of policemen on hand to guard the event. Lieutenant Wise, whose charge was the fire brigade, also nodded his approval. I suspect that deep within his sporting heart, the Earl would have enjoyed nothing better than to see the real racers wage battle, having glimpsed the titans at war earlier that morning.

Amateur photographers, in spite of the public warning not to take photographs at the meeting, were not easily dissuaded from trying their hands at action photography. They appeared with a tremendous array of cameras, hand-me-downs from grandfather's loft. Some of these early 'image catchers' were extremely unwieldy. Early in the day, one chappie was spotted grappling with a Murray & Heath 'box camera'. He must have suffered so much camera shake that his photographs would have been blurred beyond recognition. Later in the day, the same fellow was seen standing on a garden wall using his friend's head to steady his camera!

The French certainly showed off with their relatively compact stereo-plate cameras (the size of a large shoe box) made by Society des Gaumont in Paris. There was plenty of 'Let's see through yours' during the day which broke down the language barrier. Since most cameras were named after the makers, some people were adroitly 'panning' their heavy Meaghers and the W Watson model was prevalent in numbers. It was three years away from the popular Thornton Pickard era which, along with George Eastman's American Box Brownie cameras, heralded photography for the masses. Early examples of the little 'light boxes' were seen poking from underneath macintoshes. Unlike some of the big Bertha's present, they did not need a tripod.

What degree of success any of these 'shutter bugs' attained may never be known. The emulsion was slow to record the exposed images. Combine this problem with the dull weather. Shutter speeds would have been somewhere between a quarter and an eighth of a second. Owners of cameras with focal-plane shutters were better equipped for creating an acceptable image. However, for most people, the time for photography had been cut down to the short bright periods when a watery sunshine filtered through the clouds. The real buffs erected their tripods and busied themselves picturing willing custodians seated upon their motor cars.

Typically, the supporting cast which made up the Touring Section, were given the honour of baptising the new course. Ironically, it was the motor bicycles in Class FII for machines weighing not more than 112 pounds. There were nine entrants. These included the 2 hp Werner and a 1.75 hp Phoenix; and the winning 2 hp Humber was ridden by a Mr H Belcher. He romped home so easily that there was nothing for the growing throngs to get excited about. After a few heats, pressmen observed an air of indifference among the spectators who had come see the big boys in action. The programme was by no means adhered to, for reasons best known to the organisers. Colonel Crompton's telegraph board on top of the Chalet which should have given the results of each heat played up, the crowds were completely in the dark as to who was winning or losing. As for even trying to identify the cars by their numbered cards affixed to the vehicles, these proved to be too small, and some of them got blown away during a race.

By the time of Class D for Voiturettes — cars weighing less than 15-cwt — umbrellas were collapsed as the sun poked through. This encouraged Mr Archer, the official photographer of *Autocar,* to mount the steps onto the Chalet balcony. From there he secured a lovely panoramic shot of Mr D M Weigel's 8 hp Clement. The driver enjoyed a runaway win in his heat, and he waved madly at the crowd as he crossed the finishing line. In the final, Weigel beat the 12 hp Gladiator driven by Mr Perman by a mere 18 inches at the tape. Although the morning's proceedings were slow, to say the least, with Weigel's time being posted at 1 min 14 seconds, the crowd were getting into good voice. By the time Class C (for Light Cars weighing less than 18-cwt) got into its stride, Colonel Crompton had the beasties sorted out of the timing system in time to record the then distinguished pilotes like Jarrott, Mayhew, Captain Skeffington-Budge assembled for the start line in a selection of cars that included a 7 hp Panhard, 12 hp Humber, a sprinkling of Benz's, New Orleans and the MMCs.

With speeds on the increase, the crowd, even the most immovable were stirred. The sight of these throbbing creatures rushing along the track, each driver with his head bent into the wind, and his passenger crouched at his feet to create less wind resistance, was something new and bold to behold. As each car approached the finishing tape, up would go their heads, and if they led the race, they would quickly turn to see the extent of their victory, then reduce speed sufficiently to whisk past the cheering crowds on both sides of the De La Warr gates. As they motored through the melée, every crew would punch the air and draw enough breath to let out a guttural cheer. It was heart-rending stuff, because right then, the romance between the spectator and the sporting motorist was cemented. While the early events were unfolding, the first train-loads of eager fans were disgorging into Bexhill, and they searched the streets for the action — not of course realising that the races had already started. As fashionable ladies and gentlemen from London mingled with the so-called riff-raff on the walk along Sea Road and Devonshire Road to the promenade, one man's name was clearly audible above all else: 'Serpollet'. It was as if nobody else existed. The national press had previewed the races around his star. Just before the revered Frenchman took a light lunch at the Sackville Hotel, he held court with the British press avid to learn of his record-breaking run in Nice just one month before. The correspondent of the *Bexhill Chronicle* managed to quote Leon Serpollet:

> I was a little nervous before the start, because I had not been able to test my machine over the course in Nice before hand. I knew the car (the Easter Egg) was alright, and I knew how to get the maximum out of it. Previous to the trial I had noticed a little shed by the roadside, about one hundred yards from the starting point, and I said to myself That is where I must go full speed ahead. I was quite calm at the moment of departure, and when I reached the shed I pulled the lever to let the car go. A second or two later I was conscious of a great sensation of speed that can only be called fearful. I felt the machine shoot forward like a ball from a cannon mouth, and as I sped along it seemed as if I were astride an arrow. In all my previous experiences I have been able to calculate pretty nearly the speed at which

I was going, by the whistling of the air in my ears, but this time I heard and saw nothing. Platforms, trees, people I saw none of them. The one sensation I did experience was the leaping of the car. The slightest unevenness in the roadway when it is going at such a frightful pace — sure my speed was at the rate of over eighty miles per hour at the finish — is sufficient to make the machine jump, and I positively felt the wheels bound off the cement several times, as a stone ricocheted along the surface of the water. But from the start to the finish I had no time to feel uneasy, and almost before I realised what had happened I was past the post.

According to the 'tongue-in-cheek' comment of the *Daily News* correspondent, his fellow scribes looked upon the dark, middle-sized man with a fringe of dark beard, open-mouthed and almost drooling as he reiterated his astonishing experience. By two o'clock an enormous crowd of sightseers flanked both sides of the course. It was estimated that people were standing nine deep in the open areas below Galley Hill up to Bolbrooke Road. The Automobile Club viewed the huge congregation from the roof of the Sackville and reported to the press that some 12,000 people were actually watching the races, while the same number again milled about the streets of Bexhill simply gazing upon the hundreds of parked motor cars.

Every now and then, racers under the guise of 'testing the machinery' did a lustful burst along the course between the touring car heats, Baron Henri de Rothschild driving his 40 hp Mercedes enlivened proceedings and caused the spectators to draw breath when he 'side-slipped' under full power around one of the curves. A babble of excited chatter erupted in his wake.

'D'ya see the buck whills (back wheels), th'lmost slid up the fence'. That was one audible comment, other outrageous claims were made by a simple countryman who reckoned that the Merc was doing at least 'Undred moiles per 'our — and then some'. Now the adrenalin was flowing freely through the crowd. In one afternoon final between Sir Jasper Penders's 20 hp Darracq and a similar car driven by the Hon C S Rolls, the crescendo of cheering reached a deafening volume as both drivers gave their cars everything they had, and drove 'flat out ' along, the winding course. The two Darracqs were so evenly matched that in horse racing it would have been termed a 'photo-finish'. Neither Pender nor Rolls gave an inch as they bumped and lurched through the curves, both coming perilously close to colliding with each other. The crowd was driven to ecstatic euphoria. The waiting, the long train journey and the hanging about in the damp had been justified. They bellowed for an encore.

'By George, if this is motor racing', waffled a toff to his fancy lady, 'I want to have a go'.

Unfortunately, not every heat was debated with such vigour or so finely balanced between man and machine. So when the time came for the competitors in the Speed Section of the entry to show their muscle, anything less than a head-to-head contest would be considered a travesty. Perfectly aware of the crowd's passion for true combat, Earl De La Warr and Mark Mayhew spoke with Edge and Jarrott again. It was finally decided that to tempt fate at what was building up to be a fine hour in the early history of British motor racing might kill it off should a terrifying accident happen. The tourers had made a memorable dress rehearsal, but without a form of public address system, the Earl was frustrated by not being able to communicate with the mass that it was sheer speed now, and a race against the clock for safety's sake.

Weather conditions during the afternoon improved no end, although ladies were heard to observe that it was just as wet under foot because certain unscrupulous 'gentlemen' insisted upon peeing under their long coats virtually where they stood. The gentlemen dare not move in fear of losing their vantage point. As the track dried out with the combination of a strong wind from the south-west and the constant use of cars, a racing line was detectable. The heats for the electric cars opened the speed section. The difference between tourers and racers was that the bread'n'butter shopping cars had to appear 'ex-factory' with no modifications, whereas the racing cars looked more 'brutish' without their mud-guards, exhaust-box and general passenger comforts. This also opened the door to a handful of 'specials' like Serpollet's 'Easter Egg'. Heats for electric cars kicked off the speed section rather like a damp squib. Apart from not emitting throaty roars and filling the air with octane petrol, Mr E Hart in his 15 hp British Electromobile won in tranquil style at an average speed of 22.2 mph with a Kreiger driven by Mr R W Wallace in second place.

As the afternoon raced on, restive spectators awaiting the appearance of 'the gladiators' started a fuss over the repetitious nature of the loud explosions which denoted the start of each race. Driven to distraction by the constant whistling by the twenty two course marshals, an element of the casually interested throng, probably damp and footsore, started to create mischief. Dubious overtures were made to attractive young ladies. The sound of obscene lyrics wafted on the prevailing wind, upsetting the dedicated enthusiasts.

There was claustrophobic congestion along the cordoned off section of the De La Warr Parade in front of the Sackville which served as the assembly area. Many of the racers congregated in the 'paddock' before and after their runs. This provided the onlookers with a rare opportunity to admire and photograph these brave men and their wondrous racing machines.

Hundreds of people occupied the bank leading down to the road which was one of the best free stands along the course. At this spot it was a matter of the greatest difficulty to move about. The crowd in this area were mainly good-tempered and well-behaved, but a few 'local oik's' managed to squeeze in and became loud in their profanity, whereupon select guests did not just 'tut' in disgust at their behaviour, one matronly lady turned on them and screamed 'Oh take a bloody jump in the sea you stupid twerps' — an impassioned appeal that was issued with all of her Kensington bearing and evoked nods of approval from more reticent guests.

While these colourful distractions went along with the social intercourse, the races continued with the motorcycles buzzing along the course. The best time was made by A A Chase astride his 4.5 hp Soncin. Just as Mr Chase was about to receive the Motorcycling Cup, a note was handed to Mr Mayhew, who duly announced that the machine was disqualified because it was not fitted with a proper silencer. Its progress along the course was described as reminiscent to a Gatling Gun. Consequently, the trophy was awarded to a surprised unknown owner of a 2.75 hp Excelsior. The race for motor tricycles and 'quads' was won by Mr Ralph Jackson on an Eagle tandem. Then it was the De La Warr Cup event, for racing voiturettes. After much juggling of wires, Colonel Crompton eventually announced that Mr J S Overton's 10 hp Richard won the prestige trophy while a hotly debated second place was given over to the 9 hp Novelty car driven by Mr T B Browne. Animosity between these two competitors was caused when Mr Browne was heard to accuse Mr Overton's machine of dropping all its oil over one of the curves, causing him to skid and lose time. He may have had a justifiable complaint, because the way the Novelty had been 'skeletonised' to reach the weight-limit of 7-cwt 3.50-qr created no small degree of amusement.

Things began hotting up in the County Gentleman's Cup races for light cars under 12-cwt 3-qr 5-lbs. The entries included three new 20 hp Darracqs, which proved to be veritable fliers. The winning car was driven for Captain Lloyd by Baras, who covered the course in 43 seconds which was the equivalent to 52 mph — the fastest run for petrol cars at that stage of the proceedings. The odd thing was that the thousands present did not get steamed up at the actual performance, but they cheered wildly when the figures went up on the telegraph board. This must have been one of the occasions when everything clicked into place, because around mid-afternoon the press were griping about a distinct lack of information. If the great Fleet Street scribes were having fun unravelling the programme, then utter bewilderment and confusion must have reigned among the thousands camped on Galley Hill where no back-up information was relayed or posted on a similar telegraph board. One happy snapper showed his contempt for the organisation when he was spotted on the pebbled beach photographing the 'purty luttle musses' who were making the most of the sunny periods by showing a knee!

The next race was the *pièce de resistancé* for racers under 19-cwt 2-qr 20-lb for The Car Cup, subject to the one-kilometre course being covered in not more than 40 seconds. Since this weight was the maximum limit for racing vehicles under Continental rules, it followed that entries included the very latest models of the big racers.

They comprised Mr Harmsworth's 40 hp Mercedes and the same make of car driven by Baron Henri de Rothschild, Mr Jarrott's 40 hp Panhard, Mr H Austin's 30 hp Wolseley and the Hon C S Rolls's 40 hp Mors.

A great moan went up around the track when the Rolls Mors, of which great things were expected, had a cylinder-head joint give out just before the event. Many willing hands worked at the side of the track and fabricated another joint, but that also packed up. Not to deprive a hushed audience, Rolls soldiered on in spite of one cylinder retaining a certain amount of water, which in turn was leaking into the carburettor. This caused the engine to misfire badly, so that it could attain nowhere near its maximum speed. However, Rolls faired well with his do-or-die attitude. The winner was Charles Jarrott on his 40 hp Panhard with Rolls second, and highly commended for his effort, while Mr Harmsworth's Mercedes driven at the witching hour by his friend Mr Muir was third. The new Wolseley was fourth, driven by heaven-only-knows-whom because the driver was reported to have been last seen sleeping off a liquid lunch in the Sackville. While no driver actually cracked the 40-second barrier, the proprietors of *The Car* magazine decided to award the cup to Charles Jarrott for his winning time of 44.5 seconds — an average speed of about 51 mph.

Time was fast drawing nigh to the climax of the Bexhill Races. Once again people were all eyes trying to spot the ghostly Serpollet, but before the race for steam-driven cars began, the two 'heavy-weights' rumbled into view: Rolls with his second car, the 28 hp Mors which he used in the Paris-Berlin race and Selly Edge in his 50 hp Napier: both were two-seater cars, each weighing over 19-cwt 2-qr 20-lbs. Straight away two camps of supporters surged forward as the cars tore down the track on their respective runs. Londoners showed an inclination to shout for Jarrott, while Bexhillians adopted Edge as their son. By this time of day, the road surface was past its best — not that it had been that good all the weekend. 'Tramlines' of rutted gravel were conspicuous, making it extremely hard for these monsters to remain on a good racing line. Rolls gave his all as expected. He had to 'back-off' slightly round the curves in fear that one big slide would eject him and the car into the crowd on the 'sea side' of the track. Edge with his eyes firmly fixed upon the *Daily Express* Cup, shot down Galley Hill much faster than Rolls. Into the first curve amid a funnel of wildly waving hands urging him on to greater speed, the Napier got away from him. Jiggering the wheel hither'n'thither, he fought the car out of the confounded ruts where he could be heard cursing to the wind. After a final lunge for the finish line, Edge sat back in the full knowledge that his hour of glory had not dawned. Rolls had taken up the gauntlet to win by 1.75 seconds at 48.6 mph. One of the first people to welcome him into the competitors' enclosure was Serpollet, anxious to learn of the state of the road surface. The Frenchman was either going to take the fastest time of the day with ease or die of shame against his opponents L Perry-Keen in the 6 hp Gardner-Serpollet and Mr A Ginder in his Locomobile made by the Company in America.

As early evening approached, the clouds seemed to disperse, with the sun gradually dipping in its natural arc towards Beachy Head and the westside of Eastbourne. Small pockets of people were starting to wend their way homeward. Many still remained to make Galley Hill more like an ant-hill of humanity. They were determined to see the hero, Leon Serpollet, and there was still wild conjecture at the prospect of the Frenchman breaking his Nice record at Bexhill in spite of the totally unrealistic condition of the course.

Walking in the opposite direction of the small trickle of spectators strolling up Sea Road was Mr William Mayner. He had just arrived from his home in Hove to spend a few 'quiet days' at his weekend residence along the De La Warr Parade. He turned into Cantelupe Road and cursed the many vehicles that were parked higgledy-piggledy along the curb, up the pavement and at every angle. Cars not being so manoeuvrable, chauffeurs simply spotted gaps and parked their cars without thought for others. As Mr Mayner approached the crowded sea front he found his path blocked by a policeman, who informed him that his orders were to keep people away from the area around the Sackville. Not unnaturally, Mr Mayner became indignant and made the point to the officer that he owned a property along the Parade and that he had every right to gain access to his residence.

The policeman stood firm and merely shrugged his shoulders which caused Mr Mayner to rant on that he had chosen Bexhill as a weekend retreat to escape the madding crowds of Brighton and Hove. Such was the man's rage, before he left the helpless constable, he warned that he would take legal advice about the possible action against such an irresponsible sporting occasion cluttering his freedom of access to Bexhill in the future.

What was believed to be a storm in a tea cup was later to have a considerable effect upon the future of motor races in Bexhill.

Oblivious to the confrontation, the crowds at Galley Hill strained to catch sight of the Serpollet approaching for its first run. The three competing cars in the Steam Class had entered at the end of the original cycle track, and at the top of the hill they were assembled to await starter's orders. Throughout the day, the signal had changed from a discharge out of a pistol, to explosions of maroons supplied by the Coastguard. By the time of the steam cars, the starter had reverted to a large white pocket handkerchief. Mr Ginder was first away in the Locomobile which proceeded sedately, averaging 28.3 mph Mr Perry-Keen made the second run in the Gardner-Serpollet, and, try as he might, could only persuade it to achieve a speed of 38.5 mph. Since many onlookers thought that Mr Perry-Keen was in fact Serpollet himself, there were groans of disappointment at such a meagre effort. They soon woke up when the white-painted car was seen whistling back towards Galley Hill, this time with Leon Serpollet at the helm. The press were later informed that Mr Perry-Keen was under Monsieur Serpollet's order not to show any heroics, because he first wanted to try for the FTD (fastest time of the day) in the more conventional car in which he had more confidence.

Since it was so vital that Colonel Crompton's equipment was working at peak efficiency, there were several false alarms. The starter's 'hanky' was replaced by the gun. At last the white speck on the crest of the ramp was seen to move forward. A cry went up! 'Serpollet is coming!' and the assembled thousands stood, not daring to miss the greatest moment in motor racing history. The white speck grew larger, and instantly the car swept past like a meteor, screaming its way through the air. They spotted both Serpollet and his riding mechanic crouched low to cut down wind resistance, stretching forward, almost physically urging the car to greater speed. The driver crossed the line jubilant. Serpollet felt deep in his bones that he had set the fastest time of the day. Just as they crossed the finishing line, an oil bottle was upset, and the mechanic scrabbled about trying to retrieve it. Suddenly, without warning the car burst into flames. Leaping down after pulling to a halt, Serpollet used his gloved hands to beat the flames out.

For the many spectators, this was real drama happening before their eyes. A man with a box brownie elbowed forward to try to secure a 'scoop picture'. Everybody was extremely animated and jostled about unaware of the potential danger. Fortunately the great Frenchman had the situation under control amid huge cheers. He then left the car and mounted the famous 'Easter Egg' to make his second run. In his keenness to get started, Serpollet barely registered the garbled message from Mark Mayhew that he had already achieved the fastest time at 41.50 seconds with a speed of 54.5 mph.

Serpollet motored the 'Easter Egg' towards Galley Hill amid a cauldron of cheers, people waving sodden programmes and wielding their folded umbrellas in the air. Surely he must be even more inspired to make his phallic-looking projectile break all records, they wondered out loud. They waited in expectant calm before the car was finally manhandled into its correct position on the start line. *The Daily Telegraph* correspondent from his vantage point on the start line eulogised romantically at the sight spread below him:

> A broad band with sweeping curves, bordered by deep black lines. As the pistol fired, the crowd leant forward, the Serpollet silently moved away in a cloud of steam. With great rapidity, the white car turned into a dot. It hurtled along the course amid a forest of people waving and roaring the car on, as it whisked by them like a projectile. Whistles peeped, dogs barked, ladies screamed. These sights and sounds left a deep impression upon my mind. Racing automobilism has arrived.

Serpollet's second attempt was much slower. Afterwards he said: 'The corners, they are nothing, but the road after the Hotel Sackville' — he waved his hands expressively to illustrate its bumpiness — 'I had to cut off the fire. I think in the last 500 yards before the finish line, my speed was in the region of 80 mph.'

The French driver had barely crossed the line when the huge crowd started to disperse. Many of them swore that they had seen a day of 'heroic proportions'. As the sun reddened, there was one more event for the diehards to watch in front of the Sackville. After Leon Serpollet was presented with the Paris Singer Cup, which in spite of his not breaking the 40-second barrier, was handed over for the Frenchman's sportsmanlike effort. In the background, beautifully prepared and polished motor cars swept onto the track in readiness for the Concours.

* * *

Most of the racers retired to their various garages, then onto havens of rest to relax before a complete change of apparel in readiness for The Automobile Club Ball at the Kursaal. As a curtain falling upon a memorable day, some sixty motor cars regally glided past the grand enclosure to start the Concours d'Elégance. For most spectators living beyond Bexhill, this namby-pamby parade was akin to having a spring fashion show after a bare-knuckled bout of pugilism. The appreciative audience who remained were the dedicated local citizens and those who had emerged from the bridge parties to take the air.

The procession was a most imposing display of handsome motorised carriages representing that era. Each model appeared absolutely 'spick'n'span' — the paintwork gleamed in the evening sun and brasses were polished to dazzle. The custodians with their grooms and valets had done themselves proud. Several times the cars were elegantly driven around the streets that encompassed Sackville Hotel to enable the judges to cast their critical eyes upon detail. It was certainly gratifying to see well-maintained automobiles driven with qualified experience. The total entry was whittled down to twenty cars that were passed as being first-class in general appearance. Then the judges had the final six cars pass and repass the table at least four times before they unanimously agreed upon the order of merit among the last trio of finalists.

The House of Commons Premier Award was presented to S F Edge, whose handsome Napier prepared by Coupe Company received a popular accolade for the minuscule attention to every detail. Then Mr W J Peall, the celebrated billiards player, won great admiration for the Mulliner-designed body on his 12 hp Daimler, and was duly handed the Bexhill-on-Sea 'Welcome' Cup. The coachwork on Mr Alfred Harmsworth's lovely New Orleans was judged to be a credit to the Twickenham body shop.

As the final outdoor activity came to a close, one astute onlooker gazed longingly at a car not judged to be in the reckoning which had an attendant who in his uniform sat behind the driver like a footman. When it came to parking, the man would dismount and by arm signals instruct his driver to park pretty much the same way as a controller indicates to a jet-airline pilot where to place his craft in the taxi bay.

Over cocktails in the Sackville bar, Baron Henri de Rothschild and Leon Serpollet expressed their considered opinions of the Bexhill Race Course to an attentive audience in Earl De La Warr and Mr Mark Mayhew. They uttered diplomatically couched suggestions like: 'Lovely location, pity the course could not be lengthened' — an observation made by the Baron, while Serpollet interjected with the idea: 'The outsides of the curves might be banked up so as to maintain speed.' The French suggestions were taken on board with appropriate respect, but as British drivers joined the conversation, a rift of ideas appeared, Jarrott and Edge were adamant that: 'The corners were no drawback, and the course length was adequate.' Before the French could respond, Jarrott, speaking on behalf of his fellow racers, imparted a solidarity at any future meeting in Bexhill, to race the big cars two abreast.

Such a unified front from the British produced circumspect response from the French with the track as it stood. Nevertheless, they realised what 'crowd pleasing' meant from previous experience in their homeland. As the alcohol mellowed sharp minds, Leon Serpollet lightened proceedings by mulling over the idea of 'flat' and 'jump' events to draw a comparison with horse racing. This produced expressions of incredulity from everyone. Then Serpollet told of his experience while 'jumping the bunkers' on a private Sunday evening test run, when he ran out of brakes and had to swerve on to the golf course at Galley Hill. His passenger at the time was Mr Roger Wallace who thought that such an idea was appropriate to the 'Bexhill Grand National'. The Earl suggested that the party disperse before anymore crackpot ideas were inspired... dinner was due to be called.

The London and local press representatives were left to debate gregariously upon the ifs'n'buts of the race meeting among themselves. Fleet Street had been generously fortified throughout the day with ample spiritual inspiration by the Earl De La Warr. So these hugely self-opinionated scribes by evening time were able to elaborate upon the event through the rosiest coloured spectacles.

Members of the specialist motoring press kept a discreet distance away from the daily newspaper feature writers and society columnists sharpening their pencils for the Pink Domino Ball. Matters of a motoring nature peppered their barbed comments. Since they were able to draw comparisons with Continental events, the consensus of opinion between the respective editors of *Autocar* and *The Car* magazines was that Bexhill had emerged from this historic day in sports motoring considerably better off than the Race Committee of the Automobile Club.

Each writer, himself an august club member, pronounced bravely on Dutch courage extracted from a bottle, and alleged that parts of the organisation were downright shambolic. Strong language came from Mr H Walter Staner, whose observations of the mechanically propelled road carriage had to be respected. That is, of course, unless you are the editor of *The Car* publication, who naturally diluted this stream of bile by confessing to his counterpart that he had already committed to copy paper, that the Bexhill Races were 'an emphatic success' — a comment that had Mr Staner choking upon his double gin and Angostura bitters. His argument was against Colonel Crompton's totally inadequate timing equipment, which he later admitted performed tolerably well within its experimental brief.

As for the race organisation, that not only served to bamboozle the motoring writers, but must have left the great British public in permanent suspension as to exactly what was happening. *The Car* magazine published constructive suggestions to encourage a need for clear information to be delivered promptly for official and public consumption at future meetings. The opinion based upon the fact that even at this hour of the evening, no list of times or speeds had been posted. As for the assumption made by the Club that the public were better informed upon automobilism than was the reality, that was a bungle of monumental proportions. Everybody agreed that the telegraph board was a washout. Having aired their dirty washing, goodwill was reinstated before dinner and the festivities across the promenade. So the respected scribes swept the gremlins under the carpet and agreed to continue their arguments on the printed page.

Under the cloak of twilight, couples could be detected cavorting along the Marina from various hostelries, looking for all the world like phantoms advancing upon the opera. Many of the ladies were mysteriously adorned in high masquerade. These flamboyant mantles were Dominoes, delightful creations of every shade of pink, elaborately trimmed with flowers and made from gorgeous silks and satins. Flouncing along the sea front upon their gentlemen's arms, they evoked a touch of magic, the mystery enhanced by a small mask to set people guessing about their identity.

A handful of gentlemen were also decked in fancy dress, some military, some lovely pompadours with powdered wigs and patches. One gentleman was wearing hunting attire and there was even a Pierrot seen walking past the The Farm Tea Shop along the formerly named East Pier Avenue. The *Daily Telegraph* witness noted beneath his own flowing black cloak 'a totally unreal ambience created by beautiful pink butterflies gliding through the Bexhill streets, was the gas-light prelude to the Grand Domino Ball.'

With appropriate bearing, the aristocrats of motoring made their respective entrances into the Kursaal. Lady De La Warr had laid before them a spectacle of breathtaking beauty. It was a fairyland of pink flowers threaded through the ornate arches at intervals upon delicate green leaves. All festoons were illuminated by a myriad of scintillating electric lights. The orchestra platform was banked with a mass of pink bloom, it was heaven, and moved Baron Henri de Rothschild to comment: 'Even Nice rarely blushed as demurely as Bexhill tonight'. The sensational decor served to flatter the Dominoes perfectly. One particular French Domino worn by Madame Serpollet was carried out in rose-pink accordion-pleated chiffon, real pink carnations and a tastefully arranged crook of similar flowers combined to achieve an enchanting effect. The Domino parade took place just before supper to the strains of a spirited march performed by the contestants and their cavaliers. Earl De La Warr asserted that all the ladies had won his heart, but the judges had set theirs upon the winning Domino that was a blaze of pink satins and roses covered with various sprigs of white hyacinth against a dash of rose-coloured petals.

The waning hour of Monday was played out with a flourish by Mr J M Glover and his hearty musicians, who were conducted by Mr Otto Ferschal. Distinguished guests worked up an appetite dancing to polkas, the Lancers, the popular Valse and (by ever popular request), the Cakewalk. Supper arrangements were carried out by the Sackville Hotel and light refreshments were supplied by Fuller with no expense spared. So at midnight they had the choice of *Consommé Riche en Tasse, Filet de Boeuf Renaissance*, along with light *Sandwiches assorties, Patisserie Variées, Granite au Café* and *Petits Fours a là Sackville*. And the night was still young!

Tuesday morning emerged misty, the sun a diffused ball over the Channel horizon to the East. The very last of the revellers departed the Kursaal to the sound of waves braking upon the pebbled shore. Apart from that, an eerie silence had fallen upon Bexhill — now collapsed into beds, wrapped in car rugs on the beach and curled up in shop doorways. Still dozens of cars parked haywire as space allowed, were scattered along the promenade and along the side streets. The charming butterflies nestled their weary heads upon broad shoulders.

For the racing motorists, Tuesday was going to be oblivion.

17

Fetched up in a Kitchen Garden

WITHIN THE month of savouring the most supreme week of events in the entire history of Bexhill-on-Sea, the legal advisors to the Earl De La Warr convened a meeting. They sombrely advised him that Mr William Mayner had objected to the use of the De La Warr Parade as part of a race track. The solicitors letter went onto say that, on Whit-Monday 1902, Mr Mayner had found that his access to a property which he owned along the parade was restricted on the day of the race meeting. Mr Mayner then stated his intention to secure an injunction in the Lord Chancellor's court against the use of the De La Warr Parade for such motoring events in the future.

After sensational press reports of the premier Bexhill Races and the receipt of numerous letters of congratulation, the utter frustration suffered by the Earl at this sabotage of his ambition to make Bexhill the mecca for sporting automobilists can only be imagined. This mood must have deepened when the case was put before Mr Justice Farwell in the Law Courts. Mr Mayner secured his injunction. The decision was not just felt by the Earl and the Automobile Club, but the *Bexhill-on-Sea Observer* put into print the feeling of anger and frustration felt by the town's hoteliers, trades-people and any ordinary citizens when it published: 'Another instance of the overwhelming difficulties which confront the progress of automobilsm.' It was also pointed out that it was not only unfortunate for the Automobile Club which had leased the track for a number of years, but a shattering blow to the hopes of those who sought to benefit Bexhill by making it the racing centre for English motorists. Displaying venom until the last, the *Observer* summed up: 'Thus at the caprice of one individual, the pleasure or perhaps the interests of thousands have been sacrificed'. A proposed August Bank Holiday meeting had to be cancelled.

Notification of that unhappy event for Bexhill was posted upon the notice board in front of the Automobile Club premises at 119 Piccadilly it simply read: 'In consequence of the decision of the High Court in the action of Mayner-v-Earl De L Warr and the trustees of the Bexhill Estate, the Automobile Club have decided that the competitions which were proposed to be held in Bexhill shall — by kind permission of the Duke of Portland — be held at Welbeck on Thursday 7 August, at 10.30 am — Claude Johnson, Secretary.'

Upon confirming the notification of this fixture, the Duke was a sporting enough gentleman to send the Earl De La Warr commiserations upon the circumstances and stating in so many words that such an outcome would not have been his personal wish, and that Bexhill would remain the centre of motor sport in the kingdom.

In 1903 an effort was made to overcome the deadlock: the Automobile Mobile Club carried out a series of weekend contests restricted to the cycling track, which was the Earl's own freehold, to which an extension had been made in 1902 at the Galley Hill end, thus rendering the use of the De La Warr Parade unnecessary. As a result of this move, it was possible to organise a motor carnival in August 1904.

The intervening period between 1902 and 1904 witnessed a definite change of attitude towards the motor car. People living in London and the South of England during this time became thoroughly imbued with the still-novel mode of transport. Away from the so-called sophisticated south of the kingdom, the automobile, though a common sight in towns and on arterial roads, could still turn people's heads and provoke comment in the rural districts — all the more so amid the uplands of Wales and Scotland where the motor car was put to its most stringent test, horse-drawn carriages were still the norm and the car was an exception.

Working upon the assumption that the 'unconverted' were either circumspect, or a motor car was beyond their budget, the Automobile Club continued a 'soft propaganda' exercise by organising short reliability runs. Sporting heroes were invariably made guests to participating car owners. The great England and Gloucestershire county cricketer Dr W G Grace joined a 'crew' of four gentlemen straight after the 1902 Cheltenham Cricket Festival for a 140-mile circuit between Crystal Palace and Folkestone at every stop en route the towering bearded 'wonder of the willow' would enthral crowds by discussing the virtues of the motor car. He confessed to not having any knowledge of the mechanical intricacies of his adopted steed, but W G lowered his ample frame behind the steering wheel to indicate the space and comfort while a riding mechanic explained the system of controls to the mass of onlookers.

In America Oldsmobile had entered into 'mass production' of reliable light cars which had not gone un-noticed by two men. In England Charles Jarrott sensed a ready market, so he negotiated an agency which he opened in Marlborough Street, London, where he sold the 7 hp models for £150 on the slogan: 'You've nothing to watch but the road.'

Of a more significant nature was the ambition of Henry Ford, a son of Dearborn in America. He attracted a consortium of investors to foster the dream of a simple farmer's boy. Ever since Henry was a teenager, he had been inspired by Carl Benz. The automobile was his heart's desire — he wanted not just to own one, but to 'make an auto for the people'. The success of 'the Oldsmobile had not been lost upon him either, and he told his investors that there was room in North America and the rest of the world for a quality mass-produced automobile. The Ford Motor Company was born by a sheaf of cheques that crossed the table.

While no single motor car emerged along Britain's highways, an impromptu 'census' made by the President of the Institute of Civil Engineers revealed a growing concern. Standing on the curbside of the London-to-Brighton road just outside Horsham, he logged an average of 1,200 motorised vehicles per hour, over a four-hour period. These figures were collated to support a Bill in Parliament to regulate vehicles and drivers. That Bill enacted that private cars must be registered and numbered. Yet amazingly, the Government threw out any suggestion for a driving test or for the issuing of penalties for drunk drivers. It seemed that car owners and loaners could commit hari-kari on the roads of Britain, but race along them — never!

To judge how absurd this hypocrisy was, anybody could put a car on a ferry and enjoy the liberty of independent legislative bodies in the offshore islands to race on Jersey, the Isle of Man and Ulster — where in 1903 the Gordon Bennett Trophy was run round Ballyshannon. The Isle of Man hosted the 1904 Gordon Bennett trials and the Tourist Trophy in 1905. After the Gordon Bennett Cup Race, the first Irish Speed Trials were held in July 1903 over Phoenix Park. Dubliners had their first taste of real speed, when three drivers were separated by the blink of an eye over the flying kilometre.

If the Earl De La Warr had felt a victim of gothamist, then the demise of Nice as a straight speed trial venue may have concerned or comforted him. In March 1904 he and Lady De La Warr travelled to the South of France to attend the annual meeting which inspired the Bexhill Races. No 'bloody-minded objectors' stood in the way of the Promenade des Anglais. In the end, the famous French course became the subject of its own success and the sheer velocity of the motor car. The truth dawned when two drivers, Monsieurs Rigolly and Duray shared the wheel of monster 13.5-litre Gobron-Brillé. Their best standing kilometre at 53.6 seconds was nothing to write home about, so ponderous was the machine in getting up steam. When these fellows bounded onto the flying kilometre, a fatal mixture of shut-eyed oblivion, white-knuckled fear and a ferocious speed drove home the insanity of performing such a lethal run along the promenade that was no longer adequate to the task.

It was Rigolly's shattering pursuit that shook the living daylights out of himself and the ACF. As it gathered momentum, the massive car bounced, swerved and was only just contained within its master's control when he slammed down the kilometre within 23.6 seconds at a staggering average speed of 94.78 mph. Rigolly then had to bring the heaving brute to a juddering halt at the finishing line where he reckoned that the terminal velocity was well in excess of 100 mph. The violence under braking was fearful and having to wrestle the 13-ton vehicle into submission while attempting to hold a straight line produced 'skid marks' on delicate places other than the road surface! It had been an incredible sight and sound to behold, but Rigolly confessed that not only was he frightened for his own life along that amazing run, but he realised that the consequences of a monumental accident while hurtling between two walls of humanity, was too ghastly to contemplate. From that day onwards Nice became host to the more sedate timed manoeuvrability tests. After 1914 all was quiet along the Promenade des Anglais until 1932, when properly conducted street racing with massed starts saw the institution of the Nice Grand Prix.

The Earl returned to Sussex with food for thought. August 1904 had already been confirmed with the Bexhill Corporation for a return of the speed trials. Competitors' wings appeared to be severely clipped in that only touring cars could take part, racers were *persona non-grata*. Also the drastically revised course was much shorter, starting from the Chalet and finishing at Galley Hill. Publicity declared that this would now be the best 'viewing' course in the country in that spectators would be able to see from start to finish, whereas in 1902 the cars disappeared around the curves.

After setting such a precedent with the first races, the Earl along with his committee (chaired by Mr U Stratton) devised a Grand Motor Fête which would not only incorporate the races, include a whole range of activities like an illuminated procession, a battle of flowers, a decorated car parade, a gymkhana and another fantastic *Bal Masqué* at the Kursaal. In spite of this filigree, would the masses bother to attend races where touring cars would be droning along (albeit side-by-side) at 40 mph slower than Rigolly's breathtaking record at Nice? Talking of Nice, S F Edge reminded the Earl that evolution had ensured an advance in the speed of touring cars. The August Bank Holiday meeting could well surprise everybody — including the esteemed racing driver, especially if 'Le Patron' himself competed.

What would the Earl be compelled to drive in such an event? His very good friend, the Honourable Charles Rolls (yes, in a matter of two years, address by Christian names had become acceptable) had in May reached an amicable far-reaching agreement with a Mr Henry Royce, the power behind F H Royce (the Manchester based electrical engineers). Rolls, who had sold and repaired cars from his establishment in Conduit Street, London, became sole agent to sell Royce cars under the name of Rolls-Royce. The now prestigious partnership, then everything but a merger, was sealed at the Midland Hotel in Manchester after the two men had been introduced by Henry Edmunds, a Director of the Royce company, and protagonist of old against Rolls in his racing days. The Earl contacted Rolls with the idea of racing a Royce car at Bexhill in recognition of the partnership. Mr Royce regrettably had other ideas more up-market than racing for his two-cylinder 10 hp models.

By the time of the four-day event, the Earl had become Lord De La Warr. Through the co-operation of Mr Stratton, the Automobile Club, though not able to play host, gave the meeting its full support in terms of advice and some manpower. The Bexhill Corporation dressed the town and sea front with a riot of multi-coloured flags which fluttered gaily in the breeze, adding a carnival atmosphere to the event. By comparison with 1902, a far greater sense of 'occasion' welcomed the many thousands of visitors.

People of memory estimated that twice as many cars poured into Bexhill than before. But then there were twice as many cars on the highways as there had been in 1902. The nights being short and balmy saw umpteen folk revelling outside the pubs. Everybody was in full voice, and most pubs adopted their own 'choral society' — for want of a better word. At closing time, fifty or so drunks danced out of the *Devonshire* bar and down to the sea front, singing at the tops of their voices. On reaching the sea wall, they leapt onto the shingle beach. Then in a frivolous moment, men and women dashed into the sea fully clothed. There were no dippers to segregate the sexes. So when the happy-go-lucky souls emerged from the waves, their clothes wringing wet, they stripped down to their petticoats and draught excluders. Fortunately, darkness spared the blushes of the lady revellers .

By contrast to the common ribaldry, romance sprang eternal for a young innocent when early risers on Bank Holiday Monday witnessed a cameo to touch the heart. Imagine a school girl on summer holiday with her grandparents in Bexhill. After breakfast grandfather proudly escorted his pretty granddaughter to see the motor cars arriving along the promenade. Together they wandered among the big touring cars that were being mechanically finessed for the competitions.

Grandfather noticed that the young girl was mesmerised by one man's action as he meticulously polished the brass-work on his Napier. She then watched him mount the driver's seat while a mechanic started the engine. As she dodged other admirers to see him engage pedals and levers, he gave her a wave before driving out of sight.

The years passed by and that young girl matured into an attractive young lady. Then by a stroke of enormous coincidence she encountered the driver of the Napier. That school-girl prelude turned into a fairy-tale romance when the astonishing finalé became a life-long commitment as Mrs S F Edge.

High-jinks along with a touch of romance was part of the colourful fabric in Bexhill during race weeks. In 1904, a third, and extremely unwelcome, element crept into the proceedings — vandalism.

The shock and horror caused by the severance of the cord that contained the wires which connected the telephones between the Judges' marquee and the Chalet was perhaps over-dramatised. How could such wanton behaviour occur in such a splendid and mature resort as Bexhill? So trusting were the technicians that they had laid the cord out of harm's way along the fence enclosing the course from the throngs. It was unprotected, and therefore probably proved an irresistible temptation to scoundrels who overnight had taken cutters and severed the communications system in several places. Fortunately, the bared wires were spotted before the proceedings commenced. Confidence was considerably shaken among the hierarchy, who demanded a police vigilance along the course overnight In spite of this, the pests still committed their irksome deed on the following consecutive nights!

Since the Sackville was not the hub of operations in 1904, a 'tented village' was erected over the golf course at the bottom of Galley Hill. 'The Enclosure' as the area became known, was reserved for VIPs, the racing drivers and their families, and of course for the ubiquitous press. According to most reporters, refreshments, desks and information were a considerable improvement upon the 1902 provision. A few old 'grousers' from Fleet Street were inconvenienced from not enjoying 'on the ground' telegraphic installation direct to

London. Instead, after they had composed their stories, a messenger with a bicycle was provided to carry the press telegrams to the Post Office for transmission. That sad lack was more than made up in the huge hospitality marquee. After a few G & Ts, even the most cynical 'hacker' got into the swim.

By 2 o'clock, when the racing was due to start, a pin could not have been placed between the masses on both sides of the track. The crowd was estimated at 25,000 — many of the gentlemen were wearing straw boaters while lots of the ladies sought shade beneath colourful parasols.

Though entries were numerous, the programme was carried through with commendable dispatch. Since the races started from the Chalet end of the track, and there were no flying starts, the pace was perhaps congenial with the sweltering conditions. The racing was never deliriously exciting. By comparison with 1902 with Serpollet the 'carrot' to lead the horses, there appeared to be no logical 'star' upon which to hang a story.

This state of affairs was soon remedied as the racing progressed. From the enthusiasts' viewpoint, a definite improvement was the almost instant announcement of results. Each heat was posted by telephone. Runners then attended a series of blackboards placed along the course and times were registered.

Lord De La Warr featured in the class heats for cars priced between £550 and £750: he drove an immaculate 18 hp Daimler and convincingly won his heats in the first three rounds. His Lordship was always roundly cheered by everybody as he raced by, but on the second heat the ladies in the crowd reserved their goodwill when he beat the only lady competing in the races. Mrs Manville, driving her husband's Daimler, had actually won her first round amid screams of delight from the many ladies watching. So when the Lord deftly held his position in the second round, the enthusiasm among the females was sharpened by feigned scorn.

There was some stirring contest in the class for cars priced between £750 and £1,000 — S F Edge, driving his new Napier, found himself the subject of an all-to-rare protest. He won his heat by 12 seconds from Sir Archibald Mac-Donald's 36 hp Daimler.

Sir Archibald, along with a couple of cronies, lodged the protest which alleged that Edge had not declared the horse power of his car correctly and suggested that the Napier cost over £1, 000.

What is interesting to reiterate here is that the entire shimozzle was conducted by a series of formal letters delivered by a messenger commuting back-and-forth between respective hotels and private homes.

First of all Sir Archibald registered his feelings with Mr W R Jefferies, the Secretary to the Judges. He combed the race regulations to ensure that Sir Archibald's gripe was justifiable. Having found that the titled citizen had a possible foundation for argument, Mr Jefferies then sent the messenger boy packing with a letter to S F Edge.

The great British racing hero instructed the messenger to wait while he drafted out his indignant reply, a paragraph which bears reading:

Rees Jefferies Esq;
Secretary of the Judges.

Dear Sir,
In regard to the protest of my entry in Class G. I am not aware that in any way I have infringed the rules and conditions under which I have entered, and I am prepared to answer any specific charges brought against my car or myself. I personally, have no power to give such an assurance as you ask for, being the matter of a strictly technical basis but my company S F Edge Limited can prove that my entry is perfectly in accord with the conditions under which I entered. I will give you an assurance on their behalf that anything the rules or regulations under which I rode call for, will be honourably met.
Yours truly, S F Edge.

The messenger boy was kept extremely busy cycling between hotels and running between rooms in the Sackville Hotel. Rees Jefferies, along with his fellow judges was not going to be intimidated by a virtuoso. They insisted that he supply documents proving that he sold Napier chassis to the public for £850 as stated on his entry form. Then he got on his hind legs and requested that such a documentary proof should be delivered to the judges by first light next morning. Failure to do so would incur S F Edge in disqualification from Class G.

In a curt reply Edge wrote: 'Naturally under the conditions at the moment, I accept their (judges) ruling, and I am pleased to undertake that chassis like that which I have run in Class G today will be supplied to the public at £800 each if so desired.' There was a post-script to Edge's letter which was rather telling: 'May I have a copy of the rules dealing with the matter, so that I may be in a position to place a protest on record in accordance with such rules, against some other competing cars?'

With that final statement severely underlined, S F sprinted down to the beach and heaved a motor boat into the sea, fired up and took off like a dose of salts to where he was staying on the Isle of Wight. The jet-set had not yet arrived by fifty years, but the boat-set did things in style. Next morning, Edge caused a commotion among spectators as he loomed at speed from out to sea aboard his Napier Minor after a relaxing night at Ryde away from petty bureaucracy.

There is nothing on record to suggest that S F Edge managed to deliver the required document for the race judges' perusal. However, 50 years on when Mrs Edge mooted the idea of a jubilee commemoration event in 1954 to the Veteran Car Club, she donated the premier award of the day, the 'S F Edge Bexhill Trophy'. This turned out to be the 90-ounce bowl which her late husband won in the class 'G' (Large cars priced between £750 and £1,000) at the 1904 meeting. So presumably Edge was not disqualified. He must have established contact with his company in London by telegraph from either Bexhill or Ryde, and managed to persuade somebody to deliver the document to Rees

Jefferies, which probably knocked Sir Archibald's protest into a cocked hat.

Revenge obviously sharpened the air on the Tuesday because in the class for cars irrespective of price, Mr A L Guinness in a 60 hp Mercedes won the first prize, its time being 46.4 seconds. That beat Mr A Dew's 24 hp Bollee by 12.4 seconds. In the semi-final it shot from the start to cover the course in 47.4 seconds, thus defeating S F Edge's Napier whose time was 52.3 seconds. Edge was thus eliminated, although Mr Dew, who ran a bye in 59.1 seconds, got into the final where he won second prize. Edge then lodged a protest for being started against a 60 hp Mercedes. The judges suggested to the competitors in the semi-final that they should run off the final altogether, because they objected that the protest was too late. Disgruntlement filled the air, so the judges referred to the race committee who gave the thumbs-down to Edge's protest. The notoriously petulant driver showed his disgust by not attending the prize-giving ceremony. So as the successful competitors received their trophies, when presentations came to Mr Guinness and to Lord De La Warr, there was a gap in the parade.

Mr Edge had enlisted a marshal to send a message stating that he declined to attend personally to receive the prizes he had won, and wished them to be sent to London! Was such unsportsmanlike behaviour to be a portent of things to come in modern racing when 'prima-donna' drivers fly in the face of officialdom. Or was S F miffed by the fact that Rees Jefferies was not only the Secretary to the Judges, but also the Press Officer as well! This is a loaded question which will forever go unanswered.

In retrospect, it is clear to see how the court injunction secured by Mr William Mayner prematurely curtailed Bexhill's time as a longstanding venue for motor sporting events. The place of resorts as the country's centre for racing would have been overtaken anyway by the Kingdom's first purpose-built track in Surrey. Nevertheless, Bexhill can still take enormous pride in having played host to the very first races in Britain — that gloss will never tarnish in the archives of history.

The metamorphosis from horse to combustive power created a noticeable incoherence of opinion between the motorist and laws enforced by government legislation. This cleavage of opinion forced a new movement that sought to protect the freedom of the automobilist. In 1905 a body of influential motorists who were growing in concern at the prejudices of hostile police, banded together to start the Automobile Association. The pronounced objective of the 'AA' as it became known was: 'the protection and advancement of motorists and opposition to restriction on their use of the roads'.

Over fifty of the most distinguished drivers in the land were invited to provide weight against an intransigent attitude struck by Prime Minister Arthur Balfour's cabinet. Even the leaders attitude at this time seemed caught betwixt and between. Only three months before the AA was formed, Balfour had attended a preview of the 1905 Motor Show in the company of the Prince and Princess of Wales, both royals being acknowledged for their enthusiasm for the motor car. It was this combined presence at the exhibition that faced down the last militant stronghold of the anti-motoring league.

Among the distinguished guests who gathered for the launch at London's Trocadero Restaurant were Walter Gibbons, founder of the London Palladium Theatre and Selwyn Edge who had been appointed the General Manager of Dunlop Tyres. Everybody present agreed to pay an annual subscription of two guineas to support the new club. Mr Edge informed the present company that he fully supported the AA because it had pledged to assist motorists in avoiding the increasing number of speed traps set about the country by officers of the law. Special patrolmen on bicycles appointed by the AA would be vigilantes in their areas to check roads for such traps. Edge went on to say that the methods of measuring a motor car's speed were questionable because the police used conventional stop watches to 'roughly estimate' the velocity of passing cars when enforcing this ridiculous 20 mph speed limit.

Unfortunately, in spite of these good intentions for the motorist, a legality ruled against the fledgling organisation stating that scouts were flagrantly interfering with police officers going about their course of duty. The AA circumvented the issue by introducing a revised clause: 'If an AA Scout fails to salute you, stop and ask the reason.' Some hilarious situations were created when motorists quizzed the patrolmen, who would blithely say: 'Glad you felt able to stop, sir, just thought you should know the road's extremely rough a mile or so on'.

* * *

In 1905, the *Bexhill Chronicle* correspondent rose well above the occasion when his opening paragraph coloured the lily. 'The third car race meeting held over the Whitsuntide was highly successful. At least sixty competitors took part and some exceedingly good times were made.'

I can only surmise that when the remainder of their year is occupied with recording the affairs of the council, the Women's Institute, the latest guests at the Manor, births, marriages and regretted deaths; motor cars breaking wind over your editorial patch can stir the red corpuscles of the most jaundiced local newspaper reporter. As with a classic painting that has been allowed to fade in the sunlight, after that epoch-making 1902 event, anything less than spectacular would reduce the attraction. In 1905 only dedicated opportunists went down to the sea, on a glory run of 'pot hunting'.

Then personal feeling could be detected permeating the *Chronicle*'s report. 'Compared with the crowds that witnessed the 1904 August Bank Holiday meeting, the track was sparsely lined with people in spite of the beautiful weather. Only a few huddled figures dotted the reserved enclosure at Galley Hill'. Such a sad scene must have caused concern for the Automobile Club who hosted the event.

Although the entire weekend went without a hitch, the keen enthusiasm that burned with the pioneering spirit was all but extinguished. There was a lackadaisical attitude it had been decided not to publish the ties of the cars in each heat, but only those of the class winners. Consequently, the races were robbed of interest for the spectators. However, for the first time since 1902, race-prepared cars were back in harness. After watching the tourers rip up the course from a standing start in 50.3 seconds — which was pretty impressive — the die-hards anticipated sensational speeds from the racing monsters.

Only a handful of heroes arrived. There was a Napier that had come straight from the speed trials on the Isle of Man chauffeured by Cecil Edge. A brand-new 90 hp Mercedes driven with great panache by Sir Ralph St G Gore during practice got the tongues wagging, while Mr J E Hutton, the gangling driver who later became a hill-climb exponent, drove a very similar car. Last but not least was the sensation of the August 1904 races — Mr A Lee Guinness aboard a Darracq that was built for the French driver Barras.

The racers were to have been allowed to 'open up' along the full kilometre course. But an untoward incident put paid to this privilege. The change of heart by the Club happened after a practice run when Guinness had a private dice with Hutton. Guinness suffered a rush of froth to the head to beat the Mercedes driver down. He dropped the clutch of the Darracq just as he crossed the finish line, and with brakes grabbing him in all directions, he crashed through a fence. A hired gardener leapt for safety as the errant beast bounced over the potato plot, through several rows of carrots and fetched up in a cabbage patch.

The landowner was a fiercesome lady who issued the aggrieved Guinness the sharpness of her tongue. 'You crazy nincompoop, you could have killed my gardener', she shrieked, 'you only did that to annoy me'. Guinness manfully handed the venomous woman his calling card, and told her 'Please let me have the bill, but don't send it until after tomorrow, I may end up here again'. The upshot of this amusing incident was that the course was shortened to a standing half-mile, the shadow of Mr William Mayner having clouded the Automobile Club's judgment.

For most of the day, cars were timed satisfactorily by an electrical appliance which registered the time as each vehicle passed over a flat rubber tube that contained wires. Trouble began when the racing cars under hard acceleration, ripped up the tube and made mincemeat of the wiring system. After the first heat, the timekeepers had to revert to stop watches. In the event, an egg-timer would have adequately measured the Darracq's superiority, because after three heats, the accumulated times of each car were added together and 'Algy' Guinness was almost 4 seconds faster than Edge's Napier. The rest wondered what had hit them.

The deceptively young-looking Guinness with his Bohemian air, marched off with the Bexhill Town Rose Bowl graciously presented by Lady De La Warr. To the immense amusement of those gathered for the trophy presentation, the Rose Bowl was filled with potatoes and carrots to remind the young tearaway of his obligation to refurbish the kitchen garden of one irate lady resident. At the end of proceedings, the Automobile Club Ball proved more memorable than the racing itself. Lord De La Warr offered a prize of £10 for the best 'Cake Walk' and in spite of the intricate steps, competition was hot. One wag was heard to comment 'Forget the brakes, let's take the cakes' — which summed up most people's opinion of the weekend. Conversation amid

236

the fun and games of the Kursaal 'Do' was dominated, by rumour and counter-rumour concerning to proposal to create a purpose-built track. No doubt both ideas were inspired from the frustration of not being able to beat government legislation that forbade racing on public roads in the kingdom. At this Bexhill meeting, Lord De La Warr received substantial first-hand information of a plan by Mr Hugh Fortescue Locke-King to construct a 'banked' test track on his 'Brooklands' estate at Weybridge in Surrey. This ambitious £150,000 'motor course' was being laid ostensibly for British motor manufacturers properly to test their vehicles on paved circuit away from the claustrophobic 20 mph speed limit.

Within Bexhill his Lordship was not slow to notice a restive minority who were taking exception to the regular upheaval caused by motoring events within their vicinity. As a token of good public relations, plus an awareness of the shrinking impotence of the course along the parade, Lord De La Warr intimated in the press a plan to construct a National Motor Course, largely centred on marshland where today the Cooden Beach Golf Club is firmly established.

With the prospect of Brooklands stealing the Bexhill thunder, his Lordship was goaded into action with architects and planners. The baronial coffers had been sadly depleted — the only collateral that remained was the estate and the Manor House. In spite of financial difficulties, he pushed on with the plan which, true to his character, had to be the biggest and the best race venue in the country.

Meanwhile, work had started at Brooklands by the autumn of 1906. Tons of earth had been bulldozed to form the high banked bends through the wooded estate. The Brooklands project made for a full circuit of basically 2 miles 1,350 yards, which was estimated along a fifty-foot line, with a main straight of 991 yards. Overall, the full lap would be 3.25 miles.

Judged from the early earth works, Brooklands was impressive as a 'futuristic' venue where cars could be tested to well over 100 mph. It was the banked sections that drew breath from experienced racers like Hutton, Rodakowski, Napier, Edge and Lord Montagu. The 'Home' bank was almost too steep for a man to walk up, and he was on his hands and knees before he could strike for the rim. The Byfleet arc was shallower and both had a radius of between 1,000 feet and 1,550 feet respectively. S F Edge and Napier were already plotting to establish a publicity coup upon the opening of the new track.

A small delegation led by Lord De La Warr went to Surrey for a cursory look at Brooklands.

The chastened party returned to Bexhill having seen the full extent of Mr Locke-King's course and how near it was to completion. So much wind had been taken out of their sails, that there was little heart left to hold a debate.

Lord De La Warr called for an extraordinary meeting at which plans of the National Motor course were placed on display. The drawings indicated that a 7.5 mile long multi-purpose race facility would run parallel to the coastal railway that connected Hastings and Bexhill to Eastbourne. The outline of the

237

circuit had the appearance of a dumb bell, Two long straights were planned to be connected at each end by two 180° curves. Speed trials could be held along the home straight and there could be a feeder lane leading back to the pits along the return stretch. For lesser meetings, a complete oval could be cordoned off and from a cathedral-like grandstand, resplendent with hospitality suites, club-room and ballroom, plus a restaurant overlooking the entire circuit with the South Downs in the background, and the pits to both sides, the idea had the makings of a super track. The Cooden scheme was put forward to the town planners by the National Motor Course Company.

In one last thrust to do the 'Brooklands Boys' down, extravagant claims were made about what would happen after the course had been opened as a profitable business: 'the motor course will be extended to the range of hills ending at Beachy Head, for which satisfactory surveys have been made. It will include hills 575 feet above sea level, giving a gradual ascent of nearly two miles length, with a gradient of as much as 25% in some parts. The extension to Beachy Head would increase the course length to over 20 miles.'

This bold scheme even with the moral support of Lord De La Warr inspired the reporter of the *Sussex News* to pen these reflective personal thoughts: 'I can relate to my father's futility when he witnessed the paddle steamer 'General Slocum' sink beneath of the waters of New York Harbour after a fire on board and nearly 700 people were drowned. For many onlookers attending the Granville at Bexhill today, there was a similar emotion. We could only stand, listen and wonder as the demise of Bexhill, the motoring centre of the country, dawned upon its brave pioneers.'

Unlike the merchants of doom and gloom at the failed National Motor Course, the incurable romantics were determined to perpetuate the Bexhill shrine to the sporting motorist. After the 1905 Whit-weekend meeting, the flamboyant August Bank Holiday was turned into another riot of colour with a Battle of Flowers. The well-patronised event was postponed for 24 hours because of thunderstorms. Bent, be-draggled but unbowed, the 'Hooray Henry's and Giggling Gerties' flocked to Bexhill determined to have a good time. There was no racing on that occasion, but more a celebration for cars, carriages, mail carts and goat chaises. If nothing else, the flower traders rubbed their hands in joy at a profitable weekend.

Having spent a lot of energy and resources on the aborted National Motor Course, Bexhill entered 1906 quietly much to the relief of the citizens. Not that Bexhill degenerated into a back-water. As a social centre, it was still a fashionable place to go at bank holidays.

1907 was to become a red-letter year for Selwyn Francis Edge. Events unfolded straight into the hands of the egocentric British racing driver. Edge and Napier had already secretly hatched an inspired publicity stunt which they played by sleight of hand in case another driver or manufacturer got a whiff of their plan. They had booked the entire facility of Brooklands for two days in June after the official opening.

Their scheme was to establish an unprecedented high-speed, 24-hour nonstop, single-handed record around the new circuit. To the outside world it was described as a low-key reliability test programme arranged by Napier, using the Brooklands track in the spirit to which Mr Locke-King had bequeathed the circuit. Edge had surreptitiously introduced a competitive element to the exercise in creating the opportunity to secure for himself a page in the record books at the dawn of a new era in motoring at Brooklands.

At the dusk of Bexhill, Lord De La Warr was approached by the hitherto unknown Crystal Palace Automobile Club to organise a race meeting over the Whitsun weekend. Delighted to respond, he opened the estate gates and agreed to co-operate having seen the new adventurers 'permit issued by the Automobile Club. Bearing in mind that almost anybody could form a motor organisation without too many whys-and-wherefores, it was probably a decision which his Lordship lived to regret.

The Crystal Palace organisers elected to run races for three cars at a time, a format never attempted before at Bexhill. All classes of tourer and racing car were invited to enter. Notification was sent at random to various clubs in the country and on the continent.

Shortly after the races were announced in the early spring of 1907, S F Edge made contact with Lord De La Warr to arrange a visit to Bexhill. Upon arrival at the resort in his Napier, Edge, with his Lordship, drove down from the Manor House for a good look at the course. Since 1905, almost the entire length of the course to the bottom of Galley Hill had been resurfaced. Edge was mindful of Leon Serpollet's outright record for the standing kilometre which had stood at Bexhill since that trail-blazing day in 1902. He told Lord De La Warr that five years of development had improved the overall performance of the Napier. The overall power was better generated at the driving wheels and Dunlop in turn had produced much better tyres with a glue-like grip. Edge imparted his confidence that Serpollet's record was for beating, even from a standing start.

The two men returned to the Manor House in a very optimistic frame of mind. Regardless of what else went on at the Whitsun weekend, Edge emphasised to his titled friend his determination to set the record book straight by staging the fastest time over the Bexhill track — in a British car, or course driven by a British driver. They toasted to a potentially epoch making event Lord De La Warr was fully aware that his racing driver friend was sufficiently fired with personal ambition to realise a truly outstanding record.

Regretfully, the meeting was described in the press as a shambles, totally chaotic and moved the *Sussex Daily News* to remark that it was the 'worst farce ever conducted in the name of a motor car race meeting.'

Motoring enthusiasts pondered over S F Edge's desire to feature at Bexhill, especially with the prospect of the longest-ever race in history looming (between Peking, China, and Paris, France) only a matter of days after the Whitsun holiday. His reason for preferring to race at Bexhill was not made public. Only a handful of trusted friends were informed of his assault upon Brooklands. Clearly a free spirit not reputed to follow trends, Edge pursued his own priorities while some of his more durable competitors fought for 'safe passage' papers in Peking, and sign their lives away on a pledge that they were not the forerunners of an invasion of China by the West!

At Bexhill as proceedings slowly reduced the meeting to chaos, Edge understandably dissociated himself from the organisation. He sought refuge away from prying eyes in the bowels of the Sackville Hotel. Edge's invisibility caused speculation among the frugal crowd that he intended to appear at all, let alone that he was present and had deigned to sign-on.

About an hour before he was due to compete, the bewildered and extremely bothered gentlemen of Crystal Palace wrote the approximate time of Mr S F Edge's attempt upon Leon Serpollet's Bexhill record. Then Edge, punctual as ever, caught the starting official off balance as the driver steered the 80 hp six-cylinder Napier into the marshalling area by the Chalet.

The maestro then dismounted from the car and wandered casually over to the timekeepers to ensure to his own satisfaction that the apparatus was functioning properly.

Having returned to his station behind the steering wheel, showing great aplomb, Edge more or less dictated his own proceedings. He methodically lowered his goggles, adjusted his head-dress, wriggled comfortably into the drivers seat, then signalled his readiness.

The nervous starter raised his pistol to arm's length above his head while Edge focussed his attention upon the trigger finger. Whether he dropped the clutch and floored the accelerator before the shot rang out will never be known. The Napier's brute force was phenomenal by comparison with the sedate take-off of the touring classes. Grappling at the controls, bent double at the wheel, Edge and his passenger bodily urged the throbbing monster on to maximum speed within the given distance. The faithful few hollered and waved the Napier on. Edge called upon every ounce of cubic capacity up to the finishing line before dropping every anchor, man-handling the wheel with his left hand while punching the air with his right. Every stressed sinew in his body knew that he had captured the record.

Lord De La Warr jogged over to the official timekeepers in the Chalet, all of whom were ferociously calculating a committee decision as to the result. Suddenly, one man triumphantly stood up and announced that: 'Mr Selwyn Francis Edge driving a Napier registered a speed of 73.4 mph.' The redoubtable British driver had hoisted a British-made Napier ahead of Serpollet by 19 mph regardless of the shambolic day, most was forgiven in the name of justice having been done against the French. No wonder the Channel Tunnel Bill (1907) had been thrown out from the House of Commons, three months after the War Office had declared its opposition. The nation needed all of its defences intact after this thoroughly British coup!

Although Bexhill was to play host to other motoring events in the years to come, S F Edge returned home satisfied in the knowledge that his record would stand the test of time.

Throughout the winter of 1906-7, an army of workmen hewed the earth from the undergrowth at Brooklands while hundreds of trucks dumped mountains of rubble that had to be raked and rolled into place as the solid foundation. It was the wrong season of the year, for 200,000 tons of cement to be laboriously laid as the top surface. The expected date of completion was deferred because the track surface cracked in many places, especially on the banked sections. In some areas where wet cement was exposed to the harsh winter frosts, the frozen moisture caused powdering when the warmer daytime air thawed the concrete and it became porous.

While workman were endeavouring to remedy the ravages of winter, over two hundred carpenters were enlisted to erect safety fences and spectator stands. The sanity behind this huge endeavour at winter time was often questioned. Despite the extreme cold and the short daylight hours, the logistical headaches — though sometimes almost insurmountable — were overcome with resolution. For example, when Colonel Holden's drawn plans indicated that the steeper banking over the River Wey necessitated a ferro-concrete structure to bridge the gap, he called in L G Mouchal, a specialist structural engineer, to solve the problem.

While the construction of the world's first enclosed circuit slowly advanced, small parties of distinguished persons from within the motor industry travelled to Brooklands for a view of progress from specially located vantage points. For some of the more conservational minded gentlemen, the deliberate felling of 30 acres of delightful woodland for the accommodation of such an obtrusive facility was questionable. Several comments were noted that surely a flat road circuit would not have destroyed the landscape while the trees would have absorbed the noise of motor cars circulating.

Other less informed opinion was quite sure that automobiles would not remain stable on the banked sections and that when a near-verticle angle was attained, vehicles would tend to tip over. There were some comments made that Brooklands had been forsaken for a 'wall of death'. More favourable judgment positively glowed at Mr Locke-King's advanced concept. Nobody ever discovered what exactly provoked his generosity in permitting such a monstrous, almost alien structure to loom over what had been a picturesque stretch of woodland. After all, Hugh Fortescue never drove a motor car himself, in spite of being surrounded by a family of macho-motorists who shared a reckless passion for overpowering cars like intimidating Italas. His wife Dame Ethel was no exception. She was a spirited lady, who during the First World War was a dedicated humanitarian. Hundreds of people had reason to be thankful for her help and dedicated work for the Red Cross. Her deeds were recognised when she was made a Dame of the British Empire. Dame Ethel, along with other members of the family, loved nothing more than continental touring holidays.

By contrast to his free-spirited wife, Hugh Fortescue was a singularly shy man who was content to occupy his leisure hours as a master of jigsaw puzzles. He found the occasional foray abroad with Dame Ethel at the helm enlightening, but he travelled badly and was always relieved to return home — where his speciality was the breeding of pedigree French poodles.

It was after one particular sojourn in Italy that the family noticed the rugged speed and superiority of the locally manufactured motor cars. As against the British models, which were tried and tested on roads restricted by speed limits, the Italians were able to 'open their motors up' along straight, unrestricted roads and developed an enviable record for reliable grand touring, whereas the British cars were prone to breaking down after sustained motoring across Europe.

It was Dame Ethel who reputedly planted the germ in Hugh Fortescue's mind, to convert the wild patch of woodland on the estate into a high-speed test centre for the British motor industry. The rest of the family were surprised when Hugh Fortescue agreed to the suggestion — and so Brooklands was born.

Up along St George's Hill, Weybridge, well-heeled residents had, until the summer of 1907, slumbered in their rather secluded enclave. The motor car was nothing novel to them — in fact some of them had made a purchase, and were known, on high days and holidays to give their molly-coddled vehicles a run. Passing drivers were known to 'honk' as some batty sign of fraternalism which many motorists did, even more when drivers of a similar make of car encountered each other. Other than this ritual of ownership, the people upon the hill kept very much unto themselves. There were few triflings to disturb their peace apart from the song birds in the trees and hedgerows.

Comment was made upon the hive of industry which was fast appearing on the Locke-King's estate. No secret had been made of the development. Inquisitors at the early stages were informed in the press of a test facility for the motor industry to use occasionally. There were corners of pride in that Weybridge might contribute to the development of the motor car. The truth came out after the official opening on 17 June 1907. But even the buzz of excitement and a multitude of motor cars assembled did nothing to cause undue concern on St George's Hill.

The word 'racing' had never been mentioned during the planning stages of Brooklands. A certain amount of disquiet among the residents of Weybridge was caused at the news that Lord Lonsdale had formed a committee which was duly christened the 'Brooklands Automobile Racing Club' at the inaugural meeting on 12 December 1906 at their appointed offices on Regent Street in London.

A taste of what was to come brought about a rude awakening when, for an entire 24-hour period, through the witching hours as well as during the daytime, S F Edge celebrated the opening of the track with his single-handed attempt to establish a record of his own. The constant drone of the 60 hp Napier circulating became monotonous to those sensitive ears not enamoured by the din of the Napier's 'intensive test run'. But in the stillness of the night the constant thunder right through the wee small hours soon taunted the insomniacs on St George's Hill.

As it was, the 'busy little bee' sought his record and conquered fatigue, aching muscles, and a head fit to split, to write the Napier into the glory books after covering 1,581 miles, 1,310 yards — the latter being small change, but vital to the attempt against the clock. Edge, a man of gargantuan stamina and mental concentration, rested his weary limbs when he pulled off the course for the servicing of tyres, replenishment of fuel and repair of sundry mechanical faults that were rectified by the Napier mechanics. He covered the equivalent distance from London to Constantinople at an average speed of 65.905 mph. They lost count of the gallons of fuel consumed, but six sets of tyres bore testimony that Dunlop still had a lot to learn in finding a durable mix of rubber compound.

While endurance records were all very laudable, the sleepless on the hill infinitely preferred the short, sharp burst in pursuit of lap records. Percy Lambert was the first man to attain an average speed of 100 mph when he jarred his gritted teeth over the notorious Brooklands bumps at the wheel of his 25 hp Talbot in 1913. After the First World War the growing hysteria on St George's Hill had reached deafening proportions. The Brooklands authorities had to kowtow to their neighbours just at the time when Edge had bet *The Motor* magazine a bronze medal that he could improve upon his record set by the Napier. A new ruling set against 24-hour non-stop records stipulated that drivers must observe the 'Double Twelve Record' whereby a car had to be locked up during the hours of darkness. So it came to pass that in 1922 Edge performed his marathon spin, wielding a Mayback-engined Spyker. He easily beat his old record at 74.27 mph thus collecting his self-proclaimed bronze medal forged by the editor of *The Motor* magazine.

18

Bexhill Reincarnated

MY UNABASHED affection for Bexhill unquestionably stems from the fact that I innocently stumbled upon its motoring heritage. So it was not by choice that I moved from the area of Brands Hatch to a place that overlooked the finishing straight of the original Bexhill course. The surprise evolved over a period of time, and is still reluctantly giving up its secrets now. By contrast, although Dad had spoken often of Brooklands and even suggested that we should go there to take in the sights, my pilgrimage to the Brooklands shrine came in 1964. A week or so after Innes Ireland had returned from the United States Grand Prix, we met at a pub in Richmond. After a fairly hearty luncheon he suggested we might spend the afternoon 'poking about' at Brooklands.

Together we walked the entire outer course. I was staggered at how it had deteriorated into an overgrown ruin where many parts of the famous bankings were crumbling and cracked, with weeds and small spruces seeking daylight. Innes was full of unbounded enthusiasm for the track. He would stand on parts of the banking, eyes ablaze, a grin upon his rugged face, shouting to me: 'Boy, just imagine old Felice Nazzaro belting the guts out of the mephistopheles around here'. We would meander further, then he would run his palm over the moss-covered slope, and exclaim: 'Jesus Christ, what a thrill to watch Henry Birkin thunder around this lot in his big old Bentley. His eyeballs would have bounced in their bloody sockets. He would be steering from over to under steer as the car bounced over the concrete slabs. Fantastic stuff.' Without Innes painting a vivid canvas, I might have felt an impostor at Brooklands. The ghosts were laid low on that grey misty afternoon. I felt sure that if Innes had seen a beckoning mirage of Sir Henry, that he would have flung his arms around his hero like a long, lost father returned home. Staring at the banking with a perplexed look on his face, Innes wondered how on earth Colonel Holden conceived the idea of a banked circuit.

From my scant knowledge, there was no precedent like Montlhery, Avus or Daytona, since they all emerged after Brooklands. Reflecting upon the 1902 Bexhill Races, it is enlightening to note that Baron Rothschild and Leon Serpollet recommended that the curves along the De La Warr Parade should have been 'banked' to attain a faster and safer drive. Obviously the principle of banked corners had been explored elsewhere. While at least for myself, the ghosts of S F Edge, Felice Nazzaro, S C H Davis, Earl Howe and John Cobb remained dormant at Brooklands, the sight of those towering edifices left us with a great sense of wonderment, a spasm of awe and a healthy respect for those doyens. For Innes, I could detect a bristling sense of frustration. There was a massive urge burning within his soul to clear up the unholy mess, take one of his beloved Bentleys for a 'good old belt around' the hallowed oval. Brooklands had rightly been commended as the spiritual 'man-made' home of British motor sport. After the Second World War the outer circuit and the mountain course naturally became entwined with nature's undergrowth, a sad, crumbling monument to the generosity of Hugh Fortescue Locke-King. If a headstone was ever engraved, it would read 'Brooklands 1907-1939 RIP'.

Because Bexhill is a road course, it will never rest in peace. For the total stranger wandering along the De La Warr Parade, there are no landmarks (update: see pp 255-256), no gouges in the road surface, no derelict stands or service bays to create even a suspicion of its early contribution to motor racing history. The dedicated curiosity-seeker with the aid of faded sepia monochromes, may detect points of reference from remaining buildings like the Sackville and Marina Mansions, find the spot and claim 'this was where Leon Serpollet crossed the finish line on his record breaking run.' By relating to old photographs I was amazed to find that the original 'Finish' post was, give or take a yard or two, directly below the lounge window of Number 21.

Today the ornate Cycle Chalet and the magnificent Kursaal are gone for ever. The parade is a public road upon which anybody can drive because the De La Warr gates were demolished in 1913. Only a remnant of the original bandstand remains as a shelter from the elements. On cold winter days, when the south-westerly doth blow and the famous curves approaching Galley Hill are lashed by a foaming sea and peppered by flying shingle, the Bexhill Races seem a figment of the imagination. Cold, withdrawn and drowned, the resort stands hostile. Come the balmy days of summer, the images fall into focus. Standing on the spot where Gunner Milligan was stationed just below the Coastguards hut at the crest of Galley Hill, the course is spread beneath, and only then do the pioneering spirits conjure in the eye of the beholder.

For several years during the early 1920s, the Kent and Sussex Light Car Club organised restricted speed trials along the straight West Parade past the clock tower. When the Club applied for a permit to run a trial in 1925, the Royal Automobile Club refused to issue or renew any more permits for motor car competitions on public highways. The circumstance recalled the difficulties of holding road races at the turn of the century. Bexhill was fortunate in that the East Parade was on the Sackville Estate which belonged to the De La Warrs, and was not therefore a public thoroughfare. Attitudes by the citizens and visiting public had changed by the 1920s. The *Bexhill-on-Sea Observer* commented that: 'Most pedestrians think that motor cars are quite speedy enough in their ordinary usage without arranging special demonstrations of their capacity in this direction. Speeding on public thoroughfares should not be encouraged'.

In spite of the sea change, once courted, some of the pioneers of motoring gravitated to Bexhill to consummate a marriage with the resort. One such person was Mr H J Mulliner who lived at 'Bayworth', Terminus Road. He had been a motorist since the days of the red flag. There was a day when he and Charles Rolls drove around Grosvenor Square in London, led by the man with the obligatory red flag. The next day, November 14, he watched the start of the historic run to Brighton to celebrate the legalising of the motor car on British roads.

The Veteran Car Club made Mr Mulliner an honorary member for his services in the development of the motor car. The citation read: 'In the 15th Century Mr Mulliner's ancestors kept pack horses. They progressed into the 17th Century as coach builders. At the turn of the last century, his family company helped to speed the mechanical evolution by directing their attention to developing the 'horseless carriage'. They understood the requirements of the age and provided for its flourishing success. A founder and honorary life member of the Royal Automobile Club, Mr Mulliner set up as a motor carriage builder in Brook Street London in 1896. From his workshop, he fulfilled orders from the late Queen Mary when she was the Princess of Wales, Indian Rajahs and a fair sprinkling of those listed in *The Debrett*. From those beginnings sprung his firm of H J Mulliner and Company Limited from which he severed connection when he moved to Bexhill and retired in 1910'.

Occasional off-the-road motoring functions would occur in Bexhill. During the momentous year of 1937, when amid great pomp, King George VI and Queen Elizabeth were crowned at Westminster Abbey, an elegant gathering formed on the lawn of Egerton Park when a Concours d'Elegance distracted the bowls on Egerton's rinks and the boating people left the lake to admire the congregation. Although evidently well patronised, the event was low key in newspaper coverage. A young Swedish enthusiast who happened to be in England with his parents for the Coronation, by chance visited the event. Harold Fornaeus, a keen amateur photographer, sold his pictures with a story to a national Swedish newspaper, which made more fuss over the occasion than the infamous *Bexhill-on-Sea Observer*: not a bad effort by a 16-year-old young man with his Zeiss-Ikonta 3 — and he continued to make it pay 46 years later when he unearthed the same collection of pictures and sold a similar feature to a British magazine!

In 1952 when Frederick Bennett was the President of the Veteran Car Club of Great Britain, he was officiating at a club rally when his Vice President called him aside for a confidential chat. Mrs S F Edge had been widowed and after Selwyn's death she moved to Bexhill. She proposed the idea of a 50th Anniversary rally and speed trial at Bexhill to commemorate the 1904 races at which her husband had distinguished himself.

Frederick had over the course of fifty happy years of accident-free motoring frequented Bexhill. He savoured blissful memories that turned back to 1903 when he first visited the Sussex resort driving a Cadillac in the 1,000-mile Trial. Smitten by the place, Frederick became a fairly regular guest at the Sackville where motoring types fraternised over long summer weekends. He competed in two more commemorative runs in celebration of the 'One

Thousand'. They were happy jaunts, one in 1913 and the Jubilee 'charge of the chittys' in 1953.

Frederick thought that Mrs Edge's suggestion of a 'S F Edge Trophy Meeting' for the Whitsun Holiday weekend of 1954 was a capital idea. So when the President of the VCC motored into Bexhill in September 1953 along the 1,000-mile Jubilee Trial, the time was ripe to announce the meeting. Accompanied by Mrs Edge and the Committee, they jointly informed the gathering of the Club's proposal. The reaction was given in a spontaneous cheer from the numerous veteran enthusiasts assembled in the Sackville to hear the news. What was more, the event was openly endorsed by the Bexhill Mayor and Corporation and was co-promoted by the Hastings and East Sussex Car Club.

A jovial mood engendered by alcohol prompted Frederick to introduce a note of caution to his members. Police then employed the dubious method of humiliating suspected drunk motorists by asking them to recite tongue-twisters while attempting to walk a straight line. Naturally, this caused some stifled amusement among officers. So Frederick warned the merry company that the Bexhill constabulary had apparently not had a good laugh for ages. He recommended vigilance as they drove back to their respective hotels. A year later, doctors were lobbying Parliament for a proper form of breath or blood test for drunkenness.

I wondered how many drivers who arrived at Bexhill on 19-20 June 1954, apart from the President of the VCC and his lady Vice President could boast of being at the races fifty years back. It might have been reminiscent of old times for the elderly citizens and veteran motorists. Arriving at the resort from places as far-flung as Exeter, Bristol, Yeovil and Langton-Matravers in Dorset, most were in time for preliminary proceedings on the Friday. Small crowds of people jostled within the doorways of garages L Russell's, Caffyns, Marina Garage and the lock-ups behind the Sackville Hotel as the cars were dust-wrapped for the night garage following the rally section.

Competitors for the speed trials had to present their vehicles in the paddock area along Brookfield Road for inspection and presentation of plaques by the Town Mayor, Councillor Mrs J O Alexander, on the Saturday afternoon.

Not everybody was on time. What made it a military exercise for the drivers was that they were compelled to sign a declaration of their starting point, whether it was from home or from a nominated place. Each veteran car had to be driven the entire distance under its own power, and could start out no earlier than 6 am on the Thursday prior to the meeting. It was hoped that there would be honour among members in that nobody cheated by embarking upon their journey a minute earlier than the stated time — a temptation for some who wished for a leisurely drive in modern traffic conditions to reach Bexhill by 10.30 am on Whit-Saturday. Late arrivals were automatically penalised or disqualified from the rally if they arrived after 11.30 am.

Even as recently as 1954, the Veteran Car Club imposed a tough regime. So when eighty entries were accepted from owners of cars manufactured up to 1916, it was a clear indication that most members took up the gauntlet.

Most drivers trundled from Poynton, Macclesfield and Crewkerne, arrived in Bexhill with time aplenty to spare, to enjoy a fraternal binge on the Friday evening, whereas the vast majority of competitors, driving from within a 100 mile radius on the Saturday, suffered palpitations on the penalty of lateness. After all, the event happened just before the motorway came of age. So the veterans motored along the arterial roads which passed through towns and villages. Bank Holiday traffic converged into bottle-necks which caused all manner of dire mechanical failure. People from Sidcup, East Peckham and Bognor Regis were disqualified for being late because they were caught in solid traffic along the Hastings and Eastbourne coastal roads. As for competitors from Brighton and all towns further west, progress along convoluted roads really tried the patience.

There would have been no reason for Mr A W F Smith not being punctual. He had the choice of eighty veteran masterpieces, and opted to drive his 90 hp 1913 Mercedes from Wychurst Gardens. He arrived with moments to spare from the family home in Bexhill, to a chorus of 'Tea-up' bellowed by other club members. Mr Smith had been a member of the VCC for twenty years, ever since he decided to collect and restore veteran cars as a hobby. Even as a schoolboy when he visited the Motor Show in 1912, he set his heart upon owning a motor car. Mr Smith matured into a high-powered businessman and in 1920 he purchased a 1912 German Alpine Audi. Bexhillians have grown accustomed to seeing Mr Smith arrive in town with something different for each day of the week. The trouble was that he could not find enough garage space in Bexhill, so he left cars in London and throughout the Home Counties. Having arrived just before the 10.30 am deadline, Mr Smith vowed to keep his German steed under strict rein at Bexhill: 'Didn't want to give her a bang in front of the home crowd.' Besides the 550-yard course was not given for heroics.

Bexhill is renowned for having a higher proportion of centenarians than any other place in Europe. These people could recall days before the horseless carriage was emancipated. Charles 'Rivers' Davis lived in Brassey Road when I first met with him. Rivers had been flowing on for 101 years, his brain was sharp as a tack. He was looked after by his youngest daughter who was 79 years of age. Rivers recalled the Friday afternoon before the trials in 1954 when he eavesdropped upon a conversation between a Fleet Street reporter and Mr J A Masters, the Steward of the Meeting for the VCC. The journalist was merely trying to seek clarification of the regulations. Little did he know, according to Rivers who still chuckled at the telling, almost half an hour later the poor chap left the steward, his head spinning with figures, and utterly flummoxed.

The reason for his bewilderment was, according to Rivers, because the reporter was no mathematician. In casual conversation, the senior citizen learned that only a few weeks earlier, the same writer had been in Oxford to witness Roger Bannister, a 25-year-old medical student, become the first runner on earth to break the four-minute mile. So he made the rather naive observation: 'Why could not the Veteran Car Club simply acclaim the winner who was fastest past the post?' Unfortunately, in attempting to calculate a handicap system to render all cars equal, the formula does become a mosaic of figures.

The rally and time trials were combined by a method of marking, whereby the results in the four classes were calculated by a system of points. For the rally, one point was awarded for each land mile between the competitor's place of departure and the finish in Bexhill, as measured by a straight line on a map. Then 6% of the total was added to the score for each year of the car's age before 1916. To the ignorant outsider, according to this theory, drivers travelling from all points north or west in some early bone shaker had the dice heavily loaded in their favour. Indeed, that was how the results of the rally panned out. The winner was Mr M E Davenport who spiritedly drove his 1901 Progress from Macclesfield to score a maximum of 381.4 points. Sir Alec Coryton had a terrific weekend driving a 1902 De Dion Bouton from Langton-Matravers to finish second in Class A with 230.92 points and went on to gain second place in the same class in the speed trials.

In comprehending the formula for the speed trials, I quite appreciate the reason for my fellow-writer's brainstorm. You see the formula was based upon: (Time – Bonus + Penalty) x Horse Power (Classes A and B) or Cubic Capacity (Classes C and D) over unloaded weight in lbs.

It must have been at this juncture that the reporter's eyes glazed over. In the case of Classes C and D the outcome of the formula was divided by 112. Bonuses were allowed for cars with belt-drive, solid tyres, automatic inlet valves, fewer than six cylinders and fewer than four forward speeds and on age. Penalties were incurred by all classes with cars fitted with carburation or ignition systems, contact breakers, transmission, clutch, or lubrication or cooling systems that departed from the original design, or with raised compression ratios, light alloy pistons, lightened or altered connecting rods, roller or ball bearings that replaced the original plain bearings. Rivers, some thirty years younger when this event had occurred, still had the mental capacity to fathom it out for the demented reporter. It left the impression that all veteran enthusiasts must be the sons and daughters of the great Pythagoras!

Spectators and officials were habitually consulting their ready-reckoners and their slide rules, and to their collective amazement, the unexpected winner of the S F Edge Trophy was Phillip Fotheringham-Parker who had travelled less than 12 miles to the event. The extremely popular Sussex rallyist had sedately driven an 1899 Century wearing a Flying Officer Kite helmet and split goggles as appropriate to the regulations. Drivers of later cars had to don proper 'modern' crash helmets much against their historic esteem. In all honesty Fotheringham-Parker was equally perplexed at his achievement. Having recorded a best time of 60.4 seconds, he hadn't exactly 'bombed' down the course by comparison with S E Sears's FTD in his 1914 Sunbeam at 23.8 seconds to claim the Bexhill Chamber of Commerce Award. Apparently, the Mayor was heard to chortle over dinner and presentations in the Sackville on the Saturday evening: 'It really was a weekend for the connoisseurs'.

As a teenage student I recall how Dad constantly reminded me of why he took up arms in the Royal Air Force during the Second World War. A fierce patriotism drove men to fight for the King and Country to provide future generations, regardless of their political persuasion, with a free and democratic society, where everybody had a voice and were able to fight for their own principles. I was a head strong lad at college then, who did not appreciate a proud parent preaching to me about my liberties. But my grandfather George often substantiated this opinion. As a grown man I have come to realise that what the fatherly figures said was true which made me appreciate what the Second World War was all about. Dad died in December 1994. Unfortunately, after Mum's passing, we never became close. But I was glad to have the opportunity just days before his passing, to say how appreciative I was for his engendering of national pride. Something that is intangible, but a feeling that grew with every time I heard the National Anthem abroad when a British driver claimed victory in a race. I never realised national pride could bring tears to the eye, but when a British competitor has mounted the winner's rostrum, it is overwhelming, and should be the same for all nationalities. Today I bore my own children with patriotism and so life turns the full cycle.

Sadly we placed our cosy little eyrie on the property market through Brian Hazell, a local estate agent. He later became instrumental in adding another chapter to Bexhill's motoring heritage. While our view changed from the blue briny to overlooking the open playing field of St Richards, a Roman Catholic school, the tendrils of motoring even managed to ensnare me there. Part of the curriculum was the design and technology of electrically-based motor cars under the tutelage of Mr Peter Fairhurst. A born motoring fanatic, he loved nothing more than enlightening his pupils upon the rudiments of basic automobile design. Ever since 1976 the school had been entered into BP's Build a Car Competition, which was designed to help senior scholars to study for a career in industry. The first car, a city car called the 'BEE' was mini-based and by Fairhurst's own token, a 'bit-of-a-botched-job'. Next was The Electropet, an electric-petrolhybrid built upon three Austin 1300 subframes enveloped by a Vauxhall Viva bodyshell. Later, a fully electric car christened the Electrosix blazed the trail for the 'Richelle', another city motor that was powered by a unit salvaged from a milk float. This little masterpiece was based upon a Fiat 900 camper floorpan and it swept St Richard's to victory in the 1990 Build a Car finals.

Not a school to sit back on its laurels, St Richard's in 1991 set a purpose to its ambition. Peter Fairhurst told his class of a World Record for lightweight (500 kg) electrically-propelled vehicles which then stood at 100.242 mph. Planting the idea of 'world records' into the minds of 16-year-olds can either intimidate or inspire pupils. Eventually, a hard core of four scholars gravitated to the purpose. The obsession burned brightly in the minds of Vicki White, Chris Duncan, Bella Harrison (who had a brother, Matthew Harrison, an ex-St Richards pupil turned Lotus engineer) and Ben Richardson. So a target was set by Mr Fairhurst for an attempt at the record along the Pendine Sands in Wales for September 1993. Although project 'Volta' was conceived in design by Peter Fairhurst, the actual cost of making it, with outside sponsorship and school funds, was £35,000 and it was achieved virtually 'in school'. Bella could not resist the temptation to tell brother Matthew about the Volta, and naturally intrigued, he paid the school a visit, in order to cast his experienced eye over the concept and its aerodynamics. It was arranged for the body shape to be perfected in the Motor Industry Research Association's wind tunnel near Nuneaton, Warwickshire.

Deta of Alfreton supplied the eight lead-acid batteries which were aligned behind the driver's seat. The pack weighed 165 kg from the total vehicle's weight of 440 kg. Set astern, the power supply was a 96-volt Nelco motor which had been adjusted to supply 60 hp to the rear wheels. A micropressor-based 'thyristo chopper' unit controlled the 600-amp charge which was spent within 70 seconds — just enough to propel the Volta over the flying kilometre. Two Kawasaki motorcycle trailing-arm wheel-and-chain units formed the narrow rear-end track. A home-built front beam axle was mated to Fiat 126 stub axles and special wheels. The considerable work-load during the two years was spread between the school and Peter Fairhurst's garage at his home in Bexhill. There his hard-working quartet also went during weekends and school holidays.

Roughly half-way through the Volta's construction, Matthew and his Lotus colleague Richard Hill advised the team upon small modifications to the body shape which had been formed in Kevlar, (a skin similar to that used in Formula One cars), in order to gain better straight-line stability.

Rudy Thomann, a Lotus test driver, was elected to try the Volta and also to drive it on the record attempt. He gave the car a brief burst at the Hethel test track in Norfolk and declared himself confident of the machine. All that was needed was a parachute to provide compact stopping power after the high-speed run.

Land speed records had been attempted over the Pendine Sands along the coastline of Carmarthenshire during the twenties.

Sir Malcolm Campbell twice established world land speed records there in his Sunbeam and later the beloved J G 'Parry' Thomas drove his special 'Babs' into the record books along the shore (where he died after a crash believed to be caused by the collapse of a rear wheel). From a purely historical aspect, Peter Fairhurst thought that Pendine was the appropriate low-tide venue. According to local advice, the sands had deteriorated, so the record run was switched to the unlikely setting of the former cruise missile base at Greenham Common, Berkshire, where the lady anti-nuclear protesters were still camping. They viewed the cigar-shaped projectile being towed through the gates in to the base during September 1993 with feigned indifference.

The team approached the grey, slightly windy day with the mixed emotions of apprehension and great expectation. After unloading the Volta, then making a few last-moment adjustments, Rudy elected to go for an exploratory spin. Since every turn of the specially shod Michelin wheels was misspent power, the RAC affiliated timekeeper recorded all the runs whether they were performed as a warm-up or a valid attempt. The team were perfectly aware that in spite of carrying six sets of batteries, nothing should be spared or a wasted effort.

After Rudy's initial 'shake-down' everybody crowded around the Volta to hear his assessment. Meanwhile, the timekeeper strolled over to inform the team that the record had already been broken on the first run at 103 mph. Everyone stood in open mouthed disbelief, and protested that it was only a practice run. A feeling of unreality and then of anti-climax filled the air. World records are rarely served up on a plate. Rudy and Peter were delighted, knowing that there was more potential on tap. A new set of batteries was set and Rudy charged down the runway a second time. After this run the RAC official recorded a speed of 104 mph. It was ridiculous. Two years of hard work was meant to be rewarded with jubilation and a sensation of euphoria. Vicki, Ben, Bella and Chris had become spectators to their own effort. Rudy must have sensed their mood of limbo, and while Chris and Ben changed the batteries for a third time, he perked the girls up by saying that he intended to make a final big thrust in order to put their record beyond the reach of any pretender.

The slim white projectile was unleashed as the small huddle stood lonely with their thoughts amid the vast concrete acreage. Within what appeared to be an extraordinarily short space of time, Rudy exploded the parachute and gradually the object of their ambitions, hopes and deeds slowed to a final halt. The timekeeper grinned broadly and with all the authority he could muster, announced a speed of 106.74 mph. At last the Fairhurst Four gave vent to their achievement. Hugs, kisses and real tears welled up as the moment of truth dawned. They had set a real World Record. Not many children of sixteen years could boast that and get their 'A' levels in the bargain. Rudy Thomann, his face radiant with pride, observed upon completing the record-breaking runs: 'I feel great to have been part of this incredible story. These Bexhill youngsters have shown amazing commitment and ability: they deserve the record'.

From the time of moving house in 1984, I came to know that Brian Hazell had a sense of historical righteousness. When a lull appeared in the property business, on warm summer evenings we sat in his office overlooking the Marina putting Bexhill to court. We mutually regretted how the town's recent heritage along the De La Warr Parade had either been subject to the demolition squad or simply left to ruin. The Sackville had been rescued from its former decay by a developer who over the course of two years had restored it to an inkling of its former pride. To re-open the grand old place as a classy hotel again was perhaps expecting too much from business people who wanted to realise their investment by selling off renovated apartments.

I suppose it was the Sackville's place in the context of Bexhill's motoring heritage that introduced 'The Races' into our conversations. Brian was intrigued enough to read my story in *Thoroughbred and Classic Car* which had caused quite a stir among motoring historians when it was published during 1979.

As Brian perused the pages, I sensed his amazement at the revelation unfolding before his eyes. One of Brian's main extra-curricular interests is philately, which explained his natural quest for the past as depicted on stamps. He may not have been a dedicated pilgrim to the shrine of motoring, but I believe that from that moment of realisation, lightning struck.

'That's fantastic', he exclaimed after reading the story, 'to think Bexhill was the pioneer of road racing in this country!' As Brian grasped the significance of the story, his gaze centred upon infinity beyond the office window, somewhere out to sea. Bexhill-on-Sea during the latter 'eighties had virtually slipped into oblivion as a retired person's residential resort. People who motored along the A259 between Dover and Brighton would certainly pull off to sample the delights of Hastings and Eastbourne. It seemed that once the newly constructed King Offa Way was opened, the town was not only by-passed, but it was effectively ostracised from the nomadic world. The dear old place had been consigned to anonymity.

After a period of contemplation, Brian lashed out: 'This place needs to be put back on the map. What would an annual commemoration of 'The Races' do to help raise our profile and invigorate trade?' The first seed of the 'Bexhill 100 Festival of Motoring' had been sown.

Following that burst of inspiration, Brian arranged a meeting with five other likely candidates, who in their respective roles not only knew far more about motoring than he did, but shared the mad notion of starting from scratch and physically organising the first 'Bexhill 100' on the Whitsun Bank Holiday of 1990. They had four months flat, a week or so more than Earl De La Warr had had eighty years earlier, to cajole the slumbering mass into action.

The first key to lock-up the De La Warr Parade was Derek Smith, a motoring type personified from the same mould as Kenneth Moore's *Genevieve* character, who, in September 1989, had been enlisted by Rother District Council (the Bexhill Corporation had long been defunct) as the tourism marketing officer. His task was to persuade a chamber of belligerent councillors whose mandate was to maintain Bexhill as an asylum of refined tranquillity, not resurrect the spirit of unbridled automobilism. Eyebrows hit the ceiling at this new upstart's suggestion, but Derek successfully employed his powers of diplomatic persuasion, and convinced those still listening that such an event was in keeping with the deep-rooted tradition of Bexhill. He secured the rubber stamp.

Next in line of priority was the individual who could attract glamour, distinguished personages and the necessary media awareness to emblazon 'Bexhill' in big, black letters of ink. These credentials were found in Shelagh Milligan, the long-suffering wife of ex-Gunner 954024, late of the Galley Hill patrol, currently a vigilante over the Cinque Port of Rye. Shelagh had spent fifteen years on a production team making television documentaries for the BBC and was well accustomed to handling the media and celebrity liaison, Spike by the penance of marriage was beholden to turn up, even if it was in a battered army truck!

I thought that it was appropriate to introduce Paul Foulkes-Halbard to the proceedings. He had recently moved into a pile that was an old family heirloom at Filching Manor. Apart from his encyclopaedic knowledge of early racing, Paul also was in the process of building his own museum of motoring memorabilia and agreed to enter some of his own relics from the stable.

The Storkey family is almost synonymous with contemporary Bexhill. May Storkey survived her husband to become the matriarch who with her two sons Ron and Brian presided over The Bexhill Club and the Continental Restaurant with its Cellar Night Club. Brian was given charge of the marketing and hospitality which he handled with great flair. To establish the festival annually, the Bexhill 100 needed to stamp itself firmly on the British motoring calendar. A wide variety of up to 350 motor cars performing over two days before crowds of around 50,000 would make it commercially viable.

Funds had to be raised by token sponsorships, renting allotted spaces on the promenade lawns to car dealers, corporate hospitality and amusement attractions for children. Another potential source of revenue was the sale of programmes. Since the event was being organised along a public highway, there was no income to be derived from charging admission: the festival was free — just like the original.

Derek had set himself the task to invite a £25,000 sponsorship for the meeting. The shortfall was £24,000 or so. Maybe that was a blessing in disguise. Big money would have created obligations, which would have spoilt the spontaneity of the weekend. The reality turned into a glorious jamboree when a can or three of Carlsberg, Castrol R or Coca Cola were raised in gratitude to the esteemed 8th Earl for pioneering the excuse to clog Bexhill's streets with the clatter, whine and growl of combusted engines and ignited exhausts.

The festival was envisaged as two days of 'eventing' along the original course up to Galley Hill. Derek wanted to create a friendly family atmosphere among the crowds who enjoy watching motor cars. The same ambience was needed to enthuse the car owners to come again and relish the opportunity to drive along a historic road course that is closed to the public for two days.

Short on cash the first Bexhill 100 may have been, in accordance with the 1902 tradition and working on Gunner Milligan's old axiom that 'it'll be alright on the night', it worked. Despite shortcomings and blissful ignorance Shelagh ensured that it was buoyed by the bountiful assets of Barbara Windsor who cooed at everyone within earshot: 'Cor, innit great 'earing all them big ends rattlin'. Snooker's whispering Ted Lowe, then a resident of Cooden, was 'only here for the beer' and could hardly make himself heard above the purr of a Rolls-Royce. As for Barry McGuigan, a driver of no mean ability himself, he freely admitted to making 'a caille for an enjoyable clack'.

The 1990 Whitsun Bank Holiday was summed up by the plummy commentator who observed 'This is Bexhill on a bright May morning. Along the promenade of this normally quiet seaside resort, the still air is awakened by the roar of powerful engines'. Certainly a motley assortment of automobiles assembled along the De La Warr Parade paddock. Some of the veteran entries arrived with mortal wounds inflicted in the course of a treacherous journey in modern traffic conditions. A 1903 Oldsmobile driven by a splendid be-whiskered character was presented 'on tow' after its crankcase shattered along the way. The genial eccentric still managed to relate his tale of woe with a smile on his face and put his misfortune down to a veteran fact of life.

Among the pre-1900 vehicles that arrived under their own steam was one of only two 1893 Benz Victorias in the world, closely followed by an 1898 Orient Express. Each had completed the journey from Filching Manor, whereas the vintage Bugatti owners arrived with their racers sans trailers. After many years of loving care have been lavished upon such vehicles, their value to their owners was measured by the time and cost of restoration equated against the distance from home to Bexhill. Nevertheless, everybody enjoyed the re-enactment of the uphill sprint and the downhill free-wheel races.

Even the most cynical enthusiast could not help being charmed by the smiling naivety of the organisation so eager to please. Shelagh Milligan welcomed a veteran owner with a shrill note of authority: 'Ah, now this must be one of the Victoria Benz'. To which the erudite driver replied, 'Sorry my dear, you're looking at a Mercedes similar to the one driven by Lautenschlager for victory at Dieppe in 1908.'

Everybody fell about laughing because nobody came to Bexhill to nit-pick within such a gorgeous garden-party atmosphere. Regard for spectator safety had taken a low priority because of funds. So the commentator went hoarse warning people off the course while cars were on parade. Considering that anything from Captain (later Sir) Malcolm Campbell's single-seat Ford, a gift from a magnanimous Henry for a small Blue Bird favour, to the last survivor of the eight Hastings Trolley buses made in 1928 were footling up-and-down the course; it was small wonder that nobody in the 35,000 crowds who patronised the two day cavalcade got more than their toes clipped as they stood at the curbside.

The Bexhill 100 has grown annually in popularity ever since. Yet there were still a few cynical historians who question that such a pioneering event had happened in 1902 along the rather featureless stretch of English coastline. Today, Bexhill only offers a glimmer of the extravagant past. Beyond Bolbrooke Road the Edwardian architecture is mostly replaced by unimaginative shoe-box apartment blocks that rise up to Sutton Place where they overlook part of the old golf course.

Since the only evidence of a historic happening in 1902 can be found in fading print, Brian Hazell's sense of history forced him into creating a more tangible awareness for people to refer to as they walked along the De La Warr Parade.

Visitors to Bexhill came with the thought — well, this is where motor racing in Britain was born, but where did the races start and where did they finish?

Several methods to provide solid and informative evidence were considered that would mark the original track. Eventually it was decided to mount two rock based obelisks precisely where in 1902 the racers came under starters orders at Galley Hill and define the spot where Colonel Crompton's timing gear registered on the finishing line below Marine Mansions.

On a bright autumnal day in September 1994, a gathering of distinguished guests who represented the world of motoring, assembled to witness the obelisks being unveiled. The occasion was celebrated by an appropriate speech made by Raymond Baxter and attended by the Mayor and Mayoress of Bexhill and Lord Edward Montagu of Beaulieu. The formal unveiling ceremony was performed by Ivor Brampton of Cooden in his capacity as the Deputy Lieutenant of Sussex. A fine selection of veteran, vintage and modern racing cars were on display in front of the Sackville. These included the Marlboro McLaren MP4 that was driven by Ayrton Senna in 1991 and appropriately presented by Neil Trundle who worked with Brazil's champion driver at the time.

That day Bexhill-on-Sea really came of age, to be recognised officially as the cryptic nucleus of early sporting automobilism in Britain.

An occasion the 8th Earl De La Warr would have undoubtedly approved.

The Chequered Flag

Endpiece

The recognition of Bexhill has gone one stage further just prior to this book going to print. Official new road signs have been erected at each approach to Bexhill-on-Sea, proudly proclaiming the town as the 'Birthplace of British Motor Racing'.